Columbia Essays in International Affairs

VOLUME V

The Dean's Papers, 1969

Columbia Essays
in International Affairs

VOLUME V

The Dean's Papers, 1969

BY STUDENTS OF THE

FACULTY OF INTERNATIONAL AFFAIRS

COLUMBIA UNIVERSITY

EDITED BY ANDREW W. CORDIER

DEAN OF THE FACULTY

NEW YORK AND LONDON

Columbia University Press

1970

Copyright © 1970 by Columbia University Press
Library of Congress Catalog Card Number: 66-14078
International Standard Book Number: 0-231-03487-3
Printed in the United States of America

Foreword

One quality required of a well-trained student or practitioner of international affairs today is to be alert to the interaction of all or many aspects of human affairs. This in turn requires a substantial capacity for relating historical, political, legal, sociological, economic, and cultural forces and phenomena to each other, in order the better to understand the past and prospective evolution of political systems and entire societies. This is a heavy demand. As recently as the eighteenth century a person of powerful intellect could hope to "take all knowledge as his fief." Today no one mind can encompass all the disciplines that are potentially relevant to analysis and action. Nevertheless, both scholars and men of affairs recognize, more than in the past, the importance of mastering more than a single discipline and of having at least a passing acquaintance with several others.

The interdisciplinary approach to the understanding of world affairs has for this reason, been central to the educational philosophy of the School of International Affairs and the affiliated Regional Institutes—now eight in number—ever since the founding of the School and the first of the Institutes, in 1946. No one can or would be so complacent as to claim for their programs a fully satisfactory measure of success in this challenging endeavor. Nevertheless, the values to be gained through making this effort have been demonstrated, over the past twenty or so years, in scholarly or action-oriented careers pursued by hundreds of talented young men and women, Americans or citizens of many other countries alike, who have gained systematic training and received intellectual stimulus through their experience in the School of International Affairs and the Regional Institutes, which together constitute the Faculty of International Affairs within the Columbia family. This philosophy and this experience have been studied by numerous other institutions, in the United States and elsewhere, and the interdisciplinary pattern initiated at Columbia has exerted a broad influence on the development of training and research in the postwar decades.

Ever since the founding of the School and the Institutes, a good many of the reports prepared by students have, in breaking new ground, resulted directly in the publication of articles of scholarly merit and public interest, in a wide variety of journals. As a result of this experience, in 1965 the Dean and the Faculty of International Affairs launched the first of the annual volumes of *The Dean's Papers,* under my editorship, with the dual purpose of encouraging able students to put forward their best scholarly efforts, stimulated by the prospect of early publication, and of bringing to a wider public a sampling of the best research by our students, usually in their second year of professional training.

The present volume of *The Dean's Papers,* the fifth, offers a selection of the best written work accomplished in the academic year 1968–1969 by students enrolled in any course or seminar conducted by a member of the Faculty of International Affairs. The range of topics, and therefore of disciplines represented, tells something of the developing interests of young scholars, within the broad field of international and comparative studies, in seeking out new subjects and applying new methods of research.

The world of the twentieth century would have been a vastly different one if Britain and France had pursued their political and colonial rivalries, so acute in the 1890s, to the level of all-out war. "French and British Diplomacy, 1895–1899: The Fashoda Crisis," by Trevor J. Hope, brings a fresh perspective to bear on a much-studied theme. Among other values, his essay throws new light on the nature and operation of "brinkmanship" as practiced in a political and military setting different from that of today. It also illuminates the complex interaction between professional diplomacy and public opinion, in a situation of grave and prolonged crisis.

Men have long been concerned to discover the roots of aggressive behavior by social groups, in order to determine whether these phenomena are "innate" to human nature or are due to learned habits or "nurture." Many studies of human aggression cite the Eskimos of Greenland as an example of peaceful behavior by social groups in a setting close to that of man "in a state of nature." This widely held view is challenged forcefully and convincingly by Edmund Beard in his study of "Warfare among Eskimos."

The epistolary tradition in literature has long constituted an important genre in itself, as well as providing an indispensable and inexhaustible source of insights into the artistic and psychological processes of creativity and into the social and spiritual values that move men and women of talent and sensitivity. In a study of

"Gogol's Epistolary Writing," William Mills Todd presents a reappraisal of this neglected part of the intellectual heritage of a genius, whose remarkable insights into the minds and hearts of men often speak even more eloquently to the present time than they did to his own.

For the one-third of mankind living under various types of Communist rule, and for the future relations of the Communist countries with the rest of the world, the question of the nature of "democratization," its scope and consequences, is of crucial and controversial importance. In an examination of "Democratization in European Communist Countries," Karel F. Koecher presents a challenge to scholars to define the meaning of this widely used term more explicitly than in the past. He develops a fresh system of categories which is useful in both describing the concrete processes of present and possible change and in endeavoring to predict their consequences.

Yugoslavia, under Tito's leadership, plays an important role in several arenas: in the grouping of Communist countries, in the European balance of power, and in the "uncommitted world." The problem of the succession to this charismatic leader, now in his late seventies, is therefore both crucial to the future of his own country and of great importance elsewhere in the world. In "The Succession Crisis in Yugoslavia," Anna Willman sketches in impressive detail the interplay of political, economic, strategic, and nationality problems and forces that will be in the forefront of Yugoslav politics when the change of leadership takes place. The author concludes that, after Tito, Yugoslavia may best survive in the form of a confederation rather than that of the federal but decentralized regime of today.

The development of Zionism as a national and political movement within Jewry and the creation of the state of Israel have introduced new factors, of far-reaching impact, into the evolution of both Europe and the Near East. In "Kadimah: Jewish Nationalism in Vienna before Herzl," Harriet Z. Pass presents an acute analysis of the social and intellectual conditions and influences that stimulated and shaped the emergence of a Jewish national consciousness within the Hapsburg Monarchy. Treating the complex Jewish community in Vienna as a microcosm, this study provides new insights into the decline of the liberal, assimilationist tradition of the Enlightenment and examines the forces which led, with Herzl, to the emergence of a new political and irredentist movement within Jewry, especially in Eastern Europe.

The early decades of Brazil's emergence as a leading power in the

Western Hemisphere and the evolution of the unique traditions of Brazilian society have attracted the attention of many historians and sociologists. In "John Armitage: An English Historian's Interpretation of Early Nineteenth-Century Brazil," Roberta Marx Delson reexamines the significance of Armitage's *History of Brazil,* published in 1836, gives a sensitive appraisal of the author's reliability as a firsthand observer of the moving forces of Brazilian society and politics, and concludes that this early account of independent Brazil has been subject to undeserved neglect both as a source and an interpretation.

The common and divergent factors in the interpretation of internal and international conflicts are the subject of an essay by Alan D. Berlind, "Domestic and International Conflict." In a brief study of a complex area of interdisciplinary studies, he comments on a number of new explanatory theories that have been put forward by political scientists, social psychologists, and psychoanalysts and singles out several aspects of conflict analysis that are in special need of further investigation.

One of the neglected aspects of the history of Chinese Communism has been the industrial and proletarian sources of support for the scattered but highly militant worker movements that preceded, and at the time overshadowed, the formal establishment of the new left-wing party. In "Anyuan: The Cradle of the Chinese Workers' Revolutionary Movement, 1921–1922," Lynda Shaffer Womack has made an important contribution toward defining the concrete issues and forces involved in the interplay between social and economic discontent and the emerging movement for political revolution and between workers and intellectuals. She evokes the situation of the emergent proletariat and describes a fascinating phase of the revolutionary baptism of Mao Tse-tung, Liu Shao-ch'i, Li Li-san, and other future Communist leaders, many of whom gained their first experience on the political and social battlefield of Anyuan.

One crucial and little-studied aspect of African history in the colonial period has been the wide range of variation in the absorption of, or resistance to, institutional changes offered or imposed by the European rulers and administrators. By developing an ingenious model of interaction between the preexisting social and power structure and European-inspired innovations, and by applying this schema to the concrete study of educational development in Buganda, Jacob van Lutsenburg Maas has challenged a number of easily accepted generalizations. In "The Restructuring of State Education in Buganda before Colonial Overrule," the author throws new light on the evolution of an important African society and on the formation of an African elite in a precolonial setting.

Analysts have traditionally viewed elections to local government bodies, under the Soviet system, as, at worst, a mere window-dressing or, at best, as a symbolic gesture through which the rulers assure themselves and the ruled of the "legitimacy" of dictatorship. In "Political Participation in Soviet Local Government," Theodore H. Friedgut examines some of the functions of Soviet district and borough elections and suggests some ways in which the local people may at times influence the administration of policies, despite the insistence of "the Center" on controlling everything within the reach of the Communist Party's own apparatus.

In "The United States and the Yemen Crisis in 1962," Joseph A. Stork reexamines the conflicts of purpose that led, while the civil war was still being waged within Yemen, to what some critics regarded as a somewhat hasty and, for the time being, unproductive act of recognition. In this, as in many cases of recognition or nonrecognition, legal considerations and political traditions were important but not conclusive. The author disentangles the many divergent interests, both domestic and world-wide, that influenced the course and outcome of the debate. The upshot was a decision that disturbed as few as possible of the conflicting interests at stake.

As the Western powers impinged more and more insistently upon the Chinese Empire, bringing very different military, juridical, and commercial concepts and techniques to bear, the treaty ports became a major focus of conflict between the two systems. They were also an arena of commercial and political rivalry among the intruding forces. In her study of "Humphrey Marshall in China, 1853: The Failure of an Independent American Policy," Dale K. Anderson traces the diplomatic efforts, in the end abortive, of a Kentucky colonel turned diplomat to set in train a distinctive American approach to a China caught up in the turmoil of the Taiping rebellions.

"Soviet Foreign Trade: Law, Practice and Financing," by Charles J. Moxley, Jr., presents a brief review of the juridical character of the Soviet foreign-trade apparatus, from the central role of the Council of Ministers to the legal status, under Soviet law, of contracts between foreign contractors and the various Soviet foreign-trade associations, or combines.

The selection of these fourteen essays for publication in *The Dean's Papers 1969* was based upon careful review in three stages. After being recommended by their sponsoring professors, the studies submitted were examined by committees appointed by the Regional Institutes or, in the case of subjects of a functional or nonregional type, by a committee designated by the Committee on Instruction of the Faculty. The final selection was made by a committee of the Faculty of International Affairs, consisting of Louis Henkin, Chairman, Hamilton Fish Professor of International Law and Diplomacy, and Istvan Deak, Associate Professor of History and Director of the Institute on East Central Europe. It is a pleasure to express my appreciation to this committee for the care they took in fulfilling this responsibility. I am happy, also, to express my thanks to Marguerite V. Freund, Administrative Assistant of the European Institute, who again provided very efficient liaison between student contributors, faculty, the selection committee, and the Press. I wish likewise to thank Phyllis Holbrook of the Columbia University Press, who edited and supervised proofreading of *The Dean's Papers 1969*.

Andrew W. Cordier
Dean

July 1970

Contents

Columbia Essays in International Affairs

VOLUME V

The Dean's Papers, 1969

French and British Diplomacy, 1895-1899: The Fashoda Crisis

TREVOR J. HOPE

Today's observer, reviewing the relations between Britain and France in the last decade of the nineteenth century, cannot fail to be impressed by the apparently genuine desire of both countries, at least as expressed in the diplomatic correspondence, for friendly co-operation in all matters affecting their mutual interests. Obstacles existed, but none was considered insurmountable in the pursuance of good relations between these two powers. Economic and colonial rivalry was marked, but, then, there was hardly a single great power which could not be considered a potential rival to the British Empire somewhere in the world. This was hardly surprising when one takes into account those vast territorial expanses of ill-defined, and frequently undefined, frontiers, over which the British claimed "special rights" of one sort or another. Due cognizance was taken in both capitals of the ever-present danger of colonial ambitions leading to a serious confrontation, although since the Berlin Conference of 1884–85 few statesmen believed that these difficulties could not have been resolved through diplomacy, or that they were inevitably leading the two countries toward a future armed conflict.

However, a careful scrutiny of the official documents and correspondence in this period would reveal only half the picture. For, by the close of the nineteenth century, public opinion was beginning to assert itself and was becoming very much a factor of importance in the considerations of politicians on both sides of the Channel. This was an age of empire building, and the exploits of various adventurers, missionaries, and explorers, especially on the Dark Continent, seized the popular imagination in a manner scarcely equaled by the space explorers of our own times. Public excitement over exploratory missions was intense and carried with it the expectation that the national government would give full backing to these explorers as a matter of national pride and in recognition of their heroic achievements. Therefore, however much good will there might have been between governments, public opinion was something that neither dared ignore, and there were few issues that could arouse national passions more than colonial questions. Wrote L. Penson: "On colonial questions public opinion in England was now [in 1895] stronger than the personal predilections of any statesman." [1] And this could equally be said of the French, if not more so.

Yet public opinion in France over colonial issues was a far more complex phenomenon than it was in Britain. Colonization was accepted in Britain as the logical expression of that country's might and was supported by economists and politicians, without the type of opposition that characterized the French debates on the colonial question. An anticolonial feeling had always persisted in France, even in the days of the first French overseas Empire, with the arguments of the Physiocrats, Philosophers, and Revolutionaries. S. H. Roberts maintains that

the anti-colonial feeling—this positive revulsion—has been the most important feature of French colonization. . . . It is difficult nowadays to conceive the bitterness and the emotional intensity of this feeling, because colonies have never evoked in England . . . such a concerted furore of opposition as they have in France since 1870. The feeling has almost been a passion, and moments have not been lacking when to advocate colonization almost branded one as a traitor.[2]

The colonial question in France after 1870 was seen as a distraction from the main object of French attention, the recovery of the "lost" provinces of Alsace and Lorraine. Most economists endorsed the popular view that colonies were an unjustifiable expense, a burden for present and future alike. Another reason had been the reaction against the high-flown ventures of the Second Empire. Yet such feelings could not entirely resist the vast changes taking place in the last quarter of the nineteenth century; and gradually, although the general outlook toward colonies continued to be as antagonistic as ever, an attitude of greater comprehension was pressed upon the

[1] Lillian M. Penson, "The New Course in British Foreign Policy 1892–1902," *Transactions of the Royal Historical Society,* XXV (1943), 129.

[2] Stephen H. Roberts, *The History of French Colonial Policy 1870–1925* (London, Frank Cass, 1963), p. 9.

country, largely through the work of Jules Ferry. As a result, expansion came to be tolerated even if still viewed as undesirable.

On the other hand, once the colonial problem had been posed, the French had a tradition and a legacy with which to face it, namely, their first overseas Empire, and with it, the memory of the long combat with Britain for primacy in the New World. The tradition, declares Roberts,

was rather a rose coloured view of past grandiose schemes. The Frenchman liked to dream, and liked to intensify his dreams by the sense of injustice under which he laboured. Hence the strength of the tradition, and hence the curiously poignant way in which this colonial question was regarded. It was on a plane of emotional intensity unknown in England of that time; it was a living passion because nowhere is a tradition created as quickly as in France, and nowhere does national self-delusion on any desired theory reach such an intensity.[3]

The lure of Africa mesmerized everyone, politicians and public alike, during the course of the 1890s, and it was no great surprise that the continent should have become the focal point of the final Anglo-French showdown before the establishment of the Entente in 1904. Lord Salisbury, as early as 1889, developed the instinct which his daughter, Lady Gwendolen Cecil, labeled "the call of the Nile."

It now (1889) became a central episode in his calculated prevision of events . . . from this date, the necessity of safeguarding the Nile valley from the intrusion of other white powers begins to appear in his correspondence as a separate and dominating factor in his policy . . . he did not mean to allow France either to force England out of Egypt or to force her into a quarrel over Egypt.[4]

His motives were clear—British policy should seek to preserve the long and the short routes to India. It was for this cause that British troops were to fight in the Sudan and South Africa. It was also the reason why British policy was so conciliatory and flexible in West Africa, while just the reverse in north East Africa.[5] The whole pattern stemmed from the occupation of Egypt:

[3] *Ibid.*

[4] Lady Gwendolen Cecil, *Life of Robert Marquis of Salisbury* (London, Hodder and Stoughton, 1932), IV, 139–40.

[5] Elizabeth Monroe, *Britain's Moment in the Middle East* (London, Methuen, 1965), p. 18.

The Mediterranean and Indian interests, like a driving wheel in some vast machine, were now engaging the lesser wheels of East-Central Africa, and connecting them one by one to their own workings. At the turn of Salisbury's strategy, these once remote and petty interests in the Sudan, Uganda, and the northern hinterlands of Zanzibar, were changing into safeguards of Great Britain's world power.[6]

If Egypt was seen by Salisbury as vital to Britain for reasons of imperial strategy, it was vital to France for reasons of tradition and prestige. The "Egyptian question" had been dramatized by no less a man than Napoleon Bonaparte in 1798. Although Britain had persistently intervened to prevent a permanent French occupation, it had not installed its power there, and Egypt had remained under the nominal suzerainty of the Turkish sultan. The opening of the Suez Canal (1869) increased French prestige enormously, since to a large extent the work was the responsibility of French engineers and French finance and since it had been completed in the face of continual British skepticism and opposition. By 1882, about 80 percent of the traffic using the canal was British, and the British stake had been further increased by Disraeli's purchase of Khedive Ismail's shares in the canal, in November 1875. By this action Egypt was brought into the mainstream of European power politics.[7] Cooperation between Britain and France was achieved through the coincidence of interest that each had in Egypt, and there was no reason to suppose that this could not have been continued. However, the bankrupt state of Egyptian finances, coupled with the anarchic state of the khedive's domains, necessitated military intervention if the lives and property of Europeans were to be safeguarded. Uncontrolled riots by Egyptian nationalists prompted Britain and France to send a joint naval squadron to Alexandria in May, 1882. Further riots provoked a British bombardment of the town. At the last moment the French ships withdrew in protest, and Freycinet's Ministry was defeated in the Chamber over the question of an Anglo-French occupation of the Canal Zone. The field was left wide open to Britain alone, which now became the master of Egypt. The British had originally had no intention of occupying the country. According to the Prime Minister, Gladstone, on August 10, 1882, an

---

[6] Ronald Robinson and John Gallagher, with Alice Denny, *Africa and the Victorians; the Climax of Imperialism* (London, Macmillan, 1961), p. 289.

[7] L. P. Wallace and W. C. Askew, eds., *Power, Public Opinion and Diplomacy* (Durham, N.C., Duke University Press, 1959), pp. 47–91.

indefinite occupation "would be absolutely at variance with all the principles and views of Her Majesty's Government, and the pledges they have given to Europe, and with the views, I may say, of Europe itself." [8] The promise that Britain's occupation was only temporary, "was repeated sixty-six times between 1882 and 1922," according to A. J. P. Taylor.[9]

France had brought defeat on itself in Egypt, but this only increased the humiliation Frenchmen felt over the failure to take up Bonaparte's legacy. Thus the Egyptian question came to occupy a rather special position in the eyes of the French. Not that this in itself meant that an Anglo-French conflict was in any sense inevitable after 1882. There is no evidence to suggest that the French wanted to take up the position previously rejected in 1882, of joint occupying power, or even less of replacing Britain as sole occupying power in Egypt. French policy was directed toward eradicating its sense of humiliation either by securing a British withdrawal or by obtaining compensation elsewhere, in a manner befitting a great power which had, by default, relinquished its rights in Egypt. While Britain's physical position was one of overwhelming strength, its moral position was weak. Britain had to deny that Egypt belonged to it in order that no excuse might be given for the partition of the Ottoman Empire elsewhere and also because it needed the consent of the powers, on behalf of the foreign bondholders, if Evelyn Baring was to reform Egyptian finances.[10] This essentially simple position became more complicated with every year that passed, and Britain, for an increasing number of reasons, became ever more deeply involved in Egyptian affairs in the years that saw the pacification of the Sudan and the death and defeat of General Gordon in 1885. The main significance of this episode was to involve British public opinion emotionally in the Upper Nile region.

The "Scramble for Africa" in the late nineteenth century left the European powers laying claim to huge, unexplored regions and gave rise to any number of ambitious projects for the establishment

---

[8] A. J. P. Taylor, *The Struggle for Mastery in Europe 1848–1914* (London, Oxford University Press, 1954), p. 289.

[9] *Ibid.*

[10] Sir Francis Evelyn Baring, created 1st Earl of Cromer in 1892. Lawrence J. L. Dundas, The Marquess of Zetland, *Lord Cromer, Being the Authorized Life of Evelyn Baring, First Earl of Cromer* (London, Hodder and Stoughton, 1932), pp. 33–134.

of great, transcontinental, colonial empires. Thus, by the 1890s, Africa was penetrated on all sides by explorers, adventurers, missionaries, and traders. One by one the European powers were coming to realize, if a little tardily, the importance of the area. In 1893 "Africa" became a separate heading in the correspondence files of the British Foreign Office, and that Ministry gradually built up a considerable control over policy, which it often conducted without reference to the Colonial Office. This indicated the international as opposed to the strictly colonial nature of African affairs.[11] The growing importance of, and the need for greater specialization in, African affairs, prompted the French to settle their African experts in the new Colonial Ministry at the Pavillon de Flore in 1894. Thereafter the control of French policy in Africa fell more and more into the hands of colonial experts like Théophile Delcassé, who were in Monson's phrase, "extremely combative" toward Britain.[12] Previous French attempts to establish such a Ministry, in 1887 and 1892, had failed. The growth of a colonial administration was slow but steady in Britain, whereas in France it was very haphazard. The 1890s marked a turning point in the history of France's second colonial Empire, in that they marked the commencement of a genuinely constructive interest in colonial questions. "In 1899 Jules Ferry complained that all the French knew or cared about their empire was the belly dance!" [13] Eugène Étienne, the Under-Secretary for the Colonies, 1887–92, laid the foundations for the great colonial advances of the 1890s. A decree of November 23, 1889, set up the École Coloniale to train students who wanted to take up colonial appointments, and the Advisory Colonial Council followed in 1890. Colonial societies and their publications were just beginning to appear: the *Comité de l'Afrique Française* (1890), with its *Bulletin du Comité de l'Afrique Française;* and the *Union Coloniale Française,* which became the *Quinzaine Coloniale* in 1897.[14] Colonies began to be looked

---

[11] Z. Steiner, "The Last Days of the Old Foreign Office," *The Historical Journal,* VI (1963), 60.

[12] G. P. Gooch and Harold Temperley, eds., *British Documents on the Origins of the War 1898–1914* (London, His Majesty's Stationery Office, 1927), I, 158.

[13] Christopher Andrew, *Théophile Delcassé and the Making of the Entente Cordiale* (New York, St. Martin's Press, 1968), p. 53.

[14] Henri Brunschwig, *Mythes et réalités de l'impérialisme colonial français 1871–1914* (Paris, Armand Colin, 1960), pp. 116–17, and 124–25.

upon as schools for military training, and the French military provided some of the keenest exponents of expansion.[15]

Britain and France were in the vanguard of this colonial activity, and to some extent each stimulated action on the part of the other. It was largely the fear that British evacuation of Egypt would be followed by either French occupation or chaos, or both, that perpetuated the British occupation, at least under the Liberal governments of Lord Rosebery and Gladstone, 1892–95. Evelyn Baring's arguments found a ready echo among the Imperialist group within the Unionist government, 1895–1902, led by Joseph Chamberlain. The complications of British involvement in Egypt grew commensurately with the realization that, just as Britain needed control of Egypt to safeguard the route to India, so Egypt needed the control of the whole Nile valley in order to maintain its own security. This only served to increase French animosity. Although Britain was in no hurry to reconquer the Sudan, it would not leave Egypt until it had been effectively secured against control by any other European power. As J. D. Hargreaves pointed out,

precisely so long as Britain remained in Egypt, French colonists would not give up their hope of forestalling her on the Upper Nile, seeing there a possible weapon to secure evacuation. If this vicious circle could once have been broken the other Anglo-French disputes would have settled themselves.[16]

In the early 1890s it was apparently the British government's policy to consolidate its African possessions by diplomacy: thus, the Heligoland-Zanzibar Treaty of 1890, the Anglo-Italian agreements of 1891, the agreement with Germany over the eastern limits of the Cameroons in 1893, and, rounding off the policy, Lord Rosebery's agreement with King Leopold II to lease the strategic Bahr-el-Ghazal to the Congo Free State in May, 1894.[17] All served to exclude France from the upper reaches of the Nile and to shatter the dreams

[15] Andrew, p. 36, and also Roberts, pp. 21–22.

[16] J. D. Hargreaves, *"Entente Manquée,* Anglo-French Relations 1895–1896," *Cambridge Historical Journal,* X (1953), 66.

[17] *Agreement between Great Britain and His Majesty King Leopold II, Sovereign of the Independent State of the Congo, relating to Spheres of Influence of Great Britain and the Independent State of the Congo in East and Central Africa,* Signed at Brussels, May 12, 1894 (London, Her Majesty's Stationery Office, 1894), Treaty Series No. 15, p. 77.

of some Frenchmen of a Trans-African French Empire stretching from the Atlantic Ocean to the Red Sea and Indian Ocean. The Congo agreement was the weak link in the British government's chain and opened the door to serious misunderstandings. The French quickly spotted the inconsistency. If Britain insisted that the Upper Nile region was under Ottoman sovereignty, as its government undoubtedly did, then it had no right to lease it to King Leopold or anyone else. On the other hand, if it was claimed to be ownerless, the French had as much right to penetrate it as any other country. The Congo Free State was unpopular with Belgian ministers, and in August, 1894, under both French and German pressure, King Leopold agreed not to take up the lease, which would have barred the path of the French from the west to the Upper Nile.[18]

Yet, the policy of Gabriel Hanotaux, the French Foreign Minister, was to obtain French objectives in cooperation with Britain, rather than in competition with her. Indeed, 1894 was a highwater-mark in Anglo-French relations, and a *modus vivendi* was almost reached on the French expeditions in Africa.[19] Instructions were issued from Paris in July, 1894, that the expedition then being fitted out must not penetrate "le bassin du Nil, de façon à ce que la question du Soudan égyptien reste entière et complètement réservée." [20]

Agreement had been reached on most other outstanding colonial problems, including the frontier between Dahomey and what later became Nigeria, although the final terms were conditional upon the settlement of the Upper Nile problem. When this settlement proved impossible, negotiations over West Africa were suspended on November 17, 1894.[21] The French did not intend to allow this bargaining card to slip through their hands and, therefore, proceeded with their original plans for sending out an expedition toward the Upper Nile. "The nearest that Britain and France came to agreement between the occupation of Egypt [1882] and the successful *entente* [1904]" had passed.[22]

[18] M. P. Hornik, "The Anglo-Belgian Agreement of 12 May, 1894," *English Historical Review,* LVII (1942), 227.

[19] *Documents Diplomatiques Français,* First Series (Paris, Imprimerie Nationale, 1870–1900), XI, 273–75.

[20] Delcassé's instructions to Monteil, July 13, 1894, *Documents Diplomatique Français,* XI, 277.

[21] Note of Hanotaux's interview with Dufferin, November 7, 1894, *Documents Diplomatiques Français,* XI, 411.

[22] Taylor, p. 353.

The year 1895 opened with a noticeable deterioration in Anglo-French relations. There were repeated pronouncements in the French press and the National Assembly in favor of an advance to the Upper Nile, as the only way to settle the Egyptian question. The *Comité de l'Afrique Française* had been pressing for an expedition to the Bahr-el-Ghazal for a long time; in 1892 Prince d'Arenberg and Hippolyte Percher (whose *nom de plume* was Harry Alis) had been drumming up support among the leading colonists. On February 20, 1893, the new French minister of the colonies, Delcassé, took the decision, relayed by telegraph to the authorities of the French Congo at Libreville: "Suis disposé organiser mission destinée à renforcer solidement Liotard et pénétrer région M'Bomu afin d'atteindre le plus rapidement possible bassin du Nil." [23]

Interest in the Bahr-el-Ghazal was undoubtedly stimulated by the paper "Soudan Nilitique," delivered on January 20, 1893, by Victor Prompt, a French engineer in Egypt, to the Institut Égyptien. Under the title "Operations dans le Haut-Nil dues à la malveillance," Prompt stressed the possibility of constructing dams on the Upper Nile, which could cause either a drought or a flood in Egypt. Advanced lithograph copies of this paper were circulating in the Paris ministries early in 1893, and Prompt sent a copy of the paper to his old friend, President Sadi Carnot.[24] It was in this atmosphere that the Monteil mission got under way, undoubtedly designed to exert subtle pressure on Britain, and thus "re-open the Egyptian question" by the implicit threat of interference with the Nile waters.[25]

The successful French advances in West Africa, along the Niger River,[26] alerted Britain to the increasing threat to the Nile. The connection between activities in East and West Africa in the minds of politicians on both sides of the Channel, attests to the great sensitivity these movements aroused. The suspicion and hostility which greeted these actions in Britain is reflected in the *Cambridge History of British Foreign Policy,* written a quarter of a century later:

[23] Jean Stengers, "Aux origines de Fachoda: l'expédition Monteil," *Revue Belge de Philologie et d'Histoire,* XXXVI (1958), 444.

[24] Keith Eubank, "The Fashoda Crisis Re-examined," *The Historian, A Journal of History,* XXII (1960), 145.

[25] G. N. Sanderson, *A Study in the Partition of Africa: England, Europe and the Upper Nile 1882–1889* (Edinburgh, Edinburgh University Press, 1965), pp. 142–43.

[26] C. W. Newbury, "The Development of French Policy on the Lower and Upper Niger, 1880–1898," *Journal of Modern History,* XXXI (1959), 18.

It has been the systematic policy of France, when neighbours equally energetic have anticipated her in the acquisition of desirable portions of the Dark Continent, to endeavour to cut off their hinterlands, and so to gain control of the rivers upon which the prosperity of the lower territories largely depended. Colonization by this dubious method was attempted to the prejudice of Great Britain in the case of Lagos, Gambia and the Gold Coast, to that of Spain in the case of Morocco, and to that of Italy in the case of Tripoli. In 1897, it was attempted in relation to Egypt. No longer able, owing to her own want of decision and foresight, to enter the Nile region by the front door, France tried to enter from the rear; and she did this by part of a deliberate design of obtaining control of the Nile, the very source of Egypt's life.[27]

In 1895, during question time in the House of Commons, one member declared that a race had begun for Trans-African dominion, between France working from the west and Britain working from the north and south. Britain had to win this race, since any power holding the Upper Nile would hold Egypt at its mercy. The Under-Secretary of State at the Foreign Office, Sir Edward Grey, urged in the Commons' debate in March, 1895,

I cannot think it possible that these rumors deserve credence, because the advance of a French expedition under secret instructions right from the other side of Africa, into a territory over which our claims have been known so long, would not be merely an inconsistent and unexpected act, but it must be perfectly well known to the French government that it would be an unfriendly act, and would be so viewed by England.[28]

Grey's "fameuse manifestation" was itself prepared in expectation of a question on French activities in West Africa. As Grey himself stated, "[I] . . . transferred to the subject of the Nile the firmness I had been authorized to show about competing claims in West Africa." [29]

Although the French had an alliance with Russia after 1892 while 1894 saw something of a détente in Franco-German relations, nevertheless, France's international position was still too weak to permit a reply in kind to the British challenge.

France took the preliminary steps in entering her claim to the Upper Nile without adequate diplomatic preparation. Neither the government,

[27] Sir A. W. Ward and G. P. Gooch, eds., *The Cambridge History of British Foreign Policy 1783–1919* (New York, Macmillan, 1923), III, 250.

[28] *The Times* (London), March 29, 1895.

[29] Viscount Grey of Fallodon, *Twenty-Five Years, 1892–1916* (New York, Frederick A. Stokes, 1925), I, 19.

nor the press, nor public opinion was prepared to arrange a satisfactory basis of cooperation with Germany, although her aid was essential to the success of France's purposes.[30]

On April 1, 1895, Baron de Courcel, the French ambassador in London, was officially informed that the ultimate reconquest of the Sudan would be undertaken by Egyptian troops and would be followed by an Egyptian administration. He replied, "Qu'importe si ces troupes et cette administration sont dirigées du Caire, et que l'Angleterre soit au Caire." [31] The French ideas concerning the rights of the sultan and the khedive could easily become a weapon in British hands, so long as Britain was in control of Egypt. While Hanotaux could not afford to quarrel seriously with the British, he realized that French ambitions for the Upper Nile were futile unless the evacuation of Egypt could be secured. Increasingly, by mid-1895 an isolated settlement to the controversy over the Upper Nile became more and more remote.

The return of Lord Salisbury and the Unionists to power in June, 1895, increased French misgivings. The powerful Imperialist lobby attached to that party made the British government's stand even more intransigent with regard to colonial questions. Yet, for the time being Salisbury was satisfied to go along with de Courcel's suggestion to create, "une disposition plus sensée à juger des choses d'après leur valeur propre, souvent minime, et non d'après les imaginations échauffées qui trop longtemps avaient grossi outre mesure les objets débattus entre nous." [32] Discussions took place on the Niger, Tunis, and Siamese problems, but only the last produced any real measure of agreement (January 15, 1896); true, the Convention on Siam did provide for negotiations on the Niger and Tunis questions. French demands for a *quid pro quo* on the Upper Nile brought the talks over West Africa to a halt by November, 1895. The agreement over Siam was indicative of the genuine desire to clear up Anglo-French differences in Indo-China. Yet, the hope that this might lead to a more comprehensive understanding was thwarted by the African situation.

The "doctrinaire anglophobes of the Right" brought pressure to

[30] E. M. Carroll, *French Public Opinion and Foreign Affairs, 1870–1914* (New York, The Century Company, 1931), p. 168.

[31] De Courcel to Hanotaux, April 2, 1895, *Documents Diplomatiques Français*, XI, 649.

[32] De Courcel to Berthelot, February 19, 1896, *Documents Diplomatiques Français*, XII, 460.

bear on the new French Minister of Foreign Affairs, Marcellin Berthelot, to allow a French expedition to penetrate the Bahr-el-Ghazal and establish itself as a bargaining factor against the British in the Upper Nile. The Pavillon de Flore had been hatching this plan for months under the promptings of Captain Marchand and the *coloniaux,* who, as early as September 11, 1895, had submitted a detailed project to the Minister of the Colonies, Chautemps.[33] The political object of the mission was described by Marchand in his September note:

En dernière analyse, c'est par des moyens pacifiques, mais sûrs, de mettre l'Angleterre dans la nécessité d'accepter, sinon de provoquer elle-même la réunion d'une conférence européenne au sein de laquelle serait discuté et fixé le sort réservé au Soudan égyptien, c'est-à-dire à la vallée du Nil. En outre de l'intérêt que l'obtention d'un pareil résultat présente pour la colonisation française en Afrique, dont l'avenir est si gravement menacé par les ambitions anglaises, n'est-il pas permis d'espérer que la question de l'évacuation de l'Égypte découlerait tout naturellement de celle du Soudan égyptien et s'imposerait avec une force nouvelle aux délibérations de la conférence? [34]

Apart from the *coloniaux,* two other sources of pressure were bearing down upon Berthelot, "that most anglophile of French Foreign Ministers," [35] namely, the Sultan of Turkey, and Butros Ghali Pasha, the Egyptian Foreign Minister, who would have welcomed French troops on the Upper Nile as a way of putting pressure on the unwelcome British. Reaction in London to the rumors of the plans for the Marchand mission had been one of official skepticism, and the work of Salisbury and de Courcel, in London, and Berthelot and Dufferin, in Paris, seemed to proceed smoothly, until Anglo-French reconciliation was rather abruptly compromised by an unforeseen difficulty in the Niger negotiations. Here was a perfect example of not knowing what department and who were at the back of French policy. As Lord Dufferin said, it was one of the greatest difficulties in the negotiations with the French over Africa that "One never feels oneself face to face with the real persons who are determining policy." [36] Dufferin was not far wrong, the Africanists entrenched in the French Ministries were, in their own field, gradu-

---

[33] Chautemps to Hanotaux, September 21, 1895, *Documents Diplomatiques Français,* XII, 206.

[34] Captain Marchand's note, November 10, 1895, *Documents Diplomatiques Français,* XII, 280.

[35] Sanderson, p. 272.   [36] *Ibid.,* p. 232.

ally able to dominate African policy completely, to the detriment of the government's main line of foreign policy.[37]

A serious rift was finally brought about neither by the rumors of another French mission nor by the breakdown in the Niger talks but by the intrusion of external events. Germany, increasingly worried by the signs of Anglo-French friendship, tried to enlist British support for Italy, hard-pressed by the Dervishes. The Italian defeat at Adowa on March 1, 1896, forced Britain's hand.[38] Anxious not to disappoint the Italians again, as had happened over the closure of the British-controlled port of Zeila on January 2, 1896, and so drive the Di Rudiní government into the hands of France, the British government determined on the Dongola expedition, the excuse for which was to be the threat of the Dervish forces to the security of Egypt. It was an adroit move by Salisbury, who cared little about the Italian plight. As he was to explain later, "we desire to kill two birds with one stone, and to use the same military effort to plant the foot of Egypt further up the Nile." [39] Nor was that all, the British added insult to injury for France by applying to the *Caisse de la Dette* for 500,000 pounds sterling, to finance what was said to be a "joint Anglo-Egyptian force." [40] Russia brought pressure to bear on France to resist this British request, for Russia was not happy to see France cooperating with her main Asiatic rival, while Germany exerted pressure on Britain to take the initiative. These moves and counter-moves defeated all attempts by French diplomacy to save the improved relationship with Britain. Berthelot resigned on March 28, 1896, and Bourgeois became Prime Minister and Foreign Minister, continuing the drift toward a continental combination. Even the return of Hanotaux to the Quai d'Orsay a month later, failed to reverse this trend.

The dispute on the Nile was reflected in Anglo-French relations everywhere else. In the Niger Commission Britain made an attempt to break the deadlock, only to find that France had increased her original demands, upon which the discussions were again deadlocked.

[37] *Ibid.*

[38] See Arthur Marsden, "Salisbury and the Italians in 1896," *Journal of Modern History*, XL (1968), 91–117.

[39] M. Shibeika, *British Policy in the Sudan 1882–1902* (London, Oxford University Press, 1952), p. 355.

[40] The *Caisse de la Dette* was the Cairo-based commission of the European powers, established to supervise the settlement of Egypt's debts and finances.

The Tunisian Commercial Treaty was held back until September, 1897, while French commercial activity in Madagascar, which irritated the Manchester cotton trade, culminated in the annexation of the island by France in May, 1896. Egypt was at the heart of all the trouble. The French and Russian success in their juridical appeal against the majority decision of the *Caisse de la Dette,* while causing some embarrassment to Britain, made their task more difficult in the long run, since British money was in consequence committed more deeply than ever in the Nile valley. It was amid these recriminations that Captain Marchand left Paris on April 25, 1896, to begin his two-year march toward Fashoda (see map).

Meanwhile, Sir Herbert Kitchener's forces took Dongola on September 23, 1896, and were in favor of pushing on to Khartoum. France, it was believed, would not press its objections for fear of alienating the Egyptians, and the many and varied reports, usually exaggerated, of French activities in the direction of the Nile from both west and south, prompted Salisbury to acquiesce. The Italian upset had also opened the way to a French advance from Abyssinia in the east, as well as from the west and south.[41] Lagarde, the Governor of French Somaliland, was entrusted with a mission to Abyssinia, which resulted in what Hanotaux called, "un veritable traité d'alliance," [42] signed on March 20, 1897. Needless to say, the following month, a British mission led by Rennell Rodd arrived in Addis Ababa, and on May 14, Rodd signed a treaty of "amity and commerce." [43] French press reports in January, 1898, sounded the alarm over the expeditions of Lord Delamere and Macdonald, which were pressing upon the Upper Nile region from Uganda and the south.[44] *Le Temps* saw this as part of a British "expansion methodique sur le Haut-Nil," and, with regard to the Delamere mission, asked,

[41] G. E. Underhill, "Abyssinia Under Menelik and After," *The Quarterly Review,* No. 407 (1922), p. 33.

[42] Gabriel Hanotaux, *Le Partage de l'Afrique* (Paris, Flammarion, 1909), pp. 133–35.

[43] J. Rennell Rodd, *Social and Diplomatic Memories, 1884–1919* (London, Arnold, 1922–25), II, 87.

[44] See R. W. Beachey, "Macdonald's Expedition and the Uganda Mutiny, 1897–98," *The Historical Journal,* X (1967), 237. Evidence that the goals of this mission were not quite as innocent as indicated in the Foreign Office Confidential Prints, can be found in, A. T. Matson, "A Further Note on the Macdonald Expedition, 1897–1899," *The Historical Journal,* XII (1969), 155.

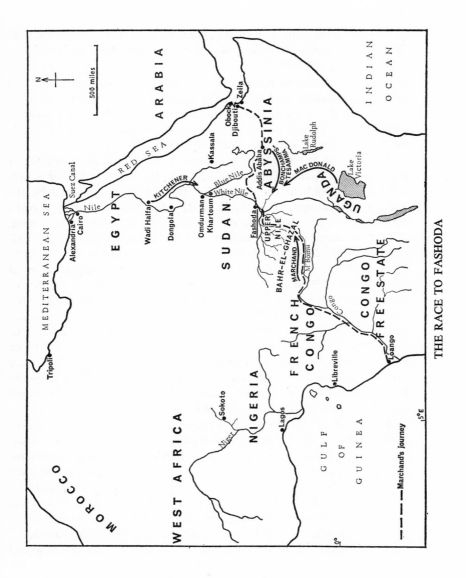

THE RACE TO FASHODA

Si le drapeau britannique avait été aboré par lord Delamère sur les rives du Nil, croit-on que le Foreign office dans les négociatiôns diplomatiques, négligé l'utilisation d'un tel fait? [45]

A rebellion among Sudanese troops terminated Macdonald's mission rather disastrously, and completely upset Britain's original plan for sealing off the Upper Nile by agreements with the other powers. Military action alone remained, for the advance into the Sudan made an Anglo-French conflict seem all but certain.

The French had not been backward in taking advantage of Italy's misfortune in Africa. On April 27, 1896, the construction of a railroad from Obock to the Abyssinian frontier was authorized by the French government. The Pavillon de Flore financed two expeditions to the White Nile, one of which, led by Dejazmach Tesamma, almost reached Fashoda twelve months before Marchand.[46] Evidently, by late 1896, the Pavillon de Flore had reinstated Fashoda as Marchand's goal, and the other expeditions were designed to meet up with him. Likewise, they hoped to gain the support of the Negus Menelik II of Abyssinia to block Britain's southward expansion. Missions matched rumors with confusing results. There was even a belief circulating in Paris, in 1896, that the French would be able to make allies out of the Mahdists. In the summer of 1897 the Pavillon de Flore strongly backed an "unofficial" mission to Abyssinia by Prince Henri d'Orléans, who reported that a buffer state could and should be set up with that territory occupied by Marchand, which would entirely exclude the British from the Upper Nile.[47]

The Pavillon de Flore was virtually conducting its own foreign policy so far as the Upper Nile was concerned, an undesirable situation at best, but one that was almost inevitable, given the problems of communications between the home country and the representatives on the spot. Hanotaux was openly opposed to invoking the assistance of the Abyssinians. He knew that even moderate British opinion would never tolerate what might be presented as a plot to call in the Mahdist "warlike hordes," against Kitchener's "civilizing mission." Hanotaux persisted in his belief that only international action would solve the Egyptian question and its Sudanese complications. He wrote to Cogordan, the French representative at Cairo:

N'est-il pas permis de penser que d'autres Puissances en viendront à leur tour à reconnaître la communauté de leurs intérêts et des nôtres

[45] *Le Temps,* January 13, 1898.
[46] Underhill, "Abyssinia Under Menelik and After," p. 40.
[47] Sanderson, pp. 302–3.

dans cette partie de l'Orient et qu'ainsi les questions relatives à l'Égypte se poseront un jour, dans leur ensemble, devant l'Europe entière? Une évolution naturelle tend en effet, depuis un certain nombre d'années, à accentuer encore le caractère européen de la question d'Égypte. Le développement des affaires commerciales et des établissements coloniaux intéresse de plus les principales Puissances à la liberté de la navigation dans le canal de Suez et la Mer Rouge.[48]

Furthermore, the excited state of French public opinion during 1897–98, deliberately inflamed by the *Bulletin du Comité de l'Afrique Française* and similar journals, made it virtually impossible to divert French interest from the Nile valley at this time, by the offer of a colonial swap. Remarked Salisbury, one year before the crisis actually broke, "If we ever get to Fashoda the diplomatic crisis will be something to remember, and the 'What next?' will be a very interesting question." [49] Consequently, all other problems were relegated to secondary importance, and some were actually resolved, as in the case of the West African disagreements.

The idea that one could not "afford to have more than a limited area of heather alight at the same time," forced Salisbury to seek more actively a solution to the problems in West Africa.[50] This annoyed Chamberlain (Colonial Secretary 1895–1903), whose "checkerboard diplomacy" in Nigeria was paying dividends, thanks to Lugard and his West African frontier force.[51] Yet, whatever Salisbury's difficulties with Chamberlain may have been, at least the Prime Minister knew what his Colonial Secretary was doing. Hanotaux was not so fortunate. He was sometimes deliberately misled by the officials at the Pavillon de Flore, who on occasion secretly modified the text of instructions which had been previously agreed upon with the Quai d'Orsay. This freedom of maneuver was one of the side-effects of the high casualty rate among French governments; there were six in the four years preceding the Fashoda crisis. It gave Sir Edmund Monson cause to complain that "in France, questions of serious international moment [were far too often] dependent upon manipulation . . . by irresponsible officials." [52] It was factors

[48] Hanotaux to Cogordan, November 16, 1897, *Documents Diplomatiques Français,* XIII, 592.

[49] William L. Langer, *The Diplomacy of Imperialism* (New York, A. A. Knopf, 1935), II, 549.

[50] J. A. S. Grenville, *Lord Salisbury and Foreign Policy: The Close of the Nineteenth Century* (London, The Athlone Press of the University of London, 1964), p. 122.

[51] *Ibid.,* p. 123.   [52] Sanderson, pp. 321–22.

such as these that led to the incident in January, 1898, when Sokoto was "invaded" by Captain Cazemajou. At that time neither Hanotaux or Salisbury wanted to force the issue in Nigeria, the latter remarking to Chamberlain, "it will be a pity if we break off the negotiations [over West Africa], for it will only add to our difficulties in the Nile valley." [53]

On the Upper Nile Salisbury had long recognized that he would have to be prepared to threaten war, although he believed a peaceful outcome both possible and in Britain's best interests. War with France would have raised a multitude of problems, among them the price Britain might be called upon to pay Germany for its quiescence in the dispute. It was Salisbury's aim, therefore, to limit the issue to the Upper Nile, in the hope that France might be willing quietly to withdraw. If the problems in the Upper Nile once became tangled with those in West Africa, anything might happen, and, given the volatile state of public opinion in London and Paris, it would probably be for the worse. Calm and patience paid dividends with regard to the latter problems, when unexpected concessions from the French suddenly hastened negotiations with the British Niger Commissioners to a successful conclusion, and secured the signing of the West Africa Convention on June 14, 1898.

The clearing of the decks for the final showdown continued, with Salisbury's demand that Chamberlain prevent Milner from stirring up trouble in South Africa, and his refusal to force a conflict with Russia in the Far East after the Russians occupied Port Arthur in March, 1898. The "surrender" over Port Arthur was resented in Britain, and Salisbury lost valuable support. But in so doing, Salisbury was ensuring that Russia would not intervene on the Upper Nile. The gamble paid off, for at the critical moment in 1898 Russia refused its French ally the backing it needed.

Throughout the first half of 1898 the prolonged West African wrangle continued to disturb Anglo-French relations, and even the expected improvement following its settlement on June 14 was not forthcoming because the French Chamber decided to postpone ratification. The settlement was generally welcomed with relief in both countries; even the *Bulletin du Comité de l'Afrique Française* expressed satisfaction, though it could not resist the opportunity to include a small map showing the extent of the French colonies in Africa, prominently including the Bahr-el-Ghazal, Fashoda, and a

[53] *Ibid.*

shaded line connecting these points with Djibouti, all within the French sphere.[54] The next stage in the drama was set.

British public opinion was becoming increasingly bellicose by the mid-1890s, encouraged as it was by a jingoistic popular press and by flamboyant political leaders of the Joseph Chamberlain ilk, whose supporters soon earned the title of "War Party." [55] In the gathering diplomatic storm that was to break after the meeting between Kitchener and Marchand at Fashoda on September 19, 1898, the press played a key role in both countries. Indeed, the inflamatory press language became a war of words and contrasted sharply with the firm, but conciliatory, tones of the diplomats. There was much in the Fashoda crisis to justify the opinion that

The diplomatists and foreign ministers of Europe would get on perfectly well together, and settle their own differences comfortably, but for the new journalists intermeddling and stirring up international jealousy and spite.[56]

Writing years later, Sir Edward Grey declared,

Any government here, during the last years of the century, would have been able to have war by raising its little finger. The people would have acclaimed it: there was a fever of excitement, and a rush of blood to the head.[57]

The newspapers could take much credit for this public mood.

Lord Salisbury tended to sneer at the popular press, whose leading representative, The *Daily Mail,* he called a journal "written by office boys for office boys." [58] But Chamberlain and the Imperialist lobby had no inhibitions about using the press, "popular" or other, and urged upon Salisbury the necessity of calling in the newspapermen to consolidate public opinion behind the government. The danger of doing this was

the possibility that publicists, politicians and journalists might take the bit in their teeth and run away with public sentiment. Exclude the public,

[54] *Le Bulletin du Comité de l'Afrique Française,* July, 1898, p. 209.

[55] Thad W. Riker, "A Survey of British Policy in the Fashoda Crisis," *Political Science Quarterly,* XLIV (1929), 65–67.

[56] T. H. S. Escott, *Masters of English Journalism* (London, T. F. Unwin, 1911), p. 338.

[57] Letter from Sir Edward Grey to Theodore Roosevelt, December 6, 1906; quoted in Pierre Renouvin, "Les Origines de l'expedition de Fachoda," *Revue Historique,* CC (1948), 195.

[58] Kennedy Jones, *Fleet Street and Downing Street* (London, Hutchinson, 1920), p. 284.

and the game was comparatively safe; turn on the publicity and a mole hill quickly became not simply a mountain, but a rocketing volcano.[59]

To a large extent, this is what happened in the fall of 1898. With emotions running high in France over the Dreyfus affair and in Britain over the victories at Omdurman and Khartoum, the acid-tongued journalists, often in league with politicians, pushed Salisbury and Delcassé to extremes, making all the more difficult the task of devising a peaceful solution.

The same situation held true in France, where the journals of the colonial societies were vying with the dailies in rousing public support for their cause. The influence of the colonial journals was out of all proportion to their circulation. However, an assessment of opinion in the French press was complicated by the practice, common among newspapers and individual journalists in Paris, of receiving bribes as a normal source of income.[60]

The newspaper war and public opinion could not alter the diplomatic realities of the international situation. If Britain was "splendidly isolated," France was "depressingly isolated." Russia turned its back on France's colonial problem on August 24, by publicly announcing the Tsar's scheme for a conference on the limitation of armaments, without so much as a prior hint to the French. The *Pall Mall Gazette* joyfully reported that

Paris can scarcely be enjoying this week. It began with the Tsar's strange circular, practically throwing over that ambition of which his faithful ally has tried not to speak, but has always thought; it will end, or next week it will begin, with the fall of Omdurman.[61]

Nor were Franco-German relations likely to provide the kind of support necessary to French designs. Finally, France had to face growing internal troubles, which cause Monson to report in May, 1898, that France might turn to war as an escape from the "racking agony of the Dreyfus affair." [62]

Yet, by June, 1898, there was already a shift in the position of the *parti colonial,* that "very noisy group, [which] has very able exponents in the press." [63] It had been recognized that the support of

[59] Oron J. Hale, *Publicity and Diplomacy with Special Reference to England and Germany, 1890–1914* (New York, D. Appleton Century Company, 1940), p. 7.

[60] Andrew, p. 42.   [61] *Pall Mall Gazette* (London), September 1, 1898.

[62] Sanderson, p. 321.

[63] Monson to Salisbury, August 4, 1898, *British Documents on the Origins of the War,* I, 161.

Russia alone would, in any case, not be sufficient in Egypt, and since August, 1898, the *Bulletin du Comité de l'Afrique Française* had urged the need for German diplomatic support also. But 1898 saw an Anglo-German *rapprochement*, not a Franco-German one, and it seemed more unlikely than ever that Germany would support any French initiative to oust the British from Egypt. This encouraged some French *coloniaux* to press for territorial compensation, an idea they previously had always rejected. On June 30, Henri de Blowitz, the Paris correspondent of the London *Times*, reported,

No-one in France has now the slightest illusion as to the [British] evacuation from Egypt. There exists in the Chamber, however, a considerable party (*le parti colonial*) which regards the Egyptian question as a problem for solution, and they think that it can, and should, be solved by some compensation.[64]

In August, 1898, the *Bulletin du Comité de l'Afrique Française*, led by the small pressure group under Eugène Étienne, suggested that only in Morocco could France find adequate compensation for abandoning Egypt to the British. In its October issue it declared its readiness to recognize Egypt as British, in return for similar terms for France in Morocco,

nous n'aurions pas nié la supériorité de la situation de l'Angleterre dans la vallée du Nil si elle avait voulu avoir, ailleurs, les mêmes égards pour la nôtre. Quelques personnes même avaient pensé au Maroc et autres territoires de l'Afrique occidentale comme étant le terrain sur lequel l'Angleterre pourrait montrer à la France des complaisances, en échange de la reconnaissance par notre pays de la suprématie britannique sur l'Égypte et toute la vallée du Nil.[65]

Thereafter, the *Bulletin du Comité de l'Afrique Française* continued to hope that "il ne serait pas encore possible peut-être d'amener l'Angleterre, désireuse de fermer sûrement sur elle la porte égyptienne, a consentir à nous laisser ouvrir la porte marocaine." [66]

At the same time as these ideas were first being mooted in France, Salisbury was becoming even more intransigent to the thought of compromise. On June 3, 1898, he suggested to Cromer that

we might treat Khartoum as the capital of the Mahdi state, and the capture of Khartoum would deliver by right of conquest, the whole of

64 *The Times* (London), June 30, 1898.
65 *Le Bulletin du Comité de l'Afrique Française*, December, 1898, p. 358.
66 *Ibid.*

the Mahdi state, from Halfa to Wadelai into the power of the capturing army. . . . That army consists of two allied contingents.[67]

This implied that the "Mahdi state" had been independent and sovereign, and therefore no longer a part of Egypt or the Ottoman Empire. This novel concept would have destroyed the claims of all but the two conquerors to decide a final settlement, thus completely undercutting the French position.

Both sides had maneuvered themselves into a situation in which neither could give way without humiliation. On July 10, 1898, the Marchand mission arrived at Fashoda. By September, Kitchener's Omdurman victory had brought the two forces into contact. Salisbury's famous "What next?" now became the question facing both governments as the crisis moved into the critical stage.

Cromer had received the British government's instructions on August 2, 1898,

in dealing with any French or Abyssinian authorities who may be encountered, nothing should be said or done which would in any way imply a recognition on behalf of Her Majesty's Government of a title to possession on behalf of France or of Abyssinia to any portion of the Nile valley.[68]

The British government's views were explicitly stated to France in a note delivered by Monson to Hanotaux as early as December, 1897:

[Her Majesty's Government] must not be understood to admit that any other European Power than Great Britain has any claim to occupy any part of the valley of the Nile. The views of the British Government upon this matter were plainly stated in Parliament by Sir Edward Grey some years ago . . . and were formally communicated to the French Government at the time. Her Majesty's present Government entirely adhere to the language that was on that occasion employed by their predecessors.[69]

Equally firm was the message sent by Salisbury in response to Sir Edmund Monson's report that the French Foreign Minister, Théophile Delcassé (in office again since June, 1898), had for the first time mentioned the possibility of an Anglo-French clash. Salisbury

[67] Sanderson, p. 266.

[68] Salisbury to Cromer, August 2, 1898, *British Documents on the Origins of the War,* I, 159.

[69] Quoted in Salisbury to Cromer, August 2, 1898, *British Documents on the Origins of the War,* I, 160.

bluntly warned that "by right of conquest" the territories of the Khalifa passed to the British and Egyptian governments, and on this point there could be no discussion.[70]

The French government was still disinclined to yield, believing that the legal arguments were in their favor and that in any case Britain would not fight. Indeed, the sharp tone of the British government and press only encouraged the French to stick obstinately by their policy. As the *Contemporary Review* had commented in April, 1898, "There is not a serious politician on the continent who believes our present government would risk a war however great the provocation."[71] Salisbury believed that if the French government understood that Britain was ready to fight to ensure Anglo-Egyptian control over the Nile valley, then there was less chance of it taking up an inflexible stand. The problem was in trying to get the French to take this possibility seriously enough. This unequivocal attitude received zealous support both in the press and in the street. British jingoism had reached its zenith. "With an unanimity rarely equalled, both the government and public opinion insisted that Marchand must be withdrawn prior to any negotiations."[72] As an expression of his absolute earnestness, Salisbury took the unusual step of publishing two Blue Books (on October 5 and October 25, 1898), while negotiations were still proceeding.

In France there was similar popular excitement in the boulevards, which the cabinet often found embarrassing. No doubt from the outset Delcassé had worked for a peaceful solution to the crisis and ultimately for a comprehensive understanding, but his delicate position was made more so by the unrestrained speeches of British politicians and the clamor of the British press. As E. M. Carroll wrote later, "It was Britain's grim determination, expressed without any considerations for French sensibility . . . which, to a large extent, stimulated resistance in France."[73]

British reaction to Marchand's presence at Fashoda certainly disconcerted the French by its unanimous vehemence. Since Omdurman, declared the moderate *Journal des Débats,* on September 20, 1898,

[70] Salisbury to Monson, September 9, 1898, *British Documents on the Origins of the War,* I, p. 164.
[71] Anonymous, "The Failure of Our Foreign Policy," *The Contemporary Review,* LXXIII (1898), 461.
[72] Riker, "A Survey of British Policy in the Fashoda Crisis," p. 57.
[73] Carroll, p. 172.

"the French press had maintained an attitude toward England of
perfect courtesy [*sic*]. . . . It has been answered . . . by an ex-
plosion of rage and hate." [74] British opinion still resented the humiliation of the Port Arthur incident and was determined not to repeat
the experience. In March, 1898, Francis Bertie, Assistant Under-
Secretary and Head of the African and Far Eastern Departments
at the Foreign Office, wrote, "Unfortunately, France, Russia and
Germany have got it into their heads that we shall never stand up
to one First Class Power, much less two or three." [75] The idea was
rampant that France had to be put in her place; quipped G. N. Sanderson,

In 1897 Chamberlain reacted to French claims in West Africa by the
marginal comment, "Cheek!" At Fashoda the French were giving "cheek"
in the most flagrant manner possible. Kitchener's reporting their claim
to occupation seemed an impudent fraud; and on the strength of bogus
occupation, secretly launched, the French were challenging deeply held,
if rarely expressed, convictions about the relative rank of Britain and
France as Powers.[76]

The hand of the Brisson government in Paris was being forced
by the growing problems of the Dreyfus affair, and a new trial had
been ordered with the revelation, on the eve of the crisis with
Britain, of Colonel Henry's forgeries. October 25, 1898, was a day
of acute crisis in France; the government was defeated in the
Chamber and threatened by an anti-Dreyfus mob in the streets.
Monson thought that the fall of Brisson might well be the signal
for a military *coup d'état*. A government of generals, he reasoned,
might force a war with Britain, if they could in this way stave off
the revision of the Dreyfus case, with all its explosive possibilities
for the French military.

The British, who had already ordered the manning of the reserve
fleet, now began to intensify their naval preparations. On October
27, the cabinet decided that the fleet should be placed on a war
footing. After the cabinet meeting of that day, Salisbury told de
Courcel that there could be no compromise or negotiation whatever
so long as the French flag flew at Fashoda and that he could neither
give nor imply any promise of British concessions after its removal.
Salisbury was demanding what Delcassé, in an interview with

[74] *Ibid.,* p. 173.
[75] Steiner, "The Last Years of the Old Foreign Office," p. 69.
[76] Sanderson, pp. 396–97.

Monson on September 27, 1898, had called "the impossible," namely, the unconditional withdrawal of Marchand from Fashoda.[77] In contrast with Britain, there existed a considerable division in French public opinion over Fashoda. The working classes were concerned more with achieving the advancement of their economic position than in going to war against their more prosperous British counterparts over a collection of mud huts on the swampy reaches of the Nile. From mid-October onward there emerged a movement in favor of evacuation, a trend that was led by the provincial press. President Félix Faure exercised what influence he could in support of conciliation and encouraged Delcassé's decision to continue in the new Dupuy Ministry and to order the evacuation of Fashoda. Commenting later on the crisis, Faure declared, "Nous avons été comme des fous en Afrique—entraînés par ces gens irresponsables qu'on appelle les coloniaux." [78]

In any event, the weakness of the French position was clearly displayed when Delcassé had to ask Salisbury if he would permit a telegram from the Quai d'Orsay to be forwarded by the British-Egyptian Agency up the Nile to Marchand. "Her Majesty's Government," read Salisbury's classic reply, "cannot decline to assist in forwarding a message from the French agent in Egypt to a French explorer who is on the Upper Nile in a difficult position." Salisbury pressed his point home by always referring to Marchand as plain "Monsieur." He was "an emissary of civilization and a pioneer," although at the same time, his was "the secret mission of a handful of men." "Monsieur Marchand had got himself into an impossible position . . . in so false and unreasonable a position," and so on.[79] The hard facts of Marchand's helplessness forced the French to accept the bitter truth that he could neither be reinforced or removed without British help. The discussions continued throughout September and October until finally, on November 3, 1898, the order of recall was sent to Marchand from Paris.[80]

The Dreyfus affair has sometimes been accredited as the major

[77] Monson to Salisbury, September 30, 1898, *British Documents on the Origins of the War*, I, 172.

[78] Félix Faure, "Fachoda (1898)," *Revue d'Histoire Diplomatique*, LXIV (1955), 34.

[79] Salisbury to Monson, September 28, 1898, *British Documents on the Origins of the War*, I, 170.

[80] Monson to Salisbury, November 3, 1898, *British Documents on the Origins of the War*, I, 188.

factor in Delcassé's ultimate surrender, and it is true that its divisive effects upon French society considerably weakened his hand. Paradoxically, however, it also made it more difficult for the French to climb down. Also, it may well have increased Anglo-French tension by arousing fears in London of a military *coup d'état* and thereby speeding up naval mobilization, although this step could not have been long delayed had the French persisted in maintaining their position at Fashoda. Above all else, the naval inferiority of France made a fight for the "marécages malsains de Fachoda" a hopelessly unequal contest without the assistance of others.[81] When this was not forthcoming, war could only have been an irrational gesture of defiance.

The tension lasted for almost six months, during which time the British did nothing to spare French feelings. Chamberlain's speeches, the publication of the Madagascar Blue Book, and Monson's rather indiscreet statement before the British Chamber of Commerce seemed deliberately planned to injure French susceptibilities.[82]

The war scare lasted right through until February, 1899, and there was in this intervening period no relaxation of British and French so-called "defensive preparations." Each country was suspicious of the other's armaments. Neither government seriously thought of going to war, but a vicious circle of fear had been set in motion by the military and naval preparations.[83]

The Anglo-Egyptian agreement establishing a condominium over the Sudan in January, 1899, was a compromise between direct British annexation of the Sudan and the continued treatment of the Sudan as a part of the Ottoman Empire. For France, this meant not only that it had been humiliatingly ejected from Fashoda but that it also had to accept the practical substitution of British for Egyptian authority in the Sudan. The worsening internal situation dictated that the French government terminate the talks and concentrate its attention on the domestic situation. The vision of Marchand as a second Boulanger haunted the Republicans. The situation came to a climax in Paris with the sudden death of Presi-

81 Andrew, p. 58.

82 Monson to Salisbury, December 9, 1898, *British Documents on the Origins of the War*, I, 194–95.

83 Arthur J. Marder, *The Anatomy of British Sea Power: A History of British Naval Policy in the Pre-Dreadnought Era, 1880–1905* (New York, A. A. Knopf, 1940), p. 320.

dent Faure on February 16, 1899, and the failure of Déroulède's attempted *coup d'état* a week later. The Franco-British Convention was finally signed on March 21, 1899, with the north-south dividing line between British and French spheres being the watershed between the basin of the Congo and the Nile rivers.

French policy in opposing Britain because of her occupation of Egypt had been dictated by wounded pride rather than by any rational assessment of French interests or of French diplomatic and military resources. Few believed that cooperation with Germany could reverse the verdict of Omdurman. Yet the Fashoda crisis served to clear away the age-old problem of Egypt as a serious obstacle to Anglo-French friendship. However, Britain was now in "isolation," and any move toward the type of relationship that emerged in 1904 had to come from Britain.[84] The Marchand mission and the Fashoda episode were spectacular manifestations of the "imperialism of prestige," which had increasingly guided French and British colonial expansion in tropical Africa in the last two decades of the nineteenth century and had led the two countries to the brink of disaster. Nor was the dominant motivation, attributed by J. Stengers to the French drive toward the Upper Nile, totally absent from the thinking in British colonial circles; the belief that "Ne pas agir, ne pas s'étendre, c'est se décerner à soi-même un brevet d'incapacité, prélude à la décadence politique." [85]

---

[84] C. H. D. Howard, *Splendid Isolation: A Study of Ideas Concerning Britain's International Position and Foreign Policy during the Later Years of the Third Marquis of Salisbury* (New York, St. Martin's Press, 1967).

[85] Jean Stengers, "L'impérialisme colonial de la fin du XIX⁰ siècle: Mythe ou Réalité?" *Journal of African History,* III (1962), 484.

Warfare among Eskimos

EDMUND BEARD

The current interest in animal aggression and warfare has created a
renewed interest in primitive human warfare. In light of such renewed discussion this seems an apt moment to dispel one particularly
widespread myth concerning primitive warfare—the belief that
Eskimos do not fight wars. This belief usually takes one of two
forms: a general belief that no war exists among Eskimos and a
refined version which restricts the claim only to Greenland Eskimos.
This widespread assertion concerning Eskimos is important because
it is often used as prime evidence by those who wish to prove that
men must not necessarily and inherently fight wars. The assertion
that Eskimos in general refrain from war will be readily shown
false. The claim for the Greenland Eskimos must be considered in
greater detail.

Among the more careful adherents of the "no Eskimo warfare"
thesis, wars among Eskimos or between Eskimos and Indians are in
varying degrees of enthusiasm, admitted. But the Eskimo of Greenland is held to be different. Isolated from other groups, particularly
certain warlike Indians, he is said to have lived without the practise,
or even knowledge, of war.

However, the evidence in favor of this more restricted claim is
also found wanting. Warfare existed among Eskimos on Greenland
just as it existed among them elsewhere in North America. If
there is a case to be made for the possibility of a human society
without war, the Eskimos should not be defense exhibit number one.

The belief that Eskimos do not fight war is shared by widely
disparate groups; from those who seize upon it in an attempt to
prove that man in his primitive state is peaceful and gentle, to those
who feel that men, although perhaps not innately generous and
cooperative, can learn to live together peacefully. It even extends to
those who view conflict between human beings as inevitable and

dismiss the Eskimo example as an exception quite aptly proving, and indeed all the more emphasizing, the rule.

In *The Evolution of War,* Maurice Davie states:

The classical example of the absence of war is that of the Eskimos. Among the Greenlanders warfare is unknown . . . cooperation in the struggle for existence is absolutely imperative in their case . . . because of the hardships of life they must place the utmost confidence in one another. Consequently they are characterized by a high degree of integrity. Among themselves they almost never steal or lie . . . fighting and brutality are unknown, and murder is very rare.[1]

Davie is for the most part merely drawing upon another source. A more striking example of the tendency to generalize beyond the evidence is found in Quincy Wright's *Study of War.* Discussing the theory of the "children of the sun," Wright says:

The assumption that the food gatherers were peaceful is supported by observation of certain foodgathering people who remain such as the Eskimos, the Veddahs of Ceylon, and certain California Indians, who are said to indulge in neither individual nor group hostilities.[2]

Wright then quotes W. J. Perry, *The Growth of Civilization:*

When inquiry is made at the beginning, when the food gatherers of the earth are examined, a remarkable result follows. Instead of spending their days fighting, these people, one and all, live peaceful lives when left undisturbed. They use no violence in their personal relations, and they do not fight as communities. The unanimity with which men and women who have lived among such peoples and know them well, testify to their honesty, their fidelity to the marriage tie, their kind treatment of children, their respect for the old, and their peaceful behavior in all their relationships, is one of the most striking phenomena of ethnology. When confronted with facts drawn from every part of the globe, from all the food gathering communities already mentioned . . . it would seem that peaceful behavior is really typical of mankind when living simple lives such as those of the food gatherers.[3]

In a footnote on the same page containing the above quote from Perry, Wright notes that Elliot Smith in *Human History* "writes to similar effect" and quotes him as saying:

[1] Maurice Davie, *The Evolution of War* (New Haven, Conn., Yale University Press, 1929) pp. 46–47. Davie draws primarily on Nansen, *Eskimi Life* (London, 1893).

[2] Quincy Wright, *A Study of War* (Chicago, 1942), p. 472.

[3] *Ibid.,* p. 474.

the food gatherers . . . live under conditions as varied as it is possible
to be—ranging in climate from the tropics to the arctic, and in environment from the tropical heat of the continent of Africa . . . to the icy
regions of Greenland . . . as there is no reason for supposing that all
these varied peoples have lost a culture that they once enjoyed, it seems
justifiable to assume that they represent the survival of the state that
was common to all mankind before civilization was created . . . free
from the common causes of exasperation, envy, and malice, the innate
goodness and kindness of Man found unhampered opportunities for expression. Men were happy and peaceful, kind and considerate.[4]

Harry Holbert Turney-High also believes the Eskimo to be
usually pacific and makes little distinction between the Western
and Central Eskimos and those in Greenland. On the functions of
battle units, he states:

Let us first regard the Eskimo tactically. For the most part they were
too pacific to have any battle practices worthy of the name. Their groups
were too small for combat effectiveness. Their social organizations made
no provision for real chieftainships with authority in the other walks of
life, and they were practically without motives for making war on anyone. They were capable of effective and fierce resistance when attacked,
as the Indians who tried to persecute them found out. The Eskimo were
therefore, practical pacifists. They did not relish an open fight, but would
stand up to one if necessary. In such cases they relied on fire without
movement. They could deliver arrow fire in great volume, and, a phenomena far from common in America, by volleys. . . . Since they did
not rush an enemy discomfited by fire, the winning side would be that
which delivered the best fire and the most of it, had the largest number
of archers and stores of ammunition. If one side became weary or wished
to eat, it would hoist a fur coat on a stick as a signal for an armistice.
If agreeable both sides would then rest, posting guards to see that the
truce was kept. After all had enjoyed their leisure, they went at the fire
fight again. Such behavior was obviously unmilitary and was more of an
athletic event.[5]

Turney-High attributes what war does occur involving Eskimos to
contamination with "un-Eskimo" ideas, a common theme in much
of the Eskimo literature.

Let us first consider the Eskimo, for he was so pacific that elaborate
battle practice was too much for him. However, contacts with un-Eskimo

[4] *Ibid.,* p. 474*n.* See also Wright's own talk of peaceful food collectors
being driven to the ends of the earth, pp. 99–100.

[5] Harry Holbert Turney-High, *Primitive War* (Columbia, S.C., University
of South Carolina Press, 1949), p. 91.

ideas did contaminate the west Eskimo to the extent of having some kind of method.[6]

The adherents to the no-war among Greenland Eskimos thesis are more cautious. They admit of certain wars between Eskimos or between Eskimos and other social groups and recognize the often violent and unrestrained nature of the Eskimo temperament. Their pronouncements are limited to claiming that only the Eskimo in Greenland does not fight wars, although he may well be often violent and abusive. Illustrations of this belief can be found in works of E. Adamson Hoebel [7] and Margaret Mead. In advancing her theory that warfare is only a social invention, Dr. Mead says:

There are peoples even today who have no warfare. Of these the Eskimoes are perhaps the most conspicuous examples. . . . The Eskimoes are not mild and meek people; many of them are turbulent and troublesome. Fights, theft of wives, murder, cannibalism, occur among them— all outbursts of passionate men goaded by desire or intolerable circumstance. Here are men faced with hunger, men faced with loss of their wives, men faced with the threat of extermination by other men, and here are orphan children, growing up miserable with no one to care for them, mocked and neglected by those about them. The personality necessary for war, the circumstances necessary to goad them to desperation are present, but there is no war. When a traveling Eskimo entered a settlement, he might have to fight the strongest man in the settlement to establish his position among them, but this was a test of strength and bravery, not war. The idea of warfare, of one "group" organizing against another "group" to maim and wound and kill them was absent. And, without that idea, passions might rage but there was no war.[8]

It must be admitted that there is a reasonable amount of first-hand evidence to support certain of the above statements. Maurice Davie cites primarily Nansen's *Eskimo Life* in which Nansen states:

The Greenlanders cannot afford to waste time in wrangling amongst themselves: the struggle to wring from nature the necessities of life . . . is there harder than anywhere else and therefore this little people has agreed to carry it on without needless dissensions . . . the Greenlander's first social law is to help his neighbour. Upon it, and upon their habit of clinging together through good and ill, depends the existence of the

[6] *Ibid.,* p. 124.

[7] E. Adamson Hoebel, *Man in the Primitive World* (New York, McGraw-Hill, 1949), pp. 517–19.

[8] Margaret Mead, "Warfare is Only an Invention," in Bramson and Goethals, eds., *War* (New York, Basic Books, 1964), pp. 270–71.

little Greenland community . . . good humour, peacefulness, and evenness of temper are the most prominent features in his character. . . . His peacefulness even goes so far that when anything is stolen from him, which seldom happens, he does not as a rule reclaim it, even if he knows who has taken it . . . the result is that there is seldom or never any quarreling among them. . . . They hold it attrocious to kill a fellow creature; therefore war is in their eyes incomprehensible and repulsive, a thing for which their language has no word; and soldiers and officers, brought up to the trade of killing, they regard as mere butchers.[9]

Davie also cites Franz Boas' observation on the Central Eskimos. "Real wars, or fights between settlements, I believe, have never happened, but contests have always been confined to single families," and another author who states that the Koksoagmuut of the Hudson Bay Territory are likewise "usually peaceful and mild tempered. Among themselves affrays are of rare occurence." [10] H. J. Nieboer's belief that "Among the Greenlanders warfare is unknown" is also mentioned by Davie.[11] Nieboer himself bases his conclusions on David Crantz's 1767 *Historie van Groenland*.[12]

However, the belief that Greenland Eskimos do not fight wars is in the first case contrary to the evidence available—evidence that organized battle did occur everywhere, including Greenland, everytime a suitable enemy presented himself—and in the second and further case merely a distinction without a difference, a distinction based on a definition of war which automatically excludes the Eskimo from consideration.

General Instances of Deceit, Theft, Murder, and War among Eskimos

In the passages from *The Evolution of War* cited above, Maurice Davie is careful to distinguish between the Alaskan Eskimos and those in Greenland and readily recognizes the numerous wars which occurred among the former.[13] However he does cite the Boas state-

[9] F. Nansen, *Eskimo Life* (London, 1893). Quoted in Davie, pp. 46–47.

[10] Franz Boas, "The Central Eskimo," *Annual Report Bureau of Ethnology,* VI (1888), 465. Also L. M. Turner, quoted in Davie, p. 47.

[11] Davie, p. 46.

[12] H. J. Nieboer, *Slavery As an Industrial System* (The Hague, 1900), p. 251.

[13] Davie, p. 47.

ment about lack of wars among the Central Eskimos with no qualifications. Yet Boas himself modified his comment by noting

One tradition only refers to a real fight between the tribes. On the steep island Sagdluagdjung, near Naujatelung, ruins of huts are found on the level summit. They are said to have been built by Eskimos who lived by the seashore and were attacked by a hostile tribe of inlanders. The tradition says that they defended themselves with bows and arrows, and with boulders which they rolled down upon the enemy. The occurrence of huts upon the top of an island is very unusual, and this tradition is the only one referring to any kind of fights or wars. Even the tradition of the expulsion of the Tornit, a fabulous tribe said to have lived with the Eskimo on these shores, does not refer to a combat.[14]

Moreover, Boas' original statement is weakened further by his inclusion in [the same work of] a later section on "Tales and Traditions," which contains the story of "The Emigration of the Sagdlirmiut." Boas' own rendition of this story states that

Near Ussualung there are two places, Qernigdjuaq and Exalugdjuaq. In each of these was a large house in which many families lived together. . . . Once upon a time it happened that the men of Qerqdjuaq had been very successful, while those of Exaluqdjuaq had caught scarcely any deer. Therefore the latter got very angry and resolved to kill the other party.

Having thus decided, the men of Exaluqdjuaq sneaked up on the men of Qerniqdjuaq while the latter were hunting and killed all of them. Thereafter the women and children of Qerniqdjuaq "resolved to follow the advice of an old woman and to flee from their cruel neighbors." This they managed to do, albeit with some difficulty.[15] Since this story bears no resemblance to a group of Eskimos rolling stones down a hill onto the heads of hostile inlanders, it must be assumed that Boas did not really mean his earlier statement that the first story "is the only one referring to any kind of fights or wars."

Furthermore, Edward Weyer cites evidence from Rasmussen, Klutschak, and Mathiassen of wars occurring all over the area of the Central Eskimo.[16]

Between these Netsilingmiut and other Eskimo groups in former times there was continual war. . . . Klutschak mentions that the Netsilingmiut

---

[14] Boas, "The Central Eskimo," p. 465.   [15] *Ibid.,* pp. 618–20.
[16] Edward M. Weyer, *The Eskimos* (New Haven, Conn., Yale University Press, 1932), pp. 158–63.

through long war had conquered their neighbors the Ukusikssillik Eskimos after greatly depleting their numbers. Similarly, for a long time the Netsilingmiut and the Eivittik Eskimos (Aivilingmiut) have been in a feud. . . . The Aiviliks and the Qaernermiut are reported to be peaceful toward each other generally, though one quarrel, arising through blood vengeance, assumed tribal proportions.[17]

The earlier quoted passages from Turney-High, however, display a much greater misrepresentation of the evidence. Turney-High had cited Nelson's "The Eskimo about Bering Strait" as support for his thesis that the Alaskan Eskimo was a practical pacifist who would never start a fight, whose wars were not really wars but rather athletic contests, and who engaged in battle only as a result of contamination by other (Indian) societies.[18] What Nelson actually says, however, is

In ancient times the Eskimo of the Bering Strait were constantly at war with one another [page 330] . . . the defeated party was always pursued and, if possible, exterminated [page 329] . . . when possible, night raids were made by the villages on both sides, and the people were usually clubbed or speared to death [page 329]. . . . The Magemut always carried off the women after a successful raid . . . the conquered village was always pillaged, and if a warrior saw any personal ornament on a slain enemy he seized it. . . . If one of the conquerors happened to see a woman wearing handsome beads or other ornaments, he would brain her and strip them off [page 329] . . . sometimes the women were put to death, at other times they were taken home by the victors, but the men and the boys were always killed [page 327]. . . . Battles took place usually in summer, and the victors killed all they could of the males of the opposing side, even including infants, to prevent them from growing up as enemies. The dead were thrown in heaps and left. The females were commonly spared from death, but were taken as slaves [page 328]. . . . The people of the coast interior from the Yukon mouth to Kotzebue Sound have many tales of villages destroyed by war parties of Tinne [page 327].[19]

Although some of these battles ocurred between Indians and Eskimos, many of them were purely Eskimo affairs and some were said to have begun within the same village and over quite trivial matters.[20]

[17] *Ibid.*, p. 161.   [18] Turney-High, pp. 19, 91, 124.

[19] E. W. Nelson, "The Eskimo about Bering Strait," *Annual Report Bureau of American Ethnology*, XVIII: (1896–97).

[20] *Ibid.*, p. 328.

Other evidence of warfare in Alaska and the Western regions comes from Hubert Bancroft who notes, "The Northern Indians are frequently at war with the Eskimos and Southern Indians for whom they at all times entertain the most inveterate hatred," and "the occupants of the several islands were almost constantly at war." [21] Similar observations are made by Edward Weyer,[22] and Kaj Birket-Smith.[23]

In fact Weyer finds so much evidence of fighting that he is surprised not by the absence of conflicts but by their number.

It is clear from the foregoing [a long list of instances of distrust and suspicion of strangers among Central Eskimo groups] that relations among groups in this Central region are not always harmonious. This is more striking in view of the fact that we have been considering only the attitude of Eskimos toward Eskimos and not toward Indians. It must not be supposed, however, that hostilities take the form of organized battles. The blood feud seems to be the basis of inter-tribal animosity where it exists, among these groups and also in Baffin Island. Relations approach closest to war when the feud expands to include whole settlements.[24]

This last quotation raises the most important point in this whole discussion. That point is the various definitions of the word "war" employed by the writers here discussed.

The predisposition to regard the blood feud as a thing apart from "war" is the single most important factor behind the statements that Eskimos know no war. But this distinction is invalid in Eskimo society, if indeed it is valid elsewhere except as a means of further classification within the broad concept called "war."

In contrast to the opinions cited by Wright that food-gathering Eskimos "use no violence in their personal relations," are the following observations. Edward Weyer says that "Murder is fairly common among the Eskimos. Life has not the sacredness which is generally attributed to it among highly civilized peoples . . . murder . . . with its corollary, the blood feud, has always been frequent." [25]

In *Across Arctic America* Knud Rasmussen observes that "Mr. Clark and I once made enquiry among the inhabitants of one en-

---

[21] Hubert H. Bancroft, *The Native Races* (San Francisco, 1883–1890), pp. 120, 91.

[22] Weyer, pp. 153–58.

[23] Kaj Birket-Smith, *The Eskimos* (London, Methuen, 1959), p. 145.

[24] Weyer, p. 162. [25] *Ibid.,* pp. 220–21.

campment, and found that out of fifteen families, there was not a single full-grown man who had not been in some way involved in the killing of another." [26] The motive, Rasmussen says, was invariably some quarrel about a woman. At another point he makes a large list of murders and attempted murders in another settlement, while the book is full of mention of Eskimo quarrels and fights.[27]

E. Adamson Hoebel devotes seven pages of his *The Law of Primitive Man* to examples of Eskimo murders.[28] Kaj Birket-Smith states that his " 'adoptive father' on the Barren Ground . . . had in cold blood exterminated the whole of his first wife's family because it had opposed the marriage." [29]

From these and innumerable other examples it is clear that the Eskimo is, or was at the time of these studies, far from peaceful and gentle; indeed murders often occurred for the most trivial reasons.[30] And once a murder had occurred the universal Eskimo practice of blood revenge insured that another and another would be forthcoming. "Blood revenge executed by kinsmen of a murdered party is expected among all Eskimos (so far as the data go) save the Copper, Igluilik, and East Greenlander. Among these latter it is optional according to the 'strength' of the surviving kinsmen." [31] "One crime cannot, however, be smoothed over in the ordinary manner, and this is murder. It always requires blood vengeance. As we have already seen, murder is by no means uncommon among the Eskimos in their aboriginal state." [32] "Among all Eskimos the duty of blood vengeance is strong." [33] "Blood, the only atonement for offense, must be washed out by blood, and the line of vengeance becomes endless." [34]

It is this factor of universal blood revenge that becomes so important in any discussion of Eskimo warfare. The next section, "The Nature of Eskimo Society," shows that the basic, and in many ways the only, Eskimo social or political unit is a form of the extended family. Apart from this they have no formal social structure, no

[26] Knud Rasmussen, *Across Arctic America* (New York, 1927), p. 250.

[27] *Ibid.,* pp. 233, 235, 60–61.

[28] E. Adamson Hoebel, *The Law of Primitive Man* (Cambridge, Mass., Harvard University Press, 1961), pp. 85–91.

[29] Birket-Smith, p. 138.

[30] Hoebel, *The Law of Primitive Man,* pp. 87, 88, 99.

[31] *Ibid.,* p. 87.   [32] Birket-Smith, pp. 150–51.

[33] Weyer, p. 222, and he cites several authors to this effect.

[34] Bancroft, p. 91.

larger organization composed of these extended families, no government except the familial ties an individual chooses to recognize. Eskimo social units, Eskimo settlements, are simply loose family groups. Therefore blood revenge or blood feuds practiced between these units are in actuality "wars" between sociopolitical groups in the Eskimo context—wars between the only groups existing in Eskimo society. This point is the basis of this essay.

Those who hoped to portray Eskimos as treating everyone, young or old, with equally great kindness simply misrepresent the evidence. In addition to the murders noted above, Eskimos regularly practice both infanticide and senilicide.[35] They are widely known to resort to cannibalism (with the children being eaten first) in dire emergencies.[36] Special note of their failure often to aid another in acute need or danger, instances of general lying and deceit, and more evidence of widespread murder are discussed in my later section on Greenland.

The Nature of Eskimo Society

We have now seen that "wars" do occur among all Eskimos and that contrary beliefs were the result of a failure to define properly "war" in the Eskimo context. War is generally defined along the lines of "organized assault by one social group upon another with the intention to further the interests of the one group at the expense of the other through willful destruction of life and goods,"[37] or "the sanctioned use of lethal weapons of one society against members of another. It is carried out by trained persons working in teams that are directed by a separate policy-making group and supported in various ways by the non-combatant population."[38] Of course in the most primitive societies, for instance the Eskimos, the noncombatant direction and support may be much less extensive and distinct than they are among more modern groups. As an example, the policy-making group may participate in the actual fighting without damaging the conflict's status as a war. War is, however, in

[35] Weyer, pp. 132, 137, 151; Hoebel, *The Law of Primitive Man,* p. 79.

[36] Boas, "The Central Eskimo," p. 574; Weyer, pp. 117–24.

[37] Hoebel, *Man in the Primitive World,* p. 508.

[38] Anthony F. C. Wallace, "Psychological Preparations for War," in *War: the Anthropology of Armed Conflict and Aggression, Natural History,* December, 1967.

some sense, organized and sanctioned assault by one society against another.

But William Graham Sumner warns that "when we talk about primitive society we should conceive of it as consisting of petty groups scattered separately over a great territory . . . The group may consist, as it does amongst Australians and Bushmen, of a man with one or possibly two wives and their children, or it may have a few more members." [39]

This is precisely the case among the Eskimos. Therefore, as Weyer notes, "The designation 'tribe' is not exactly applicable to the social organization of the Eskimo . . . Eskimos do not think in terms of large population units . . . *rather groups tend to be only an extended family.*" [40] Another observer notes:

The Eskimos provide one of the favorite ethnographic examples of a society in which it is said there is "no government." Actually, social control and regulation occur, as indeed they must to some degree in any viable society; but it is true that no specified social structures exist which embody group law and have a monopoly over the legitimate use of physical force. Social control is accomplished by actuation of diffuse sentiments in most Eskimo groups, sentiments which are translated into behavior by the impromptu social support given by kinsmen. [41]

Further observations on the difficulty of referring to Eskimo "tribes" are provided by Birket-Smith and E. Adamson Hoebel. Birket-Smith writes,

We speak of Eskimo tribes; but in a political sense there are really no tribes. What is meant by this word is merely geographic groups. . . . Thus among the Eskimos there is no state which makes use of their strength, no government to restrict their liberty of action. If anywhere there exists that community, built upon the basis of the free accord of free people of which Kropotkin dreamt, it is to be found among these poor tribes neighboring upon the North Pole. There is no rank or class among the Eskimos. [42]

This same problem is recognized by Hoebel when he says, "Although we speak and write of the Eskimos; there is no Eskimo tribe. . . .

[39] William Graham Sumner, *War and Other Essays* (New Haven, Conn., Yale University Press, 1911), p. 7.

[40] Weyer, pp. 203–4, italics added.

[41] Charles Campbell Hughes, *An Eskimo Village in the Modern World* (Ithaca, N.Y., Cornell University Press, 1960), p. 284.

[42] Birket-Smith, pp. 144–45.

Contacts between local groups are fleeting and temporary. No super-structure of social organization embracing several local groups has ever come into being." [43]

Birket-Smith's failure to perceive that blood feuds between familial settlements are actually wars in the Eskimo context (a fact which Weyer in the long passage quoted above was beginning to recognize) can be seen in his belief that although "in some cases blood vengeance may grow into feuds between the settlements," [44] the Alaskan Eskimos acquired their warlike inclinations through contact with the North West Coast Indian culture.[45]

Although the above observations on the Eskimo social structure include the Greenland Eskimo, there is one study of a Greenland group in which the social unit appears to be even smaller than the extended family. In a study made in 1884 of the then 371 Ammassalik Eskimos, Jeannette Mirsky states,

The Ammassalik have achieved a society that is highly individualistic. Each couple is a self-sufficient economic unit in a community with a minimum of social forms, and there are no effective social sanctions to regulate murder, competition for women, or economic activities. There are occasions for cooperation which are implicit in their relations with the environment, but when they occur actual cooperation is minimized . . . social cohesion is at a minimum. . . . They have no political unity, no organized leadership, no social stratification. They have no complicated relationship system nor any set of kinship attitudes that defines by its terms the rights and obligations obtaining among its members. There is no set residence. The biological family constitutes the only recognized bond. With each new marriage a new household is set up so that a family of adults does not function as a group.[46]

The fact is that the Eskimos hardly needed to learn to fight wars. In the context of their society they fought innumerable wars. The refusal to equate blood feuds between the only Eskimo social groups which exist—the family or partly extended family—with war is the crucial error made by those who claim Eskimos have no war.

[43] Hoebel, *The Law of Primitive Man,* p. 67.

[44] Birket-Smith, p. 151.

[45] *Ibid.,* pp. 144–45. Weyer characterizes blood feuds which occurred between Eskimos and Indians as wars, but it is unclear if this is a conscious identification or just casual use of the word.

[46] Jeannette Mirsky, "The Eskimo of Greenland," in Margaret Mead, ed., *Cooperation and Competition among Primitive Peoples* (Boston, Beacon, 1961), pp. 54, 77–78, 61.

Where other social or social-politicial groupings occur which encompass or supercede the family, such exclusion of blood feuds from
"war" might be valid, particularly if the nonfamily societal groupings
engaged in nonfamily fighting with each other. Then such exclusion
would prove necessary to avoid confusion and retain the primal
sense of "war" as intersocietal conflict. But in the case of the Eskimo
there is no larger social grouping to supercede the family. Therefore interfamily battles *are* fights between social groups, "tribes,"
or whatever term applicable in the Eskimo context. That such conflicts happen, in this case, to be precisely blood feuds among families
does not alter this fact. It is interesting to note that in another
context Margaret Mead, one of the foremost proponents of the
thesis that Eskimos do not fight wars, is quite ready to class blood
feud as a type of warfare.[47] Yet in the case of the Eskimo, apparently
she is not.

Specific Case of Greenland Considered

FACTUAL EVIDENCE

Maurice Davie's evidence for the supposed peacefulness of the
Greenlander is Nansen and H. J. Nieboer, the latter citing in turn
David Crantz. Nansen, as noted to some extent earlier, says Greenland Eskimos never lied to each other, that "the Greenlander's first
social law is to help his neighbor," that "good-humour, peaceable-
ness, and evenness of temper are the most prominent features in his
character," that he "never utters a syllable of abuse" nor contradicts
another, and in all ways refrains from offending his fellows. In sum,
fighting, brutality, and even quarreling are unknown or very rare.
"They hold it atrocious to kill a fellow creature." [48]

However, Nansen's bias is immediately apparent, as he notes, "I
have again and again sought to impress upon the reader that the
Eskimos are a peaceable and kindly race." [49] Unfortunately almost
every other observer of the Greenland scene disputes him. Even
Margaret Mead's admission that fights, theft of wives, murder, and
cannibalism occur there has been noted. Much more explicit evidence
is available from all sides. Thalbitzer tells of several murders, and

[47] Margaret Mead, "Violence in the Perspective of Culture History," in
J. H. Masserman, ed., *Violence and War* (New York, Grune & Stratton, 1963),
p. 94.

[48] Nansen, pp. 158, 162, 101, 109, 116.   [49] *Ibid.*, p. 186.

thefts occurring between Greenland Eskimos, numerous occasions where Eskimos informed on one another, and drum dances (ritual Eskimo form of judicial settlement where the two litigants face each other before a crowd and sing taunting chants back and forth in an effort to win public opinion to their side of the argument) which became brutal.[50] Erik Skeller notes that at the time of Holm's discovery of the Angmagssalik, "Many young men lost their lives in numerous family feuds." [51] Skeller also refers to ancient hostile relations between Eskimos and Indians and Eskimos and Norsemen.[52] Mirsky states that among the Ammassalik "no sickly child, or one without a mother, is allowed to live, and in times of stress it is understood that children must be sacrificed before their parents . . . [page 75] the orphan in tales and in fact is hungry, ragged, and abused. He may be killed or abandoned [page 72] . . . a father may provide for his son, and this is the usual picture, but he may also abandon him. A mother may aid her daughter in getting a husband or may compete for her daughter's husband [page 63]." [53] Furthermore,

Women are taken by force with the rewards going to the most powerful man. . . . Women are the primary source of quarrels, and such quarrels may lead to murder, to revenge by theft, or to a drum match. . . . Murder is of frequent occurrence. . . . In 1884 there were three murders within the Ammassalik group. . . . One young man . . . killed his stepfather because the father abused his mother. . . . The two other murders were done because in one case a brother resented the harsh way his sister was treated by her husband when she broke a tabu; and in the other case a man killed his father-in-law, after he had been divorced from the man's daughter, because the older man had frightened him badly years before.[54]

Although Mirsky claims blood revenge did not occur among the Ammassalik,[55] Rink notes its existence in Greenland.

Murder, and under certain circumstances, witichcraft, were, as a rule, punished with death which was carried out in two different ways—either as revenge of blood, or being duly deliberated upon by the inhabitants

[50] William Thalbitzer, "The Ammassalik Eskimi," *Meddelelser Om Granland,* XXXIX (1914), 144–46, 127.

[51] Erik Skeller, "Anthropological and Ophthalmological Studies on the Angmagssalik Eskimos," *Meddelelser Om Grønland,* CVII (1940–54), 26.

[52] *Ibid.,* pp. 28, 30.   [53] Mirsky, pages in text.   [54] *Ibid.,* pp. 67–70.

[55] *Ibid.,* p. 70.

of one or more stations . . . to fulfill the blood revenge was the duty of the nearest relative.[56]

Instances of animosity between groupings larger than simple families also occur. In discussing Holm's findings, Weyer states, "We read that in East Greenland 'the people of one settlement form, as it were, a society by themselves which often is at enmity with the folk of another settlement,' and a people one side of a fiord will volunteer the information that those on the other side are bad men." [57]

This same tendency is described by Jeannette Mirsky

The attitude of suspicion and slander that exists between the Ammassalik and their nearest neighbors, the southwestern Greenlanders, is the same within the Ammassalik group. The attitude contrasts strikingly with their behavior. . . . Under the pattern of extended hospitality runs the ever present note of suspicion and slander. It is present between the group as a whole and the outsiders, between members of one settlement and all the other settlements, and between an individual and the rest of the group. The lack of political unity is carried to such extremes, the marked individualistic nature of the people is so opposed to the slightest suggestion of cohesion that the same attitudes and feelings are found intratribally as well as intertribally.[58]

Full-scale wars with Indian tribes also seem to have occurred in the Greenland Eskimo past. Birket-Smith observes that "All Eskimos lived permanently in a state of war with the neighboring Indians, and even the Greenlanders preserve the memory of these wars from the time when their forefathers lived on the mainland. . . . There was no chivalry in these wars, which were merely a series of treacherous attacks and brutal massacres on each side." [59] Traditions of these wars are more fully discussed under "Folklore" in this section.

A similar instance of possible past warfare occurs even in the case of the Polar Eskimos, a group of only 250, who, at the time of their discovery by Ross in 1818, believed themselves to be the only inhabitants of the universe. They were extremely afraid of Ross's party and alternately threatened to kill the newcomers and begged not to be killed by them. Observing their isolation Weyer states: "It is not strange, therefore, that John Ross could not make clear to these Eskimos the idea of war." Weyer observes that

[56] H. Rink, *Tales and Traditions of the Eskimo* (London, 1875), p. 35.
[57] Weyer, pp. 168–69.   [58] Mirsky, p. 62; see also p. 65.
[59] Birket-Smith, p. 151.

according to Birket-Smith, however, "legends prevailing among these people seem to suggest that an old trading communication with the Upernivik region was interrupted by hostile encounters." [60]

It would be hardly surprising that a group of people who believed they were the only people in the universe could not imagine fighting a war with another society. However, in light of the fact that manslaughter and blood revenge were reportedly known and practiced by these people within their group of 250,[61] it is difficult to accept them as nonviolent. Indeed they seem to have fought with and killed members of the only group of people they were aware of—themselves. However, there is poor evidence as to what form this violence took, if it occurred at all; so little can be said concerning them and "war," even of a blood-feud nature. However, it seems likely from what we have seen thus far, that the blood feud would be one of the causes of their murders.

A final indication of Nansen's bias (it being Nansen's statements, primarily, which occasioned the above opposing evidence) can be seen in his explanation of the fact that when Eskimo murders do occur, much to his dismay, the victim is usually stabbed or otherwise waylaid from the rear. Nansen explains such an apparently cowardly practice by the following. "It does not accord with the Eskimo's character to attack another face to face, not so much because he is afraid as because he is bashful, and would feel it embarrassing to go to work under the other's eye." [62]

Another earlier noted expression of belief in the peaceful Eskimo cited David Crantz's 1767 *Historie van Groenland.* Unfortunately Crantz is simply so internally inconsistent that it is impossible to tell what he thinks. Certainly he does say that Greenland Eskimos are complaisant, jovial, gentle, loathe to give offense, friendly, and unboisterous.[63] They show little

. . . disobedience, obduracy, ingratitude, or neglect towards their parents [page 186] . . . we but seldom hear of any lying, cheating, or stealing; and as for violent assaults or highway robberies, they are quite unheard of there [page 185]. . . . They are an upright people and seldom tell an untruth knowingly [page 186] . . . nor have they a single word

[60] Weyer, pp. 165–66.

[61] Erik Holtved, "The Polar Eskimo: Language and Folklore," *Meddelelser Om Grønland,* CLII (1951–54), 302–8.

[62] Nansen, p. 163.

[63] David Crantz, *The History of Greenland* (London, 1767), pp. 170, 185.

in their language by which to utter abuse or cursing [page 171]. . . . Neither is there any handle of war, violence, oppressive injustice, chicanery, or such things [page 184].

Then, having voiced such high praise, Crantz turns about directly and states, "if they are accused of a thing, one can seldom get the truth out of them" [page 186]. In fact, "lying and slander are quite common among the women" [page 190]. Crantz then cites certain instances of barbarous treatment of poor widows and orphans and of stealing from widows [pages 191–92]. He also mentions murder, even from pure envy, and blood revenge in which cousins and friends get involved [page 193]. After all the talk about how loathe they are to give offense, Crantz says "You will scarce find a Greenlander do good to another, without the mercenary hope of some speedy retribution [page 188]. In fact, Greenlanders will often not help a drowning man and are even entertained by his plight [page 189]. To finalize the about-face Crantz sums up: "Some of them are considerate, judicious, beneficent people, but such are very rare. On the other hand, those are not rare that lead a confessedly culpable, nay a vicious and unnatural life, when they have once conquered modesty and shame, and have no retaliation to fear." [page 190].[64]

FOLKLORE

We have seen evidence of Eskimo warfare, in its blood-feud form and involving groups larger than the extended family and between Eskimos and Indians or the early Norsemen. Now let us examine further evidence of Indian and Norsemen wars as well as purely mythical wars with mythical creatures as found in Greenland Eskimo folklore. The special significance or cultural function of the various types of myths will not be particularly investigated. Rather they are cited here simply as further evidence that the Eskimos in Greenland do seem to have fought wars (both as blood feuds and on a much larger scale) in the past, are fully acquainted with, and not particularly opposed to, the phenomenon, and, indeed, seem to have fought wars with every possible enemy that presented itself.

There are several stories referring to early battles with the first Norsemen. Crantz mentions them [65] and Rink includes four of them in his *Tales and Traditions*. In the first of Rink's stories, "Ungortok, the Chief of Kakortok," the Greenlanders sneak upon the Kavdlunait

---

[64] *Ibid.,* pages given in text.   [65] *Ibid.,* p. 263.

(Norsemen) by floating down to their camp in driftwood. This story reveals a series of encounters, as the above attack is in counter revenge after the Norsemen have retaliated for an original Greenlander murder of a Norseman. Another of Rink's stories, "Encounter of Kaladlit with the Ancient Kavdlunait on the Ice," notes that "it is said that the Kaladlit (Eskimos) of the South Country at times were attacked in the Autumn season" by the Norsemen.[66] Franz Boas also notes that "in South Greenland the memory of the contests between the Eskimo and the Norsemen which took place between 1379 and 1450 survives." [67]

Many Eskimo tales refer to great battles with the fabulous Inlanders, with other mythical creatures, or with Indians. Speaking in general terms and not particularly about Greenland, Boas says:

The fabulous tribes described in Eskimo folklore are numerous. Those most frequently mentioned are the Tornit, the Adlet or Erqigdlit and the Dwarfs. The Tornit are described as a race of great strength and stature, but rather awkward, who at an early period inhabited the country jointly with the Eskimo, but who were ultimately driven out. On the whole they are good natured, and the stories tell mostly of friendly visits, although hostile contests also occur. . . . The Adlet or Erqigdlit are described as having the lower part of the body like that of a dog, while the upper part is like that of man. They are ferocious and fleet of foot, and encounters between them and Eskimo visitors always terminate in a fierce battle which generally ends with the death of the Adlet.[68]

One of the most widely known stories is that

of the Iavaranak which is known in Greenland, Cumberland Sound, and in Labrador. It tells of a girl of a tribe of inlanders who lived among the Eskimo, and who betrayed them to her own tribesmen. One day, while the Eskimo men were all absent, she led her friends to the Eskimo village, where all the women and children were killed. She returned inland

[66] Rink, pp. 308–21, 320.

[67] Franz Boas, *Race, Language, and Culture* (New York, Macmillan, 1940), p. 512. In private correspondence with the author, Edward Weyer also notes that "one theory of the disappearance of the Norse colony in Greenland in the 14th century is that the Eskimos exterminated them," but adds, "This is a big order because there were probably 5,000 or 10,000 Norse in Greenland at the height of the settlement; there were probably other causes—perhaps plague, intermixture with the native population, unfavorable climatic cycle, etc.—but there are legends among the Eskimos that may tie in with the theory of massacres."

[68] *Ibid.*

with her friends, but eventually was killed by a party that had gone out to take revenge.[69]

Two versions of this story are given by Rink. In the North Greenland version, after the initial Inlander attack, the coastal Eskimos desire revenge and go inland where they find and surround the inlander camp.

They waited until all had entered the tents, and then they made their attack. Arrows came flying from both sides; but those of the Inlanders soon grew fewer and fewer in number, and the coast-people remained all unwounded. When they had done with the men they went inside, killing women and children; and having thus satisfied their revenge, returned home.[70]

Rink tells of a similar version of this story occurring in South Greenland and relates one from Labrador in which an Indian woman originally lived with the Eskimo.

And so it happened that all the inhabitants were put to death by Jaavraganak's Indian countrymen. Many of them sought refuge in a cave where some were suffocated and others murdered. On their return the men found their wives and children all killed, but shortly afterwards they set out to kill the murderers.[71]

These stories very clearly illustrate the difficulty in attempting to differentiate between blood feuds among Eskimos and something else called a "war." In these stories whole settlements decide to attack one another and do so in concerted, organized fashion. This, then, is war. Whether the individual reason for acting may have been in many cases the desire to avenge a personal loss, the sum total was a concerted group attack on another group. Each man did not run off by himself in pursuit of the Inlanders. They went together and acted together. In this case the result of the blood-revenge impulse is very clearly intersocietal war.

Once the Greenlanders had left the mainland and found themselves alone on Greenland, they continued to practice intergroup war, but on a smaller scale between extended family units. And in this isolated, non-Indian context, feuds between families were

---

[69] *Ibid.*, p. 511.   [70] Rink, pp. 174–75.

[71] *Ibid.*, p. 176. Another Indian version with an interesting difference in that this time an Eskimo girl betrays her own people is found in Rasmussen, *Across Arctic America*, p. 253, "Navarano, the Eskimo girl who Betrayed her people to the Indians."

wars—wars between the only social groups that existed. When Indians and Norsemen were around, the Eskimos fought them, and when they were no longer available, the Eskimos continued to fight with the only people left—themselves.

Many other tales tell of battles with Indians, Eskimos, Inlanders, and mythical creatures. In a collection of Greenland Eskimo folklore, Knud Rasmussen tells the story of "Atarssuaq" who sees "many Kayaks appearing from the northward" in pursuit of him and his family.[72] At another point he tells of organized, field warfare between the Dwarfs and the Inlanders, showing the concept was known to the Greenlanders. "And then the dwarfs went out to fight, and took up their posts on the plain, one party opposite the other, and none said a word." [73] Thalbitzer notes that Jeannette Mirsky's Greenland Ammassalik Eskimos have tales of fights with the Inlanders,[74] and Rasmussen includes a native drawing of "an 'inland dweller' half dog, half human, pointing out a settlement for destruction." [75] Rink also relates various other stories illustrating general hostility between the coastal Eskimos and the Inlanders.[76]

Furthermore, there seems to be a close link between certain Greenland Eskimos and those of Baffin Land and the Hudson Bay region. According to Boas, there is a "close relationship between the culture of the Northeast coast of Greenland and that of Ellesmere Land, Northern Baffin Land and the Northwestern part of Hudson Bay. The similarities are . . . far reaching." [77]

In another work Boas then describes many traditions of group conflicts involving these Baffin Land Eskimos with various mythical creatures, including Dwarfs,[78] Adlet,[79] and Tornit.[80] The tale of the battle with the Tornit, which arose over a territorial question, is particularly gruesome. "At one time while the people were off hunting, the Tornit came to their houses and killed the women and

---

[72] Knud Rasmussen, *Eskimo Folk Tales* (Copenhagen, 1921) p. 142.

[73] *Ibid.,* p. 70.

[74] William Thalbitzer, "The Ammassalik Eskimo, Part II," *Meddelelser Om Grønland,* Copenhagen, XL (1923), 412. "Aqattiaq and the Inalilik."

[75] Rasmussen, *Eskimo Folk Tales,* p. 96.

[76] Rink, p. 265, "The Girl Who Was Stolen by an Inlander," and p. 268, "The Child that Was Stolen by the Inlanders."

[77] Boas, *Race, Language, and Culture,* p. 592.

[78] Franz Boas, "The Eskimo of Baffin Land and Hudson Bay," *Bulletin American Museum of Natural History,* XV (1901), 201.

[79] *Ibid.,* pp. 204, 207–8, 212–13.   [80] *Ibid.,* p. 315.

children." Upon their return the Eskimos went after the Tornit and, after a ruse,

killed them with their spears. One of the Tornit, who had not been wounded, pretended to be dead; but the men went up to him and stabbed him with a knife, which made him turn quickly. Then they despatched him. After all the men and women were dead, they took all the Tornit children home. On their way back, whenever one of the children became tired, the people would drill a hole in its forehead. Most of them were despatched in this way. Only two arrived—one boy and one girl.[81]

Another Boas version of the betrayal story noted above, involves an Adla girl who helps the Adlet to massacre the Eskimo women and children. The Eskimos "went secretly in a round-about way to the village of the Adlet," and killed them all. Then one shouted, "That is nice! They gathered up all the property of the Adlet, carried it home, and reported what they had done." [82]

The widespread belief that Eskimos do not fight wars takes many forms. Some assume that all Eskimos do not fight wars and extend the assumption further to say that Eskimos are universally honest, kind, gentle, and friendly. Others say that only the Greenland Eskimos fit the above description. Still others say only that Greenland Eskimos fight no "wars," although they are at times given to violence, deceit, and murder.

The results of an examination of the evidence produced to support these contentions are unmistakable. Eskimos have always fought "wars" in the basic sense of organized, sanctioned conflicts between societies. When "tribes" of Eskimos happened to develop as large groups, as in the Alaskan area, there were battles between them. When Indians or Norsemen were available, the Eskimos fought with them also. When Indians and Norsemen were not available or were eliminated, as in Greenland, and the "tribes" never developed beyond the extended family, these extended families fought. And because these extended families were the only social or political groupings in the Greenland context, the conflicts which occurred between them were "wars."

Indeed, far from being peaceful, the surprising thing about the Eskimos may be the amount of fighting they do engage in, often in the face of strong reasons against it. As Hoebel says:

[81] *Ibid.*   [82] *Ibid.*, pp. 207–8.

Food gatherers and lower hunters just do not possess enough property to make booty raids worthwhile, and victors in fights among the lower nomads do not have the means to carry surplus goods with them. Hence there is little advantage in appropriating such goods as the vanquished may possess.[83]

Eskimos are fishermen primarily and have no need of strict possession of territory. In fact if the fishing goes bad in a given area, being forced to remain there would be a major disadvantage. They have no need of property beyond the barest essentials, and, as noted above, could not carry it if they had it.[84] They have no need of slaves because unskilled labor is of no value to them and food is scarce. Furthermore they have certain "unemployment" difficulties of their own without slaves.[85]

Their mode of life leaves little time for fighting. "The general sparsity of population precludes war parties of considerable size. A further hindrance may lie in the fact that both factions are so poverty-stricken and harassed by the common hardships of the antagonistic and ungenerous habitat that inter-tribal fighting but poorly repays even the victor for the time and energy it consumes." [86]

Nevertheless they fight, in groups and individually. In many respects it might be more apt to cite Eskimos for their violence rather than their passivity. At any rate it is not true that they know no war. Unfortunately,

in a society in which man power is desperately needed, in which occupational hazards destroy more men than the society can well afford, there is additional tragic waste in the killings which the inchoate system permits—indeed encourages.[87]

The question remains, of course, why has the belief that Eskimos do not fight wars become so widely and deeply held. The answer seems to be the dynamic inertia of an original incorrect or biased observation gaining legitimacy through a pyramiding process. Coupled with this was the desire of certain persons to believe that men might live without war leading to their eager and unexamined acceptance of any evidence to that effect.

The present study should not act in the opposite manner, causing despair by questioning one of the few bits of hopeful evidence. But

[83] Hoebel, *Man in the Primitive World*, p. 517.
[84] Rink, p. 43, Mirsky, p. 55.   [85] Nieboer, pp. 252–55.
[86] Weyer, p. 162.   [87] Hoebel, *The Law of Primitive Man,* p. 99.

it should promote impartial inspection of evidence rather than its uncritical embrace simply because it is pleasing. If men are to live together in peace, the answer may lie in creating new forms of human society, which take account of the twentieth century, rather than in longing after some supposed innocent past.

Gogol's Epistolary Writing

WILLIAM MILLS TODD

Gogol's nearly fourteen hundred letters constitute over a third of his total writing. It is probable that many more of them have not come down to us. They span thirty years of his life—a decade before and a decade after his major fiction was completed and published. Gogol wrote much of his critical and didactic prose in epistolary form, and, although he never wrote an epistolary novel, letters are occasionally used in his imaginative works. In this essay I shall give an outline of the Russian epistolary tradition of the eighteenth and early nineteenth centuries, then briefly survey Gogol's letters and suggest a number of approaches to them: their relationship to epistolary convention, special features, evolution, and place in his *œuvre*.

In any Soviet critical edition of a writer's works correspondence occupies a prominent place. The recent Academy of Sciences edition of Gogol devotes five of fourteen volumes to his letters.[1] Nevertheless, students of Russian literature have virtually ignored epistolary writing. There is no article on letters in the Soviet literary encyclopedia, they are not listed among the many seminar topics proposed by N. K. Piksanov,[2] nor are they given a separate section in the *History of Russian Literature* bibliographies of the eighteenth and nineteenth centuries.[3]

The meager scholarly work on letters as a literary phenomenon was fertilized by the Russian Formalists and has addressed itself to the disrespectful relationship of personal correspondence to the

[1] N. V. Gogol, *Polnoe sobranie sochinenij* (Akademi ja Nauk, 1940–52). Subsequent citations from this edition (volume and page) will be included within the body of the essay in parentheses.

[2] N. K. Piksanov, *Dva veka russkoj literatury, 2-oe izd.* (Moscow, 1924).

[3] *Istorija russkoj literatury XIX veka: bibliograficheskij ukazatel'*, ed. K. D. Muratova (Moscow-Leningrad, 1962). *Istorija russkoj literatury XVIII veka: bibliograficheskij ukazatel'*, ed. P. N. Berkov (Leningrad, 1968).

changing genres of the early nineteenth century.[4] Recently, intro-
ductory articles in editions of the major authors' collected works [5]
and linguistic analyses [6] have monopolized the study of epistolary
forms.

Almost all such studies insist *en passant* on the literary significance
of epistolary genres in the eighteenth and early nineteenth centuries
and tell how the writer would polish the rough drafts of his letters.
The studies give one or two interesting characteristics of the letters
in question, then proceed to illustrate theories on the writer's biography or relationship to his social and intellectual milieu. A common
scientific metaphor for the creative process reveals the Formalist
heritage; Griboedov's letters are a "laboratory" for the language of
Woe from Wit,[7] the intimate letter of the early nineteenth century is
a "laboratory" for linguistic experiment,[8] Pushkin's are a "laboratory" for his prose and poetry,[9] Gogol's are a "laboratory" for
Selected Passages from Correspondence with Friends ("Vybrannye
mesta iz perepiski s druz'jami").[10]

These conclusions about the individual writer's creative evolution
and biography cannot usually be denied, and at times the letter
does serve as a type of writing more disrespectful of literary
decorum than other types. Nevertheless, these are far from the only
possible treatments of epistolary writing. It can be examined as a
field of literary endeavor with its development, rules, and classifica-
tions by period, structure, style, theme. One may ask not only how
the writer rebels against the decorum of his age but to what extent

[4] N. Stepanov, "Druzheskoe pis'mo nacala XIX v.," *Russkaja proza*, ed.
B. Ejenbaum and Ju. Tynjanov (The Hague, Mouton, 1963), pp. 74–101.
Also in N. Stepanov, *Poety i prozaiki* (Moscow, 1966), pp. 66–91. Stepanov's
"Pis'ma Pushkina kak literaturnyj zhanr" is also in *Poeti i prozaiki*, pp. 91–100.

[5] G. M. Fridlender, "Pis'ma Gogolja," in N. V. Gogol, *Sobranie sochinenij v
semi tomax* (Moscow, 1966–67), VII, 5–30. I. Semenko, "Pis'ma Puskina" in
A. S. Puskin, *Sobranie sochinenij v desjati tomax* (Moscow, 1959–62), IX,
389–407. S. I. Vavilev, "Predislovie" and L. B. Modzalevskij, "Ot sostavilelja"
in M.V. Lomonosov, *Sochinenija* (Akademija Nauk, 1891–1948), VIII, 1–40.

[6] I. Il'inskaja, "O jazyke pisem Griboedova," in *Literaturnoe nasledstvo*,
Nos. 47–48 (Moscow, 1946), pp. 285–96. V. A. Malaxovskij, "Jazyk pisem
Puskina," *Izvestija A.N.S.S.S.R., otdelenie obshehestvennyx nauk*, Nos. 2–3
(1937), pp. 503–68.

[7] Il'inskaja, p. 285.   [8] Stepanov, "Druzheskoe pis'mo," p. 76.

[9] Semenko, p. 401. Malaxovskij, p. 505. A. Z. Lezhnev, *Proza Puskina* (Moscow, 1966), p. 247.

[10] Fridlender, p. 23.

he observes it. Such adherence would be proof that the writer considered letters a form of literature. Are his letters "subjective" (dealing with the inner life, thoughts, feelings) or are they "objective" (concerned with the external world, topical matters, things outside the mind)? This is an especially important question to ask of any writing of Gogol's age, and G. M. Fridlender does so in his introduction to Gogol's letters.[11] Does the writer alter his letters for different correspondents, or does he direct his entire arsenal of styles and subjects at any one of them? Finally, when dealing with an author who takes pride in his use of the written word, who realizes that his letters may someday be published, one should not fail to consider a point raised by Northrop Frye in connection with autobiography: "most . . . are inspired by a creative, and therefore fictional, impulse to select only those events and experiences in the writer's life that go to build up one integrated pattern." [12]

While modern literary theoreticians and critics have consigned letters to writers of etiquette manuals, their eighteenth-century predecessors did not. They attached great importance to the letter, invented and preserved rules and categories for it, and used it for a number of purposes our age no longer does.

The value of correspondence in early eighteenth-century Russian society with its small reading public, ecclesiastical and secular censorship, and limited printing facilities is not difficult to imagine. Small literate groups could copy letters numerous times and circulate them easily, thus escaping the censorship.[13] Even when literacy and interest in secular literature spread throughout the country, and more printing firms were established, occasionally repressive censorship made this type of letter attractive to such radical polemicists as Belinskij, whose unpublished "Letter to Gogol" ("Pis'mo k Gogolju," 1847) passed through many hands in thousands of copies. Such works, most appropriately called "open letters" since their audience is clearly expected to exceed the person or group to which they are addressed, are still popular among the Soviet Union's intellectuals.

These public letters transmitted some of the most important

[11] *Ibid.*, p. 7.

[12] Northrop Frye, *Anatomy of Criticism* (New York, Atheneum, 1966), p. 307.

[13] Avvakum's letters, a number of which are preserved from the seventeenth and early eighteenth centuries, are early examples of sucr circulation.

scholarship and criticism of the eighteenth century. Lomonosov's "Letter on the Rules of Russian Prosody" ("Pis'mo o pravilax rossijskogo stixotvorstva," 1739) virtually founded this field of study in Russia. His "Introduction on the Use of Church Books in the Russian Language" ("Predislovie o pol'ze knig cerkovnyx v rossijskom jazyke") was originally planned as a letter to his Maecenas, I. I. Shuvalov.[14] In the "Introduction," Lomonosov became one of the first Russians in the eighteenth century to treat the letter theoretically. This treatment, however, is brief and limited to a discussion of lexical levels permissible in two types of letter. The first consists of "familiar verse letters" (*stixotvornye druzheskie pis'ma*), for which a middle style is presecribed—Church Slavonic known to literate people, words common to both Church Slavonic and Russian, Russian words used by cultured people, and nonvulgar colloquialisms.[15] The second is "familiar letters" (*druzheskie pis'ma*), for which Lomonosov specifies the lowest of his three styles (the last two levels of the middle style).[16]

Lomonosov's critics delight in showing the inadequacy of the theory of the three styles and his own violations of it.[17] He had intended the low and middle styles to imitate conversational speech, and they did not come close, to judge by the few examples he gave. This was a matter of literary decorum. Nevertheless, the theory was significant for Russian letters because it placed them directly in the tradition of Western European correspondence, which developed from the classical epistolary ideal of "the easy informality of friendly conversation." [18]

Lomonosov's contemporaries collected and posthumously published some of his letters in the first scholarly edition of his works. During his life, Lomonosov himself was not unaware of their appeal.

---

[14] Lomonosov, IV, 236 nn.   [15] *Ibid.*, p. 228.

[16] *Ibid.* A. P. Sumarokov's "Epistle I" ("Epistola I," 1748) expressed similar ideas on prose letter writing. See *The Literature of Eighteenth Century Russia*, ed. Harold B. Segel (New York, Dutton, 1967), I, 225.

[17] V. V. Vinogradov, *Ocherki po istorii russkogo literaturnogo jazyka XVII–XIX vv* (Moscow, 1938), p. 97.

[18] *Dictionary of World Literature*, ed. Joseph T. Shipley (Paterson, Littlefield, Adams, and Co., N. J., 1960), p. 250.

Classical stylistic theory was available to Lomonosov through a seventeenth century Slavonic "Ritorika" (1620). A. I. Gorshkov, *Istorija russkogo literaturnogo jazyka* (Moscow, 1965), p. 99. He could also have encountered it through French manuals published in 1714 and 1736. Lomonosov, LV, 239 nn.

One of the sterner, more rhetorical letters warns: "if you do not spare him from defamation this letter will be sung in songs and circulated around the city like a *pièce d'éloquence.*" [19] His letters reflect the personalities and interests of their recipients, a feature of neoclassical letter writing. Those written to fellow scholar Teplov tend to be blunt, vernacular, yet not without rhetoric; one to the Archbishop of Archangelsk is convoluted, self-effacing, and lofty in diction. Letters to foreign scientists are in German or Latin. The ones to Shuvalov feature classical allusions, sober reminiscences, humor, and poetry.

A letter to Shuvalov dated July 26, 1753,[20] is one of the most popular in Russian: Pushkin admired it and Grech used it as a model, remarking that only the language had become outdated.[21] Describing the death by lightning of the scientist G.-V. Rixman, it is a paradigm of the neoclassical letter's integration of theme, style, and construction, as well as one of the best narratives of its century. Lomonosov opens without any polite formulae. He alters the usual ending to fit the situation: "Your Excellency's most humble servant, in tears." The first sentences, disturbed and confused manifestations of *neglegentia epistolarum,* are striking in that Lomonosov was normally a lucid, articulate man: "that I am writing to Your Excellency consider a miracle; for the dead do not write. I still do not know, or at least I doubt, whether I am alive or dead." The third sentence introduces the subsequently intertwining parts of the story—the effects of the lightning bolt on Lomonosov and on Rixman: "I see that Prof. Rixman was struck down by lightning in those same circumstances which I was in at the same time." The heirs of the two men, Rixman's son and Lomonosov's infant (secular learning) dominate the second half of the letter.

There are a few manifestations of the tortuous syntax of Lomonosov's age present, but generally he composes with terse sentences describing as many as several actions contiguous in time: setting a table, observing the conducting wire as the cabbage soup grows cold, heeding pleas to come in to dinner. At the center of the letter comes

[19] Lomonosov, VIII, 218. This remark was not included in the letter's final version, which was sent to G. N. Teplov on Jan. 30, 1761.

[20] Lomonosov, VIII, 129–31.

[21] N. Grech, *Uchebnaja kniga rossijskoj slovesnosti ili izbrannye mesta iz ruskix sochinenij i perevodov v stixax i proze,* 4 vols. (St. Petersburg, 1918–21), I, 59.

a magnificent long sentence encompassing a much greater period of time and assembling all the fathers and heirs:

The proximity of my own death, his pale corpse, our past accord and friendship, the lament of his wife, children, and household were all so painful that I could not give a speech or answer to the multitude who gathered as I looked at that man with whom I had sat for an hour in the Conference and discussed our future public act.

Then Lomonosov the scientist clinically records the results of his colleague's "lamentable experiment":

The first flash from the suspended line had entered his head, where a cherry-red spot was visible on his forehead; the lightning's electrical force had gone out of his feet into the floor. The leg and toes were blue, the boot torn, but not burned . . . and so by a lamentable experiment he proved that the electricity of lightning can be deflected.

A plea to Shuvalov to educate Rixman's son ("who already shows good promise"), to seek a pension for the widow, and to protect the sciences, lest Rixman's "fine death" have been in vain, conclude the letter. One wonders if anything so tragic, yet so directly grounded in the everyday world (cabbage soup, torn boot) could have been written in any other recognized genre of the mid-eighteenth century.

The second half of the eighteenth century witnessed the rise of Sentimentalism in Russia, and personal correspondence reflects this to no less an extent than other genres. Comparison of a theme (children) common to Lomonosov's letter above and to a letter by Radishchev, who stood close to the Sentimentalist movement, illustrates this development. Lomonosov's concern for Rixman's son is related to the son's adult life, that he should fulfill the "good promise" he had shown at the age of *five years*. There is scant feeling involved in the description of this little man. Lomonosov need not be considered a pedantic pedophobe—this is the way the child was treated in the literature of his time. Radishchev's outpouring reflects a different decorum, although the reference to the utilitarian Helvetius and a request in the postscript for meteorological instruments shows that Radishchev's interests were not entirely satisfied by contemplating his own emotions:

But what power has the intellect over feeling? From myself I now see that reason follows feelings or is nothing other than they are: according to Helvetius's system, it revolves around one thought, and all my reasoning, all philosophy disappears, when I remember my children. Be charitable to them, dear sir; if your mercies touch and have not yet ceased to pour out onto their unhappy father, do not deprive them of the same, edify and instruct them. I feel that being deprived of their father, they are deprived of so much I cannot imagine it. . . . Before a sensitive soul I pour out my grief.[22]

Through this display of Radishchev's own emotions and his projection of them into his correspondent, even less emerges about the children than does in Lomonosov's letter—only vague fears that his brother will exert a bad influence on them.

This type of letter deserves a new classification—sentimental, introspective, or subjective—as opposed to Lomonosov's objective letter which expressed his emotions in actions—speechlessness, crying, confusion, At the same time a compositional principle has remained unchanged—Radishchev's personal letters, like Lomonosov's, tend to deal with but a single topic, unless they reply to a series of questions the addressee has asked. Radishchev's adherence to this convention produced a somewhat ludicrous letter to A. R. Voroncov (May 2, 1791), in which the postscript on literature is twice as long as the body of the letter, a discourse on the Siberian economy.

The possibility of using the personal letter as a vehicle for portraying the inner life and serious events with some informality was not lost on eighteenth-century novelists. Richardson, who wielded enormous influence on the European epistolary novel, contends in his Preface to *Clarissa* (1747): "all the letters are written while the hearts of the writers must be supposed to be wholly engaged in their subject . . . so that they abound, not only with critical situations, but with what may be called instantaneous descriptions and reflections." Ian Watt correctly points out that despite Richardson's assertion, literary convention does not entirely unhand the epistolary novel.[23] An early Russian example, F. A. Emin's *Letters of Ernest and Doravra* ("Pis'ma Ernesta i Doravry," 1766) illustrates this. The characters have foreign names, and the lexicon of Sentimentalism—feelings, fate, the heart, tears—drenches the novel. Emin's characters generalize more than give instantaneous descrip-

[22] A. N. Radishchev, *Izbrannye sochinenija* (Moscow, 1952), pp. 526–27. The letter was sent to A. R. Voroncov on Oct. 20, 1790, as Radishchev was traveling to exile in Siberia.

[23] Ian Watt, *The Rise of the Novel* (Harmondsworth, Middlesex, England, Penguin, 1966), p. 199.

tions of nature. Ernest spends considerable time virtually citing Rousseau on the problem of the civilized man's place in nature, and the letters tend to turn away from the external world, as he admits: "All these deliberations quelled the cruelty of my poverty, and of necessity I began to philosophize." [24] Emin's novel is not nearly as successful as some of its Western European predecessors, but it shows how the inward direction of the modern novel in part owes its existence to intimate Sentimentalist correspondence.

A number of other offshoots from the familiar prose letter flourished in the eighteenth century. N. I. Novikov took advantage of Catherine II's momentary weakness for satirical journals to flay her ample vanity in his own journals (1769–74). The primary scourge was imaginary letters from the readers, a voice that could not be equated with the editor's, especially after allegorical names (Pravdoljubov, "lover of truth") gave way to funny or nonsignificant ones. That the Empress was not writing under her own name made her an inviting victim—she is referred to as "great-grandmother" and accused of inability to write Russian.[25] Furthermore, Novikov invented an ungrammatical, brilliantly ironic private correspondence between members of a provincial family. They considerably lowered the tone of this fiction from that of Emin's novel and thus parodied the rural idylls and didacticism which frequently found their way into epistolary novels. The family does not act out a parody of the epistolary novel's love triangle, however.[26]

Fonvizin's "Letters from France to P. I. Panin" ("Pis'ma iz Francii P. I. Paninu," written 1777–78) is an example of another form of ironic letter, one with indirect commentary and indirect address. While treating French situations with scorn, Fonvizin obviously touches actual Russian problems (superstition, tax farming, corruption, rule of favorites), expressing little praise for his homeland.

Nonironic travel letters were also popular. A writer could collect or invent them and, as in the epistolary novel, create "instantaneous descriptions and reflections." Karamzin's *Letters of a Russian Travel-*

[24] *Xrestomatija po russkoj literature XVIII veka,* ed. A. V. Kokarev (Moscow, 1965), p. 583.   [25] *Ibid.,* pp. 237–38.

[26] There is merely a hint at a potential forced marriage for the son Falalej. *Ibid.,* p. 257.

The naïve letter as a form of fiction has not been lost in subsequent Russian literature, as Chexov's "Letter to a Learned Neighbor ("Pis'mo k uchenomu sosedu") and Babel's "Letter" ("Pis'mo") testify.

ler ("Pis'ma russkogo puteshestvennika," 1792) consists of such units, varying in mode, but generally touching one scene and related topics.[27] He maintains the illusion of correspondence by intimate nicknames and mention of received letters, but often dispenses with such devices, perhaps to aoivd repetition. Moreover, Karamzin makes little attempt to reveal the interests and personaities of his correspondents, a situation which occurs in familiar letters as they turn from neoclassical politeness to increasing subjectivity.

By the 1790s, writers less frequently resorted to epistolary forms for depicting their characters' inner lives. "Stream of consciousness" and inner monologue eventually assumed this function. The modern Russian novel's subsequent development was such that not only did the epistolary form gradually disappear during the course of the nineteenth century, but even letters within the novel generally fell into disrepute as plot components. Dostoevsky's epistolary *Poor Folk* ("Bednye ljudi," 1846) remains an effective counterexample: the sentimental letters of Julie and Marija in *War and Peace* are an exception justified by the period in which the novel is set.

It is with some reservations that one calls the personal correspondence of the Arzamas group a new step in the evolution of Russian epistolary writing. I. Semenko's conclusion that their familiar letters were "connected with the escape from neoclassicism's lofty genres and expressed the personal, intimate, 'domestic' side of human life," [28] ignores the fact that such letters were a neoclassical genre, that Russian neoclassicism had a number of lowly genres anyway, and that letters had been associated since the fifth century, B.C., with the characteristics he lists. Lomonosov's middle and low styles were, after all, intended to imitate conversation and portray everyday life within the limits imposed by literary decorum.

Like Lomonosov, Pushkin tended to write letters objectively and kept the recipient's personality in mind.[29] Like Lomonosov, he included verse, wit, and material from various linguistic levels. The essential difference between the two authors is in the nature and extent of the wit, in the interests and literary styles not necessarily in the attitudes toward personal correspondence. One of Pushkin's most oft-quoted letters vividly reveals these changes:

[27] Hans Rothe, *N. M. Karamzins europäische Reise: der Beginn des russischen Romans* (Berlin-Zurich, 1968), p. 157, lists five modes: idyllic, tragic, ironic, mixed, and informational.

[28] Semenko, pp. 405–6.   [29] *Ibid.*, pp. 397–98.

In the wilds, worn out by a life of fasting, with a
broken-down stomach, I do not soar like an eagle—
I sit and am ill of diarrheic idleness.

I am saving a supply of paper; I am foreign to the
effort of inspiration; I rarely go onto Parnassus,
and only for great need.

But your ingenious manure tickles my nose pleasantly;
it reminds me of Xvostov, the father of toothy
pigeons, and it invites my soul again to the
defecation of my former days.

Thank you my dear fellow, and I kiss you on your poetic little a——.
Since I have been in Mixajlovskoe I have guffawed only twice: at your
critique of the "New Poetics of Fables" and at the dedication of your
s—— to s——. How can I help loving you? How can I help groveling
before you? However, I am ready to grovel, but no matter what you say
I shall not copy—it would be the death of me, and nothing else. Con-
gratulate me, my dear fellow, upon my romantic tragedy. In it the principal personage is Boris—Godunov! My tragedy is finished; I reread
it aloud, alone, and I clapped my hands and shouted, 'at a boy, Pushkin,
'at a boy, you son of a bitch! My holy fool is a very funny young
fellow. Marina will make you get a h—— —— — because she is a Pole
and very good looking (of the type of Katerina Orlova, have I told
you?). The others are very appealing, too, except for Captain Margaret,
who swears obscenely all the time—the censorship won't pass him.
Zhukovskij says that the Tsar will forgive me, as a result of my tragedy—
hardly, my dear one. Although it is written in a good spirit, there's no
way I could hide my ears completely under the pointed cap of the holy
fool. They stick out! Your criticism of Krylov is killingly funny: be quiet,
I know that myself, but that rat is an old crony of mine. I have called
him a representative of the *spirit* of the Russian people—I don't vouch
that it does not stink in some respects. In antiquity our common people
were called *smerd* [stench] (cf. Mr. Karamzin). The point is that Krylov
is a most original carcass, Count Orlov is a fool, but we are bumpkins,
etc., etc.

I wrote you from Pskov a killingly funny letter, but I burned it up.
The bishop there, Father Evgenij, received me as the father of Evgenij.
The governor was also extremely gracious. He gave me his own verses,
sir, to correct. What do you think of that! Farewell, my dear one.[30]

---

[30] Pushkin, IX, 213–14. to P. A. Vjazemskij on approximately Nov. 7,
1825. The translation is from *The Letters of Alexander Pushkin*, trans.
J. Thomas Shaw (Bloomington and Philadelphia, University of Pennsylvania
Press, 1963), pp. 261–62. The opening three paragraphs are in verse in the
original.

The literary criticism is characteristic of the Arzamas letter, as are the *ex abrupto* opening, the abundance of scatological imagery, the in-jokes, mock compliments, conversational cadence, and the lack of a closing formula.[31] The letter can only be said to have unity in that it replies to points Vjazemskij raised or else in that it is preoccupied with literature.

The Arzamas writers were a small group and represented but one trend in the letter writing of the early nineteenth century. A somewhat different, more conventional and comprehensive approach is found in N. Grech's section on letters in his *Textbook on Russian Literature or Selected Passages from Russian Works and Translations in Verse and Prose*.[32]

Followers of the textbook and the Arzamas writers would agree in defining the letter as a one-sided conversation written as its author would speak. Grech, however, follows the Sentimentalist school's doctrine of "pleasantness" (prijatnost') and avoidance of bombast, which the Arzamas writers consciously violate with obscenities and Church Slavonicisms for comic effect. The Arzamas group's practice generally coincides with Grech's dictates that the letter should be a whole, that it should be written with the recipient in mind, that it should have one governing tone. But there is considerable difference of opinion on the role of the feelings or the heart. Little was exempt from irony or parody in the Arzamas correspondence; little inner life was revealed in their letters. Stepanov sees no psychology at all in those of Vjazemskij, Pushkin, and A. I. Turgenev.[33] Grech, conversely, insisted that the personal letter be an arena for the heart and mind, cautioning only against excessive sentimentality, and declared feelings and serious thought off limits for humorous letters.[34]

Grech, whose Russian grammar required eighty paradigms to cover the noun system, was more succinct in categorizing epistolary forms. First he divides them into "personal" and "literary," the latter using the outer form of the letter to afford the author greater freedom of structure and expression. Nevertheless, he makes the important concession that the boundaries are unclear between the two. As examples he lists of the former "business," "polite," "friendly," "humorous," and "instructive" letters: of the latter, "travel," "description of important events," "critical," "important

---

[31] Stepanov, "Druzheskoe pis'mo," p. 86.
[32] See note 21 for the Russian title.
[33] Stepanov, "Druzheskoe pis'mo," p. 86.   [34] Grech, p. 56.

concepts which touch the heart and imagination." These fuzzy distinctions serve only to justify his inability to draw a hard and fast
line between "personal" and "literary" letters, for there is really
little difference in the potential content of the two types. An important omission, for a study of Gogol and Romantic letter writing,
is the confessional letter. The list's primary value lies in its indication of the usual content of letters in the early nineteenth century.

Grech gives a number of set forms for polite letters, such as could
be found in any modern book on etiquette, and notes their frequent
insincerity. His examples of literary letters from the eighteenth century are not too different from those in Soviet school anthologies.

Several conclusions may be made before discussing Gogol's correspondence. First, throughout the eighteenth and early nineteenth
centuries, Russian literary theoreticians treated the letter and recognized it as a legitimate form of literature. Second, the letter was
from the beginning of this period a flexible form, adaptable to many
subjects from the sublime to the scatological. Third, the letter, despite
its canonized freedom and traditional conversational orientation,
was still subject to literary decorum. Fourth, as was seen by the
epistolary novel's example, the letter could inspire innovation in
other genres. Fifth, by the 1820s there existed a clear distinction in
personal correspondence between "objective" and "subjective" letters. The former let little escape lampooning and paid little attention to the inner life; the latter refrained from irony and satire, but
observed and gave vent to feelings and emotions.

The variety of Gogol's letters in style and theme can scarcely be
imagined by a reader who knows him only from his stories, plays,
and novel, in which letters are generally humorous. The nonsensical,
alogical petitions in "The Tale of How Ivan Ivanovich Quarreled
with Ivan Nikiforovich" and the mayor's note to Anna Andreevna
written over a hotel bill in the *Inspector General*,[35] for example, are
ironic comments on the characters who send and receive them as
well as on the not entirely defunct epistolary tradition in fiction. The
dogs' letters in the "Diary of a Madman" also serve a variety of
purposes—pricking Poprishchin's vanity ("Papa sometimes sends
him out instead of a servant" [36]) or exposing Sophie's emptyheaded-

[35] *The Collected Tales and Plays of Nikolai Gogol,* ed. Leonard J. Kent,
trans. Constance Garnett (New York, Modern Library, 1969), p. 627.

[36] *Ibid.,* p. 464. The letters are, of course, also the product of Poprishchin's
diseased mind.

ness. Indeed nobody in the story is left unscathed: these letters are written better than those of the department head, they mock "papa's" glory-seeking. Despite their sentimental intention of conveying feelings and impressions ("an idea taken from a work translated from German," [37] says Porprishchin), they reflect a banal canine world equivalent to the human one they ridicule.

The note Chichikov receives in chapter VIII of *Dead Souls* is a parody of the graveyard sentimental love epistle—a parody in the meaning of the Greek word from which it is derived, "to sing beside," since the narrator's naïvely ironic commentary accompanies the cliché-ridden epistle:

The letter began in very positive terms, precisely as follows: "No, I really must write you!" After that it went on to say that there is such a thing as a secret affinity between souls; this verity was clinched wtih a number of full stops that took up almost half a line. Then followed a few thoughts, quite remarkable for their incontrovertibility, so that we deem it almost indispensable to make an abstract of them: "What is our life? A vale of sorrows. What is the world? An insensate human herd." Next the fair writer mentioned that she was bedewing with tears certain lines written by her angelic mother—five-and-twenty years had gone since she had passed from this world; she called on Chichikov to come out into the wilderness, to leave forever the city, where people in stifling enclosures cannot breathe the free air; the end of the letter even echoed downright despair and concluded with the following lines:

> Two turtledoves will show thee
> Where my cold corpse lies;
> Their lovelorn cooing tells thee:
> She died amid tears and sighs.

There wasn't much meter, especially in the last line: this, however, mattered but little—the letter was written in the spirit of that time. Nor was there a signature of any sort, either first name or last—not even a date line. The postscript merely added that his own heart ought to surmise who had written these lines, and that at the Governor's ball, which was set for the morrow, the writer herself would be present.[38]

Since the unknown admirer never appears, this passage constitutes another of the novel's violations of traditional plotting.

Gogol used the letter form twice in a second area of his work, critical and didactic writing: "An Excerpt from a Letter Written by

[37] *Ibid.,* p. 461.

[38] Nikolai V. Gogol, *Dead Souls,* trans. B. G. Guerney (New York, Modern Library, 1965), pp. 201–2.

the Author to a Certain Littérateur Soon after the First Performance of the *Inspector General*" ("Otryvok iz pis'ma, pisannogo avtorom vskore posle pervogo predstavlenie 'Revizora' k odnumu literatoru," 1841) and *Selected Passages from Correspondence with Friends* ("Vybrannye mesta iz perepiski s druz'jami," 1847). But, as the titles of the works (excerpt, selected passages) indicate, many of the letter's formulae were cut out. This would come as no particular shock to the Russian reader; Karamzin had done it fifty years earlier in his *Letters of a Russian Traveller*. The "Excerpt" takes advantage of the letter's intimacy to reveal Gogol's frustrations with his play's staging in more personal terms than he did in other articles on the *Inspector General*. He opens and closes on highly emotional notes:

. . . The *Inspector General* has been performed—and things are so dim and strange in my soul. . . . I anticipated, I knew in advance, how the affair would go, and from all this a sad and vexingly distressing feeling enveloped me [IV, 99].

For Heaven's sake come soon. I will not go without bidding farewell to you. I need to tell you much more than I can say in an unbearable, cold letter . . . [IV, 104].

This "letter," Gogol told S. T. Aksakov, was sent to Pushkin, whom Gogol never did see again after the *Inspector General* was staged. Gogol dated it May 25, 1836. As he composed the rough drafts for the "Excerpt" in 1840–41, it is unlikely that the final plea was made to Pushkin. Certainly the tone of the "Excerpt" differs so much from the generally humorous tone of his letters to Pushkin that this claim is not inconceivably a figment of Gogol's creative imagination.

The *Selected Passages* use epistolary techniques in different ways, although like the "Excerpt" each chapter in varying degrees dispenses with devices which give the illusion of letter writing. Two (XXXI, XXXII) destroy it entirely. Sometimes Gogol maintains the illusion merely by using second-person pronouns (III) or by referring to an addressee in the chapter title (V). Other chapters contain personal allusions (XXIV), while chapter XXX ("Parting Words") tantalizes the reader with an untold story about the addressee in debilitating combat with the bureaucracy of a vulgar town.

The epistolary format enabled Gogol, who had been seriously ill, to finish the book quickly; much of it had already been written in his familiar letters during the years 1843–46. It also gave a mass of material an acceptable form. At the same time, the letters allowed him to create the persona of a moralizing adviser in contact with representatives of Russia's cultural, political, economic, and religious institutions and to depict their problems in perfecting these diseased organs of his society. It should be noted that Gogol himself invariably referred to the book as his "letters," although he did confess to Vjazemskij that they contained some things inappropriate to letters and were somewhat of a sermon. (February 28, 1947). Nevertheless, he did resort to that convention of correspondence by which the author adheres to a single topic, tailored to the needs, interests, and personality of its recipient. This motivates and justifies different approaches and certain inconsistencies between the chapters which would be impermissible in another form, such as a journal or treatise. The fascinatingly contorted scholastic apology for secular literature in chapter XIV, for example, is motivated by the religious interests and monastic outlook of its recipient ("Count A. P. T. . . . oj"), established in that chapter and in chapters III, VIII, and IX, which were also addressed to him. In fact, Gogol had specifically hoped to bring "characters and subjects" (XIII, 209) to the fore, he asserted, not himself. He did not succeed in this for his contemporaries because the censorship eliminated five chapters and numerous negative evaluations of the church, state, and gentry from the published book. So although the restored version is not without its obnoxious passages ("[this] book, which perhaps half of literate Russia will read," VIII, 343), we should not be overly influenced by the famous devastating reviews it received in Gogol's own lifetime.[39]

The relationship of Gogol's personal letters to tradition is more complicated than was the case with letters in his fiction, which tended to parody the Sentimentalist letter, and with letters in his expository writing, which creatively used tradition but did not violate it. Gogol on occasion revealed his attitude toward the letter in his correspondence. His prescriptions for others by no means always equaled his own practice.

In friendly letters of the Arzamas type, the style of the correspondent's letters or the works he had enclosed with them were generally criticized. In objective, humorous letters, Gogol followed this convention throughout his career, as to this young girl of partly

[39] They are summarized in Jesse Zeldin's introduction to his translation of N. Gogol, *Selected Passages from Correspondence with Friends* (Nashville, Vanderbilt University Press, 1969) and in Vsevolod Setchkarev, *Gogol: His Life and Works* (New York, New York University Press, 1965), pp. 79–80.

foreign descent: "I like to read your letters very much. Although declensions in them are more often than not free and do not sometimes obey your lawful power, your thought is always clear and sometimes expressed so felicitously that I envy you" (XI, 180. M. P. Balabina. Nov. 7, 1838).

Nevertheless, Gogol took less interest in the style of his correspondents' letters than in their content. From his early youth to the end of his life he pestered family and friends for descriptions—of Petersburg, of the Ukraine, of Russian life on all levels—and for criticism of his works. A number of these descriptions were used in his fiction, from *Evenings on a Farm near Dikanka* to the second volume of *Dead Souls,* for which he once demanded information from Rosset lest his own "nose poke out" of the book (XII, 279, April 15, 1847). In short, he asked for critical, objective letters somewhat in the Arzamas tradition.

In the 1840s, when Gogol was occupied with the second volume of *Dead Souls* and new problems presented themselves, the nature of his requests changed. On December 24, 1844 he described to A. O. Smirnova what sort of letter young Jurij Samarin should write him: "in the letter there should be almost a diary of thoughts, feelings, and sensations, a lively understanding of all people he happens to meet, his opinions about them, and the opinions of others about them, and finally incidents and skirmishes with them. In a word, so that I may *hear life itself"* (XIII, 412). This very demand for some sense of the inner life is implicit in Gogol's criticism of P. V. Annenkov's *Parisian Letters:* "recently I read your letter about Paris. There was much keenness of observation and accuracy, but daguerreotype accuracy. The brush which painted them is not sensed; the author himself is unformed wax. . . . In a word, it is not evident from your letters why the letters were written" (XIII, 363. Aug. 12, 1847). This dovetails with Gogol's desire, expressed in the same letter, to portray the whole Russian man as a psychological phenomenon.

Gogol rarely comments on his own letters. It is not until the 1840s, when epistolary forms begin to constitute the greatest part of his writing, that he reflects on their role in his life and work. In an especially introspective letter to V. A. Zhukovskij, Gogol promises: "about the everyday trifles of my life I say nothing to you; there are almost none of them, and incidentally, thank God I do not even feel or perceive them." [40] (June 26, 1842) Significantly, with this departure from the detail of an objective letter, Gogol announces that his soul's education is on the road to completion and proclaims his grandiose plan for further volumes of *Dead Souls.* Not long thereafter Gogol writes Smirnova: "I live in work, partly in letters, partly in my own inner work" (XII, 420. Dec. 24, 1844). He refers not to *Selected Passages,* which he had not yet begun, but to the private correspondence he was churning out at an astounding rate. This particular letter is ten pages long in small print.

During these same years there occurs a change in his attitude towards his letters. The long-established practice of passing letters from hand to hand has been described already. Gogol does not himself discuss it until a letter to S. T. Aksakov on August 18, 1842: "let this letter be for both you and Olga Semenovna, but do not show it to others. The lyric movements of our soul! . . . It is unwise to communicate them to just anyone" (XII, 97). Within two years Gogol had lost almost all such shame. In *Selected Passages* he mentions having asked friends to save and publish his letters, starting from late 1844, the year he began to write many of the didactic letters which form the basis of the book (VIII, 222). And during the years 1843–48 he several times asked his correspondents to pass his letters on to others, to reread his previous letters, or to save them. He actually held his letters of the period in which he wrote *Selected Passages* and the surviving drafts of the sequel to *Dead Souls* [41] to be of greater importance than the stories of the 1830s which made him famous.

Gogol's final references to the letter are connected with *Dead Souls,* on which he was working with some frustration. The same

[40] *Letters of Nikolai Gogol,* ed. Carl R. Proffer, trans. Carl R. Proffer in collaboration with Vera Krivoshein (Ann Arbor, University of Michigan Press, 1967), p. 115. Proffer's preface presents the letters as having primarily autobiographical significance.

[41] There has been some controversy amongst Soviet scholars over the date of the surviving five chapters. I favor the 1843–45 date proposed by M. V. Xrapchenko, *Tvorchestvo Gogolja* (Moscow, 1959), pp. 475–76, and by E. S. Smirnova-Chikina, *Poema Gogolja "Mertvye dushi"* (Moscow, 1964), pp. 205–6. Reliable memoirs support this date. The editors of the Academy of Sciences edition suggest 1848–51, although they believe the surviving fifth chapter came from the earlier period, VII, 402, 415–21. E. S. Smirnova-Chikina finds his handwriting in this chapter most similar to that of the early 1840s, p. 283.

letter to Pletnev that records his impatience voices discontent with
the letter too: "a letter is rubbish. It can never express even the
tenth part of a man" (XIV, 160. Jan. 21, 1850). As expressing the
whole man was one of the problems he had set himself in the second
part of *Dead Souls,* this outburst implies that Gogol might have been
trying to achieve the same goal in his letters. Indeed, Gogol later
asked P. A. Pletnev for all the letters he had written him about the
novel (XIV, 220. May 6, 1851).

This meager collection of attitudes and information is of some
help in determining Gogol's relationship to letter writing. First, it
shows he had a tendency to distinguish two broad categories of
letters, as did his contemporaries, those describing the external world
("everyday trifles"), such as I previously call objective, and those
involving matters internal to the mind, thoughts, "expressing the
man," character, and feelings (subjective). Second, it shows that
Gogol treated correspondence with respect and associated it with
other components of his *œuvre.* He stopped short of defining that
association explicitly for his own letters, but on occasion told his
correspondents that their letters had to provide material for his
fiction or else demanded that the nature of their letters (objective or
subjective) answer the needs of his work in progress. Let us now
examine an expansion of these two problems: a classification of
Gogol's letters and the relation of them to his other writings.

Gogol's implied differentiation of objective and subjective letters
is a good starting point for classification despite the difficulties involved in defining the two words. With it we have some basis for
comparing his with traditional uses of these categories. Nevertheless,
just as his fiction is marked by its disrespect for plotting conventions,
so are many of his letters. Condolences, normally the subject of
polite form letters, are inserted into friendly ones which quickly
shift to other topics.[42] Transitions can be extraordinarily abrupt and
not motivated by the requirement of replying. There can arise
combinations of subjective and objective elements in equal portion,
such as in a letter to G. I. Vysockij with a florid self-portrait as an
internal émigré, grotesque descriptions, mock heroic characterizations, a humorous periphrastically related spanking, a romantic pro-
testation of disgust for the vulgar crowd, and a request for the price

[42] Examples are letters to Pletnev on Sept. 27, 1839, and to S. T. Aksakov
on Dec. 28, 1840.

of the "very best frock coat in the latest fashion" (X, 97–103, June 26, 1827).

At least one characteristic of Gogol's letters cuts across this line of classification—verifiable prevarication abounds in both objective and subjective letters, as all of Gogols biographers note. Some can be interpreted as attempts to please his correspondent or his own vanity—letters to his mother, for example, improve his social position. Other falsehoods seem born as much of a fictional impulse—to make the letter a good story—as of the desire to explain an action; such is the ecstatic love for a divine "she" in the letter to his mother of July 24, 1829 [43] (X, 147–48). Such frenzied mystification enters his fictional characters: Xlestakov in the *Inspector General* or Chichikov, the momentarily compulsive liar of *Dead Souls,* part II: "Chichikov became utterly muddled and lost his head; he all but spat in disgust and said to himself; 'Lord, what sort of rubbish am I spouting!' " [44] Whether "the artistic type of schizoid personality" gives birth to this prevarication is not our present concern.[45] Sometimes an artistic purpose justifies it: in a letter to A. O. Smirnova it fits Gogol's neatly composed self-portrait as a persecuted artist and helps justify his treatment of literary friends to write that he never spoke to any of them about his spiritual condition, but it is hardly true.[46]

Nevertheless, a number of Gogol's letters fall into the humorous, objective category. He used features of this type even before he came into contact with the remnants of the Arzamas group in Petersburg. He would have been led to this writing by his own fertile sense of humor and perhaps by the little gentlemen of his school. Vysockij for one was a wit and writer of comic verse (X, 404). Like the Arzamas letter, Gogol's objective letters can include puns, humorous alterations of opening and closing formulae, nicknames based on private associations, parody, obscene literary criticism, hyperbolic compliments, and ironic treatment of lofty diction. His first letter to Zhukovskij provides an example of this:

If . . . there were to appear in the area around Petersburg some tramp or night-time bandit and steal this unbearable twenty-four versts from

---

[43] V. Gippius, *Gogol* (Leningrad, 1924), p. 24, presents an interesting, but unconvincing challenge to the fictitiousness of "she."

[44] Guerney translation, p. 376.

[45] Proffer, pp. 212–13, lists symptoms of this illness.

[46] *Ibid.,* p. 154. Dec. 28, 1844.

Petersburg to Tsarskoe Selo, and take to his heels toward the edge of the world with them—or that some starved bear would hide them in his bearish belly instead of breakfast. Oh! With what ecstasy would I then brush off the dust of the earth from your boots with my hair, with what ecstasy would I prostrate myself at the feet of Your Poetic Excellency and with greedy ear catch the sweetest nectar.[47]

Such letters to his schoolfellows tend to be even less restrained since Gogol may have felt some reserve in writing to the older literary figures Zhukovskij and Pushkin. However, this is belied by the letter he once wrote Pushkin telling him how to conduct a conversation.[48] Gogol, nevertheless, lacks one essential feature of the Arzamas letter, self-irony. He reveals none of it except for comments on his "bird-like name" [49] and on the appreciation of his work by snorting typesetters [50] and by the French press, who sandwiched a review of his stories between pill and pomade advertisements.[51]

While Gogol wrote humorous, objective letters throughout his life, they came less frequently as his disenchantment with his early works grew, as he became more concerned with spiritual matters, and as he left Moscow, Petersburg, and his Russian literary friends behind. The majority of his letters were written from abroad, and most of these may be classified as "subjective."

Some distinction must be drawn between them and the sentimental subjective letters Gogol had more or less abandoned before he left school and had lampooned in *Dead Souls*. Although they preserve the convention of humorlessness (except for unintentional self-parody), it is fairly clear that they portray something deeper and more complex than the pleasant awareness of one's own sensitivity which permeates Sentimentalist writing. Gogol's subjective letters contain emotionally heightened self-dramatization, a complex of confessions (not always demonstrably reliable), and a gallery of deep and positive heroes. Ivan Turgenev, admittedly hostile to the ideas in them, at least understood something of their variety:

oh, what a great service their editor would have done if he had thrown out two-thirds of them [Gogol's posthumously published letters], or at least those written to society women—there is a no more hideous mixture of arrogance, servility, sanctimoniousness and vanity, prophetic and cringing tone in all literature! [52]

[47] *Ibid.*, p. 40. Sept. 10, 1831.
[49] A *gogol* is a type of duck.
[51] *Ibid.*, p. 161. Jan. 8, 1846.
[48] *Ibid.*, p. 49. May 13, 1834.
[50] Proffer, p. 38. Aug. 21, 1831.

[52] *Turgenev's Literary Reminiscences*, trans. David Magarshack (Minerva Press, 1968), p. 163.

The writing of such letters commenced in Gogol's youth (1827–28). Here is one of his most complex self-portraits:

When I used to visit you at home, I always purposely tried to display absent-mindedness, capriciousness, etc., so that you would think I had acquired little polish and was pressed by evil. But there is probably not anyone who suffered so many ingratitudes, stupid injustices, ridiculous pretensions, cold disdain, etc. I bore everything without reproaches, without grumbling; no one heard my complaints; I always even praised those who caused me grief. Truly, I am considered a riddle by everyone; no one has found me out completely. There at home I am considered capricious, some kind of unbearable pedant who thinks that he is more intelligent than anyone, that he is created in another way than most people. Do you believe it, inside I laughed at myself along with you. Here they call me a humble one, an ideal of modesty and patience. In one place I am the quietest, the most modest and polite; in another I am gloomy, pensive, uncouth, etc.—in a third garrulous and annoying in the extreme. Some think I am smart; others think I am stupid. Consider me what you like, but with my real career you will discover my real character; believe only that noble feelings always fill me, that I have never debased myself in my soul, and that I have destined my entire life to Good. You call me a dreamer, rash, as if inside I didn't laugh at them myself. No, I know people too well to be a dreamer. The lessons I have learned from them will remain ineffaceable forever, and they are the true guarantee of my happiness. You will see that with time I will be able to repay all of their bad deeds with good deeds, because in me their evil turned into good.[53]

While there is a certain amount of truth here—Gogol is such a complex person and accomplished ironist and actor that no biographer will ever "find him out completely"—this collection of poses is as much a portrait (or parody) of the complex romantic hero as a piece of serious self-analysis. Indeed, such posing led M. P. Pogodin in 1836 to tell Gogol he was becoming a comic actor (XI, 372).

As Gogol continues to write this type of letter, he tends to limit the number of poses per letter, but the mixture of sober self-analysis and hyperbolic self-dramatization continues. One wonders in reading them whether these and subsequent postures are self-delusion, conscious use of the mask to observe and control those who believe they are watching him, or literary composition. The answer is probably an inseparable mixture of these possibilities and others, but only the last two concern us here.

[53] Proffer, pp. 27–28. March 1, 1828. The translation accurately reproduces Gogol's clumsy style.

One aspect of this self-analysis most critics would accept: Gogol's frequent recognition of such problems and weaknesses in his style as these: "if you do not fasten down a beauty, her features will be too ethereal, indefinitely general, and therefore without character" (X, 217. Jan. 1, 1832), or "treasured feelings somehow become banal when they are clothed in words" (Dec. 28, 1840),[54] or "misunderstandings have come about because it occurred to me too early to speak of that which was extremely clear to me, but which I could not express in my stupid and vague speeches" (May 16, 1844).[55] A letter to his family summarizes his troubled situation—he will no longer write them of external matters, which bore him, and he cannot write of his inner occupations because they will be incomprehensible (XII, 320. June 12, 1844).

Throughout his career, Gogol turned to his letters to contend with these and other problems. His objective letters clearly relate to his fiction of the 1830s in their use of comic techniques, which occur in letters previous to his earliest surviving stories. It is possible that he developed some such techniques in lost and destroyed stories from his school days. Leon Stilman asserts that Gogol first isolated images in a famous letter comparing Petersburg with Moscow and European capitals which he had never seen (Jan. 3, 1829).[56]

The letters on occasion must also have served in developing his fictional characters for the early stories. The legendary "she," for example, appears in relation to the letter's author in part like the prostitute to the artist Piskarev in "Nevsky Prospekt," which was written in 1833–34 but conceived earlier in the decade.

After leaving Russia in 1836 Gogol was reduced to rare visits from literary friends and correspondence instead of the close personal contacts he had profited from in Petersburg. His letters, as we see, served to solicit information, "statistics," and criticism for the writing he did while outside Russia. They also served during this period (1836–48) as virtually rough drafts for the characterizations and, to a lesser extent, for the plots and imagery of his other writing: "Rome" ("Rim," 1842), *Selected Passages,* and the second part of *Dead Souls.*

The published fragment "Rome," his first work to be both con-

---

54 *Ibid.,* p. 100.   55 *Ibid.,* p. 138.
56 Leon Stilman, Nikolai Gogol. *Historical and Biographical Elements in his Creative Personality* (Columbia University Dissertation, 1952), pp. 225, 252.

ceived and written abroad, draws on letters, as G. M. Fridlender briefly notes. From objective humorous letters Gogol takes such details as the grotesque trousers made from a jacket (XI, 202. late Feb., 1839); from other letters he transplants attitudes towards France, Russia, Germany, and Italy for the prince, as well as such moments in his characterization as praying, playing roles, and touring Rome as a foreigner (XI, 140–7, April, 1838). In answer to Belinskij's criticism of the fragment, Gogol denied that the prince's attitude was his own, because of their different national origins (XII, 211. Sept. 1, 1843). If so, Gogol had practiced empathizing with the prince in his letters. Anyway, the story's subjectivity can be seen by the congruence of attitudes in it towards Rome's Christian civilization and Gogol's attitudes towards Russia's in his later writing. Indeed the subjective geography of "Rome" removes Italy from Europe, just as it would later remove Russia.

A comparison of the letters with *Selected Passages* shows the indisputable stylistic superiority gained in the book through the use of Biblical imagery and language, proverbs and vernacular expressions, and many of the devices of Russian rhetoric, such as anaphora, rhetorical questions, and long polysyndetic sentences. A very presentable composition resulted, especially when one considers the generally poor quality of post-Pushkinian critical writing (Belinskij's, for example) and the often sloppy diction of Gogol's correspondence.[57] Gogol was developing in the letters not rhetoric so much as the ability to write about "characters and subjects," to redeem these characters, and to articulate abstractions. His own comments on letter writing justify these conclusions.

The personal letters clearly precede *Selected Passages*. Establishing their full relationship to the second part of *Dead Souls* is forever complicated by the fact that only a part of two drafts of the 1843–45 version survives. *Selected Passages*, which draws on many of the same personal letters, outlines more social and cultural strata than the novel does and has greater thematic scope. A potential chronological problem also arises in discussing the relationship of Gogol's letters to the second volume of *Dead Souls*: What was written first? Actually, we may ignore this; the complicated drafts of the novel are

[57] For a tantalizingly brief parody by Gogol of such criticism see Proffer, pp. 38–39. (Aug. 21, 1831). There is a very thinly veiled mockery of V. G. Belinskij in *Dead Souls*, Vol. II, as "a certain aesthete who never finished his studies," Guerney translation, p. 359.

more polished than the letters. Nevertheless, the drafts show Gogol rearranging the relationships between his *raisonneurs* [58] and their potential converts, which is one of the chores Gogol struggles with in his letters of that period. For example, the major changes in the last chapter come not in the humorous scenes, at which Gogol had two decades of practice before this, but in the confrontations of Murazzov with Xlobuev and Chichikov. And Gogol tends to write letters when he is having problems with his writing. After several years of begrudging members of his family only several short notes a year, Gogol suddenly dropped an eight-page letter on them (XII, 315–23. June 12, 1844). Its content parallels that of the last chapter of the sequel to *Dead Souls*.

The question of whether Gogol tailored his letters to suit his correspondents' tastes and interests can be answered affirmatively only in the broadest sense. To certain readers Gogol addressed specific types of letters, both subjective and objective. [59] The priest Matvej Konstantinovskij never received a scatological review of Kukol'nik's works, while letters to Balabina were replete with sensual imagery and generous references to Gogol's nose. A letter to the elderly Sentimentalist I. I. Dmitriev is a model of this technique: it features a tone of light sentimentality and makes polite mention of Karamzin (X, 238–40). Nevertheless, life-long friends such as Zhukovskij were subject to the full range of Gogol's epistolary imagination. Especially during the 1843–45 period, but at other times as well, Gogol seems sometimes to adjust the recipient to his letters, not only the letters to the recipient. The correspondents are often accused of being slothful, impious, one-sided, sinful. It may be true that they were, of course, but they had not been served thus previously. Sometimes the accusations appear unjustified, [60] such as one to his mother

[58] This term is used by Rufus W. Mathewson, Jr., *The Positive Hero in Russian Literature* (New York, Columbia University Press, 1958), pp. 18–19. It should be noted, however, that the *raisonneurs* are placed in a much nore ironic setting than in the neoclassical drama. The first fruit of Murazov's correction of Chichikov is to find him in a prison cell eating a catered meal from faience containers. The unnamed prince, unlike the prince *ex machina* in Molière's *Tartuffe*, ultimately begs; he does not command. The long-winded Konstanzhonglo puts part of his audience to sleep.

[59] Stilman, pp. 349–50, answers this question affirmatively using Pushkin (to whom Gogol wrote for several years and with no change of circumstances) and Zhukovskij.

[60] S. T. Aksakov was amazed at Gogol's accusations. S. T. Aksakov, *Istorija moego znakomstva s Gogolem* (Moscow, 1960), p. 265. Gogol confessed to

just after her daughter had died, in which Gogol expounds on the laziness and ignorance of his surviving sisters (XII, 315–23. June 12, 1844). Gogol's prescription for the provincial girls (looking after people of various social stations and telling Gogol about them) is virtually Murazov's advice to Xlobuev. Finally, Gogol played with the various patterns of coercion which evoked Turgenev's wrath in his personal letters; combinations of accusation, humble confession, instruction, illustration, pleading, and encouragement. Gogol also used these in structuring personal relationships for the second part of *Dead Souls.*

The vocabulary of the novel (and of *Selected Passages*) is ground out with relentless repetition in the letters. Words such as "soul," "service," "mission," "calling," "post," "order," "need," or "enlightenment," which occur up to fifteen times each in a single letter, enter the speech and descriptions of Murazov, Xlobuev, the prince, the earnest young clerk, and the teacher Aleksandr Petrovich. Imagery from the letters, medicinal for example, is also used in the novel. The wise teacher and Murazov are both connected with this particular imagery. Even incidents in the plot of the novel can be found in the letters: in that long epistle to his poverty-striken mother Gogol suggests that if she were given a million rubles, no good would come of it. Murazov cuts the sum, but tells the bankrupt Xlobuev the same story. The difference is that the incident takes place with better transitions and more sympathy in the novel, suggesting that the letter was an antecedent of the novel's incident or, if not, that Gogel was so engrossed in *Dead Souls* he related to the outside world through it.

The author of these letters of the 1840s casts himself in a number of roles—prophet unhonored in his own country, merciless social critic, dislocated artist, penitent sinner, impatient missionary, and several others. In these roles we sometimes recognize variations of the characters of the second volume of *Dead Souls:* the shifty, sometimes cynical, sometimes penitent Chichikov; the reasonable, pious Murazov; the practical, boring Konstanzhonglo; the dreamy Tentetnikov filled with projects for never-to-be-completed works; the stern, reforming prince; and the wise teacher. Other personae of the letters might have entered the projected third volume of the novel, in which scoundrels and misers were to be reborn. In any event, it is no

Aksokov's wife (Nov. 29, 1842) that he loved to accuse his friends. *Ibid.,* p. 92.

wonder that Gogol cursed the letter when he was having trouble with *Dead Souls,* and wanted to see his old letters about it. These were the short forms which were to have paved the way for the psychological variety he longed for.[61]

Gogol's relationship to epistolary tradition is irreverent, unpredictable, and most of all creative. This we would expect from treatment of literary convention in his other imaginative works. He uses few letters in his fiction in keeping with the general trend away from them. What ones there are often parody the Sentimentalist letter or the use of letters as a plot component.

Nevertheless, Gogol found the conventions of letter writing helpful for his expository works; they provided a justification for the emotions in his "Excerpt . . . after the First Performance of the *Inspector General,*" and a speedy means of assembling the content of *Selected Passages.* In this book he created a number of addressees and molded the chapters to their interests and personalities in accordance with the rules of polite correspondence.

Gogol was aware of the distinction between objective and subjective letter writing. He interwove both types with the rest of his *œuvre* on many more occasions than could be cited in this essay. In his letters he solicited material for his works, developed imagery, the expression of abstractions, plot elements, and characterizations. Gogol wrote few humerous letters in the Arzamas style after he had perfected his comic technique. A lack of self-irony limits their appeal compared to that of his predecessors, especially Pushkin.

Emotionally heightened subjective letters with their fictional heroes and addresses were his most original contribution to the development of the Russian familiar letter. In them Gogol became a superb ironist, regarding from behind a cloud of symptoms and a plethora of masks an audience which can perhaps be ultimately convinced only of Gogol's own words: "I live in my work, partly in letters, partly in my own inner work."

[61] Gogol's desire to show psychological depth through moralizing on the part of his characters was decidedly old-fashioned. Cf. Emin's Doravra: "Your description . . . is full of moralizing judgments which reveal your mind." Kokarev, p. 582.

Democratization in European Communist Countries

KAREL F. KOECHER

The Notion of Democratization

The notion of democratization, unless it is reserved for processes resulting in actual establishment of a modern democratic society in the Western sense, is a relative term of a considerably wide extension. It comprises all sociopolitical changes which broaden the scope of recognized civil rights of citizens or which augment the citizen's participation in the government on any of its levels. The study of democratization is, therefore, closely tied to the study of social and political controls exercised in a given country. It should be noted that in the case of communist countries, there is a direct conceptual link between the notion of democratization and the totalitarian model of communist societies.[1] The totalitarian model is concerned with the organization and methods of control in the service of communist ideology, and it is the change of these factors which is the very essence of democratization.

I have pointed out that democratization in the usual sense is a relative term. One of the consequences is that a process of democratization within a communist society does not have to represent a departure from its totalitarian nature. The system may well go through a stage of democratization and yet remain a totalitarian autocracy, though a more rational one.[2] Khrushchev-inspired de-Stalinization in Czechoslovakia before 1968 or in the Soviet Union is a good example of such development. There can hardly be any doubt that the disappearance of crude terror in the Soviet Union

[1] As defined in C. J. Friedrich and Z. K. Brzezinski, *Totalitarian Dictatorship and Autocracy* (Cambridge, Mass., Harvard University Press, 1965), p. 17.

[2] The possibility of emergence of a rationalist totalitarian dictatorship has been pointed out in Z. K. Brzezinski, *Ideology and Power in Soviet Politics* (New York, Praeger, 1967), pp. 53–63.

after 1956, the bridling of secret police, proliferation of local administrative bodies such as comrade courts, and the like permitted a broader participation of population in the running of Soviet society. However, this eliminated only the redundant and unnecessarily harsh means of control, while indirect control replaced, in some instances, direct supervision. But as a whole, the control of the population by party leadership remained total.

For some authors, the continuation of totalitarian dictatorship in the Soviet Union after the Khrushchevian reforms was a reason to reject the view that a democratization took place.[3] It is, of course, only a matter of definition, but it seems to me somehow unfortunate to conceive of democratization solely in such a narrow sense. The only reliable way to tell whether a particular process was or was not that of democratization would then be to examine the results to which it has led. If the results are not yet visible or if their character is uncertain, it is not possible to make the desired evaluation. The latter conception would also mean that the notion of democratization would differ from society to society, because the outcome of social and political reforms depends not only on their content proper but also on outside factors such as national tradition, average education, and the like. Such a notion of democratization would be of little value to comparative analysis, because it would not offer a uniform standard on the background of which could be distinguished the specific features of the examined societies. What we are concerned with is not whether a particular reform can be regarded as a step which will eventually lead to the establishment of "genuine" democracy but rather, whether, and to what extent, it represents a move toward the lower extreme of totalitarian control, whether it is potentially capable of becoming a base for a departure from totalitarian dictatorship, and why. All these questions can be dealt with if we conceive of democratization as a relative term in the sense in which it was defined in the beginning.

Typology of Democratization

When conceiving of democratization in the communist countries as a change in the sociopolitical controls, what we have to realize above

[3] See, for instance, Jeremy R. Azrael, "The Party and Society," in Allen Kassof, ed., *Prospects for Soviet Society* (New York, Praeger, 1968), p. 68.

all is that these controls serve—as in all totalitarian societies—the goal of building a new mass society according to the blueprints of ideology. There are two principal functions which the controls fulfill in the service of ideology. The first is oriented entirely toward social transformation; its concern is the destruction of the old and the formation of the new. One of the provisions of communist ideology is, of course, that the process of revolutionary transformation can be accomplished only under the guidance of the communist party. That brings us to the second function of sociopolitical controls, which is essentially conservational. Its task is to ensure that the domination of party leadership is preserved no matter what ideological turnabout the latter will make or what measures it will adopt. Consequently, democratizing measures can be also divided into two basic groups: first, those which affect the transformative level of controls; and, second, those which are related to the conservational level.

The preceding differentiation does not, however, make possible an evaluation of the role which the reforms in question play with respect to the nature of the regime itself. It does not provide for a distinction between mere formal reforms, not capable of producing any substantial change, and those which have the potential of affecting the totalitarian essence. That, however, should not be a major problem. Since what makes a system of extensive sociopolitical controls a totalitarian one is its subservience to a revolutionary ideology. A change in ideology is the basic prerequisite of any alteration of the totalitarian character of the system. Processes of democratization can be thus divided according to their potential of altering the totalitarian structure into two main groups: into those which are embodying a change of ideology and those which are not. The final scheme for the classification of democratizing measures will then have the following form:

a. Reforms not embodying changes of ideology
   i. Oriented toward social transformation
   ii. Oriented toward self-government

b. Reforms embodying changes of ideology
   i. Oriented toward social transformation
   ii. Oriented toward self-government

Actual Democratizing Measures

REFORMS NOT EMBODYING IDEOLOGICAL CHANGES

Abolition of mass terror enacted in the first years after Stalin's death in all European communist countries except Albania has certainly been a democratizing measure. But how fundamental is it with respect to the totalitarian system? That terror, as such, is deeply connected with totalitarian ideology is well known. It is its "determination to achieve total change that begets the terror." [4] It is also undeniable that Stalin's theorems of the intensification of class struggle and of imperialist encirclement were used as justification of draconian penalties, pressures, and threats existing under his rule and that together with the abolition of drastic forms of coercion and purges, both theorems were declared invalid. However, that does not still prove that the abolition of crude terror was an embodiment, or direct consequence, of this change of ideology. It is perfectly conceivable to stick to Stalin's dogmas without extracting false confessions, sending thousands to labor camps, and the like, just as it is possible to assert that there is "ideological subversion" and not to massacre people for being suspected of reading smuggled Western literature. In this connection, it is not without relevance that the existence of acts of crude terror was never publicly admitted during the years of its occurrence, although the theory of the intensification of class struggle and capitalist encirclement was preached in every conceivable manner. Also, it should be noted that mere abolition of unbridled mass terror does not by any means represent a total abandonment of terroristic practices. The trials of Siniavski and Daniel or of dissenters condemning the intervention in Czechoslovakia can be rightfully considered acts of terror to the defendants and terroristic threats to the rest of the population. There was an ever-present menace posed to common citizens in the Soviet Union, Poland, Bulgaria, and other communist countries by the vigilance of activists, potential confinement to mental institutions, loss of position, forced participation in public demonstrations of loyalty in innumerable meetings—all clear instances of terror. The crudeness was replaced by a more sophisticated, individualized, and bureaucratized approach.

From the preceding arguments, it is possible to conclude that the

[4] Friedrich and Brzezinski, p. 162.

abolition of crude mass terror, although accompanied by changes of ideology, was not in any way their necessary expression. With respect to the totalitarian structure, it was a formal reform and not a substantial one. For the same reason, it cannot also be considered a measure increasing the degree of self-government, since the dominating role of the Communist Party, remains as absolute as before. What the abolition of unrestrained mass terror has accomplished is a decrease in the speed of social transformation, which can now proceed at a rate and in forms which are closer to the natural process of development.

Increase of legal security should be distinguished from the suppression of crude forms of terror, although it is true that to a limited degree the latter implies the former, as numerous inhuman practices were illegal even under Stalinist laws. There have been, however, additional and more substantial increases of legal security in European communist countries, stemming from the reforms of law codes and procedural regulations. Although far from installing independent and unprejudiced judicial systems, they nevertheless upheld—at least in principle—the previously rejected notion of legal rights, undeniable even to the enemies of the people. Among the innovations were, for example, the right of defense, the right for a trial after a specified period of time, and the like. Because of this upholding of legal rights, all the mentioned reforms may be considered principally the same democratizing measure, in spite of the fact that their extent, time of implementation, and degree of enforcement vary from one country to another. For instance, the new Basic Principles of Criminal Procedure were adopted in the USSR in 1958 (the statute of Advokatura of the RSFSR in 1962); in Czechoslovakia, the new Penal Code and Regulations of Criminal Procedure were adopted in 1961, while in East Germany, a similar reform took place only in 1968. None of these reforms was correlated with any change of ideology: the general principle of "partisan justice" remained the leading ideological guideline for the administration of justice. This principle, together with the continuing flexibility of the definitions of crimes, guaranteed that in no way would the effected increase of legal security imply a limitation of the absolute domination of the party over all aspects of social life. However, as in the case of the abolition of mass terror, the reduction of coercive means—which the reforms do imply—affects the depth, speed, and forms of social transformation.

Decentralization of low-level decisions is implied in measures such as broadening of the responsibility of local Soviets or their equivalents, labor union committees, creation of street or bloc committees, and, to a certain extent, in the establishment of comrade and factory courts (which may recommend nonjudiciary actions). All these bodies are elected and the electoral process is relatively free of constraint. In most of the cases these bodies deal with, it is entirely up to them what decision they will take—regarding issues such as dispensation of apartments, awarding of free holiday accommodations, recommendations for personal loans, trips abroad, and the like. It is true that in some instances, these institutions turn out to be just additional oppressive organs and not tools of the process of democratization. However, such a development is largely due to the laxity and timidity of the voters who do not take advantage of the opportunity to have their will expressed. Generally speaking, the granting of authority to these bodies signifies that the party has given up its control over certain decisions; or in other words, that the degree of self-government has been increased. Of course, the party has limited the power of these decision-making institutions in such a way that no issues which may play a relevant role with respect to the sociopolitical character of the society may be considered by them. Therefore, there is no change in the ideological principle that the leading force in the society is the party. The change of control which takes place here is only a replacement of direct supervision over certain general irrelevant issues by an indirect one.

Minor electoral reform can be considered the introduction of active participation of the population in the selection of official candidates for elected public offices. Such participation may consist of an opportunity to question the qualifications of the proposed candidate, his private life, and the like, which the authority responsible for the nomination has to anticipate. It is also not unusual that there is more than one official nominee, in which case, the final decision concerning the candidacy is left to those present at the meeting. What this amounts to is a nongeneral, nonrepresentative electoral process added to the perfunctory balloting. However, with respect to the practice, according to which the candidates were appointed entirely arbitrarily by inaccessible party authorities, the procedure described above is an instance of democratization. This democratization becomes somehow more advanced when the multiplicity of choice passes from the pre-electoral stage into legitimate elections. Of this, the best example is Poland where, since October, 1956, there have always been, on the official list of candidates, more candidates than offices to fill.

As far as the type of this democratization is concerned, basically the same analysis is applicable as in the case of the decentralization of low-level decisions: no change of ideology but a voluntary restraint of the party domination over small and irrelevant decisions is noticeable, and the degree of self-government is thus increased.

REFORMS EMBODYING IDEOLOGICAL CHANGES

The ideological tenets about the abolition of the law of supply and demand, the egalitarian socialist principle of remuneration, according to the merits, and the subservience of economic planning to utopian ideological goals could never provide room for other private initiative than that connected with the execution of orders. Transition to *market economy,* even on a limited scale, thus constitutes a major ideological change. The democratizing aspect of this primarily economic reform lies mainly in the respect which market economy pays to the demands of the public and in the decentralization of the decision-making process. From the viewpoint of democratization, the *emergence of private ownership* has a similar effect—as in the case of Poland's reprivatized agriculture or in the continuing existence of private enterprise in East Germany, well beyond the initial stages of socialist construction. However, what is primarily affected in all these economic reforms is the transformation of society and not the degree of self-government. There are, of course, some low-level decisions exempted from direct party supervision, but that is not a development essentially different from that captured already in the notion of "decentralization of low-level decisions" which is described above.

Another factor delimiting the over-all extent of democratization is the attitude toward religion. *More tolerance toward religion* can result only from the restriction of the "irreconcilable struggle against idealistic ideologies" and their exponents. Thus this measure constitutes an ideological change; the consequences of which affect social transformation, while the degree of self-government remains the same.

The conception of imperialistic encirclement and the intensification of class struggle and of absolute superiority of socialist achievements had first to give way before any significant volume of *foreign travel,* first official and later private, could become part of the scene in communist states. Obviously, although remaining fully under party control, such a development has to be reflected in the transformation of society, since the latter now takes place in a less isolated milieu.

The *limitation of censorship* is the most important measure which promotes democratization in culture. It is reflected in a more liberal publishing policy, administration of show business, and the like. Here also belong public discussions in newspapers about issues previously strictly off-limits, such as economical failures, inefficiency in state organs, and the like. Another important manifestation of the limitation of censorship is the restricted regimentation of science and other scholarly disciplines.

It may seem, at first sight, that the limitation of censorship is a reform of the same type as the decentralizaton of low-level decisions: that ideology is not basically affected and that party domination is whittled. There is, however, a basic difference. A newspaper or scholarly journal, for instance, may publish an unrevised controversial work or view, but the decision to do so is not left entirely to the discretion of the editors. The party still supervises the whole scope of activity of communications media. Very often these works and views also concern highly relevant and vital issues which represent another difference from the conceding of authority over irrelevant issues to decentralized bodies. Thus, what is involved in the limitation of censorship observable in European communist countries is a certain change of ideology with respect to the control of social transformation. At the same time, there is no alteration of the party control of media, and the degree of self-government remains, in this respect, the same.

The last group of democratizing reforms are the following: total *abolition of censorship;* establishment of the right to unlimited *free travel;* institutionalization of a *worker's self-determination* through the worker's councils; and *establishment of party democracy* on all levels of party apparatus. All these reforms were fully implemented only in Yugoslavia and for a brief period, preceding the Soviet invasion, some either materialized or were prepared in Czechoslovakia. In the first wave of post-October reforms in Poland, there were also attempts to establish organs of worker's self-government, but eventually the experiment was abandoned.

It is obvious that the preceding four reforms presuppose major

DEMOCRATIZATION IN EUROPEAN COMMUNIST COUNTRIES

	democratizing measure	Yu	Cz*	Hu / Cz**	Po	E.G.	Bu	Sov. U.	Ru		type of reform
I	abolition of mass terror	▨	▨	▨	▨	▨	▨	▨	▨	no change of ideology	transformation of society
I	legal security increased	▨	▨	▨	▨	▨	▨	▨	▨		
II	low-level decisions decentralized	▨	▨	▨	▨	▨	▨	▨	○		self-government
II	minor electoral reform	▨	▨	▨	▨	▨	▨	○	○		
III	elements of market economy and private enterprising	▨	▨	▨	▨	▨	◪	○	○	change of ideology	transformation of society
III	more tolerance toward religion	▨	▨	▨	▨	▨	○	○	○		
III	limited foreign travel allowed	▨	▨	▨	▨	○	○	○	○		
III	censorship limited	▨	▨	▨	◪	○	○	○	○		
IV	censorship abolished	▨	▨	○	○	○	○	○	○		transformation of society and self-government
IV	free travel	▨	▨	○	○	○	○	○	○		
IV	worker's self-determination	▨	▨	○	○	○	○	○	○		
IV	party democracy established	▨	▨	○	○	○	○	○	○		
		12	12	8	7½	6	4½	3	2		

*in the pre-invasion period
**under Novotný and after invasion

changes in ideology. But they have yet another common specific feature: they pertain both to the controls supervising the social transformation and the degree of self-government. The two aspects in these reforms are inseparable, because the latter represent total and unconditional suppression of all controls in the area they affect. That makes them essentially different from all other democratizing measures we have so far examined. And, as the following analysis shows, this property gives them a very special place in the dynamics of democratization in European communist countries.

Comparative Survey

The preceding chart gives a survey of the democratizing measures that have been heretofore analyzed and shows their implementation in different European communist countries. The half-squares appearing in the columns of Poland and Bulgaria refer to the rather limited degree of respective reforms in these countries: censorship in Poland has attained a considerably high level; and the economic reform in Bulgaria has not departed from the preparatory stages. The chart, in addition to showing the relative advancement of democratization in given countries, suggests several interesting conclusions.

The first conclusion we may draw from the chart is that ideological considerations had substantially influenced the process of democratization in East Germany, Bulgaria, the Soviet Union, and Rumania. In none of these countries have all possible measures from Group III been implemented. All involve an ideological change, but—as the experience of Poland, Hungary, and Czechoslovakia under Novotný shows—the changes by no means jeopardize the totalitarian supremacy of the party. This ideological conservatism is a part of a broader conservative trend in Rumania and the USSR, where, in addition to a reluctance to accept ideological changes, there seems to be an opposition even to mere structural changes concerning the system of party domination.

There are three striking coincidences in the extent of democratizing measures: between Yugoslavia and Czechoslovakia during the 230 pre-invasion days; between Poland and Hungary, to which we may add Czechoslovakia before Dubček took over; and between Rumania and the Soviet Union. Neither in the case of Czechoslovakia and Yugoslavia nor in the case of Poland and Hungary, together with pre-Dubček Czechoslovakia, are we faced with countries having the same type of society and political culture. Thus, the dynamic force behind the process of democratization must be something other than these two factors. The Czechoslovakian transition from the Hungarian-Polish model to the Yugoslav one is apparently crucial for the understanding of the process of democratization in European communist countries. It is beyond the scope of this essay to try to solve this problem, but what is immediately apparent is that the transition was preceded by only one major change: replacement of leadership with very limited support, even within the party, and no record of past political and military victories by a leadership possessing these qualities (especially in the persons of Svoboda and Smrkovský). It should be also noted that neither the present Polish nor the Hungarian leadership can offer such an impressive and self-assuring background, while the Yugoslav chiefs certainly can. For this reason, it does not seem at all exaggerated to consider the consistent thrust toward more democratization a matter of leadership, rather than one of social, national, or geographical characteristics of the country. This holds also with respect to the similarity of the process of democratization —or better, the lack of it—in Rumania and the USSR. The party leadership in both countries is characterized by a degree of continuity not found in the rest of the group: neither Soviet nor Rumanian leadership includes personalities not compromised during the Stalinist era, or even persecuted.

Democratization and "Oscillating Totalitarianism"

Although the Soviet Union and the four faithful Warsaw Pact countries differ in the number of democratizing reforms enacted, they seem to be in good agreement regarding the limit of democratizing measures which are deemed to be expedient within the Bloc. It is obvious from the chart that the limit is the line separating reforms in group III, from reforms in group IV. In other words, the line which Czechoslovakia had crossed in early 1968. As I have already pointed out, reforms beyond this limit are characterized by a common specific feature, namely, that they establish total and unconditional suppression of control in the domains they affect. For this reason, they represent a departure from totalitarian dictatorship. None of the other measures has such a principal character. Abolition of mass terror, as well as increase of legal security, does not alter party domination at all, and the decentralization of low-level decisions, together with the minor electoral reform, introduce self-government only in order to offer a choice from alternatives strictly controlled by the party. Reforms in group III are partial by definition, and, as a whole, reforms in groups I to III all leave enough room for their flexible interpretation and do not destroy the party supremacy over the given area. For this reason, the line between democratizing measures accepted by the Bloc and those which are rejected is the line between totalitarianism and nontotalitarianism. In other words, the democratization introduced by European communist countries—with the exception of Dubček's pre-invasion Czechoslovakia and Yugoslavia—has not been designed as a means of gradual progress toward democracy in the Western sense.

It is conceivable that the preceding analysis may give rise to the following objection: But why then do the communist regimes in Europe introduce democratizing reforms at all? It would be absurd to assume that they are willingly weakening the totalitarian structure of their societies which is the final result of any democratizing measure, no matter how limited.

The answer is that the "expedient" democratization would produce a weakening of the totalitarian structure only if it would be *stable in its content*. Totalitarian regimes, when they implement any of the democratizing reforms, even the initial abolition of mass terror, are necessarily faced with the consequence of potential formation of oppositional forces. If the regime does not want to revert to crude terror, which in a modern industrial society is, under normal conditions, basically nonfunctional and counterproductive, it has only one choice: not to allow the oppositional forces to organize by not providing them with a stable situation which could become the unifying cause or base for a revolt. The constant change of the sociopolitical practice, alternating relaxation and tightening of the control, is typical for a new type of totalitarian society which may be termed "oscillating," because of its perpetual seesaw movement.[5] There are some indications that this is actually the case: Gomulka's turn-about from a liberal to a hard-liner; Kadar's in the opposite direction; and above all, Khrushchev's fall resulting in an increasing concern over the predictability of Soviet behavior. It seems that it might be easier to understand these developments if we see them

[5] The vacillation between relaxation and restraint in the culture of European communist countries has been thoroughly analyzed in Yorick Blumenfeld, *Seesaw. Cultural Life in Eastern Europe* (New York, Harcourt, Brace, 1968).

neither as signs of the disintegration of the Soviet Bloc nor as transitory stages between Stalinism and Western-type democracy but as current manifestations of the dynamics of a new type of totalitarian state.

The Succession Crisis in Yugoslavia

V. ANNA WILLMAN

Yugoslavia is going through its most critical period since the end of World War II. Joseph Broz "Tito," President of the Socialist Federal Republic of Yugoslavia and head of the League of Communists (the Communist party), was seventy-seven years old on May 25, 1969; and although there is little formal discussion of the problem of succession within Yugoslavia, the question intensifies and provides the underlying focus for the country's many economic and political problems.

There are two basic unsolved problems in Yugoslavia which any government must face: the nationality question and the great economic disparity among the different regions of the country. Yugoslavia, although a small country, is remarkably diverse. It combines five different Slavic nationalities (Serbs, Croats, Slovenes, Macedonians, and Montenegrins, in order of numerical importance), none of which has a majority of the population, and many non-Slavic minorities (the most important are the Albanians).[1] There are four Slavic languages and many minority languages, two different alphabets, and three major religions. Centuries of shifting borders, migrations, and invasion and occupation by peoples with vastly different cultures (Rome, Turkey, Austria) have made each nationality historically and culturally unique. Regional variations in economic development are great: in 1964, for example, per capita income in Slovenia, the richest republic, was more than twice the national average and more than three times that of Montenegro, the poorest

[1] Yugoslavia is a federation with six republics (Bosnia and Herzegovina, Croatia, Macedonia, Montenegro, Serbia, and Slovenia) and two autonomous provinces in Serbia (Vojvodina and Kosovo-Metohija). These republics and provinces are based on nationality.

republic. To further aggravate the situation, the gap appears to be widening.[2]

Politically, these two closely related problems have been significant ever since the formation of the Yugoslav state in 1918. The nationalities have at best cooperated uneasily and at worst become embroiled in open power struggles culminating in civil war during World War II. Perhaps the most durable political legacies from pre-war Yugoslavia are fear of Serb hegemony and resentment of Croatian and Slovenian economic superiority. As the succession problem brings the two basic issues into sharp focus, it becomes apparent that "Titoism," Tito's unique, revolutionary brand of socialism, has so far failed to resolve these fundamental questions.

The importance of the succession problem therefore lies not in which individuals take over the positions of head of state and head of the party but in how these individuals deal with the complicated problems facing the country and with the numerous contending groups and factions within the country. The period of succession must be seen not merely as a brief interval following Tito's retirement or death but rather as an extended political process preceding and following the formal change, with competing groups struggling for control or, failing that, for an acceptable compromise. The succession struggle first came to the surface in July, 1966, with the purge of Aleksandar Ranković,[3] and it is continuing with such vigor and confusion, that one expert on Yugoslavia, Paul Shoup, has described Yugoslavia's present situation as "one of barely controlled chaos." [4] While this assessment is perhaps too extreme, the situation is certainly critical and is likely to continue unabated until either a workable compromise on the basic issues is found or the political system collapses. Tito is currently making impressive efforts to find this compromise by revising the Titoist political machinery and by "depoliticizing" certain crucial issues. If he succeeds, he in effect will have solved the succession problem before the literal event.

[2] Warren F. Mazek, "Yugoslav Regional Development: Policies and Experiences," *The Florida State University Slavic Papers* (Center for Slavic and East European Studies, Talahassee), II, (1968), 32.

[3] Discussed in more detail below, p. 109.

[4] Paul Shoup, "Recent Political Developments in Yugoslavia" (mimeographed), paper presented at the Northeastern Conference of the American Association for the Advancement of Slavic Studies, April 26, 1969, Boston, Massachusetts, p. 2 (Henceforth referred to as: Shoup, "RPDY").

Titoism: The Political Machinery and
Its Effects on Succession

Beginning with the adoption of workers' councils in 1950, Yugoslavia's economic, social, and political institutions have been constantly changing as the country has developed its own unique variety of socialism. The evolution has been erratic, but generally rapid, moving toward increased decentralization of both economic and political decision-making, within a broad framework of federal policy guidelines. The process, which has accelerated especially since the Ranković affair in 1966, is taking place in the party as well as in the government, and also, within the necessary restrictions of military discipline, to some degree in the army.

THE PARTY

The Sixth Congress of the Yugoslav Communist Party, held in November, 1952, officially began the Titoist reform of the party, changing its title to the League of Communists of Yugoslavia (LCY) and for the first time describing its role as one of "persuasion" rather than of "handing down orders." [5] As developed in later statements, the LCY no longer is a political party "in the classical meaning of the word",[6] but the "guiding ideological force" of Yugoslav socialism. Communists are to work through all economic, social, and political institutions, where they have "equal rights" with other members of the institutions and are expected to influence decisions by presenting convincing arguments and not by issuing orders or applying pressure.[7]

Little was done to implement the new policy, however (particularly after Milovan Djilas's heresies in 1954), until the 1960s.[8] At that time reform went so far in some areas that LCY secretary Mijalko Todorović complained at the Fifth Plenary Session of the Central Committee, October, 1966, that while some local party officials

[5] Nenad Petrović, "Jugoslav Communist Party Congresses Since the War," *Review* (Study Centre for Jugoslav Affairs, London), No. 5 (1965), p. 346.

[6] Petrović, "Jugoslav Communist Party Congresses," p. 347.

[7] Aleksandar Petković, "The Socialist Alliance—A Form of Self-Government," *Socialist Thought and Practice* (Belgrade), No. 17 (January-March, 1965), p. 85.

[8] Slobodan Stanković, "Yugoslavia's Critical Year," *East Europe*, XVI, No. 4 April 1967), 17.

continued to interfere excessively in economic and political matters, others were now too passive.[9] Actual implementation of the reform apparently has caused considerable confusion among party leaders, some of whom pay lip service only to the new "guiding" role of the league, while others, unsure what is allowed and what is not, have abandoned active political participation altogether. However as the reform proceeds, the LCY seems to be learning how to be active without being coercive. This is especially true in Slovenia and Croatia, where almost all reforms are implemented first and most fully, partly because of technological and educational advantages and partly because these republics tend to be most sympathetic to reform. The effects of the party reform are most noticeable in local organizations (enterprises, social organizations, communes), for the local party cells now rarely take a direct stand on specific problems, but expect their members to argue the merits of the issues as individuals.[10]

However the reforms should not be interpreted as an abdication of power by the LCY. Tito has repeatedly stated that the LCY is more important than ever before and that its role "will continue to grow until public awareness is educated well enough for it no longer to need to be guided by the communists." [11] Even where the reform is most fully implemented, the party's role is still significant, and usually decisive. Although LCY members are frequently a minority, especially in nongovernmental and increasingly in local governmental bodies, they have many advantages over other individuals. They have the prestige of party membership and the advantage of formally organized political action.[12] Furthermore, by not taking an overt

[9] Stevan K. Pavlowitch, "The Marshal and the Lecturer: A Tourist Attraction or a Sign of the Times?" *Review* (London), No. 6 (1967), p. 476.

[10] Jack C. Fisher, *Yugoslavia—A Multinational State: Regional Difference and Administrative Response* (San Francisco, Chandler Publishing Co., 1966), p. 171.

[11] "Chronicle of Events," *Review* (London), No. 6 (1967), p. 556.

[12] On the other hand, on many important issues, nonparty members of organizations do form informal "alliances" based on particularist (localist, economic, social, etc.) interests, and, in fact, LCY members also form factions based on these interests, so that the nonparty individuals may be partially organized while the party members are somewhat disorganized, reducing the LCY's effective advantage. Thus, for example, the editorial board of *Knjizevne Novine,* a Serb literary journal, although headed and presumably controlled by LCY members, has been considerably less than "persuasive" in its support of the party-backed economic reforms. "Conservatives in Trouble," *The Economist,* CCXXVI, No. 6491 (January 21, 1968), 45.

position on particular questions, the LCY retains the tactical advantage of being available, as a last resort in highly controversial issues, as a neutral arbitrator.[13]

The LCY "guides" most effectively perhaps through the mass social-political organizations, the Socialist Alliance (SA), the trade unions, and the youth organizations. Although these organizations are formally, and increasingly actually, independent from the LCY, they have a hard core of Communists in their membership [14] and generally pursue policies closely linked to the LCY. As the commanding role of the LCY diminishes, these organizations are being given more important organizational roles in the society. For example, the 1969 electoral law [15] gives the SA the primary responsibility for organizing nominations and elections for the various representative bodies.

However, as these organizations become more important, they are also becoming more independent.[16] They are organized as self-governing bodies [17] and legally can be influenced by the LCY only by "persuasion." Unhampered by democratic centralism, the discussions within the social-political organizations appear to be quite free and lively. Their independence actually seems to be encouraged by the LCY, which apparently is becoming sensitive to the dangers of political monopoly. At the Ninth Congress of the LCY, held in March, 1969, the roles of these mass social-political organizations were increased, specifically to permit "a gradual overcoming of the one-party monopoly" without permitting "the creation of political groupings outside the self-managing socialist structure of society." [18] Thus, the LCY seems to be opting for a compromise between a one-party and a two-party system, by allowing a variety of nonparty or semi-

[13] Fisher, pp. 171–72.

[14] LCY members must belong to the SA. In 1966, there were 8 million members of the SA, including the more than 1 million LCY members. (In 1965, the population of Yugoslavia was approximately 20 million.) Nenad D. Popović, *Yugoslavia: The New Class in Crisis* (Syracuse, Syracuse University Press, 1968), p. 62.

[15] Available in Serbo-Croatian at the Yugoslav Consulate, New York, N.Y.

[16] See, for example, the new independent role of the trade unions, below, pp. 115 ff.

[17] For a definition of Yugoslav "self-government," or direct democracy, see below, p. 100.

[18] Quote from Mitja Ribicić, member of the Central Committee of the LCY, in "Current Developments: Yugoslav Party Draft," *East Europe*, XVII, No. 3 (March, 1969), 38.

party channels for political organization while simultaneously decreasing its own direct political control.

In addition to reforms in the relationship between party and government (and between party and society), the LCY has been reforming internal party relationships by allowing greater freedom of criticism through modification of democratic centralism and by partially decentralizing the party hierarchy.

Modification of democratic centralism began in 1964, when LCY members were given the right to criticize party leaders and functionaries.[19] After Ranković's ouster, a new discussion took place in the LCY, beginning at two Central Committee plenums in July and October, 1966. The discussion, which was widely reported in the Yugoslav press, questioned all traditional party dogmas, including democratic centralism. Krste Crvenkovski, the Macedonian party leader, went so far as to suggest free formation of factions within the party, interpreting democratic centralism as more democratic than centralist.[20] While the reforms at the Ninth Congress did not go this far, they made considerable inroads into centralist practices. Party members may now retain their own opinions even after a different position has been accepted by a majority within the party; and they "cannot be called to task" for any views expressed in the league. They may not, however, set up an opposing faction or try to prevent implementation of a party decision. In addition, party leaders may resign without any stigma being attached to them if they feel unable to carry out a policy contrary to their opinions.[21]

Although substantial leeway is permitted for opposition through criticism within the party, however, the criticism must remain within certain boundaries. No LCY member may attack the basic principles of the party; and criticism at all times (within and outside of the party) must be "constructive." Criticism must have "a *socialist point of departure and aim and democratic responsibility* for its influence on the current social relations." [22] It must be "scientific," objective criticism aimed at improving the operation of "scientific socialism"

[19] "Current Developments: Yugoslav Party Draft," p. 37.
[20] "Remaking the Party," *The Economist*, CCXXI, No. 6425 (October 15, 1966), 241; Stanković, "Yugoslavia's Critical Year," p. 16.
[21] "Current Developments: Yugoslav Party Draft," p. 37; "The Old Faces Go," *The Economist*, CCXXX, No. 6549 (March 1, 1969), 32.
[22] Eduard Kardelj, "Notes on Social Criticism in Yugoslavia," *Socialist Thought and Practice* (Belgrade), No. 20 (October-December, 1965), p. 60.

and not, in Tito's words, "systematic criticism for its own sake." [23]

The second aspect of internal party democratization is reform of the structure of the LCY. The reforms give the rank-and-file members a larger role in decision-making and also make the lower levels of the party (particularly the republic parties) more independent.

Since 1965, LCY members have been encouraged to participate more fully in internal party politics, through reforms suggestive of self-management practices. Reports and programs drawn up for party electoral conferences and party congresses are no longer simply written by the local party secretaries, but are the product of committee meetings and discussions with large numbers of members contributing. Elections to party positions are also more democratic, with contending candidates nominated by the basic party units and secret ballot voting.[24] Members of the republic central committees are elected only after consultation with party committees at the local levels.[25]

The same trend is occurring in relationships between top- and lower-level party officials. At the Ninth Party Congress, for example, the major reports by Tito and his colleagues were circulated to the Congress in advance; and at the Congress, the party leaders limited themselves to brief speeches, leaving three quarters of the time to special commissions for discussion of concrete problems. About 400 delegates took the floor during commission debates, and more than 200 amendments to the draft documents were discussed.[26]

As the basic issues facing Yugoslavia have become more sharply debated in recent years, the republics and local party organizations have become individually significant factors in the political system. One observer of the LCY has noted that "so much latitude has been allowed the individual republics, with their individual parties, that it could to some extent be said that there are six parties in operation." [27] The "separateness" of the republic parties was illustrated by the economic agreements signed by the central committees of the Serb and Montenegrin parties in 1964 and by the Serb and Macedonian parties in 1966. Although the agreements were the result

[23] Pavlowitch, "The Marshal and the Lecturer," p. 477.

[24] Voja Mičović, "Development of Inner Party Democracy," *Socialist Thought and Practice* (Belgrade), No. 18 (April-June, 1965), 103–9.

[25] Mičović, "Development of Inner Party Democracy," p. 112.

[26] "Triumph for Tito: Yugoslavs Gain More Freedom," *The Christian Science Monitor,* March 18, 1969, p. 9.

[27] *Ibid.*

of a party split on economic issues,[28] the negotiations involved provide a clear example of the republic parties acting as individual political entities.[29]

At the Ninth Party Congress this reality was to a great extent formalized. For the first time the republic parties held their congresses before the federal Congress, allowing the republics to bring their own programs and ideas to the federal Congress rather than merely discussing and accepting policies already adopted on the federal level.[30] At the Ninth Congress, the old 154-member Central Committee and the 35-member Presidium were abolished and replaced by a Presidium with 52 members elected by the republic and provincial party congresses. The Executive Committee (11 members) was replaced by a new 15-member Executive Bureau, with two members from each republic party, one from each of the two autonomous provinces, and the president of the LCY (Tito).[31] According to Tito, the Executive Bureau is to "work collectively and there will be no first, second or third in rank," [32] thus at least formally giving the republics equal power in the new body. The Presidium is responsible for the daily execution of policy, meeting more frequently than the cumbersome Central Committee could; while the Executive Bureau acts as "a kind of policy-drafting 'cabinet' " for the Presidium.[33]

Another innovation of the Ninth Congress is the Annual Party Conference of some 300 members, one fourth elected by the republic party congresses as permanent members and the other three fourths chosen, presumably for specific terms, by the communal party conferences.[34] The annual conference will supplement, but not replace, the party Congress, which will remain the ultimate

[28] See below, pp. 107–8.

[29] Paul Shoup, *Communism and the Yugoslav National Question* (New York, Columbia University Press, 1968), p. 222 (henceforth referred to as Shoup, *Communism.*)

[30] "Let's Blame Those Federal Chaps," *The Economist,* CCXXVII, No. 6506 (May 4, 1968), 41.

[31] Tad Szulc, "Collective Rule Proposed by Tito," New York *Times,* March 13, 1969, p. 9; Shoup, "RPDY," p. 5.

[32] Szulc, "Collective Rule Proposed," p. 9. Obviously while Tito is a member of the Executive Bureau, he will, in fact, be "first." However, the reform is clearly aimed at a time when the presidency of the LCY will be held by figures less imposing than Tito and presumably for shorter terms.

[33] Szulc, "Collective Rule Proposed," p. 9; "Triumph for Tito," p. 9.

[34] Shoup, "RPDY," pp. 3–4.

authority and will continue to meet every four to five years. Apparently the annual conference will also take over some of the long-term functions of the former Central Committee.[35] How responsibilities will be divided in practice is not yet clear, but certainly the republic party organizations have more opportunity for "individualism" in the new LCY, since they are now recognized more or less as "electoral districts" for selection of federal party leaders.

In addition to changes in party structure, the republic parties have also been given more power locally. Republic party congresses now have the right to draw up their own party statutes and, within certain limits, to formulate and implement their own policies.[36]

As Tito introduced the draft reforms at the Ninth Congress, he remarked that "some of us are rather advanced in years," [37] pointing to the most urgent aspect of the evolution of the LCY. The succession problem is clearly the most direct cause of the Titoist reforms, which are attempting, first, to reduce the possibility of one-man rule (which would be disastrous in Yugoslavia without a "Tito"), and, second, to undercut the nationalist and particularist tendencies of the republics.

Two aspects of the reform are intended to counteract centralist forces and make it impossible for one or a few men to gain control of the LCY. Democratization of the league's decision-making process, allowing open criticism and large-scale participation by rank-and-file members and lower- and middle-level officials, is expected to prevent any individual from simply dictating policy to the party. Secondly, the creation of specific republic "constituencies" for members of the highest organs of the party should establish a balance of republic (nationality) interests that will prevent any individual identified with either particularist or centralist interests from building a power base. If the reforms are successful, leadership will have to rely on compromise and conciliation of different interests rather than on authoritarian commands.

On the other hand, if particularist interests are given too much freedom in a country as diverse (and divided) as Yugoslavia, the succession could result either in chaos or in a stalemate and in stagnation of economic progress. Therefore, in a clever surprise maneuver, Tito demanded that the new Executive Bureau, which in-

---

[35] "Triumph for Tito," p. 9; Szulc, "Collective Rule Proposed," p. 9.
[36] Shoup, "RPDY," p. 5.
[37] Szulc, "Collective Rule Proposed," p. 9.

cludes the top leaders of the republic parties, be permanently based in Belgrade. Two members, Vladimir Bakarić of Croatia and Krste Crvenkovski of Macedonia, in particular, were thus brought to the capital reluctantly after long resisting offers to serve in choice federal party and government positions. By bringing these local nationalists (but also loyal Titoists) to Belgrade, Tito apparently hopes, first, to get the different republic leaders to discuss their problems directly rather than through long-distance polemics in the press, on television, or in local party meetings, and, second, to divest the republics of their most vocal potential separatists, while forcing these individuals to look at policy problems from the federal point of view for a while.[38] If Tito's tactics are successful, the Executive Bureau could become a genuinely unifying collective leadership, quite free from the dangers of centralism (considering the personalities and loyalties of its membership).[39] However, national loyalties are so strong even in the top party leadership, that this may not be possible.

THE GOVERNMENT

Change has been much more frequent in government institutions and political procedures than in the party. The trend has been toward increased democratization of procedures and toward more independent local and republic governments. Recently reforms have also given the republics a larger role in the formulation of federal policy.

Perhaps the most important tenet of Titoism is the principle of direct democracy, which evolved from self-management by the workers (through workers' councils in the enterprises) to self-government in all other "social-economic" organizations (professional organizations, service institutions, etc.), in the "social-political" organizations (the SA, trade unions, and youth organizations), and in the government (especially, the communes). Essentially, Yugoslav direct democracy means active and decisive participation by the members of an organization or a political community in selecting leaders, in determining internal rules and regulations, and in deciding policies. While the implementation of direct democratic

[38] "Tito Looks Forward, Not Back," *The Economist*, CCXXX, No. 6552 (March 22, 1969), 46, 49; Shoup, "RPDY," pp. 4–5.

[39] All 14 members are active supporters of the Titoist reforms, although there are crucial differences in emphasis. "Triumph for Tito," p. 9; "Tito Looks Forward, Not Back," p. 49.

procedures varies from one part of the country to another, it is generally recognized that, particularly on the local levels of government, self-government is an actuality (although imperfect) even in the less developed regions.[40]

Elections, which are an important part of social self-government, were first reformed substantially for the assembly elections in 1953, establishing the secret ballot and some degree of competition for office.[41] As subsequent election laws have been passed, a new emphasis has been developed, bringing the voters directly into the process of nominating candidates.[42] Nomination is considered more important than the "formal act" of voting for a candidate, since there is a wider choice at the earlier stage.[43] Technically, any citizen with suffrage may be nominated if he has sufficient backing; but from the complaints of the Yugoslav press, the local SA organizations, which are responsible for organizing nominations and elections, have not always succeeded in eliminating all authoritarian pressures from local officials, and many prospective "opposition" candidates apparently are "persuaded" to withdraw their candidacies before the election.[44]

Campaigns are carried on with speeches and public appearances, and since there are no nationwide or even republic-wide elections, campaign funds do not need to be very large. Apparently the LCY no longer officially endorses particular candidates,[45] who may look

[40] In these regions, however, interference in the self-governing process by conservative managers, local bureaucrats, and local party officials has been a continuing problem. See Popović, pp. 83–89.

[41] Thomas T. Hammond, "Jugoslav Elections: Democracy in Small Doses," *Political Science Quarterly*, LXX, No. 1 (March, 1955), 57–74.

[42] Except where indicated otherwise, information on nomination and election procedures and practices came from the 1969 Electoral Law, available in Serbo-Croatian at the Yugoslav Consulate, and from an interview with the public information officer of the consulate.

[43] There are usually at least 2 candidates for each elective post at the communal level, often 2 candidates at the republic level, and sometimes 2 at the federal level. The trend is towards an increased number of candidates. In the April, 1969, elections, there were 179 candidates for 120 seats in the Economic Chamber of the Federal Assembly. In contrast, on the communal level, in the 1967 elections, 533 candidates competed for 212 seats in the Belgrade Commune. David Binder, "Yugoslavs Elect Representatives," New York *Times,* April 14, 1969, p. 1; Popović, p. 121.

[44] Binder, "Yugoslavs Elect Representatives," p. 6.

[45] LCY members frequently compete for the same position, and presumably in such cases both would be league candidates. Before voting in the April,

to the local SA, trade unions, professional and social organizations, and the like, for support. Newspapers do not endorse candidates, since endorsement would be "impartial reporting."

The removal of the LCY from direct participation in the organization of elections and in campaigns seems to be an attempt to "depoliticize" the electoral process. Election literature emphasizes the importance of finding the "best" men regardless of their political affiliations. According to the Titoist philosophy, deputies in the various assemblies are expected to respond directly to the needs and demands of their constituencies, rather than indirectly through the policies of a political party "as is the case with multi-party systems." [46]

Although the results of the election reforms have occasionally been somewhat embarrassing to the Yugoslav authorities, with opposition candidates winning supposedly "safe" assembly seats and the number of Communist delegates in local assemblies constantly decreasing,[47] there seems to be no indication of a retreat. Instead Tito and his colleagues seem impatient with delays in the full implementation of the reforms (which as usual, are slower to succeed in the less developed areas).[48]

Another important aspect of democratization of the government is the considerable freedom of criticism allowed in the assemblies. In February, 1954, delegates were granted parliamentary immunity; [49] and the intensity and effectiveness of the debates have increased steadily since then. Even the first debates in 1954 brought about several substantial changes in the federal budget after twenty days of debates and hearings.[50]

Since 1963, the Federal Assembly has had five chambers, one which debates and votes on all bills (before 1969, the Federal Chamber, and after, the Chamber of Nationalities) and four special-

---

1969, elections, Tito told reporters: "To me they [the candidates in his district] are all equal." *Ibid.,* p. 6.

[46] Mirko Bosković, "Elections in Yugoslavia," *Socialist Thought and Practice* (Belgrade), No. 17 (January-March, 1965), pp. 99–101.

[47] Kenneth Ames, "Yugoslavia's Crumbling Federation," *The New Leader,* L (June 5, 1967), 12; Shoup, "RPDY," pp. 14, 25.

[48] Binder, "Yugoslavs Elect Representatives," pp. 1, 6.

[49] Jack Raymond, "Yugoslavia Lets Deputies Debate," New York *Times,* February 14, 1954, p. 15.

[50] Jack Raymond, "Yugoslav Deputies Alter Official Budget," New York *Times,* March 10, 1954, p. 6.

ized chambers, each of which handles only those measures relating to its specialty. Members of three of the specialized chambers (the Economic Chamber, the Health-Social Welfare Chamber, and the Educational-Cultural Chamber) are delegates elected by and from local conferences of people working in the relevant areas. Members of the fourth chamber (the Social-Political Chamber) are direct representatives of the entire voting population, divided into electoral districts.[51] Thus the deputies are legislating on matters of direct relevance to their own professional lives as well as to their constituents' lives, and this has kept the debates both informed and lively.[52]

One impressive example of parliamentary independence occurred in December, 1967, when after particularly heated debates, the Federal Assembly flatly rejected the government's major economic bills. When Tito made the vote on the measures a vote of confidence, more debate followed. Although the delegates finally accepted the bills, they did so only by a very small majority.[53] Considering the general reluctance of most Yugoslavs to hasten the event of succession to Tito, the narrow margin in the vote illustrates the degree to which the delegates are willing to go in defense of their interests.

In addition to democratization in the government, Titoist reforms have decentralized administration and policy-making. One of the most important government institutions is the commune, a direct product of the reforms. Both formally and actually the communes have great powers. The 1963 Constitution gives the communes power to legislate on all political, economic, social, and cultural matters not specifically assigned to the federal and republic governments and also responsibility for the administration of all federal and republic laws unless the law in question or the Constitution specifically requires enforcement by a higher administrative body.[54] The

[51] *The Constitution of the Socialist Federal Republic of Yugoslavia, Adopted on April 7th 1963* (Belgrade, Federal Secretariat for Information, 1963), pp. 72–73; "Amendments to the Yugoslav Constitution Adopted by the Federal Assembly, December 1968," *Yugoslav Facts and Views* (Yugoslav Information Center, New York), No. 50 (February 21, 1969), pp. 3–5.

[52] Although criticism in the assembly is expected to confine itself to "constructive" comments as described above, p. 95, there is no governmental democratic centralism, and parliamentary immunity provides further freedom. Members of the LCY, of course, are always subject to party discipline.

[53] "One Place Where the Right Things Manage to Happen," *The Economist*, CCXXVI, No. 6489 (January 6, 1968), 22–24.

[54] *The Constitution*, pp. 49–50.

considerable legislative and administrative powers of the commune are further increased by the fact that the communes are considered an equal rather than a subordinate government body, and higher administrative organs have no formal control over their operations.[55]

The functions of the communes grew steadily, extending even beyond simple local concerns,[56] until the economic reforms of 1965, which substantially reduced the administrative powers of the communes in economic matters. Prior to the reforms, the communes had played a significant (and sometimes economically damaging) role in the local distribution of federal investment funds. When the federal government relinquished this last direct control over the socialist enterprises (i.e., control of investment), the communes' administrative functions decreased accordingly.[57] Nevertheless, the communes have retained many significant powers in the economic field (taxation, irrigation projects, transportation facilities, etc.), as well as in political and social matters, so that they remain highly significant, both in terms of local policies and in relation to the higher government bodies.

The republic governments' role has also increased steadily, and in contrast to the communes they have become more powerful since the 1965 reforms. Whereas the communes lost an important tool (both for control of local economic development and for potential leverage against unpopular federal policies), the republics were simply freed from an aspect of federal intervention which was extremely unpopular at least in the industrialized republics.

A dramatic illustration of the increased power of the republics occurred in January, 1968, when Stane Kavcić, the Premier of Slovenia, publicly challenged a Federal Assembly resolution to limit both federal and republic taxation and warned that a federal attempt to force its own way would result in open political conflict.[58]

In addition to the increased independence of the republics vis-à-vis the federal government, the republics have recently been given

[55] Antun Vratuša, "Decentralisation on the Basis of Self-Government in the Yugoslav Practice" (paper presented at the Sixth World Congress of the International Political Science Association), *New Yugoslav Law* (Belgrade), XV, No. 4 (October-December, 1964), 3. Also, for a discussion of the development and practical operation of the communes, see Fisher, pp. 150–54.

[56] Vratuša, "Decentralisation on the Basis of Self-Government," p. 3.

[57] For this reason, considerable resistance to the 1965 reforms has come from local officials.

[58] Richard Eder, "Aide Challenges Yugoslav Powers," New York *Times*, January 21, 1968, p. 26.

a more direct voice in federal policy formation. Before the passage
of the 1969 Constitutional amendments, the Chamber of Nationalities had been a small dormant chamber of the Federal Assembly,
almost fully absorbed into the Federal Chamber. Although supposed
to meet separately in special session to discuss problems of importance to the republics, it was not used once between 1953 and
1967, when nationality pressures following the purge of Ranković
finally made a meeting of the chamber unavoidable.[59] The 1969
amendments transformed the Chamber of Nationalities into the
major chamber of the Federal Assembly, and abolished the Federal
Chamber. Deputies in the Chamber of Nationalities are elected by
all chambers of the republic and provincial assemblies (20 from
each republic and 10 from each province).[60]

Other recent reforms have further expanded the republics' role.
New parliamentary rules make it incumbent upon all the specialized
chambers of the Federal Assembly to consult with their counterparts
in the republics before making final legislative decisions. In addition, republics are now represented in the Federal Executive Council
and participate in the appointment of personnel to the Secretariat
of Foreign Affairs.[61]

Tito's government reforms, like the LCY reforms have recently
focused on the succession problem, countering centralist dangers
with increased democratization and decentralization, on the one
hand, and combating separatist elements by drawing the republics
into the federal decision-making process, on the other.

In addition, some specific changes, mostly after the Ranković
purge, have been made to prevent any individual from accumulating
too much power. In 1967, so many high government officials were
transferred to new jobs that only Tito and two others remained in
the same positions. These changes were apparently not the result
of any particular misgivings about the individuals involved but the
response to a new policy of reducing the number of high-level positions any one individual could hold (particularly if they were positions in both the government and the LCY) and to a decision to
eliminate certain nonessential, but potentially powerful, positions
such as the vice-presidency and the post of deputy supreme commander of the armed forces.[62]

59 "Chronicle of Events," *Review* (London), No. 7 (1968), p. 652.
60 "Amendments to the Yugoslav Constitution," p. 3.
61 Shoup, "RPDY," pp. 7, 24.
62 William D. Hartley, "Maverick Tito Prepares for Tomorrow," *The Wall*

The principle of rotation of office, limiting the number of terms [63] that a government official may hold a position, had been introduced in the 1963 Constitution for the Executive Council (one term each) and for the President (two terms, except for Tito). The 1969 amendments extended this principle further, limiting assembly delegates to two terms in the same chamber.[64]

THE ARMY

Although the army has not been active in Yugoslav domestic politics, it is potentially significant and therefore has not been neglected by Tito's reforms. In the spring of 1965, as the conflicts leading up to Ranković's ouster became more heated,[65] the Council of National Defense passed a rule that the commanding general in each republic must be a citizen of that republic. At the same time, the council reestablished republic Committees of Defense, which originally had been organized at the republic capitals during Yugoslavia's conflict with the Comintern.[66] In 1966, after it was discovered that the "Ranković group" had been proselytizing in the army "to sow dissension and foster chauvinism",[67] the federal army was reorganized, and the individual republics were given the right to maintain and command their own territorial armies.[68]

As radical as these reforms were, the Soviet invasion of Czechoslovakia in August, 1968, led to even more extreme measures, when the Yugoslavs discovered that their generals were relying on an outmoded strategy and military equipment purchased from the Soviet Union and dependent on Soviet replacement parts. During the winter, 1968/69, a number of top-level generals who had become "too friendly" with their Soviet suppliers were quietly retired on pensions.[69] The inadequate conventional defense strategy was re-

Street Journal, September 18, 1967, p. 16; *Amendments to the Constitution of Yugoslavia 1967*, supplement to *The Constitution*, p. 7.

[63] Terms for most positions are four years.

[64] "Amendments to the Yugoslav Constitution," p. 7.

[65] See below, pp. 26–27.

[66] Ilija Jukić, "Tito's Last Battle," *East Europe*, XVI, No. 4 (April, 1967), 7.

[67] From a report to the Federal Assembly, December 9, 1966. Quoted in Jukić, "Tito's Last Battle," p. 8.

[68] Stanković, "Yugoslavia's Critical Year," p. 15; Hartley, "Maverick Tito," p. 16.

[69] At least 9 members of the general staff (mostly Serbs), including the former Deputy Supreme Commander, General Ivan Gosnjak, and the Chief of the General Staff, General Rade Hamović, were purged.

placed by a partisan concept of an "all peoples' war," which was
adopted unanimously by the Federal Assembly in February, 1969,
in spite of strong opposition in professional army circles.[70]

The new Law on Territorial Defense is aimed at the preparation
of "every able-bodied citizen, male or female, to fight" in local
defense units supporting the regular army in the event of an invasion.
The law assigns military, paramilitary, or civil defense duties to
every citizen, with the intention, according to one high official, of
turning Yugoslavia into "the Vietnam of Europe" if necessary.
Financed, supplied, and organized locally (by communes, towns,
and even enterprises), the defense program will establish arms centers throughout the country. Although the law did not officially go
into effect until March, 1969, the various local groups have been
accumulating and storing weapons (in factories and local army
quarters until the arms centers can be built) since shortly after the
law first appeared in draft form in the fall of 1968.[71]

This remarkable "communization" of national defense, however,
does not mean that the regular army is exempt from further Titoist
reforms. While the local governments are taking on military duties,
the army is undergoing political reforms. Efforts are being made to
insure the loyalty of the army by increasing military participation
in LCY events. A week before the Ninth Party Congress, the first
all-army conference of the LCY met, and a good proportion of the
delegates at the Congress itself were military men of all ranks. To
acquire more support from the army rank and file, units are now
to be allowed to elect their own representatives to party conferences
instead of having them appointed from above.[72] Thus, a certain
amount of "democratization" is being introduced into the army as
well as into the party and the government.

The effects of these military reforms on succession is uncertain.
By giving the republics their own army organizations, the reforms
have irrevocably strengthened decentralization forces; although possibly, military discipline, with the President of the Federal Republic
as the supreme commander of all military forces, may be sufficient

[70] David Binder, "Yugoslavs Purge Army Generals," New York *Times,*
April 15, 1969, pp. 1, 8.

[71] "Arming of Yugoslav Civilians for Defense Units Under Way," New
York *Times,* February 23, 1969, p. 16; Tad Szulc, "Yugoslavs Move To Build
Up Regular and Partisan Defenses," New York *Times,* January 26, 1969, p. 4.

[72] "Tito Looks Forward, Not Back," p. 49.

to counteract the dangers of separatism. The decentralized military operations under the new Law on Territorial Defense seems to take a considerable amount of military authority away from both federal and republic governments, and it is too soon to guess the final outcome.

The Titoist political structure thus offers many channels for opposition and, in fact, represents a compromise between liberal and conservative forces and between local and federal interests. It is an attempt to balance the contending forces in Yugoslav society, molding them into a coherent political system in which there will be channels for a constructive exchange of viewpoints, for compromise, and for coordinated implementation of policies. However, the outcome of the Titoist attempt is still very much uncertain: the opposing political forces are very strong, and the issues are both complicated and highly emotional.

The Opposition: Forces Contending for Succession

The balancing mechanisms of the Titoist system, together with Tito's usual practice of staying above the various conflicts as an arbitrator, make it impossible to identify any group as completely "in" or any as totally an opposition group. In fact, the federal government is a popular scapegoat for all political groups in the country.[73] This has been particularly true as the succession problem has altered the focus of the contending groups from specific policies to barely concealed competition for eventual control of the government.

THE REGIONAL ECONOMIC CONFLICT

Economic decentralization, begun in the early 1950s and radically increased by the 1965 reforms, is the basis of serious conflict among the Yugoslav republics. Essentially, the conflict has arisen over investment policies, with the nonindustrial republics arguing for centralized allocation of funds and the wealthier republics insisting on decentralization of investment.[74] Officially, this debate ended to the detriment of the less-developed republics with the 1965 reforms,

[73] For example, see "Let's Blame It on Those Federal Chaps," p. 41.
[74] Almost everyone in Yugoslavia today accepts (or at least claims to accept) the general principle of economic decentralization. The differences lie in "how much" and "how fast" to decentralize.

but the full implementation of the reform has been delayed and the emotion-charged conflict is continuing. Croatia and Slovenia argue that centralized investment has merely meant siphoning funds from the wealthy republics into uneconomic, "political" [75] enterprises in the southern nonindustrial areas, while the efficient industries in the North are allowed to deteriorate for lack of investment funds. The southern republics, led by Serbia, reply that a fully decentralized economy would result in enriching the wealthy republics while the less-developed areas would stagnate or deteriorate.

The economic differences are intensified and complicated by their coincidence with nationality conflicts and particularly by the Serbs' role in the conflict. Although Serbia is not as industrialized as Slovenia and Croatia, it cannot be categorized with the nonindustrial republics either; and, it is not at all clear whether the republic would suffer or benefit from decentralization.[76] Nevertheless, Serbia has taken the lead in resistance to the reforms, most likely because Serbs tend to identify their interests with a strong, centralized federal government. Croatia and Slovenia understandably have responded to Serbia's attitude with open suspicions that the Serbs are attempting to reestablish hegemony over the country. Even Serbia's allies in the economic dispute are not altogether sure of their supporter's motivation. Macedonia, in particular, is quick to take offense at any imagined interference in its affairs.[77]

The emotional tone of the conflict is extremely high, and there have been many reports of actual physical violence in high-level party meetings on the reforms. For example, in a closed session of the Central Committee in August, 1959, Blazha Jovanović, head of the Montenegrin government, reportedly seized Slovenian leader Eduard Kardelj by the throat while the latter was explaining a decision to postpone work on a Montenegrin railroad project.[78] Again, in March, 1962, after a party plenum discussing the projected reforms, accounts circulated about Serb and Macedonian leaders facing each other at gun point.[79] Only slightly less spectacular were reports (later confirmed in a television interview with a Slovenian party official) that Slovenia (Kardelj) had threatened to secede from the federation during the conflict preceding Ranković's purge.[80] Im-

[75] For examples of political investments, see Shoup, *Communism,* pp. 242–46.

[76] *Ibid.,* p. 249.   [77] Fisher, p. 57.

[78] Jukić, "Tito's Last Battle," p. 2.   [79] Shoup, *Communism,* p. 250.

[80] *Ibid.,* p. 223; Jukić, "Tito's Last Battle," p. 4.

mediately after the passage of the 1965 economic reform, about 2,200 Serb party officials resigned in protest.[81] Although the removal of Ranković in 1966 apparently calmed the situation briefly, emotions have recently again surfaced to a degree that Paul Shoup considers the present situation at least as urgent, if not more so than in 1966.[82] In the summer of 1968, conflict was so severe that the Federal Executive Council called the Federal Assembly into session specifically to get a vote of confidence in the council and its program.[83]

The results of the conflict have been numerous delays, first in instituting the reform and now in implementing it. The March, 1962, party plenum, at which Ranković's conservative position was outvoted, showed feelings to be so strong that the reform was put off for three years. Meanwhile Ranković began covert resistance to reform through his control of the secret police and his high rank in the LCY and in the government. Kardelj (Slovenia) and Bakarić (Croatia), with Tito's implicit support, organized their forces.[84] According to one report, a preliminary showdown occurred on the eve of the Eighth Party Congress in December, 1964, when Kardelj and Bakarić thwarted an attempt by Ranković's followers to elect him general secretary of the LCY in Tito's place.[85] Ranković's hints to foreign correspondants at that time that Tito would probably announce his imminent retirement at the Congress [86] seem to support this account. After the Congress, Tito began his military reforms, and Kardelj managed to assign some of his supporters to key positions under Ranković.[87] The Serb leader, meanwhile, expanded his activities. The secret police began to keep files on all members of the LCY, checking their past and planting listening devices to ascertain how each one stood on the economic reforms.[88]

[81] *Ibid.*, p. 6.   [82] Shoup, "RPDY," p. 3.

[83] The specific cause of this unusual step by the FEC was a "show of defiance" from the Croatian assembly. This illustrates how complicated the situation has become, with all sides of the conflict acting in opposition to the federal government. The Federal Assembly adopted a resolution backing the FEC, with one deputy abstaining. Shoup, "RPDY," p. 10.

[84] Many of the political reforms (rotation, etc.) in the 1963 Constitution may have been intended primarily to limit Ranković's ability to "take over" in the event of Tito's death.

[85] Jukić, "Tito's Last Battle," p. 4.

[86] " 'Liberalization or Disintegration?' What the Papers Say," *Review* (London), No. 6 (1967), p. 369.

[87] Jukić, "Tito's Last Battle," p. 7.

[88] Although such files had been kept on suspect non-Communist citizens

In July, 1965, the long-delayed reforms were passed, but the republics opposed to the measures responded by refusing to carry them out locally. At a plenum of the Central Committee of the LCY in March, 1966, divisions in the party leadership were openly admitted, Serb nationalism was sharply attacked for resisting implementation of the reforms, and party leaders were bluntly directed to carry out the reforms without further delay. However, the reports of republic Central Committee meetings in the following weeks indicated that implementation would be slow at best. In Macedonia, after heated debates, the Central Committee adjourned without issuing even a weak resolution supporting the reforms. Serbia's reaction was particularly impressive: only days after the federal Central Committee meeting adjourned, the Serbs opened discussions with Macedonia which eventually ended in an agreement for economic cooperation similar to a 1964 Serb-Montenegrin agreement.[89]

In July, 1966, Ranković and his supporters were purged, but while the purge eliminated the most likely Serb contender for the presidency and may have eliminated the centralists' hopes for direct control of Yugoslavia after succession, it by no means ended their resistance to the reforms or their determination to influence the eventual outcome of the succession struggle.

NATIONALITY CONFLICT AND THE FEDERAL SYSTEM

In March, 1966, Bakarić stated in an interview in the party newspaper *Borba* that although the nationality question was second to the economic reform in importance, if the struggle against bureaucratic centralism was lost, the nationality problem would become the "number one question" in Yugoslavia.[90] Since that statement, however, despite the apparent victory of the economic reform in the purge of Ranković, nationality conflicts have become increasingly severe. This is due in part to the relaxation of police controls which

---

immediately after the war, such practices had been discontinued, or at least drastically reduced in the early 1950s, and had never before included party members. Nenad V. Petrović, "The Fall of Aleksandar Ranković," *Review* (London), No. 6 (1967), p. 539.

[89] Shoup, *Communism,* pp. 255–57.

[90] John C. Campbell, *Tito's Separate Road: America and Yugoslavia in World Politics* (New York, Council on Foreign Relations, Harper and Row, 1967), p. 138.

had kept many national problems hidden [91] and in part because undoubtedly for the Serbs and their allies, the reverse of Bakarić's statement is true, that is, nationality is becoming the predominant issue because the reform is beginning to be implemented.

The Yugoslav federation, which gives "the nationalities" and, therefore, their republics the right to secede,[92] is crucially affected by the absence of a unifying Yugoslav national feeling. Individuals think of themselves as Serbs, Croats, Macedonians, and the like, rather than as Yugoslavs, and there is even some sense of discrimination against those few who do think of themselves as Yugoslavs. Thus most individuals tend to give their primary allegiance to their republic rather than to the country as a whole (although in times of international crisis, the existence of powerful secondary allegiance to Yugoslavia becomes apparent). Active government attempts to create a "Yugoslav nationalism" were abandoned in 1958 because the historical association of "Yugoslavianism" with Serb hegemony made the policy more divisive than unifying.[93] Since then Tito has limited himself to occasional pleas for tolerance for those who feel themselves "to be only a citizen of Yugoslavia." [94]

The conflicts among the nationalities are complex: the republics are drawn together in recognition of the necessity of a Yugoslav union for international political viability, but they are wary of accepting too close a tie because of mutual distrust.

Serbia's situation is particularly interesting. Itself the object of almost universal suspicion (possibly excepting Montenegro), Serbia feels exploited and threatened by Slovenia and Croatia. Serbs deny

[91] David Binder, "Ranković Ouster Ended Yugoslav Fear of Police," New York *Times,* November 28, 1966, p. 9.

[92] This right has become increasingly more practical, especially since the 1966 military reforms. Even before then, its political utility was demonstrated by Kardelj's use of the threat to secede in the conflict with Ranković.

[93] This was a bitter, personal defeat for Tito, who, although a Croat, considers himself a Yugoslav and had hoped to create a Yugoslav identity to overcome the nationality divisions. Shoup, *Communism,* pp. 191, 224.

[94] Joseph Broz Tito, "Power Must Remain in the Hands of the Working Class" (speech at the 10th City Conference of the League of Communists of Belgrade, April 17, 1967), *Socialist Thought and Practice* (Belgrade), No. 26 (April-June, 1967), p. 22. See also, Shoup, *Communism,* p. 224. "Yugoslav nationalism" is strongest among the non-Slavic minority groups, among individuals of mixed Slavic nationality backgrounds, and in a particular political rather than psychological sense among Serbs. Pavlowitch, "The Marshal and the Lecturer," p. 493.

that they wish to reestablish hegemony, but feel that their unselfish efforts alone are working to keep the country together and preventing it from being divided up by neighboring states.[95] This understandable, if not altogether accurate, self-conception is based partly on the fact that Serbia's position on the economic issues seems to be independent of its immediate economic interests (since those interests are not altogether clear) and also on the very valid concern the Serbs feel about the disunity of the country. It is entirely possible that the stormy events of the March, 1962, party plenum were what influenced Ranković to take the drastic measures of police surveillance rather than the fact that he was outvoted. It certainly must have looked as if Tito had lost all control of the situation (as indeed he may have). Nevertheless, Serb "chauvinism," no matter how disinterested it seems to the Serbs, clearly is a major cause of disunity in the country.

The Serbs strongly feel that they are being discriminated against. National traditions which are permitted and even encouraged in the other republics are repressed in Serbia because of the psychological links between those traditions and Serbia's prewar hegemony. Political liberalization has had less effect in Serbia than it has had in Croatia and Slovenia, and although this is largely the result of the conservatism of Serb leaders, the Serb populace tends to blame it on a federal "anti-Serb" policy.[96] Ranković is widely regarded as the victim of a Croatian-Slovenian plot against Serbia, and after his purge he was so frequently applauded in the streets and restaurants of Belgrade that the authorities suggested he leave the city.[97]

Croatia and Slovenia regard Serbia as dangerously nationalistic, seeking to reestablish control over the rest of Yugoslavia; and, they see themselves as the sole defenders of nationality rights against Serb encroachments (via "Yugoslav nationalism"). In an interview in March, 1964, in the periodical *Nedeljne Informativne Novine* (*NIN*), Bakarić complained that "though we have rejected this 'Yugoslav nationalism' in theory, we in fact adopt it in all practical questions." [98] Although secession is advocated primarily by Croatian and Slovenian extremists, the threat of secession has been used by

[95] Philip Ben, "The Going Gets Rough in Yugoslavia," *The New Republic,* CLV, Nos. 9–10 (September 3, 1966), 16.

[96] "Liberalization or Disintegration," p. 374.

[97] Jukić, "Tito's Last Battle," p. 10.

[98] "Two Obstinate Problems," *Review* (London), No. 4 (1964), p. 220.

these republics in political emergencies, indicating the seriousness with which they regard the threat from Serbia. Croatian party leaders continually advocate more independence for the republics and especially for Croatia. In the same *NIN* interview, Bakarić announced Croatia's interest in foreign affairs,[99] and in October, 1967, the Croatian assembly formed a committee for foreign affairs.[100] Slovenia and Macedonia have followed Croatia's example, and all three republics currently engage in limited foreign policy activities. Croatia and Slovenia have carried on negotiations directly with other countries, primarily on economic matters (Croatia with Austria on "common problems" and Slovenia, through special sections of its Economic Council, with COMECON and other international economic organizations). Macedonia is now directly responsible for international diplomacy on the "Macedonian Problem" with Bulgaria and Greece.[101]

Macedonia, although generally conservative on economic issues through necessity, is also almost fiercely nationalistic and resentful of anything resembling federal (or, particularly, Serb) interference in its affairs.[102] The Macedonian Constitution refers to the republic as the "Macedonian state" and describes the realization of the rights of the Macedonian peoples to national independence and "state self-development." [103]

Montenegro, however, has so far shown little independence, following Serbia's policies very closely. Bosnia and Herzegovina has been a special situation, as a multinational republic. However, the Muslim Slavs in the area are apparently now finally to be recognized as a distinct nationality rather than as merely a religious grouping of Serbs and Croats.[104] This will give the republic more of a national character; and presumably, having gained this recognition through long agitation, the Bosnians will turn their nationalism to other issues and become equally embroiled in the general conflict.[105]

---

[99] *Ibid.*, pp. 220–21.

[100] "Chronicle of Events," *Review* (London), No. 7 (1968), p. 654.

[101] Shoup, "RPDY," pp. 8, 24.   [102] Fisher, p. 57.

[103] Shoup, *Communism*, p. 223   [104] Shoup, "RPDY," p. 8.

[105] As a multinational republic, Bosnia and Herzegovina has had no legal basis for secession, since the right is granted to the nationalities rather than to the republics. Now, however, presumably Bosnia and Herzegovina will gain this right. See Branko M. Pešelj, "Constitutional Characteristics of the Socialist Republic of Bosnia and Herzegovina," *Review* (London), No. 5, (1965), pp. 335–37.

Similar concessions are being made to the Albanians in Kosovo-Metohija (Kosmet), which, due largely to the high Albanian birth rate and to emigration by other groups, is losing its multinational character and becoming an Albanian province. Albanians are now to be allowed to have a national flag and to celebrate Albanian holidays officially. Officials in the province will have to know Albanian as well as Serbo-Croatian.[106] Bosnia and Herzegovina and Kosmet both have followed Serbia's lead economically, but national antagonisms clearly exist and certainly are likely to increase in Kosmet as long as it remains an Albanian province (no matter how autonomous) in a Serb republic.

Nationality differences are extremely intense, affecting all aspects of the society, and the important role Tito has played, keeping Yugoslavia together with minimal repression of national identities, cannot be overstated. The significance of losing Tito's unifying personality has not been ignored by the Yugoslavs, and the question of succession has been implicit in recent discussions on the possibility of replacing the federal system with a confederation. The discussion began publicly in February, 1968, in the periodical *Politika*,[107] and has been carried on in articles and speeches proposing change and defending the federation. One of the most radical proposals was made by the president of the Slovenian Supreme Court in an article in *Borba,* August, 1968. He suggested that federal powers be confined to legislation in precisely defined areas, to be enacted only after consultation with the republics. All other legislation, and all executive decrees and regulations, would be made only at the republic level.[108] Others, including Šabka Dabčević-Kućar of Croatia and Crvenkovski have publicly defended the principle of federation.[109]

While the confederation-federation discussion has not yet divided participants clearly along lines identical to the economic reform, there is likely to be considerable coincidence, with Croatia and Slovenia supporting at least a very liberal form of federation, and Serbia, backed by Montenegro, supporting the federation as it now exists or perhaps even more centralized. While Macedonia would

---

[106] Shoup, "RPDY," pp. 8, 24.
[107] "Chronicle of Events," *Review* (London), No. 7 (1968), p. 655.
[108] Shoup, "RPDY," p. 8.
[109] "Chronicle of Events," *Review* (London), No. 7 (1968), pp. 656–57.

suffer economically from confederation, it is not very likely to support a strongly centralized federation.

NONREGIONAL ECONOMIC OPPOSITION

Another type of conflict in the society which may have a profound effect on succession is opposition based not on national differences but on economic interests. One by-product of Yugoslavia's economic and political liberalization has been the proliferation of economic and professional associations, industrial lobbies, and a large variety of economic pressure groups.[110] These groups have arisen naturally from the economic pluralism created by liberalization; and the organization of the Federal Assembly into specialized chambers has encouraged these associations to be active politically through elections, through direct contacts with the delegates, and through indirect contacts such as trade journals and newspapers.[111] The trade unions, once merely another channel for party control, have become extremely forceful in their defense of workers' rights, particularly in relation to damaging side effects of the economic reforms.[112]

Although the government's attitude toward these groups has been somewhat mixed,[113] on the whole it has regarded them as a valuable counterbalance to the nationality differences. Industrial associations, combining enterprises throughout Yugoslavia, are often able to counteract local pressures more effectively than the federal government.[114] Furthermore, these groups are usually somewhat less emotional than the various nationalities, and by allowing them to take over the dialogue, the government can partially "depoliticize" the issues. For example, the trade unions will probably be brought into the process of establishing uniform wages, which the workers' coun-

---

[110] Shoup, "RPDY," p. 9.   [111] *Ibid.*, p. 10.

[112] *Ibid.* The trade unions' opposition to the reforms is based on the consequences of the reforms to inefficient enterprises and to their workers. In 1965, Yugoslav economists predicted that if the reforms were fully implemented, about 2,000 enterprises would have to shut down, and about 1 million workers (one fourth of the labor force) would lose their jobs. Jukić, "Tito's Last Battle," p. 6.

[113] For example, Vukmanović-Tempo, head of the trade unions, was dismissed in 1967 for his outspoken opposition to many government policies. Shoup, "RPDY," p. 10.

[114] *Ibid.*, p. 11.

cils have made very irregular.[115] This is a highly emotional issue among republics, but by taking it out of the realm of politics and letting the trade unions handle it, the government may find a workable compromise.[116]

Another nonregional group that has expressed itself on the economic issue is the students. Although they have been more emotional in their protests (violent demonstrations in June, 1968),[117] they have helped to strengthen the workers' bargaining position. Tito, in fact, retreated from some aspects of the reform after the discovery that "Tito's youth" were not quite his.[118] However, far more important to the problem of succession are changes in the party and the government resulting largely from the student protests. In an effort to recapture support from young Yugoslavs, Tito has pensioned off most of the old partisan party and government workers and replaced them with younger men who are more technologically competent and less ideologically restricted. The Ninth Party Congress and the April, 1969, elections were the scenes of the rejuvenation process.[119] This change will be likely to have a calming influence on the nationality problem within the government, if it is true, as one observer notes, that the younger Yugoslavs are more willing to discuss nationality problems but less likely to become too excited about them.[120]

The pattern of opposition in Yugoslavia is extremely complex, and not easily reducible into a simple "liberal"-"conservative" pattern. All groups claim to favor direct democracy, workers' councils, and the like; they are all Titoists in the sense that they recognize that a return to Stalinist socialism, even if desirable, is simply not feasible in Yugoslavia any more. Furthermore, even within the confines of this consensus, the contenders do not simply choose sides for "more" or for "less" liberalization. There are many groups that demand more political freedom at the same time that they condemn aspects

[115] Workers set their own wages through the workers' councils on the basis of the enterprise's income. Thus, wages in the profitable industries of the North are substantially higher than they are in the inefficient Southern enterprises.

[116] Shoup, "RPDY," p. 11.

[117] "But Can You Be Liberal By Halves?" *The Economist,* CCXXIX, No. 6535 (November 23, 1968), 25.

[118] Shoup, "RPDY," p. 14.

[119] *Ibid.,* p. 5; Binder, "Yugoslavs Elect Representatives," p. 6.

[120] Binder, "Ranković Ouster," p. 9.

of economic liberalization (e.g., the students, to some extent Macedonia, and certain economic associations). Even in terms of political liberalization alone, there are two issues (liberalization of federal-republic relations, and liberalization vis-à-vis the individual's role in the political process) with a possibility of four distinct positions, not counting disagreement on degrees of liberalization or even on what liberalization really is.

The problem for Tito, or for his successors, is to find some order in all of these opinions and to find a less emotional way of making policy. The 1965 economic reforms, despite the controversy they have spurred, were actually an attempt to do just this. It was an effort to "de politicize" investment decisions, a continual source of controversy, by making investment depend on scientific, nonpolitical criteria (i.e., profitability). Unfortunately, these scientific criteria are to the advantage of the more developed republics, and therefore highly political notwithstanding their objective nature. Whether it will be possible to find many truly "nonpolitical" means of making controversial decisions remains to be seen.[121]

The Succession

Although the "decentralists" seem to be greatly outnumbered, at the present they have the advantage, if only because it seems nearly impossible to retreat without unacceptable resistance from at least the Croats and the Slovenes. They have much of the country's wealth, major figures in the federal government (Kardelj is usually regarded as the likely successor to Tito, now that Ranković is gone), and, in the last resort, their own armies (which they never mention, but . . .). On the other hand, the Serbs and their allies have, in addition to numerical superiority (at least on economic issues), the marvelously effective political weapon of simply resisting policies they find objectionable.

Nevertheless, despite the extreme positions taken, there seems to be a real commitment to the Yugoslav idea even among the Slovenes and Croats. While it is very likely that they would resort

[121] A new attempt has been proposed in the establishment of a scientific Institute for the Study of the Development of the Standard of Living, which would provide objective and accurate information on the effects of current economic policies on incomes and the Yugoslavs' standard of living. Shoup, "RPDY," p. 19.

to their armies to defend themselves from overt aggression by the Serbs, actual secession, no matter how peacefully accomplished, seems unlikely except as a desperate last resort.

A more likely solution, should the exaggerated political strife continue, is a confederation. While this would deprive the less-developed republics of substantial development funds from the northern republics, it would permit them to choose policies specifically oriented towards their own economic problems. Certainly, if the reforms fail, a confederation seems the only viable alternative to Tito.

Kadimah: Jewish Nationalism in Vienna before Herzl

HARRIET Z. PASS

Liberalism and the Jews of Vienna

Liberalism was the creed of the middle-class Jews of Vienna at the end of the nineteenth century. They were not interested in Jewish nationalism; the idea of Jewry as a nationality rather than a religious community did not appeal to them, especially in its extreme form, Zionism, which advocated the creation of a separate Jewish state. The Jewish bourgeoisie was mainly German-speaking and tended to favor assimilation. They identified with the Austrian state, not with a Jewish homeland in Palestine. As liberals, they were concerned not with the rights of Jews as a national group but rather with their position as individuals and Austrian citizens under the Constitution and Bill of Rights.

The Jews of Austria had been granted full legal emancipation when the Liberal party first came to power in 1867. During the era of Francis Joseph, they enjoyed a period of unprecedented economic prosperity. All but one of the major Viennese banking houses were Jewish.[1] Jews began to crowd the liberal professions, in particular journalism, medicine, law, and later academic posts as well. They also played a predominant role in the arts, literature, and music. Some Jews even gained high positions in the civil service and in the army. Economic and political emancipation was virtually complete but assimilation was not entirely successful; certain restrictions and social barriers still remained. Few Jews were accepted in high society, and popular resentment against Jewish influence grew.

Not all the Jews in Vienna, however, belonged to the wealthy

[1] P. G. J. Pulzer, *The Rise of Political Anti-Semitism in Germany and Austria* (New York, John Wiley & Sons, Inc., 1964), p. 11.

middle class. After 1867, there was an influx of Jewish settlers from outside Vienna, especially from Galicia. The Jewish population of Vienna jumped from 15,600 (3.30 percent) in 1856 to 72,590 (10 percent) in 1880, and then to 118,495 (8.8 percent) in 1891.[2] The newcomers, for the most part poor peddlers and tradesmen, lived in the old Jewish quarter, Leopoldstadt. Their Eastern European, Orthodox manners were resented by their Westernized coreligionists. The principles of Jewish nationalism or Zionism did not particularly attract these Eastern European immigrants either, although they were more conscious of their Jewish heritage than were the native Viennese Jews. The Hasidic tradition which they brought with them from the ghettos stressed the religious aspects of Judaism; it did not favor the creation of a secular Jewish state in Palestine but awaited the arrival of a Messiah. These Jews had come to make a new home for themselves in the Austrian capital and were trying to become accepted by the society in which they were living. In the meantime they were allowed to play only a limited role in Jewish community life in Vienna. The assimilated liberals kept the leadership in their own hands.

The fate of Viennese Jewry was closely linked with that of liberalism. In 1879, the Liberal ministry collapsed after being in office for twelve years, during the reorganization and industrialization of the Dual Monarchy. Once in opposition, the Liberal party split into various factions and its importance in Austrian political life began to decline. Simultaneous with the fall of the liberals from power was the upsurge of anti-Semitism in Austria. These events did not coincide by chance: the forces encouraging anti-Semitism and those encouraging anti-liberalism were often one and the same. Liberalism was identified with the Jews and the Jews with liberalism. Liberalism had never struck deep roots in Austria. It did not gain support among the conservative aristocracy or among the masses, who associated it with the evils of industrialism, modernism, and urbanism. It was the liberals, hence the Jews, who were held responsible for the stock crash of 1873, the suffering of the lower middle class, the exploitation of the workers, and poor urban conditions.

Because neither the economy nor the society of the . . . Austrian Empire was ever thoroughly liberalized, the alliance between the ruling class and the lower middle class—officials, humbler professional men, trades-

2 Max Grunwald, *History of Jews in Vienna,* Jewish Community Series (Philadelphia, Jewish Publication Society of America, 1936), p. 67.

people, artisans—could come about. It was this strange alliance that formed the basis of political anti-Semitism.[3]

In 1879, Georg von Schönerer made his first anti-Semitic speech on the election platform. By 1882, there was a flood of anti-Semitic propaganda and two anti-Semitic organizations were created, the *Österreichischer Reformverein* and the *Deutschnational Verein*. The Jewish establishment in Vienna, the foremost rabbis, Adolf Jellinek and Moritz Güdemann, and the community leaders refrained from loud protest against these occurrences. The Jews wished to consolidate their position, not jeopardize it. The only voice to be heard in an open fight against anti-Semitism was that of Joseph Samuel Bloch, a young rabbi from Floridsdorf, a suburb of Vienna, who in a celebrated court case in 1883 successfully refuted the charges in Professor August Rohling's anti-Semitic tract *Der Talmudjude*. A year later, Bloch founded the *Oesterreichische Wochenschrift,* a weekly paper meant to be the "fighting organ for rebutting all hostile attacks against Judaism." [4] In 1885, he helped to establish the *Oesterreichische-Israelitische Union,* which accepted as the basis of its program community of race, not of religious faith, and declared its aims:

to promote a love for Jewish learning among the Jews of Austria and to further their interests; to oppose and dispel the widespread errors in regard to the Jews and the prejudices against them, and to combat the efforts to increase the severity of the religious and racial opposition to them.[5]

This defense organization, aiming to combat anti-Semitism through education and later through legal means, had only limited effectiveness. It concerned itself only with the improvement of the condition of Jews within Austria itself. Bloch never became a Zionist, although he sympathized with the Jewish national cause.

Thus the political and intellectual climate among the Jews of Vienna towards the end of the nineteenth century remained liberal, despite the undeniable presence of anti-Semitism, which liberalism was unable to hold in check. The Jews for the most part chose to be Austrian citizens of the Jewish faith; they were not prepared to accept the idea of a Jewish homeland. There was one exception to this

[3] Pulzer, p. 27.

[4] Joseph S. Bloch, *My Reminiscences* (Vienna, R. Löwit, 1923), p. 178.

[5] Ismar Elbogen, *A Century of Jewish Life* (Philadelphia, Jewish Publication Society of America, 1945), p. 193.

rule: a group of students that renounced liberalism and chose Jewish
nationalism instead. This is the story of *Kadimah*.

The Beginnings of Jewish Nationalism in Vienna

In 1883 *Kadimah,* the first Jewish nationalist organization in Western
Europe, was founded at the University of Vienna. Although the
concept of Jewish nationalism did not find a receptive audience
among Viennese Jewry as a whole, it did take root among a small
group of Jewish students, helping to pave the way for Theodore
Herzl, the founder of the Zionist movement. The purpose of this
essay is to study the academic association Kadimah, its origins, its
development, and its contributions up to the time of the First Zionist
Congress in 1897.

The University of Vienna became a hotbed of German nationalism
and anti-Semitism in the 1880s. "Throughout the nineteenth century
student opinion in Austria was predominantly nationalist; nationalist
and liberal before 1848, nationalist and illiberal after 1867." [6] Prior
to the 1870s, Austrian universities had been relatively free of anti-
Semitism, and Jewish students had played an active role in many
of the German-nationalist organizations and fraternities. To illustrate
this phenomenon, William J. McGrath, in an article entitled "Student
Radicalism in Vienna," gives an account of "what must have been
one of the most remarkable scenes in the cultural life of nineteenth
century Vienna":

a student political meeting in which Victor Adler (the Jewish future
leader of the Social Democrats) and Heinrich Friedjung (the Jewish
liberal historian) joined other young politicians in singing "Deutschland,
Deutschland ueber alles" while Gustav Mahler (the Viennese Jewish
composer) assisted with a passionate piano accompaniment to the tune
of "O du Deutschland, ich muss marschieren.[7]

Nevertheless, by 1880 the tide was turning, and Jewish students were
gradually being excluded from German student activities in Vienna.
In 1878 *Libertas* was the first fraternity to expel its Jewish members,
and in 1881 it forbade its members to fight duels with Jews. One by
one, the other fraternities followed suit and included an "Aryan
Paragraph" in their programs, so that by 1890 nearly all such organi-

[6] Pulzer, p. 248.

[7] William J. McGrath, "Student Radicalism in Vienna," *Journal of Contemporary History,* II, No. 3 (July, 1967), 183.

zations were *judenrein* (Jew-free). The anti-Semitism of the German-nationalist student body in Austria was, from its beginning, based on racial, not religious, grounds.[8] Membership restrictions for German societies in Austria applied even to baptized Jews; by contrast, the situation in Germany before the turn of the century was not as extreme.[9] Thus, anti-Semitism effectively barred Jewish students from participating in normal extracurricular student life at the University of Vienna.

The Jewish students comprised a sizable percentage of the student body at the University of Vienna (38.6 percent of the medical faculty and 23.3 percent of the law faculty in 1880[10]), but they were divided among themselves and lacked organization. The basic dichotomy was between the "Westerners," mainly natives of Vienna, and the large number of students from Eastern Europe; "while the Jews born in the Western European countries were regarded as outcasts by the non-Jewish corporations and societies, the foreign Jewish students—mostly from Russia—were regarded as outcasts by the outcasts."[11]

For the most part, the "Westerners" were assimilated and liberal, with attitudes similar to those of liberal Viennese Jewry at large. They were indifferent to Judaism and did not consider themselves as part of a separate Jewish nationality. "What marked them out as Jews was in fact only the treatment meted out to them by the anti-Semitic student societies, which hated and insulted them."[12] Finding themselves excluded from the German-nationalist organizations, some members of this group attempted to form parallel liberal student associations, which generally consisted of a large majority of Jews, with a few non-Jewish members included on the membership roster. These efforts were largely ineffective in solving the problems of the Jewish students, since, lacking a positive attitude towards their Jewish identity, these small clubs found it difficult to defend themselves against the attacks of anti-Semites. Such organizations diminished in number and in importance by the 1890s.

Unlike their Westernized counterparts, the Jewish students from

[8] Paul Molisch, *Die deutschen Hochschulen in Oesterreich* (Munich, Drei Masken Verlag, 1922), p. 118.

[9] George L. Mosse, *The Crisis of German Ideology: The Intellectual Origins of the Third Reich* (New York, Grosset and Dunlap, 1964), p. 196.

[10] Pulzer, p. 13.

[11] Nahum Sokolow, *History of Zionism 1600–1918* (London, Longmans, Green and Co., 1919), I, 283.

[12] *Ibid.*

Eastern Europe did not seek the answer to their plight in liberalism. They had never really felt themselves part of university life in Vienna and generally led a lonely and isolated existence. Coming to Vienna with a Jewish background stronger than their native German-speaking contemporaries, they identified themselves much more readily as members of a Jewish nationality. Being university students, many had freed themselves from the Orthodox beliefs and practices of the ghetto, and they did not necessarily share the views of the other Eastern European inhabitants of Vienna. It is therefore not surprising that when a group of Eastern European students organized themselves at the University of Vienna, they became the first to raise the banner of Jewish nationalism in Western Europe.

The origins of Kadimah can be traced back to the situation in Eastern Europe, as well as to that in Vienna. As a result of the bloody pogroms and harsh regulations of 1881–82 the Jewish intellectuals in Russia became convinced that the Western example of emancipation and assimilation, as in Vienna, did not solve the problem of the Jews in the diaspora, and that the only real solution was settlement in Palestine. In 1882 in Russia, Leon Pinsker, a former assimilationist, published in German the first document of political Zionism, a pamphlet entitled *Autoemanzipation,* which was to become the guidebook for *Kadimah.* He maintained that assimilation was impossible, that anti-Semitism was an incurable disease, and that the Jews, through self-help, must develop a land of their own.[13] In the same year, the first *Choveve Zion* (Lovers of Zion) association was founded in Warsaw, and similar organizations were formed in Iaşi (Romania) and in London. Simultaneously, the first Jewish colony was established in Palestine.

The Jewish nationalist philosophy was brought from Russia to Vienna by Perez Smolenskin, founder of the first Hebrew-language journal in the West, *Hashachar* (The Dawn) (1868–85). In his fight for the development of a Jewish national consciousness, Smolenskin opposed both assimilated and Orthodox Jews. He participated in the founding of Kadimah and gave the organization its name, which means both "Eastward"—away from assimilation and towards a national culture—and "Forward"—away from Orthodoxy and towards progress.

In the fall of 1882, the stage was set for the formation of Kadimah.

[13] Adolf Böhm, *Die Zionistische Bewegung* (Berlin, Jüdischer Verlag, 1937), I, 99–101.

Three students, Reuben Bierer, an older medical student from Lemberg, Maurice Schnirer, a young medical student from Bucharest, and Nathan Birnbaum, a first-year law student from Vienna, "decided to found a Jewish national student union." In the words of Schnirer, "It was not to be a drinking and speechifying union after the Teutonic model, but a very seed-bed for Jewish national thought, an educational centre for future leaders of the Jewish people." [14] After official sanction was granted by the City of Vienna, the newly created "academic association *Kadimah*" held its first plenary meeting on May 5, 1883. Of the original eleven members, a majority of whom were in the medical faculty, all were from Eastern Europe, with the exception of Nathan Birnbaum, who, although born and raised in Vienna, nevertheless considered himself an Easterner. In the words of Birnbaum:

This Eastern exclusiveness was of course no accident, but based on the fact that the young people from the East still came from a living Jewish national milieu, where there was already a movement for self-emancipation or a national rebirth. The young people from the German cultural circle, however, had seen no example of living national Judaism. To them, assimilation was a self-evident fact; the question of whether or not it was really possible never even entered their minds. To such people, a hint of independent Jewish national strivings had to appear as entirely ridiculous, reactionary foolishness.[15]

The official aim of Kadimah was "to cultivate the literature and science of Judaism, excluding all political tendencies." The real goals, however, were: to fight academic anti-Semitism, to pledge allegiance to the idea of a Jewish nation, and to further colonization of Palestine.[16] Their main purpose, therefore, as to combat assimilation and anti-Semitism by increasing Jewish awareness and national consciousness.

The new organization began its career by posting an announcement on the university bulletin board. This notice, written by Schnirer, Kadimah's first president, and Birnbaum, its publicist, read as follows:

[14] M. T. Schnirer, "The Days of Early Zionism," in Nahum Sokolow, *Hibbath Zion* (Jerusalem, Rubin Mass, 1934), p. 380.
[15] Nathan Birnbaum, "Gegen die Selbstverständlichkeit," in Ludwig Rosenhek, ed., *Festschrift zur Feier des 100. Semesters der akademischen Verbindung Kaimah 1883–1933* (Mödling, 1933), p. 30.
[16] Schnirer, "Gründung der *Kadimah*," in Rosenhek, ed., *Festschrift*, p. 17.

Brothers!

For eighteen centuries, since the Jewish nation lost its independence, ceaseless persecutions have been conducted, the goal of which is the destruction of Jewry. In these attempts, our enemies have unfortunately received all too much help from our own people. The indifference from inside Jewry itself joins forces with the enemies on the outside in achieving this goal. We can behave only defensively against our enemies, but indifference must be opposed. This is the task which the newly-formed academic association *Kadimah* has undertaken to perform; its purpose is to maintain and to protect the spiritual wealth of the nation. . . . In order to reach our lofty goals, the young association needs the moral and material support of all in whose breast a Jewish heart still beats.

Brothers! Reach out your helping hand to us in the firm conviction that you will have contributed to a great and lofty aim, to the regeneration of the Jewish nation! [17]

This appeal was greeted with jeers and laughter from all sides. From the Jewish student body, as well as from the Viennese Jewish population at large, they heard little but scorn and contempt for their project. Kadimah received token sympathy from the rabbis of the community, Jellinek and Güdemann, as well as from Bloch, but the voices of real support came only from the outside, from Pinsker in Odessa, Moses Montefiore, the Jewish philanthropist in London,[18] and Heinrich Graetz, the Jewish historian in Breslau.[19]

Undaunted by the generally unfavorable reaction, this small group of students continued with their activities. They set up a library and reading room, where they could hold meetings and discussions. The library contained approximately 700 volumes in German, 150 in Hebrew, and 120 in other languages, as well as journals of general and Jewish interest from all over the world. Their lecture schedule for 1883 included talks on subjects such as "The Jews as a Race and a Nation," "The Extent of Jewish National Thinking," "A Trip to Jerusalem," and "On Messianism in Judaism." [20] In addition to its educational role, Kadimah also served a social function for its members.

The highlight of the Kadimah calendar was the annual Maccabean celebration in December. Attendance at this event, both of members

17 *Ibid.*, p. 18.
18 Isidor Schalit, "1890 bis 1904," in Rosenhek, ed., *Festschrift*, pp. 37–38.
19 Sokolow, *Hibbath Zion*, p. 383.
20 Schnirer, Rosenhek, ed., *Festschrift*, pp. 26–27.

and of guests, was reported to be as large as 500 persons.[21] The holiday of *Chanukah* (The Festival of Lights) was chosen because of its symbolic meaning, commemorating one of the glorious moments in Jewish history, the victory of the Maccabees over the Greeks in the second century B.C. Nathan Birnbaum, in his address at the first Maccabea, which took place on December 22, 1883, spoke of the significance of the Maccabees and the need to revive their spirit. He advocated the Jews educate themselves to a life of dignity in their own land and opposed both "modern Hasidism," which stressed the religious personality of the Jewish people rather than its national character, and the assimilationsts, "the modern imitators of the Hellenists." In the theme song which Birnbaum wrote for Kadimah, the following line appears: "So darfst Du Jude, Sklav nicht sein—Du hattest Makkabeer" [22] (Jew, you should not be a slave—you had the Maccabees).

Nathan Birnbaum (also known under the pseudonym "Mathias Acher") played an important role in the history of Kadimah, especially during the early years of its development. He became the organization's second president in 1884, but he held that position for only a short time and resigned because of a difference of opinion with a majority in the group. As well as delivering speeches and writing songs and propaganda, he founded a journal in 1885, named *Selbstemanzipation* (in 1894 it became *Jüdisches Volksblatt*); for many years, this paper served as the voice of Kadimah to the outside world. Birnbaum was one of the pioneers of Zionism in Western Europe. In 1893, he wrote a pamphlet entitled "The National Rebirth of the Jewish Nation in its own Land." He was also a proponent of Jewish nationalism within Austria itself, and around the turn of the century he broke with political Zionism to become a follower of Ahad Ha'am, the spokesman for cultural Zionism. Eventually he became an advocate of the Yiddish language and of Eastern European orthodoxy.[23] Despite the rather erratic nature of his career—from a Marxian socialist freethinker to an extreme Jewish Orthodox fanatic—Nathan Birnbaum made a significant contribution to Jewish nationalism by acting as a link between Eastern and Western Jewry at the crossroads, Vienna.

[21] *Oesterreichische Wochenschrift*, I, No. 10 (Dec. 26, 1884), 7.
[22] Werner J. Cahnman, "The Fighting *Kadimah*," *Chicago Jewish Forum*, XVII, No. 1 (Fall, 1958), 26.
[23] Böhm, pp. 137–38.

The Development of Jewish Nationalism in Vienna

By the late 1880s, Kadimah was firmly established on the Viennese student scene. The first phase of its development was over and a controversy was arising within its ranks as to its future course. The organization was divided on two issues: whether or not Kadimah should become a "fighting" (dueling) society, and whether more emphasis should be placed on Jewish cultural nationalism or on Jewish nationalism with Palestine as the ultimate goal. Eventually, as the composition of Kadimah's membership gradually shifted from one of primarily Eastern Jews to one containing a high percentage of Western Jews, dueling and Jewish nationalism in Austria won out over nondueling and exclusive stress on Palestine colonization. The second stage in Kadimah's history, the "Westernization" of its membership and its program, can best be explained with the help of a comparison with developments taking place among Jewish students in Germany at the same time.

At German universities in the nineteenth century, anti-Semitism was never quite as universal and extreme as in Austria. Nevertheless, in 1881, the *Verein Deutscher Studenten-Kyffhäuser Bund* was organized along far-reaching *völkisch* lines.

Anti-Semitism was strong and central to the Verein and the fraternities. In fact, the impetus for a program of anti-Jewish prejudice, as in petitions, ostracizing of fellow Jewish students, and even violent expressions of hate, was provided by student organizations.[24]

In Germany, as in Austria, the Jewish students reacted by founding their own organizations.

In the fall of 1886, a group of Jewish students in Breslau—11 in the medical faculty and 1 young rabbinical student named Benno Jacobs—formed a Jewish fraternity, which they called *Viadrina* after the official name of Breslau University, Leopoldius Viadrina. They issued a manifesto entitled "A Word to Our Co-Religionists," which read as follows:

. . . The Jewish student has already ample occasion at the university to experience the whole weight of hatred and scorn that every Jew meets in public life. . . .
Wherever we look we see division, isolation, disaproval of one another,

24 Mosse, p. 194.

lack of self-confidence and self-esteem. We have lost the feeling for the unity of our interests. That is the reason why the Jewish undergraduate has no influence, is not respected, has neither support nor power. . . . an Association of Jewish Students . . . will raise the badge of independent Jewry and will unite under its banners all those who are of the same mind.

This association, by its mere existence, will revive the almost extinguished consciousness that we are Jews.[25]

These same feelings were held in common by aware Jewish students in both Germany and Austria. Although the founders of Viadrina and Kadimah had different ideologies, they were faced with similar situations. Kadimah in its early days had primarily directed its efforts towards education, but its members soon became conscious of the urge to defend the Jewish cause in a more demonstrative fashion. The new course which they were to adopt resembled the following program of Viadrina:

As to the practical aims of the association: we think, first of all, of physical training as a means of achieving our purpose. . . . We have to fight with all our energy against the odium of cowardice and weakness, which is cast on us. We want to show that every member of our association is equal to any Christian in any physical exercise and chivalry. Physical strength and agility will increase self-confidence and self-respect, and in future nobody will be ashamed of being a Jew.[26]

Unlike Kadimah, however, Viadrina was totally German, not Jewish, in character. It imitated all the traditions of German fraternities, including its colors, black-red-gold, and its coat of arms with all German symbols. From its beginning, it was a "fighting" society with caps, ribbons, and parades. Its manifesto asserted: "We uphold . . . the principle that we can be Jews and good Germans at the same time, and we shall prove it by our behaviour." [27] The members of Viadrina, with Western Jewish backgrounds and outlooks, were culturally German, not Jewish; they did not consider themselves as part of a Jewish nation but rather as part of the German nation, as German citizens of the Mosaic faith.

Viadrina was a German-style fraternity with all Jewish members; Kadimah was a Jewish association which gradually acquired a native

[25] Adolf Asch and Johanna Philippson, "Self-Defence at the Turn of the Century: The Emergence of the K.C.," *Leo Baeck Institute Yearbook,* III (1958), 123.

[26] *Ibid.,* p. 124.   [27] *Ibid.*

German-speaking majority. Towards the end of the 1880s, more and more students from Vienna, the Czech lands, and Bukovina began to join the organization, changing its former Eastern European—mainly Russian, Romanian and Galician—composition and outlook completely. The original members of Kadimah had been characterized by a deeply ingrained Jewish consciousness. Those who subsequently joined the organization had for the most part been raised in an assimilated atmosphere. Disillusioned by their experiences at the university, they had turned to Kadimah where for the first time their Jewish awareness developed. The early Kadimah followers were generally quiet and contemplative by nature; they were secure in their close ties with Jewish life of the time. The newcomers were more activist by nature; Jewish nationalism was for them a novel ideology and they were anxious to propagate it both by word and by deed.[28]

It is striking that to an overwhelming extent the originators and leading figures of modern political Zionism (Leon Pinsker in Russia, Theodore Herzl in Vienna, Max Bodenheimer and Kurt Blumenfeld in Germany) were former assimilationist, not Orthodox, Jews. As Nahum Sokolow points out in his *History of Zionism,* "Pinsker, like all subsequent political Zionist leaders, arrived at the idea of Zionism not through the problem of Judaism . . . but through the problem of Jewry."[29] In the case of Kurt Blumenfeld, a radical German Zionist in the early twentieth century, "it was not Judaism that made him a Zionist . . . , but Zionism that made him a Jew." Blumenfeld designated this phenomenon "post-assimilationist Zionism." According to him, "Post-assimilationist Zionism differs . . . from Zionism which had grown out of a deeply rooted relationship with Judaism"; it "includes all those who have left assimilation behind in order to gain the safety of Judaism."[30] This classification applies very well to the second generation of Kadimah members; they became the enthusiastic agitators and fighters for the Jewish nationalist movement, forerunners of the Zionist organization in Vienna.

Under the influence of these post-assimilationist Jewish nationalists, Kadimah broadened its sphere of activities. It still retained its originally educational role but expanded it to helping assimilated Jewish students find their way back to Judaism. In addition, it

[28] Schalit, in Rosenhek, ed., *Festschrift,* pp. 39–41.

[29] Sokolow, *History of Zionism,* p. 224.

[30] Shaul Esh, "Kurt Blumenfeld on the Modern Jew and Zionism," *Jewish Journal of Sociology,* VI, No. 2 (December, 1964), 236.

launched itself on an entirely new course: to combat assimilation and anti-Semitism with the sword as well as the pen.

This change took place in the early 1890s, when a small group of Kadimah members—including Siegmund Werner from Vienna and Karl Pollack from Prague, both past presidents of the organization— began to fight duels with anti-Semites, heckle Jewish liberals, and break up their meetings.[31] Such activity attracted a growing number of Western Jewish students but alienated the Easterners, who regarded dueling as "totally un-Jewish and against the spirit and tradition of Judaism." [32] They rejected the idea of *Muskeljudentum* (Judaism of the muscle)—a term coined by Max Nordau, an early follower of Herzl in Vienna—and felt that the spiritual idealism of Kadimah was deteriorating and being replaced by the power of fists. Nevertheless, in May, 1893, after a stormy battle within the ranks, the following resolution was passed at a general meeting:

The academic associaition *Kadimah* declares itself unconditionally conservative and obliges each member to give satisfaction upon insult, whenever the settlement of a dispute is not possible by means of a declaration of honour.[33]

As an official "fighting" association, Kadimah had its own fencing society, fully equipped with cap, band, and rapier. In the fall of 1893, 6 duels were fought against the Waidhof German nationalist fraternity *Philadelphia,* and, in 1894, 30 duels were carried out with the fraternity *Gothia.* By and large these efforts met with success. "The fact that Jewish students appeared in public as Jews and were ready to fight duels for the honor of Judaism . . . made a deep impression, even on Christian students." [34]

Duels played a very important part in German student fraternity life. The dueling tradition was based on a medieval caste concept, whereby only members of the upper classes had "honor" and were worthy of "satisfaction"; Jews and all other lower-class elements were excluded from participation. It was a far-reaching sign of emancipation that Jewish students were permitted to fight duels in Germany and Austria in the nineteenth century, first as members of German-nationalist fraternities and then as members of Jewish organizations. On March 11, 1896, however, the German-nationalist fra-

[31] Cahnman, "The Fighting *Kadimah*," p. 26.
[32] Schalit, in Rosenhek, ed., *Festschrift,* p. 72.   [33] *Ibid.*
[34] Elbogen, p. 712.

ternities at a conference at Waidhof declared: "Jewish students were without principles and completely devoid of honour, and accordingly no satisfaction was to be granted them." [35] Paul Molisch, an historian of strong German-nationalist convictions, justified this by stating: "If one could prove a psychological or moral difference between Aryans and Jews, then it was entirely fitting that Jews should be declared completely without honour according to our German concept." He denied that a people existed that possessed no honor at all, but claimed that "Jewish honour was not German honour." [36]

The Jewish students protested vigorously against this decision. It was not the actual issue that was important, but the idea behind it. As Bloch wrote in an editorial in the *Oesterreichische Wochenschrift,*

The duel question itself may interest certain individuals, but for the majority of the Jewish student body it does not exist. For them it is entirely a question of the insult which was heaped upon them by the declaration that all academic citizens of the Jewish faith were without honour.[37]

A general meeting of all Jewish students at the University of Vienna prepared a joint resolution by the various Jewish student organizations, which contained the following statement:

The Jewish student body rejects the accusation of lack of honour. Having honour is not dependent on belonging to the German nation or the Aryan race. The Jewish students are firmly dedicated to defending their position as academic citizens, having equal rights and full status, with all the means which are at their disposal.[38]

The Viennese Jewish community at large supported the students in this dispute. Despite differences in outlook, many liberal burghers were proud of the efforts of the Jewish nationalist students to defend Jewish honor publicly.

In 1896, on the occasion of Kadimah's "jubilee," celebrating its twenty-fifth semester of existence, J. S. Bloch concluded an editorial on this subject with the assessment:

When we thus examine the activities of *Kadimah* until now, we have to admit that we have once again to ascribe to *Kadimah* the responsibility

---

[35] Schalit, in Rosenhek, ed., *Festschrift,* p. 73.

[36] Molisch, *Die deutschen Hochschulen,* p. 125.

[37] *Oesterreichische Wochenschrift,* XIII, No. 12 (March 20, 1896), 229.

[38] Schalit, in Rosenhek, ed., *Festschrift,* p. 75.

for the inauguration of a new trend. Thanks to *Kadimah,* Jewish youth at the university begin to think and feel as Jews again. It is *Kadimah* alone that teaches Jewish youth to fight back.[39]

The Influence and Contributions of Jewish Nationalist Students in Vienna

Kadimah was instrumental in helping to found other Jewish student organizations both in Vienna and elsewhere. In 1894, its members played a leading role in the creation of the *Rede- und Lesehalle jüdischer Hochschüler in Wien,* which has to be a neutral meeting place for Jewish students from different political camps. According to Paul Molisch, this "Reading and Discussion Room for Jewish Students" was a copy of a German-nationalist institution of the same type, *Germania,* which had been established in Vienna the previous year.[40] The need for such a meeting room was pointed out by Bloch in an editorial:

It is true that there already exists a Jewish organization, the academic association *Kadimah,* at the University of Vienna, which in the last years has been of undeniable service to the Jewish students. Nevertheless, due to its set program and its organization as a fighting society, which channels its activities in a very definite direction, it is not in a position to increase its membership beyond a certain limit. Alongside of *Kadimah,* however, a new association would be able to achieve good and necessary results. It would serve a pressing need of the Jewish student body.[41]

Despite the allegedly nonpolitical nature of this organization, a dispute arose over control. The Jewish nationalist students fought their liberal opponents bitterly on this issue, since the former "were not willing to make their creation into an instrument of a dying party." [42] The battle over the Reading Room was a long-standing one; in the end, the Jewish nationalists won out over the assimilated liberals. Kadimah claimed to be the spokesmen of the Jewish students of Vienna.

By 1896, however, Kadimah was no longer the only Jewish

---

[39] *Oesterreichische Wochenschrift,* XIII, No. 7 (February 14, 1896), 137.
[40] Molisch, *Die deutschen Hochschulen,* p. 146.
[41] *Oesterreichische Wochenschrift,* XI, No. 15 (April 13, 1894), 293–94.
[42] Schalit, in Rosenhek, ed., *Festschrift,* p. 69.

student organization in the Austrian capital. Several sister clubs were created with memberships determined along regional, professional, and ideological lines. A group of Kadimah members who disagreed with the policy of dueling broke away in 1894 to form a nonfighting, Jewish nationalist academic association called *Gamala;* their leader was Siegmund Werner, who ironically enough had been the first Jewish nationalist student to fight a duel in Vienna. In the same year, two other Jewish nationalist "fighting" associations came into existence: *Unitas,* composed of students from Moravia, led by Karl Pollack, and *Ivria,* whose members were drawn mainly from Silesia. In 1897, the Jewish students from Galicia organized *Bar Kochba,* an association which gave up its fighting colors and concentrated on learning Hebrew and promoting colonization in Palestine. Two "fighting" professional organizations were also formed in Vienna: one (in 1895) among the Jewish veterinary students called *Libanonia* and another (in 1898) among the polytechnic students called *Maccabea.*[43]

Former members of Kadimah also helped to establish similar Jewish organizations outside of Vienna; *Veritas* in Brünn, *Bar Kochba* in Prague, *Hasmonea* in Czernowitz, and *Chartas* in Graz were all modeled on Kadimah. Beyond the borders of Austria, Kadimah served also as a pattern for Kadimah in London (1887) and *Jung Israel* in Berlin (1892).[44]

Kadimah was more generally Jewish nationalist than specifically Zionist in orientation before 1896, since it gave equal weight to the diaspora and to Palestine in the movement for Jewish national regeneration.[45] Several alumni of Kadimah, among them Maurice Schnirer and Oscar Kokesch, assisted in the founding of the Palestine Colonization Society, *Admath Jeschurun,* in 1892. Two years later, this organization joined with a number of other small Zionist associations elsewhere in Austria to form *Zion,* the "Union of Austrian Societies for the Colonization of Palestine and Syria." [46] The colonization of Palestine was one of the firm planks in Kadimah's program from the very beginning; it is hence not surprising that the alumni

[43] Siegmund Werner, "Die jüdischen Studentenverbindungen in Oesterreich," *Ost und West,* I, No. 6 (June, 1901), 419–20.

[44] Schalit, in Rosenhek, ed., *Festschrift,* p. 49.

[45] Werner J. Cahnman, "Adolf Fischof and His Jewish Followers," *Leo Baeck Institute Yearbook,* IV (1958), 132.

[46] Schalit, *Festschrift,* p. 71.

of Kadimah should play an important role among the early Zionist leaders in Vienna both before and after Herzl.

The year 1896 marked a turning point in the history of Kadimah: Theodore Herzl arrived on the scene. Kadimah welcomed him warmly on his return to Vienna and presented him with their colors at a gala celebration held in his honor. The students felt a common bond with Herzl; the founder of political Zionism had been a member of the German-nationalist fraternity *Albia* during his student days in Vienna but had resigned in 1882 as a result of the outbreak of anti-Semitism. As one of the Kadimah members, Isidor Schalit, stated:

Herzl also had experienced the great disappointment as we all had, and now he found a union of Jewish students, surrounded it is true with all the outer trimmings of German student romanticism, but inwardly filled with very proud lofty feelings of national enthusiasm.[47]

A letter promising full support for Herzl's program was signed by all the affiliated Jewish organizations, including Kadimah, Zion, Unitas, Ivria, Gamala, and Libanonia. Members and alumni of Kadimah, Schnirer, Kokesch, Schalit and others, served as Herzl's co-workers at the First Zionist Congress in Basel in 1897. Nathan Birnbaum became the first general secretary of the Zionist Organization, which had its headquarters in Vienna until Herzl's death in 1904. Isidor Schalit helped to found *Die Welt,* the organ of the Zionist movement, in 1897, and Siegmund Werner became the editor.[48] The contribution of Kadimah to the early Zionist movement was thus considerable.

"The mission of *Kadimah* was fulfilled when Herzl created the Zionist organization." [49] After 1896, the real function of Kadimah was over. Zionism was no longer a purely student movement in Vienna and the students were no longer the exclusive bearers of the nationalist Jewish idea. The membership of Kadimah provided recruits for the Zionist ranks, but the organization itself had lost its unique importance; it became simply one pro-Zionist organization among many. Political anti-Semitism declined in Austria around the turn of the century, but, according to P. G. J. Pulzer, it "continued to flourish with full force in the universities, leading to frequent riots with which the forces of the law were prevented, by academic

---

[47] Berliner Büro der Zionistischen Organisation, *Warum gingen wir zum ersten Zionistenkongress?* (Berlin, Jüdischer Verlag, 1922), p. 87.
[48] Schalit, in Rosenhek, ed., *Festschrift,* pp. 85–88.   [49] *Ibid.,* p. 105.

privilege, from interfering. . . . The old enmity between Jewish and German students continued undiminished." [50] Kadimah and the other Jewish organizations tried to combat these enemy forces as best they could. The academic association Kadimah continued its existence at the University of Vienna into the 1930s, but as the years went on, its leadership seemingly deteriorated and the role it played in Jewish life in Vienna became gradually less significant.

It is interesting to note that the heyday for Jewish nationalist students in Austria occurred before Herzl began his Zionist activities, whereas in Germany the most important period for the Jewish student movement, in particular student Zionism, was after 1896. In 1896, when the Jewish liberal student organizations in Vienna had all but disappeared, the Jewish fraternities in Germany, patterned on the Viadrina model, banded together to form the *Kartell-Convent der Verbindungen deutscher Studenten jüdischer Glaubens*. By 1906, while Kadimah and the other Jewish nationalist associations in Vienna were disintegrating inwardly, two student confederations with more or less Zionist orientations were already in existence in Germany. Later, in 1914, these Zionist groups merged to form the *Kartell Jüdischer Verbindungen*. Thus in Germany student Zionists were primarily followers of Herzl, while in Austria Jewish nationalist students were mainly his forerunners.

In conclusion, the academic association Kadimah, the first Jewish nationalist organization in Western Europe and the most important Jewish student organization in Vienna, served a twofold purpose. On the one hand, it offered Jewish students the opportunity for self-defense, self-respect, and self-awareness in the face of German nationalist anti-Semitism at the University of Vienna and elsewhere. On the other, it helped to set the stage for the founding of the Zionist movement in Vienna in 1896 and supplied much of the early Zionist leadership. As a result the significance of Kadimah far transcends that of a local academic fraternity in its contributions to both Jewish and Zionist history.

[50] Pulzer, p. 254.

John Armitage: An English Historian's Interpretation of Early Nineteenth-Century Brazil

ROBERTA MARX DELSON

When the Portuguese monarchs arrived in Brazil in 1808, they brought with them a tradition of commercial privileges which had long characterized trade between Portugal and England. Although British interests were well integrated into the Portuguese economy prior to the Napoleonic invasion in 1808, it was not until the ruling Braganza family escaped the French and set up court in Rio de Janeiro that the British sought to formalize commercial relations with the colony of Brazil, in addition and apart from those agreements already reached with the mother country. The treaty which officially cemented British commercial privileges in Brazil was negotiated in 1810; after that date, Great Britain began to encourage her business houses to take advantage of the rich opportunities waiting for them in the Brazilian market.

Official sanction for the practice of favoring British economic interests continued in Brazil until 1844 (when the Brazilians refused to renew the commercial treaty with Great Britain) and was thus unaffected by the emergence of Brazil as an independent empire in 1822. Hence, when twenty-one-year-old John Armitage was sent by his employer, Philips, Wood and Co., to the firm's branch office in Rio de Janeiro in 1828, he was embarking upon a commercial venture similar to those undertaken by scores of his fellow British businessmen in the eighteen years following the signing of the 1810 Commercial Treaty. Nor was the seven-year residence that Armitage enjoyed in Brazil (during which time he was witness to the unsuccessful experiment of the First Empire) an unusually lengthy stay for a

British merchant. However, what distinguished Armitage from the rest of his commercially minded countrymen was his decision to record and interpret the momentous period of Brazilian history through which he lived. Smith Elder and Co. published Armitage's two-volume *History of Brazil* in London in 1836, a scant year from the time the author had departed Brazilian shores. It remains, today, a classic study of the Joanine period and the First Empire.

Until this century, Armitage's *History of Brazil* was one of the few works in either Portuguese or English to deal specifically with the period from 1808 to 1831. One historian notes that prior to 1920, only three historians had attempted to analyze this time span of Brazilian history: John Armitage, Francisco Adolfo de Varnhagen, and Manoel de Oliveira Lima.[1] The last two have been the subjects of great attention by those concerned with tracing the development of Brazilian historiography, while Armitage has been considered only with reference to the academic debate over the authorship of the *History of Brazil*. Although the Englishman is frequently cited, I know of no other study which has attempted to analyze his ideas nor which has ventured an evaluation of his contribution to the writing of Brazilian history.

Even more perplexing is the fact that while Armitage's work has not been subjected to scholarly examination, the *History of Brazil,* written by Englishman Robert Southey in 1822, is constantly praised for its contribution to Brazilian historiography. In an otherwise perceptive essay outlining the Brazilian historiographical tradition, Pedro Moacyr Campos devotes pages to discussing Southey's florid study, but makes no mention of Armitage at all.[2] This is a particularly curious omission since Armitage intended his history to be a continuation of Southey's investigation, which only covered the history of Brazil to the arrival of the Braganzas. Furthermore, Southey wrote his history utilizing the limited sources which were available in England; Armitage, on the other hand, actually lived in Brazil, and thus recorded the history of a country which he knew personally.

Of more historical importance than this slight to Armitage is the fact that the ideas presented in his *History of Brazil* have been instru-

[1] Stanley J. Stein, "The Historiography of Brazil, 1809–1899," *Hispanic American Historical Review,* XL (May, 1960), 236.

[2] Pedro Moacyr Campos, "Outline of Brazilian Historiography in the Nineteenth and Twentieth Centuries," in E. Bradford Burns, ed., *Perspectives on Brazilian History* (New York, Columbia University Press, 1967), pp. 44–48.

mental in shaping our traditional view of the First Brazilian Empire. For example, the thesis that Pedro I fell from power because of his inability to ingratiate himself with the Brazilian people is directly traceable to Armitage. The same thing may be said for the position that despite his shortcomings, Pedro I served a positive function in preserving the unity of the former colony once independence had been achieved. Students of Brazilian history should know why Armitage undertook to write his history; they should be made aware of the views he held of the people who were host to him for seven years; they should understand in what ways Armitage typifies the viewpoint of Englishmen resident in Brazil during the First Empire. It is with a view toward increasing our understanding of John Armitage's *History of Brazil* that this essay is intended.

First, let us consider Armitage's motivation in writing the *History of Brazil*. In the introduction of his study, the author claims to have written a book which would provide information on Brazil to his fellow countrymen. (Armitage apparently felt that his own lack of knowledge had hampered his business dealings in Brazil.) Yet, curiously, Armitage's history is hardly a guide for the commercially minded traveler; rather, it is completely oriented toward political matters and serves basically as a treatise on why the First Empire failed. The author never mentions his own business dealings specifically, but instead makes passing references to the "higher motives" of writing history. For him, historical writing had to serve as a guide for the proper governing of a nation, an idea for which he gives credit to the German historian Herschel. In this sense, Armitage's *History of Brazil* may be viewed as a statement of the author's views on Brazilian government. Armitage summarily approved of the monarchy (he was, after all, a subject of the British Crown), but demanded that the Brazilians drop their pretensions for the aristocratic trappings that presumably went along with the monarchical idea. Although the *History of Brazil* predates by eight years the now-famous essay of Karl Friedrich Philipp von Martius on "How the History of Brazil Should Be Written," Armitage's sentiments precisely foreshadow those of the German naturalist; for von Martius, as well as for Armitage, "a book should be written . . . to correctly convince them [the Brazilians] of the impracticability of their utopian plans, of the impropriety of licentious discussions about public business, of the undesirability of an unrestrained press." [3]

[3] Karl Friedrich Philipp von Martius, "How the History of Brazil Should Be Written," in Burns, *Perspectives on Brazilian History*, p. 40.

Throughout his work, Armitage utilized an oral history technique. Much of the *History of Brazil* is based on the author's private conversations with the leading figures of the First Brazilian Empire. It is known, for example, that Armitage was on intimate terms with the vocal editor of the *Aurora Fluminense, Evaristo da Veiga.* Armitage's friendship with da Veiga (whose picture adorns the first pages of Volume One, along with that of José Bonafacio de Andrada) has led many to speculate that the editor might be either the author or the translator of the *History of Brazil,* a matter considered later in this essay. Other important figures who were acquainted with Armitage include the Brigadier Machado de Oliveira, who claimed to have first met him in the Cisplatine, where the latter was observing the war between the Argentines and the Brazilians over control of the Banda Oriental.[4] Lest any doubt remain of Armitage's connections, the author himself assures the readers that

he has had opportunities of associating with some of the most eminent political figures in Brazil: he has had access to documents and stores of information open but to few; and he has also had occasion to visit the seat of the Cisplatine war, and thus been enabled to estimate the manners and character of the wild inhabitants of that district, from personal observation.[5]

Drawing upon private conversations and newspaper articles for his principal sources, Armitage was able to present a remarkable synthesis of the events of the First Empire. In one of the few evaluations made of the content of the *History of Brazil,* Armitage has been complimented for the exactitude of his information.[6] On the other hand, a thorough reading of Armitage reveals that he was not above contriving some of his data, a reflection of a somewhat romantic notion of historical writing. Such is the case, for example, of the conversation that Armitage describes between the dying empress of Brazil and the mistress of Pedro I. In vivid terms, Armitage recreates the action of the Minister of Marine who wisely interposed himself between the two women and prevented the Marchioness de Santos

---

[4] Letter of Brigadier José Joaquim Machado de Oliveira to the Barão Homen de Mello, in Octávio Tarquinio de Sousa, *História dos Fundadores do Imperio do Brasil* (Rio de Janeiro, José Olympio, 1957), VI, 200.

[5] John Armitage, *History of Brazil* (London, Smith Elder & Co., Cornhill, 1836), Preface.

[6] Rubens Borba de Morães and William Berrien, *Manual Bibliografico de Estudos Brasileiros* (Rio de Janeiro, Grafica Editora Souza, 1949), p. 424.

from entering the sickroom by counseling, "Tenha paciencia Senhora Marqueza Vossamerce não pode entrar" ("Have patience, my Lady Marchioness, you cannot enter").[7] While it is probable that Armitage received a secondhand account of this event from one of his numerous influential acquaintances, he nevertheless describes the scene as if he personally had been there. Yet we know this could not be the case, for the empress died in 1826 and the author did not arrive in Brazil until two years later.

Apart from an occasional digression (particularly to discuss the events in the Cisplatine), Armitage systematically treats the events of the First Empire in chronological order. An analysis of Armitage's view of periodization is pointless, since his work deals mainly with the ten-year period of the First Empire, but, it is worthwhile to note that the first volume contains a brief summary of events until 1820, with the remainder of the discussion devoted to events that took place up to the end of the Banda Oriental war in 1828. The second volume treats the occurrences between 1829 and the downfall of the Empire in 1831. It also contains a document section, where such items as the "Secret Instructions of the Marquiz de Lavradio" and the emperor's "Manifesto," written when he closed the Constituent Assembly, are translated by the author.

The *History of Brazil* is stylistically formal; in general, Armitage's tone is restrained, although at points he appears to be ironic. This is particularly noticeable in the passages where Armitage reports on Lord Cochrane's failure to receive just compensation for the services he rendered to the cause of Brazilian independence. There are also instances of exaggerated portraits of First Empire personalities: the Andrada brothers are made to appear the worst sort of opportunist villains, while the empress has a saintly aura, especially in comparison to the Marchioness de Santos.

Most of the events presented in the *History of Brazil* do not receive a penetrating analysis. The slave-trade treaty of 1827, for example, is considered very matter-of-factly. Notwithstanding the predominantly narrative character of the work, Armitage does manage to assume an interpretive role in discussing the reasons for the downfall of the First Empire. It is Armitage's perceptive view of the Empire that makes the *History of Brazil* more than just a routine compilation of events.

[7] Armitage, I, 266.

A weighty problem which must be confronted in assessing Armitage's *History of Brazil* is the viability of the author's claim to objectivity, based on his position as a foreign observer. An overall impression of impartiality is not the feeling that one gets from having read both volumes. On the contrary, Armitage repeatedly maintains his sympathies with the Brazilians and is consistently anti-Portuguese in sentiment. The *History of Brazil* so much favored the Brazilian people that a Portuguese-language edition of it appeared just two years after the English edition. The translation, printed in Rio de Janeiro, is signed "Hum Brasiliero," a pseudonym presently attributed to Joaquim Teixeira de Macedo, a Brazilian intellectual of the period. Nevertheless, when the *História do Brasil* first appeared, many Brazilians assumed that Evaristo da Veiga had either written or translated the work, so closely did the book's sentiments echo his own. Although it is not my purpose to establish Armitage's authorship, it is worthwhile to examine the evidence on this matter as it now stands. Both Octávio Tarquinio de Sousa and Rubens Borba de Morães should be cited for the work they have done on the problem. Morães points out [8] that da Veiga received his copy of the work in English from Armitage (then in Europe) in October, 1836, accompanied by a letter in which Armitage proves himself to be the author of the history. As to da Veiga being the translator of the *History of Brazil,* Morães denies this possibility, noting that da Veiga had died before the translation was published and that, furthermore, the editor never indicated in his correspondence that he was working on such a project (although there remains the vague possibility that translation was published posthumously). However, the strongest argument in favor of Armitage being the author of the study (and one that is overlooked by those concerned with this question) is the curious feature that despite his pro-Brazilian sympathies, Armitage was very much a typical English intellectual of his time, and the work reflects it.

Although the question of authorship of the *History of Brazil* has been mildly debated since its publication, few historians have paused to examine the material contained within its pages. Yet, outstanding Brazilian historians such as Varnhagen and Oliveira Lima were undoubtedly aware of and influenced by Armitage's observations. Varnhagen, in his *História Geral do Brasil,* makes frequent refer-

[8] Rubens Borba de Morães, *Bibliographia Brasiliana* (Rio de Janeiro, Colibris Editora Ltda., 1958), I, 40.

ence to events described in Armitage's study, but does not attempt to evaluate the contents of the book. Similarly, Oliveira Lima makes use of Armitage's research and compliments the Englishman for "tão evidente bom senso" ("such evident good sense").[9] But neither his *O Império Brasileiro* or *O Movimento da Independencia 1821– 22*, nor the more recent *Empire in Brazil* of C. H. Haring, puts Armitage's work into historical perspective. Curiously, even José Honório Rodrigues limits his discussion of Armitage in his monumental *Teoria da História do Brasil* to treating the question of whether Armitage was actually the author, ignoring the thematic portion of the *History of Brazil*. Notwithstanding these omissions, the value of Armitage's work to the understanding of Brazilian history should not be doubted; the Brazilians have paid homage to the importance of Armitage's *History* by publishing three separate editions. Thus, let us examine the thematic portion of the *History of Brazil*, rather than further considering the question of authorship. The interpretations which follow may not seem particularly novel or variant from traditional views of the First Empire. But, it is precisely this feature which makes the themes so interesting; for it is with Armitage that many of our thoughts on Brazilian history have their origin.

Three themes are recurrent in both volumes of the *History of Brazil*. In the first place, Armitage postulates that poor administration on the part of the Portuguese resulted in a discontented colonial Brazil. This theme is of course reminiscent of the *creoles* vs. *peninsulares* conflict popularized as one of the causes of the Spanish-American wars of independence. A second motif is Armitage's distrust of the creation of a titled nobility. Finally, the author sets out to prove that while Pedro I was a unifying force in keeping Brazil intact after independence was achieved, the emperor, nevertheless, caused his own demise by failing to assimilate to Brazilian ways.

The theme of rivalry between the Portuguese and the Brazilians is carefully developed. Those Portuguese (*renois*) who came to seek their fortune in Brazil and later to return to Portugal were little concerned with bettering conditions in the colonial land. A totally different attitude developed among the children of Portuguese brought up in the colony; these *mazombos* came to resent the lack

[9] Manoel de Oliveira Lima, *O Império Brasileiro* (Rio de Janeiro, Weiszflog Irmãos Inc., 1927), p. 95.

of interest displayed by the renois in Brazil, and, by the end of the eighteenth century, began to argue for an amelioration of conditions in the colony. Armitage starts his treatment of the renois-mazombos clash after the arrival of the Braganzas. While the existence of the royal family in Brazil did bring prosperity to the colony (the ports were opened in 1808 and commercial restrictions lifted), Armitage observed that the tensions between the Portuguese and Brazilians increased rather than diminished. In very uncomplimentary terms, Armitage reported that the Portuguese followers of the Braganza family were indifferent to Brazilian problems:

The new comers [sic] were but little interested in the welfare of the country. They regarded their absence from Portugal as temporary, and were far more anxious to enrich themselves at the expense of the state, than to administer justice, or to benefit the public.[10]

A further cause for mazombo discontent, according to Armitage, was the inferior status of the Brazilian troops vis-à-vis the Portuguese regiments stationed in Brazil during the Joanine period. During the brief span when João VI left Pedro I to act as regent of Brazil (1821–22), the author notes that the rivalry question was of constant concern to the young ruler. Expanding further on this theme, Armitage astutely interprets the role of this Portuguese-Brazilian competition as having hastened the advent of independence.

Another irritant to the Brazilian people was the grossly inept bargaining of the Portuguese Cortes (effectively the ruling body in Portugal in 1820), which attempted to trade its claims in the Banda Oriental (at that time tenuously held by the Luso-Brazilians) for the right to reclaim the city of Olivença, ceded to Spain by the Portuguese in 1801. Armitage reports that the population of Rio de Janeiro was "indignant beyond measure that a fertile and extensive province should thus be balanced against a paltry town." [11] Armitage concludes that annoyance with the Cortes was instrumental in causing the final break with the mother country. It appeared to him that while the Cortes maintained a liberal front in Europe, it was bent on stripping Brazil of the privileges she had obtained during the Joanine era.

In outlining the Portuguese-Brazilian rivalry during the stay of João VI and in the days leading up to the independence movement, Armitage's sympathies are decidedly with the Brazilians. It comes as

[10] Armitage, I, 15.   [11] *Ibid.*, p. 75.

no surprise therefore that he took such a harsh view toward Pedro I, who surrounded himself with Portuguese advisers, turning a deaf ear to Brazilian demands. In the remainder of the *History of Brazil,* Armitage relentlessly chides the emperor for his lack of understanding of the people whom he had guided toward independence.

A second matter which greatly disturbed Armitage was the creation of a titled nobility in Brazil. Although the practice of rewarding deserving colonial subjects with titles had begun before the arrival of the Braganzas, the titles were increasingly distributed under the guidance of João VI. There were no set criteria for receiving the titles; men who had contributed to the well-being of the colony were thus rewarded. Haring wrote that Pedro I continued the granting of titles and thus the "principal collaborators in the independence movement were so honored—barons, viscounts, marquises —and many others whose claim to distinction was less evident." [12]

In his typically liberal fashion, Armitage condemns the granting of titles as being inconsistent with Brazilian ideals and anachronistic for the age. He complains that many of the titles were relics from a feudal age and were conferred upon Brazilians having scant knowledge of the history of such medieval practices. Furthermore, the desire to receive these titles led to what Armitage believed was an unhealthy rivalry in Brazil. Early in the text, Armitage writes:

Until the arrival of the Monarch (João VI), titulary distinctions were almost unknown, and appear to have been valued in proportion to their scarcity. On being now thrown open, as it were, to all, they became the great objects of competition among the aspiring; and there was, very soon, no species of petty tyranny which was not put into active force, nor any degradation which was not cheerfully submitted to, when the object in view was that of obtaining some of these high emanations of Court favor.[13]

Continuing his polemic against the creation of a titled nobility, Armitage strengthens his argument by pointing out that those who received titles subsequently changed their life styles. Like the old aristocratic families of South America, these new Brazilian nobles would not demean themselves (and their titles) by labor. "Knights could no longer descend to the drudgeries of commercial life, but were compelled to live either on the resources already acquired or;

[12] C. H. Haring, *Empire in Brazil* (Cambridge, Mass., Harvard University Press, 1968), p. 67.
[13] Armitage, I, 16–17.

[*sic*] in default of those, to solicit for employment under the government." [14] In addition, the competition for titles created a new source of friction between the renois and the mazombos.

Armitage seems to have been particularly irked by Pedro's insistence on maintaining and augmenting the nobility. Sympathizing with disillusioned patriots, Armitage rebukes the emperor for establishing a new order of knighthood on the eve of his coronation. It appeared to the author that this was a reversion to "feudal usage," and totally inconsistent with the republican view held by the vocal patriot minority. One of that minority, Evaristo da Veiga, was particularly eloquent in voicing his disapproval of the emperor's action and produced a satirical editorial on the subject in his newspaper, the *Aurora Fluminense*. The editorial (translated by Armitage) appears in its entirety in Volume I:

The Portuguese monarchy . . . was, according to the authority of the almanack, founded seven hundred and thirty-six years ago, and had, in 1803, an epoch in which several titles had been renewed, and others recently created—sixteen marquises, twenty-six counts, eight viscounts and four barons. Brazil, in the eight year of her existence as a nation, already contains in her bosom, twenty-eight marquises, eight counts, sixteen viscounts and twenty-one barons. Now, going on as we have hitherto done, which is to be hoped, we shall have by A.D. 2551 (that is, when our monarchy will have the same antiquity with that of Portugal, in 1803), no fewer than two thousand three hundred and eighty-five marquises, seven hundred and ten counts, one thousand four hundred and twenty viscounts, and one thousand eight hundred and sixty-three barons; this, by the simple rule of proportion. Thus we have no occasion to fear for the future, since, as there is no nobility without wealth, our descendants ought necessarily by that time to be revelling in riches.[15]

It is tempting to dismiss the ire which Armitage displayed against the creation of a titled nobility as a product of his English background, in which nobility represented a stable social institution and not a recent innovation. However, there is little evidence in his *History of Brazil* to support such a conclusion. On the contrary, Armitage objected to the establishment of a titled nobility for the reasons stated above: that is, it tended to create friction between the renois and the mazombos; it caused a disdain for honest labor; and, lastly, it was incompatible with the goals of a liberally minded people.

---

[14] *Ibid.*   [15] *Ibid.*, II, 65–66.

It is with respect to the liberal principles of the Brazilian people that Armitage takes Emperor Pedro I most severely to task. He was thoroughly skeptical of the young ruler's frequent claims of "acting on the behalf of the Brazilians." The disenchantment with Pedro I occurs early in the *History of Brazil;* already noted is the author's disgust with the emperor for creating a new order of Crusaders to celebrate his coronation. Although, at first, Armitage compliments the monarch for his role in securing Brazilian independence, he later takes a more critical look at the ruler, particularly in regard to Pedro's assumed title of Perpetual Defender of Brazil. The legal claim to the title is found in the Constitution of 1824, which the emperor himself submitted to the Brazilian populace. What Armitage objected to in the title (aside from his general dislike of titles) were the dictatorial powers inherent in that name. Armitage felt that a free people should be able to defend themselves; in any event, this should be the reward for a people who have successfully achieved their own independence. "By virtue of this appellation," complains the author, "the privileges of dictatorship were apparently vested in His Majesty . . . it is easy to perceive that a venal legislature could instantaneously have invested him with almost absolute authority." [16]

As to Pedro's dismissal of the Constituent Assembly, Armitage is not openly critical, except for his observation that the emperor had succeeded in alienating the Brazilian people. While on the surface this seems inconsistent with Armitage's generally liberal views, he justifies the action of the emperor by pointing out that the ruler remained faithful to the oath he had taken at the opening of the Constituent Assembly. In that oath, Pedro I promised to defend the proposed Constitution only if he deemed it worthy of Brazil and himself. Thus, when the emperor imposed his own Constitution on the Brazilians, he was doing so because he had found the proposal of the Constituent Assembly not to his liking, an action which Armitage could understand. Furthermore, Armitage actually praises the emperor's document, claiming it a most liberal constitution for the day. Despite this exception, the over-all view that the English merchant-historian had of the emperor was decidedly negative.

The monarch's chief fault, in Armitage's eyes, was that in spirit he remained essentially Portuguese; he lacked the insight or the

[16] *Ibid.,* I, 156.

assimilative capacity for becoming truly Brazilian. In the second volume of his history, Armitage succinctly summed up his reasons for claiming that Pedro I was not "A Man of His People":

At the period of the Independence, he [Pedro I] had, when excited by enthusiasm, given utterance to sentiments calculated to flatter the nascent spirit of nationality, and his sincerity had been credited; yet his subsequent employment of a foreign force, . . . his continued interference in the affairs of Portugal, his institution of a Secret Cabinet, and his appointment of naturalized Portuguese to the highest offices of the State, to the supposed exclusion of the natives of the soil, had, among a jealous people, given rise to a universal impression that the Monarch himself was still a Portuguese at heart. The native Brazilians believed that they were beheld with suspicion, and that the Government looked principally for support to a party which they regarded as a foreign one. This struck directly at self-love, a very fastidious judge, and no nation ever pardoned such offenses. This was what originally lost the Government of Don Pedro, what first caused its policy to be regarded as antinational, and what took from it all moral force, reducing it to the state of a passive spectator of all the insults daily directed against it by its opponents.[17]

This passage is additionally important because it gives the reviewer an insight into the notions Armitage had on good government. Throughout his critique of Pedro's rule, he never questions the vehicle by which the emperor governed, that is, the institution of monarchy. In fact, he so strongly believed in the monarchy that he felt it was the only form of government which could have held Brazil together after independence was declared. However, a monarchy had to be responsive to the needs and representative of the views of the populace it governed, two qualifications which the monarchy of Pedro I did not fulfill. In a retrospective comment, Armitage points out:

The regimen to which the people were accustomed was monarchical, and the monarchy was the best instrument to introduce that civilization which was wanting, and to induce them to adopt those social ameliorations which form an inherent and essential part of the representative system.[18]

The extent to which Armitage's ideas were conditioned by his experience with the British model of government is hard to determine, since he provided few allusions to that nation's system of government.

[17] *Ibid.,* II, 104–5.					[18] *Ibid.,* II, 139.

It seems probable, however, that a predilection for a constitutional monarchy reflected the author's English background.

Reviewed together, the three major themes developed in the *History of Brazil* reveal the author as a perceptive historian for his time. Modern studies of the First Empire tend to echo Armitage's concern with the rivalry between the Portuguese and the Brazilians, the incompatibility of a titled nobility with the republican ideals of the people, and the failure of Pedro I to conform to the Brazilian ethos. A case in point is the recent interpretive history *Brazil, Land and People,* in which the author, Rollie E. Poppino, gives as a cause for the downfall of Pedro I the monarch's reputation for being too receptive to Portuguese demands. Although most of Armitage's ideas are now accepted as traditional views of the Joanine period and the First Empire, it must be underscored that while the author was writing his history these ideas had not been previously recorded. Furthermore, no Brazilian in Armitage's time had even attempted a presentation, let alone an interpretation, of the events leading up to Pedro's fall from power. Apart from documents and newspapers of the period, Armitage's *History of Brazil* is the only interpretive and analytic study of the First Empire based on firsthand information.

While Armitage gives most of his attention to the three themes discussed above, he also includes his observations on varied features of Brazilian life in the nineteenth century. His experience in the Cisplatine left him impressed with the gauchos, native to that region. In one of the rare passages in his study, which provides a glimpse into Brazilian life styles, these gauchos are vividly sketched. As if ill-equipped to deal with the behavior of the pampa men, *sui generis,* the Englishman resorts to a comparative technique and contrasts the gauchos with Europeans: the garment worn by gauchos looked like a highland kilt to Armitage; lacking a proper metaphor by which to portray the motion of the bola lasso, Armitage compared the action to that of the "governing balls of a steam-engine" (a remark which instantly reveals him as a man well-acquainted with the technical innovations of his time).

In another cursory look at pampa social organization, he observes that the social norms in Montevideo and Buenos Aires were quite different from those prevailing in Rio de Janeiro. While, in Rio de Janeiro, women were restricted from appearing in public, and socializing was at a minimum, in the Plata region Armitage notes that "every evening is dedicated either to the theatre, the ball, the tertulia or soirée." [19] The exciting night life in Montevideo is wryly interpreted by Armitage as one of the detractions which kept Brazilian forces stationed in that city in 1826 rather than out in the pampa fighting for possession of the Banda Oriental.

Curiously, he avoids making a definitive statement on the question of slavery, one of the pressing social issues of the period, and certainly one that was of chief concern to the English. He never directly criticizes the slave trade, but postulates that had the slaves been allowed to develop families on the plantations, the continuous importation of slaves would have become unnecessary. Otherwise, his treatment of the slave trade is restricted to an objective presentation of the obligations assumed by Brazil and England in the Treaty of 1827, with no attempt to predict what effect the curb on the trade would have on the Brazilian economy or social system. As to the actual emancipation of the slave population, Armitage moderately urges gradual manumission; a rash move to liberate the slaves would have resulted in anarchy, necessitating the replacement of constitutional rule by absolute government, which was of course total anathema to Armitage. It is interesting that he subscribes to the myth of racial equality in Brazil. Despite the fact that enormous numbers of *gente de côr* (people of color) were held in bondage, Armitage preferred to emphasize the rare instances of such men receiving high state offices. "In Brazil," he concludes, "where the political association is composed of such heterogeneous materials, and where honours are open to all alike, distinctions of caste have necessarily less weight than in any other civilized country." [20]

In general, Armitage takes a typically English view regarding the question of slavery. While he does not openly declare himself to be against the practice of enslavement, he gives the impression that a civilized nation (read "one which conforms to European norms") should take pains to eradicate a social system which is archaic. At one point he declares that slavery should be abolished in Brazil gradually, as the feudal peasant-class had been in Europe. Hence we can make the equation, that for Armitage, slavery was undesirable because it represented a retrograde social institution, unbecoming to a country that was emerging into the civilized community of nations. At any rate, Armitage certainly did not present any evidence that slaves should be manumitted for humanitarian reasons.

[19] *Ibid.,* I, 245.   [20] *Ibid.,* I, 368 (note to p. 285).

A typically English point of view turns up again in Armitage's treatment of Brazilian economic problems. While, as I noted earlier, Armitage declined to dedicate his study to economic matters, he nevertheless presents a definite statement on what he considered to be the principles of a healthy economy. In essence, Armitage is very much a nineteenth-century English economist; for him, as well as for most of the prominent English thinkers of his time, a laissez-faire policy was the preferred economic order. Richard Graham comments upon the influence of this British policy in nineteenth-century Brazil:

They [the British] had derived from Adam Smith, Jeremy Bentham, and other political economists the conviction that every individual should be free in his economic life to do as he pleased; . . . Britain had made great strides while preaching this doctrine, and many young Brazilian leaders believed it was the key to British success.[21]

Like the men Graham describes, Armitage was convinced that a healthy economy operated with the least amount of governmental interference. This attitude is apparent in the section of his work which deals with the rising cost of products in Brazil. Brazilians were arguing that increased importation of products from abroad (albeit at cheaper prices than in Brazil) was responsible for the constant flow of currency out of the country. These intellectuals reasoned that a protective tariff was necessary in order to stimulate manufacturing at home and thus keep currency circulating within Brazil. Armitage, however, objected to this line of thought, and through a somewhat circular process arrived at the conclusion that what was actually causing the absence of gold and silver in Brazil was not increased importation but overcirculation of currency at home. The subsequent inflation thus made it cheaper to import goods than to buy them in Brazil; the solution which suggests itself out of Armitage's reasoning is to reduce the amount of circulating currency, and not to erect protective tariffs. Again, it is difficult to determine the degree to which Armitage was influenced in his thinking by his personal business, since he made no reference to the nature of his dealings in Brazil. But logic dictates that as Armitage was working for a commercial house in Brazil (which was probably engaged in export-import transactions), he stood to gain if Brazil increased importation of goods from abroad.

[21] Richard Graham, *Britain and the Onset of Modernization in Brazil, 1850–1914* (Cambridge, England, Cambridge University Press, 1968), p. 216.

Thus, his financial philosophy identifies him as a nineteenth-century English intellectual. The ultimate expression of this attitude, however, is the height from which he surveyed the Brazilian cultural landscape. For Armitage, as for most Englishmen of his century, civilization was measured by the extent to which another society could ape British (or European) ways. Hence it is not surprising that Armitage writes in his preface that he would be tracing the development of a people from "rudeness to comparative civilization"; the qualifying adjective "comparative" is the dead giveaway. It is doubtful that Armitage ever granted Brazil the possibility of reaching the glories of English civilization. The first chapter of his study is devoted to showing the miserable cultural levels of Brazil under the Portuguese tutelage; even the churchmen lacked sufficient erudition, as their halting knowledge of Latin showed. Again, it is only to compliment briefly the emperor for his success in raising the level of Brazilian culture that Armitage digresses from his usual diatribe against the monarch. Finally, the frequent, and pejorative, references that he makes to the feudal relics in Brazil (i.e., the titled nobility, the slavery system) single Armitage out as a typical English intellectual of his time, anxious to concentrate on developing the modern, "civilized" order.

Reviewing the ideas presented thus far, it is possible to see a contradictory view of John Armitage emerging. On the one hand, Armitage seems to be an avid Brazilian sympathizer; he identifies with the patriots and is unrelenting in his criticism of the emperor's nonliberal policies. Nevertheless, it is also equally clear that Armitage is representative of a class of Englishmen who viewed Brazil in terms of their own background.

How do we reconcile this apparent duality in John Armitage? Does his British mentality preclude us from accepting what he had to say about the takeover of government by Pedro I and the subsequent failure of that regime? Answering the second question is probably the most difficult problem concerning the *History of Brazil,* for if we reject his description of the political process in Brazil, then our total view of the First Empire (which has been heavily influenced by this Englishman) must therefore be revised.

The key question to resolve is whether or not it was inconsistent for an Englishman, writing in 1836, to be favorably disposed to an independent Brazilian nation. The answer is "No" on two levels. First, Armitage probably rightly assumed that when her economic ties with Portugal had been severed, Brazil would increasingly come to rely on trade with England to insure her economic livelihood. While he took great pains to avoid writing a manual of Brazilian–British commercial relations, Armitage was nevertheless a merchant, and increasing the volume of trade between the two countries would have been to his advantage.

On another level, it is also quite possible that Armitage was honest in his feelings towards the Brazilians, in whose country he had lived for seven years. His liberal sympathies need not be doubted on this level, since it would not be at all extraordinary for a nineteenth-century Englishman to be opposed to despotic monarchical rule. There is a possibility that Armitage had read, or was familiar with, the liberal views of Jeremy Bentham, an English intellectual who had urged political reform in his country and extension of the franchise. Similarly, the young Armitage (who did not leave England until 1828) could have been influenced by the ideas of Cobbett, an early nineteenth-century exponent of the liberal British cause. Hence, it becomes tenable, and even rational, for Armitage to take the side of the Brazilian patriots and defend their cause against the Portuguese Cortes and the pro-Portuguese sentiments of Pedro I. To do so was to be consistent with the English liberal philosophy of this time.

Thus it is completely plausible for Armitage to be at the same time pro-British and pro-Brazilian in sentiment. The fact that he viewed Brazil in terms of his own English background need not, therefore, make the reader suspicious of the interpretations presented in the *History of Brazil;* Armitage's study still remains a unique firsthand report of events during the First Empire. When it is realized that no Brazilian or other foreigner at the time had the insight to record or interpret either the Joanine period or the First Empire, then the importance of his work becomes clear. It is for this reason, that any thorough discussion of Brazilian historiography must consider the contribution of John Armitage.[22]

[22] It is interesting to note that this interpretation of John Armitage allows for a final comment on the matter of authorship of the *History of Brazil.* It is highly doubtful that a Brazilian (unless he was a master of duplicity) would have written an account which classified Brazil as a "comparatively" civilized nation. Pessimism about the Brazilian cultural milieu was not to arrive until the last half of the nineteenth century, when it was accompanied by fierce racial dogma.

Domestic and International Conflict

ALAN D. BERLIND

The words *conflict* and *strife* as used here should not be read as defining a particular intensity or type of activity but rather a whole range of activity beginning with the slightest deviation from peace. Domestically, conflict includes silent protests, campus disorder, racial strife, gangsterism and gang warfare, revolutionary activity, open revolution, and raging civil war. In the international arena, conflict begins with polite diplomatic protest and encompasses the withdrawal of ambassadors, the rupture of diplomatic relations, assistance given from abroad to domestic insurgents, border skirmishes, and armed battles between national armies backed by fully mobilized economies. In short, conflict is the absence, to some degree, of peace and amity between states or of peace, unity, and cohesion within a state. In neither case is violence a necessary ingredient. Likewise, the participants may be few or many.

There are, of course, phenomena common to all conflict, domestic and international, and their enumeration would not greatly contribute to an understanding of the relationship between the two types. There are a few points, nevertheless, that strike me as being quite pertinent to a discussion of both types of conflict; they are treated briefly following this preface. Thereafter, I will devote the rest of my efforts to an exploration of causality in the interaction between domestic and international conflict.

The first of those phenomena that bear on both domestic and international conflict can be called *population density* and should be understood to include the sociological and political problems that attend it. On the domestic level, we speak of urbanization, comprehending a prior shift away from agricultural pursuits, and the dislocations and general social disorganization that follow on its heels. An American research psychologist (Philip G. Zimbardo of Stanford University) recently joined the chorus of those who find the seeds of violence and antisocial behavior in the pressures of crowded city life.[1] A series of experiments led him to conclude that city residents are more prone to criminal acts than are their country or small-town cousins, a not unexpected discovery. What is interesting, however, is that many of the transgressors did not consider their actions to be criminal. (In one test, an automobile was left in the street with the hood raised and the plates removed. Hidden observers watched well-dressed middle-class Bronx citizens reduce the car to a gutless shambles within three days, performing their vandalism in broad daylight and with no apparent fear of detection.)

Ruth Glass takes exception to the urban theory of disorder.[2] Holding that the pressures of city life have borne too much of the blame for conflict, she suggests that urban behavior only mirrors, in an exaggerated fashion consonant with the numbers involved, the propensity for similar behavior throughout the society as a whole. In defense of her thesis, she cites the fact that radical movements in underdeveloped areas often emanate from the countryside. Since she was thinking in terms of revolutionary activity rather than crime, she leaves room for the urban theory at least with regard to the latter. Karl Deutsch, however, disputes her even on the subject of revolutionary activity.[3] Contending that discontent and the potential for disorder are indeed higher in the city, he advances as a likely explanation for countryside revolts the concentration of the forces of law and order in the city, especially when it is also the seat of government. (This is not to say, of course, that a movement spurred by agrarian causes of discontent would not have its beginnings where the trouble lay.)

This academic inquiry by Glass and Deutsch was certainly not intended to deny the empirical association of urban life with crime and disorder. Crowded conditions, in French universities, Harlem, or elsewhere, bruise human souls and ripen both the opportunities and the inclinations for conflict within the group or against others. On the question of deterrence, recent experience in this country does not fit Deutsch's model (based, it is only fair to note, on a study

[1] New York *Times,* April 20, 1969.
[2] Ruth Glass, "Conflict in Cities," in *Conflict in Society,* a Ciba Foundation book edited by Anthony de Reuck and Julie Knight (London, J. & A. Churchill, Ltd.; Boston, Little, Brown and Company, 1966), pp. 141–64.
[3] "Role of Cities in Social Unrest," in *Conflict in Society,* p. 167.

made in the Philippines). In fact, the presence of forces of law and order sometimes seems to inflame incipient violence, and this is surely part of the dilemma faced by college presidents and mayors of looted cities. With or without police, urbanization as a cause of domestic conflict is more meaningful when considered along with the concomitant rupture of family and other ties and the restraints they impose.

There are two obvious applications of the factor of density to the area of international conflict. The first is adequately illustrated by citing the Nazi cry for *Lebensraum* and the Japanese quest for Chinese territory. Secondly, domestic conflict arising from urbanization (or other causes) can push national leaders into diversionary foreign adventures (discussed below). But of more immediate interest are the questions raised by the targeting and protection of cities in the thermonuclear age. The rhetoric of nuclear warfare and deterrence is replete with estimates of expected megadeaths, calculations made simply by the concentrations of populations in the cities of the industrialized world.

The second general topic I would raise here is the role of the individual as an object of study in the over-all study of domestic and international conflict. The first order of business is to call attention to the danger of personalizing groups or institutions—of endowing them with the characteristics of individual human beings. As soon as two men have entered into the equation, the resulting unit, when considered as such, is not amenable to psychoanalysis. Whether the unit (or movement) is more or less complicated than the individual can be left for debate between sociologists and psychologists; they are in any case essentially different. "Nervous governments" and "angry movements" are grist for the journalist's mill and are no doubt descriptive in an impressionistic way, but the student must beware.

That being dutifully said, it can also be said that scrutiny of the individual *per se* is a valid occupation for the student of conflict. Thomas Schelling recognizes this and the previous points in a discussion of deterrence and compellence:

Even more than deterrence, compellence requires that we recognize the difference between an individual and a government. To coerce an individual it may be enough to persuade him to change his mind; to coerce a government it may not be necessary, but it also may not be sufficient, to cause individuals to change their minds.[4]

A possible exception to this rule is the case wherein the government to be persuaded is purely a one-man operation, but even most totalitarian regimes are more or less responsive to public opinion. Another case is that in which the coercion is applied on a matter not yet in the public domain, such as during secret negotiations when the individuals involved are still free from outside pressures. This image suggests international dealings, but it may apply equally well to relations between labor unions and management or between student groups and school administrations. It may be that the former in both twosomes purposely avoid secret negotiations for the very reason that they do not wish to be isolated from their potential support. The leaders of small and vulnerable countries frequently do the same.

Schelling's interests lie in the international field, but his arguments translate easily into the language of internal conflict. From Paul Kecskemeti's *Strategic Surrender* (on Japan's defeat), he quotes: "The survival of the loser's authority structure was a necessary condition for the orderly surrender of his remaining forces." [5] In the United States, do civil authorities adopt different policies towards black militant leaders and crime syndicate chieftains depending upon the government's perceptions of the relationships of each with their respective organizations? Was the appointment of black leaders to poverty-program positions in part a maneuver to subvert their goals while keeping their followers from lapsing into an even more dangerous anarchic uncertainty? There is a foil to Kecskemeti's conclusion that in some circumstances might make better sense: destruction of the enemy's leadership destroys morale below and produces quick surrender. "Crudely speaking the questions are whether the enemy's command structure is more vital to the efficient waging of war or the effective restraint and stoppage of war, and which of the two processes is more important to us." [6]

The last aspect of individual behavior I wish to mention is one explored by Edward Hoedemaker, a psychiatrist who perceives a

[4] Thomas C. Schelling, *Arms and Influence* (New Haven, Yale University Press, 1966), pp. 85–86.

[5] *Ibid.*, p. 128.   [6] *Ibid.*, pp. 212–13.

useful analogy between interpersonal and international disputes.[7] Where valid, the analogy holds for domestic disputes as well. Hoedemaker says that when an individual exhibits pathologic distrust and behaves in an uncooperative manner, he really wants the respondent to react in a nondefensive, nonplacatory but cooperative way. Similarly, when the same individual behaves aggressively and destructively, he is only asking the respondent to stand firm, not retaliate, and remain calm, thereby allowing the relationship to progress in a constructive and fair manner. To translate this into policy, the response to distrust and aggression must consist of avoiding anger, protestations of innocence, admissions of guilt, and attempts to persuade the distrustful party that the distrust is misplaced.

Shifting the argument to the international plane, Hoedemaker selects three cases: 1) at the 1963–64 gathering of the Eighteen Nation Disarmament Conference, things might have gone better had U.S. representative Arthur Dean refrained from attempting to persuade the Russians of America's honesty and good intentions; 2) the hapless Dean, by walking out of the talks at Panmunjom in 1953 in the wake of repeated Chinese insults despite the fact that the Chinese (acting out the psychiatrist's fondest dream) actually cried out "come back, come back," failed to respond to the Chinese need for a continued working relationship; and 3) John Kennedy gave Khrushchev relief by taking a firm stand during the Cuban missile crisis and, at the end, rejecting Khrushchev's Turkey-for-Cuba ploy. "If the analogy holds, the nation toward which the distrust and the hostile intrusive behavior are directed is in a position to help the other by appropriate behavior in the face of the distrust and carefully measured limit-setting in the face of the intrusive behavior." [8]

In taking Hoedemaker's analogy under advisement, two notes of caution need to be sounded. In the first place, his interpersonal model involves an individual showing "pathologic" distrust, which in psychiatry can be taken to be mentally deviant behavior. If his theory depends upon a strict medical definition, the subsequent analogy is frivolous. Secondly, it is clear that negotiators in international or

[7] Edward D. Hoedemaker, "Distrust and Aggression: An Interpersonal-international Analogy," *The Journal of Conflict Resolution*, XII, No. 1 (March, 1968), 69–81.

[8] *Ibid.*, p. 80.

domestic disputes are fully capable of tactical demonstrations of distrust and aggression.

"What happens abroad is inescapably a function of what happens within strife-ridden societies and, conversely, the dynamics of internal wars are conditioned, perhaps even sustained, by external events." [9] So states James Rosenau, who is worth quoting again for the purposes of illustration. On the linkage from domestic to international conflict, with specific reference to the American Negroes' struggle for equal rights, he writes that "not only is each event in this dramatic episode a landmark in the nation's history; it is also a major occurrence in the cold war." [10] As evidence of the reverse flow, he notes that "the new weapons technology has forced the great powers to test each other's strength and contest each other's influence through involvement in the internal wars of small neutral nations." [11] The comprehensive coverage and abundant examples provided by Rosenau and his colleagues leave the amateur investigator with little to add, but the following two cases come to mind. When internal strife occurs, foreign visitors or residents often find themselves victimized or otherwise drawn into the fray, as active participants or innocent bystanders, bringing the foreigner's embassy either to offer an apology to or to lodge a protest with the local foreign office. Expropriations or nationalizations of property owned by foreigners are likely to have similar repercussions. Secondly, the colonial rivalries of centuries past have left a heritage of independent African states that, because they house half a nation or more than one, are today the scenes of frequent internal wars that cross borders faster than a tribal drumbeat. Needless to say, this spillover can cause domestic trouble in the neighboring state, which may then feel compelled to take the first state to task; the cycle is seemingly endless, and without time limits.

George Modelski points out that the process of internationalization of internal war has many dimensions, any of which can bring the others into play, thus intensifying and prolonging both the original internal war and the international involvement.[12] For instance, the

[9] James N. Rosenau, ed., *International Aspects of Civil Strife* (Princeton, Princeton University Press, 1964), p. 1.

[10] *Ibid.*, p. 5.   [11] *Ibid.*, p. 6.

[12] George Modelski, "The International Relations of Internal War," in Rosenau, ed., p. 18.

establishment of a base in one country by rebels from another country leads to foreign involvement in communications and supply and may produce sympathy or resentment on the part of the local population. The element of violence receives special attention from Rosenau on two counts: violence attracts publicity and therefore tends to be contagious; internal violence is taken by outsiders to confer on them the right, even the duty, to take an active interest.[13] A good case in point is the concern over Biafra shown by young Americans who ordinarily damn foreign (read American) interference in the internal affairs of others. Finally, I believe one comment made by Modelski deserves criticism: " 'Nonintervention' is not only patently impracticable but untenable in an age that cannot turn its back on outbreaks of political violence anywhere." [14] Given the demonstrated interplay between internal and international conflict— internal strife spilling over the border or, alternatively, itself being the direct result of a foreign policy decision made across the sea— moral indignation over foreign "interference" often seems anachronistic. But not all internal conflict can be linked to external phenomena, no matter how small the world stage or how Machiavellian the actors. The rule of noninterference may require some modification, but it cannot be crossed off the books while the nation-state remains the basic unit in international relations; its observance has certainly contributed to world peace, and its formal demise, sanctioned by political scientists, would remove a restraint occasionally observed by even the most ambitious world powers.

Interdependent statistical studies done by R. J. Rummel [15] and Raymond Tanter [16] would seem to belie the truths apparent to the naked eye on causality between domestic and international conflict. After subjecting to factor analysis a welter of data obtained from 83 nations on 9 domestic and 13 foreign measures of conflict behavior for 1958, 1959, and 1960, Tanter failed to turn up evidence of any significant relationship between the two kinds of

---

[13] Rosenau, "Internal War as an International Event," in Rosenau, ed., pp. 52–53.

[14] Modelski, "International Settlement of Internal War," in Rosenau, ed., p. 149.

[15] R. J. Rummel, "Dimensions of Conflict Behavior within Nations, 1946–59," *The Journal of Conflict Resolution*, X, No. 1 (March, 1966), 65–73.

[16] Raymond Tanter, "Dimensions of Conflict Behavior within and between Nations, 1958–60," *The Journal of Conflict Resolution*, X, No. 1 (March, 1966), 41–64.

behavior at one point in time. With the use of an additional technique ("time lag regressions"), he comes to a slightly modified conclusion: "Although there is still a very small amount of variance on which to make a generalization, there seems to be some relationship between domestic and foreign conflict behavior with a time lag." [17]

It is unlikely that the traditional political scientist would be satisfied with this small concession to the facts as he sees them, and it is useful to try to resolve the discrepancy between the two conclusions. It might be claimed that the advanced methodology employed by Tanter and Rummel only serves to obscure the obvious, that political phenomena are not suitable objects of quantitative measurement. The rejoinder might be that knowledge arrived at impressionistically is bound to be unscientific, vague, and, consequently, of little value. There is, I think, a calmer reconciliation between the two schools. We know from history and logic that there is a causal relationship between internal and foreign conflict behavior, and we can cite irrefutable specific cases where it has worked in both directions. We also know, however, that it is not always so and that it is not necessarily so. In fact, we cannot safely say it is so most of the time or even more than a fraction of the time. In short, one type of conflict may cause another, but Tanter and Rummel in their basically negative findings demonstrate, at least, that causality is not automatic. Beyond that, it is necessary to remember that when we search for proof of cause and effect, we are naturally attracted to major events of the kind that are rarely confined to one dimension. There is no good reason to fault Tanter and Rummel on their conclusions, which are based in large part on conflict behavior of minor consequence.

Thus far, I have tried to explore the interactions between conflict behavior in the domestic and international spheres, where conflict in one does or does not lead to conflict in the other. More intriguing is a related question: Does the absence of conflict in one sphere increase the potential for conflict in the other? Does the existence of tranquillity and cohesion at home heighten the prospects for foreign conflict? Does internal strife feed on international peace and friendship?

The first of the last two questions was stimulated by the literature on nationalism, initially the work of Z. Barbu, who constructs two

[17] *Ibid.*, pp. 56–57.

models of nationalism and relates both to the possibility of international conflict.[18] In the first model, inspired by the phenomenon of national socialism in Germany, he ties the emergence of nationalism to the progress of modernization, with its accompanying increase in social mobility, breakdown of class rigidity, and rising sense of individualism. Shorn of the comforts of narrow class identification, individuals seek psychological support elsewhere and discover it in ethnic or national pride and identity. In the process, centralized government and control paradoxically become less objectionable to the newly individualized society. The second model, taken from the Russian experience of the early nineteenth century, is somewhat more intricate. Briefly, a prestigious alien culture invades a society and is taken up and propagated by an emerging elite intelligentsia. This elite group, abandoning native culture as it embraces the imported variety, becomes marginal, conscious of its superfluousness, and obsessed with guilt. Overcompensating, the guilty "escape their marginality only by a fanatical re-identification with their native culture and people." [19] They then foster a resuscitation of an ethnic consciousness, praising the primitive native values of power and vitality and contrasting these with the now insubstantial values of the alien culture. The awakened masses respond by trying to live up to their reborn image. (This Russian model would, I think, be helpful in studies of elite behavior and nationalism in Africa or of the recent propagation of black culture by Negro leaders retreating from attempts to share in the wider American value system.)

In both cases, Barbu sees

nationalism as a psycho-historical phenomenon, as a collective reaction to social and psychological crises produced by periods of transition from a traditional, agrarian to an industrial, urban social structure, and by periods of cultural retardation and prolonged political and cultural oppression. The reaction to such crises leads to a highly emotional social solidarity and a highly idealized image of the group. A negative reference to out-groups is a characteristic feature of such collective identity.[20]

Clearly, the door to international conflict is open as a result of internal cohesion.

The thesis has been carried a couple of steps further by Daniel

[18] Z. Barbu, "Nationalism as a Source of Aggression," *Conflict in Society,* pp. 184–97.

[19] *Ibid.,* p. 194.   [20] *Ibid.,* pp. 196–97.

Levinson.[21] Extending Barbu's concept of a negative reference to outgroups to include a belief that other nations are envious and threatening as well as inferior, Levinson sees nationalism inciting fears of attack from abroad and, the penultimate step, rationalizing a belief in the inevitability of war. What follows in terms of armament and defense is plain. Levinson adds another dimension to the subject of nationalism, however, that upsets any hypothesis positing the mutual compatibility of domestic peace and international conflict. Simply, he finds that the internal cohesion produced by nationalism is only partial, that "those who tend most strongly to fear and derogate other nations will exhibit similar beliefs and feelings about various intranational groups, such as Negroes, Jews, foreigners, lower socioeconomic groupings, and the like." [22] The new hypothesis suggests that nationalism nurtures conflict at both levels.

It will be instructive at this point to take a look at the American South, a traditional breeding ground of intranational bigots and international hawks. (Again, a new dimension enters the picture as we examine a people indelibly stamped, it seems, with the legend of one of the great domestic conflicts of all time. Perhaps George DeVos had the Civil War in mind when he spoke of the "crisis period [when] self-identification becomes frozen into some kind of rigidified aggressiveness towards external objects." [23] In the South, both blacks and reds qualify.)

In reviewing two books on the South and foreign affairs (by Charles O. Lerche, Jr. and Alfred O. Hero, Jr.), Cecil Crabbe finds the authors in agreement on three basic points.[24] To begin, southerners traditionally favor the use of violent instruments in the pursuit of national policy goals. Secondly, southerners are generally skeptical about the chances for disarmament, *détente,* or achieving national goals by relying on peaceful methods. Lastly, they hold little hope for permanent stability in the new nations of the underdeveloped world. One should insert two caveats: southern opinion may be heading towards a more moderate stand; southerners may be reflect-

---

[21] Daniel J. Levinson, "Authoritarian Personality and Foreign Policy," in Leon Bramson and George W. Goethals, eds., *War* (New York, Basic Books, Inc., 1964), pp. 133–46.

[22] *Ibid.,* p. 140.

[23] "Internal Conflict and Overt Aggression," *Conflict in Society,* p. 203.

[24] Cecil V. Crabbe, Jr., "The South and American Foreign Policy: a Review," *The Journal of Conflict Resolution,* X, No. 2 (June, 1966), pp. 240–45.

ing, in an intense way, what is really a national viewpoint. Nevertheless, the South and its people are surely unique enough to provide a valid illustration of the relationship between nationalism, or patriotism, and conflict.

Closely connected to the subject of nationalism is the practice of scapegoating, a very efficient tool for intertwining the threads of domestic and international conflict. It is accurately said that national leaders sometimes invent foreign devils in an attempt to divert attention away from domestic troubles and to unify a nation. Tanter notes that several authorities are convinced of the effectiveness of this technique of maintaining internal cohesion and strengthening the position of national leaders.[25] Among this group are Georg Simmel, Lewis Coser and Quincy Wright. Karl Deutsch, on the other hand, agrees that fragmented societies seek scapegoats but doubts that internal unity results: "the people who have the greatest dislike for scapegoats are also those with the greatest dislike for considerable numbers of their own countrymen." [26] This suggests, as does Levinson's similar judgment, that the leader who resorts to scapegoating is not at liberty to pick his target at random: the scapegoat must be disliked not only by a large enough segment of the society but also by a segment that can be counted upon not to turn against the leader himself.

In discussing nationalism, I have concentrated on the possible effects of domestic conflict or its absence on international relations. Quite a different issue is involved when considering the effects of international peace on the domestic scene. This matter has just been touched upon, since international peace is understood to include the absence of provocative scapegoating. Deprived of a foreign enemy on which to vent their frustrations and anger, are members of a society apt to seek vengeance against their fellow citizens? Obviously, if international peace prevails, they will have more time to be impressed with grievances closer to home. But the question just posed contains within it a deeper inquiry into the very nature of man. Whether man is aggressive by instinct is not a matter that can be dealt with in a brief digression. I do feel safe in asserting that aggressive behavior can be induced accidentally, as in urbanization, or purposely, as in scapegoating. And once given its head, can it be reined in again at will? Can the explosive potential in urban slums

25 Tanter, pp. 42 and 58.

26 "Internal Conflict and Overt Aggression," in *Conflict in Society*, p. 208.

be disarmed by belated corrective measures? How many times must a recruit be made to shout "kill" before he learns to love his bayonet —before he refuses to give it up, even after the fighting is supposed to be over? Pregnant questions, and perhaps unanswerable, but they are of great urgency in a country where cumulative violence against itself can no longer be controlled by foreign threats, real or imagined.

I have concerned myself with the initiation of conflict, but the situation in the United States calls for mention also of the effects of internal solidarity, i.e., the absence of conflict, on the outcome of international war. Herbert Spencer had an answer long ago that still holds up under most circumstances: "As the loose group of savages yields to the solid phalanx, so, other things equal, must the society of which the parts are but feebly held together yield to one in which they are held together by strong bonds." [27]

[27] Herbert Spencer, "The Military and the Industrial Society," in Bramson and Goethals, eds., *War,* p. 301.

Anyuan: The Cradle of the Chinese Workers' Revolutionary Movement, 1921-1922

LYNDA SHAFFER WOMACK

Two distinctive and central developments of modern Chinese history
—the introduction of modern industry and the growth of revolutionary political forces—intersect dramatically in the town of Anyuan,
Kiangsi province. Here, in 1898 Chang Chih-tung and Sheng Hsuan-
huai opened up the Pingsiang Colliery. In 1908 this colliery became
part of the largest Chinese-owned industry in China, the Hanyehping Coal and Iron Company, Limited.

Along with industry grew the industrial proletariat, which, in the
conditions then prevailing in China, became the revolutionary proletariat which was to exert an important influence over the future
course of the Chinese revolution. The union organized by the
Anyuan miners was one of the four major labor organizations in
China. It was the first major one led exclusively by the Chinese
Communist Party. After the victorious strike in 1922, it became one
of the strongest and most secure Communist bases and recruiting
grounds for the early period of the revolution. Anyuan workers
were among the Communist cadres at the Whampoa Military Academy, the Peasant Movement Training School, and the Political
School in Kwangtung after 1925, the Northern Expedition, the
Autumn Harvest Uprising, and the Nanchang Uprising in 1927. In
1928 the party organization at Anyuan was forced underground,
and at one point the Hunan Provincial Committee of the party was
moved there. After Mao established his base in the Chingkang mountains, Anyuan became his relay center for all communications with
the outside and with the party center. Party documents and cadres

passed through Anyuan when entering or leaving the Soviet areas. In 1930 over 1,000 Anyuan workers joined the Red Army. The survivors joined the Long March and fought in the Anti-Japanese War.[1]

The importance of Anyuan in the history of the Chinese revolution, as interpreted by participants in the Cultural Revolution, has been illustrated vividly; the painting *Chairman Mao Goes to Anyuan* was the *pièce de résistance* of the agitprop art of this recent upheaval. In July of 1968 the workers, peasants, and soldiers of the Shanghai area held a large poetry recital dedicated to the painting,[2] and in written comments widely distributed along with reproductions of the painting Chinese authorities described how

Chairman Mao came to the Anyuan coal mines in Kiangsi province where he initiated and led the general strike of 17,000 railway workers and coal miners, which ended in great victory for the workers. He planned the world-shaking Autumn Harvest Uprising and organized the Anyuan workers for this great armed struggle. Chairman Mao led the Anyuan workers from one victory to another on the road to the armed seizure of political power. . . . The great leader Chairman Mao had opened up Anyuan as the cradle of the Chinese workers' revolutionary movement.[3]

The scant attention which the Anyuan workers' movement has heretofore received in non-Communist sources generally and even in the best Western studies of Chinese labor history reflects the limitations of Western knowledge about China rather than the true historical importance of the Anyuan events. The isolation of the major foreign communities in China from vast geographical, demographical, and economic areas of the country was the basis for the uneven coverage of important events in China. This bias of the foreigners in concentrating their attention on the events closest to them is reflected in their relatively abundant literature and thereby reproduces itself in scholarly works.

This essay is concerned only with the first chapter of the Anyuan

[1] This list of activities is spelled out by Li Jui, but most can be documented from other sources as well. See his *Mao Tse-tung T'ung-chih te ch'u-ch'i ke-ming huo-tung* (Comrade Mao Tse-tung's Early Revolutionary Activities) (Peking, China Youth Publishers, 1959), pp. 189–90.

[2] "With the Best Words Sing the Praises of Chairman Mao," *China Reconstructs*, XVIII, No. 2 (February, 1969), 17–19.

[3] The entire statement appears as the Appendix to this essay.

Communist movement, from September, 1921, when Mao first visited Anyuan, to September, 1922, when the work of the Communist students culminated in a victorious five-day strike. The topic around which the study had been organized concerns the question of how the Communist students organized and led the workers: How did the students succeed in integrating themselves with the workers? How did they attempt to popularize Marxist ideology among the workers? What were the external factors that contributed to their success?

General Background for the Years 1921 and 1922

The years 1921 and 1922 were two out of many in China described as chaotic. The period from 1916 to 1927 was the height of the warlord era. Interregional disputes between warlords had provoked fighting in both Hunan and Kiangsi. Pingsiang *hsien,* Kiangsi, on the border of these two provinces, was the site of the Anyuan coal mines. Several times it was the victim of these armies. In June of 1920, two outside armies, fighting over the Chuchow-Pingsiang railroad, cut off communications for more than eighty days. In 1921 the Kiangsi provincial authorities requisitioned labor from Pingsiang, such that the reduction in the number of miners was alleged to have affected production. In August of 1921, the provincial armies of Hunan and Hupeh were battling each other, and communications were again cut off, this time for two months. In June of 1922, the Kueichow army passed through. It demanded funds, as well as labor.[4]

The situation in Peking, nominally the capital of the country, was most unstable. In June of 1922, Li Yuan-hung, a man described by *The Weekly Review of the Far East* as the person whom the majority of the Chinese people considered the most honest official in China,[5] resumed the presidency with the aid of the warlord Wu P'ei-fu. Yet,

---

[4] These military movements were described by C. Y. Hsieh in relation to their effect on coal production at Anyuan. See his *General Statement of the Mining Industry 1918–1925,* Special Report of the Geological Survey of China, No. 2 (December, 1926) (Peking, Commercial Press Works, 1926) p. 35. This study is in Chinese with an English introduction and table of contents.

[5] S. K. Yu, "The Chaotic Political Condition of China," *The Weekly Review of the Far East,* XXIII, No. 4 (December 23, 1922), 127.

in the next seven months he was forced to reorganize his cabinet four times.

Secondly, economic conditions were deteriorating.[6] Chinese agriculture, in particular, was disintegrating. In 1920 China imported only 1,163,519 piculs (a picul is about 133⅓ pounds) of rice.[7] One year later, in 1921, China imported 10,629,245 piculs; in 1922, 19,156,182 piculs were imported,[8] constituting 8.45 percent of total imports.[9]

There are very great problems with these statistics, especially the production statistics. For example, what appears to be a steady decline in production, may have been no decline at all. There was, in fact, a decline in the number of provinces reporting to the Ministry of Agriculture and Commerce. The number of provinces reporting in each year were: 20 in 1918; 12 in 1919; 10 in 1920; and 6 in 1921.[10] However, rice imports as a percentage of production were increasing at a rate of more than 2 percent each year. These percentages are most likely underestimates. They should be based on each year's production figures, but since the production figures are hopelessly inadequate, they must be based on the estimated annual production in a good year. And, the figure of 400,000,000 piculs is even one-third larger than the production figure for 1918, when 20 provinces reported.

The reasons given for this deterioration by one writer of the period include civil wars, banditry, increased land taxes, natural calamities, high rents and interest rates, and population pressure on the land. The result was an influx of population into the urban areas.[11]

The cost of living all over China was rising rapidly. Between 1912 and 1922, the prices of some daily necessities had doubled. For example, the American Consul General in Hankow issued a price chart (see Table 2: the prices are in cash; a catty is about 1⅓ pounds).

---

[6] For a description of the Chinese economic crisis during this period, see the forthcoming study by Marie-Claire Bergere.

[7] *China Year Book 1921–1922*, p. 998.

[8] *China Year Book 1924–1925*, p. 480. [9] *Ibid.*, p. 674.

[10] D. K. Lieu, [Liu Ta-chün], *China's Industry and Finance* (Peking, 1927), pp. 85–88.

[11] Lowe Chuan-hua, *Facing Labor Issues in China* (Shanghai, China Institute of Pacific Relations, 1933), pp. 2–8.

Table 1. Rice Production, Imports, and Exports *

	1918	1919	1920	1921	1922
Gross imports	6,984,207	1,809,905	1,163,519	10,634,560	19,156,651
Gross exports	33,281	1,227,649	311,834	34,714	45,117
Net imports	6,950,926	582,213	851,685	10,599,846	19,111,534
Production	302,000,000	96,000,000	88,000,000	70,000,000	n.a.
Average production in good year	400,000,000	400,000,000	400,000,000	400,000,000	400,000,000
Net import as percent of average production in good year	1.74%	.15%	.21%	2.65%	4.79%

* Imports and exports are from *China Year Book 1921–1922*, pp. 998 and 1009; *China Year Book 1924–1925*, pp. 480, 490. Production figures are from D. K. Lieu [Liu Ta-chün], *China's Industries and Finance* (Peking, 1927) pp. 85–88. The average production figure in a good year, estimated at 400,000,000 piculs, is from *China Year Book, 1924–1925*, p. 526. The calculations are mine.

Table 2. Prices of Daily Necessities in Peking and Hankow
1902–1922 *

	1902	1919	1922
Peking			
Ordinary cloth	5	70	140
Rice/catty	40	80	100
Pork/catty	70	200	230
Cabbage/catty	2	5	7
Hankow			
Ordinary cloth	—	80	160
Rice/catty	—	110	200
Pork/catty	—	220	560
Cabbage/catty	—	30	100

* United States Government, Records of Department of State Relating to Internal Affairs of China, 1910–1929, 893.504–893. 5045/83. "Labor Conditions in the Hankow Consular District," prepared by P. S. Heintzleman in September, 1923, 893.504/77, p. 4.

Moreover, the price of rice in Hankow was climbing unsteadily in the years 1919 to 1923. In 1919 a picul was worth taels 6.132 (U.S. $7.185); in 1920 it was taels 8.376 (U.S. $11.069); in 1921 it dropped to taels 7.444 (U.S. $5.356). By September, 1923, it had risen to taels 8.498 (U.S. $6.291).[12]

Inflation was aggravated by the debased coins minted by the war-lords and provincial governments. The problem became so acute in Hankow that the Chinese Chamber of Commerce decided that the copper and some silver coinage would not be accepted at all in the principal shops.[13]

The Hanyehping Coal and Iron Company, Limited

The Hanyehping Coal and Iron Company, Limited, the owner of the Anyuan mines, was the largest Chinese-owned company in all of China. In 1922, the company was capitalized at over $60 million

[12] United States Government, Records of Department of State Relating to Internal Affairs of China, 1910–1929, 893.504–893.5045/83. "Labor Conditions in the Hankow Consular District," prepared by P. S. Heintzleman in September, 1923, p. 3.

[13] *Ibid.*, p. 5.

(U.S.) and directly employed over 23,000 persons. All the top management personnel and the shareholders were Chinese, although, after 1913, the company was greatly in debt to Japanese creditors.[14] The origin of the company lay in the three *kuan-tu shang-pan* (officially supervised and merchant-managed) [15] industries founded by Chang Chih-tung, the governor-general of the Hupeh and Hunan, and Sheng Hsuan-huai, the director-general of the Hanyang Ironworks. These three were the Tayeh Iron Mines at Tayeh, Hupeh (70 miles downstream from Hankow), the Hanyang Ironworks at Hanyang, Hupeh, and the Pingsiang Colliery on the Kiangsi-Hunan border. Such enterprises were the concrete manifestations of the philosophy of self-strengthening, a late nineteenth-century response to the West and a part of the regional economic and military development promoted by several noted viceroys after the Taiping Rebellion.[16]

Modern industry in China during the late Ch'ing period was not a creation of economic forces within the country, but was, instead, a small limb, consciously grafted onto the Chinese economy by her most forward-thinking elite, for their own purposes. Lacking any roots of its own, (such as available investment capital, a market, and an infrastructure), it required the protection and support of Chinese officialdom to survive. But, on the other hand, these officials had grafted it onto the Chinese economy for a purpose, and their aims often came into conflict with what is recognized in the West as businesslike behavior. The new enterprises were used by the officials, and later by the warlords, as providers of services (transportation or uniforms for troops), income (legitimate and otherwise), and as sinecures for friends and relatives.[17] The shareholders were, however, protected by guaranteed dividends.[18] What Westerners in China were

[14] P. S. Heintzleman, "Mining and Metallurgical Industries in Central China," *United States Foreign and Domestic Commerce Bureau Trade Information Bulletin,* II–78, No. 26 (1922), 3.

[15] The kuan-tu shang-pan enterprise, as a type, grew out of the earliest efforts of industrialization in China. The word "official" refers, not so much to the imperial government in Peking, as to the local governors-general—most notably Li Hung-chang and Chang Chih-tung. See Albert Feuerwerker, *China's Early Industrialization: Sheng Hsuan-huai (1844–1916) and Mandarin Enterprise* (Cambridge, Mass., Harvard University Press, 1958), p. 12.

[16] *Ibid.,* pp. 12–14.   [17] *Ibid.,* p. 14.

[18] Albert Feuerwerker, "China's Nineteenth-Century Industrialization: The Case of the Hanyehping Coal and Iron Company Limited," in C. D. Cowan,

quick to describe as ineptness, reckless borrowing, vanity, nepotism, and general mismanagement [19] was in fact the natural product of this objective situation.

In 1908, Sheng Hsuan-huai amalgamated the three enterprises and officially formed the Hanyehping Coal and Iron Co., Ltd. It then became at least in name a purely commercial concern (*shang-pan*), with Sheng as its largest shareholder.[20] The production process which Sheng introduced formed a triangle. The coal was mined at Anyuan and moved by railroad to Chuchow and then down the Hsiang River to Hanyang. The iron ore moved by railroad to the Yangtze River and then to Hanyang. The great bulk of the production at Hanyang was in the form of rails, but there was some structural steel produced for small purchasers in Shanghai and Hankow. In 1922, 70 to 80 percent of the steel was sent to Japan.[21]

The Hanyehping Company provides a striking example of the dilemmas faced by modern industrial concerns in underdeveloped countries. The company was inaugurated with high-quality raw materials,[22] all produced and controlled by the company, a market that was in part guaranteed,[23] and a cheap supply of labor.[24] The company began manufacturing iron and steel in 1894, but by 1913 it was well on its way to becoming little more than a producer of raw materials and intermediate products for the Japanese iron and steel works at Yawata, which had been founded two years after Hanyehping.[25]

In principle, the company was a profit-making organization, but

---

ed., *The Economic Development of China and Japan: Studies in Economic History and Political Economy* (New York, Frederick A. Praeger, 1964), p. 110.

[19] For a good example of such comments, see the remarks of the Peking correspondent of the *North China Herald. North China Herald,* March 14, 1914, pp. 759–60; quoted in Feuerwerker, in Cowan, ed., p. 110.

[20] *Ibid.,* p. 90.

[21] Heintzleman, *Trade Information Bulletin,* II–78, No. 26 (1922), 3. Lansing W. Hoyt in his article, "Blast Furnaces and Steel Mills in China: A Comprehensive Survey of China's Steel Industry," states that the coal was moved by railroad all the way to Wuchang. *The Far Eastern Review,* XIX, No. 5 (May, 1923), 316–17.

[22] Wilfred Smith, *A Geographical Study of Coal and Iron in China* (Liverpool, University Press of Liverpool, Ltd.; London, Hodder and Stoughton, Ltd., 1926), p. 71.

[23] Feuerwerker, in Cowan, ed., p. 88.   [24] *Ibid.,* p. 104.

[25] *Ibid.,* p. 79.

in the twelve years from 1912 to 1923, its books showed a profit only in the war years from 1916 to 1919, inclusive (see Table 3).

Table 3. Hanyehping Profits and Losses 1912–1923 *
(in dollars Mexican)

	Net Profit	Loss
1912		2,872,076
1913		1,538,390
1914		100,968
1915		388,106
1916	1,878,496	
1917	2,801,872	
1918	3,779,904	
1919	2,918,464	
1920		1,279,588
1921		511,835
1922		3,666,876
1923		2,952,610

* Feuerwerker, in Cowan, ed., p. 93. This table was compiled by Albert Feuerwerker and is reproduced here in its entirety.

The sources of this poor performance can be found both in external factors, such as the chaotic political and military situation,[26] and in the economic context of Chinese business practice. The company's profits were cut into by the high cost of transporting coal from Anyuan to Hanyang, the growing obsolescence of the plant and equipment, and the salaries of unnecessary managerial personnel.[27] By far the largest problems were the inadequate sources of investment and working capital, and the consequent need to borrow. In 1913 the Hanyehping Company was forced to sign a loan agreement with Japan which stipulated that it sell 600,000 tons of iron ore to Japan every year at about half the market price.[28]

The Pingsiang Colliery, located at Anyuan, was one-third of this iron and steel complex. Anyuan was the third largest coal producer in China, second only to the Japanese-owned Fushun Collieries and the Kailan Collieries, which were jointly owned by the British and the Chinese. Coal production at Anyuan reached its height in 1916 with 950,000 tons produced.

[26] See above, under "General Background for the Years 1921 and 1922."
[27] Feuerwerker, in Cowan, ed., p. 104.
[28] Heintzleman, *Trade Information Bulletin,* II–78, No. 26 (1922), 6.

Table 4. Coal Production in China's Three Largest Mines *

	Pingsiang	Kailan	Fushun
1912	400,000	1,636,085	1,471,126
1913	700,000	2,036,967	2,179,202
1914	800,000	2,798,932	2,147,692
1915	927,463	2,971,792	2,169,245
1916	950,000	2,844,610	2,044,409
1917	946,080	3,176,469	2,311,445
1918	694,433	3,262,657	2,601,849
1919	794,999	3,762,763	2,928,792
1920	824,500	4,416,009	3,129,835
1921	808,971	4,320,274	2,738,416
1922	827,870	3,657,344	3,784,200
1923	666,939	4,495,962	4,883,000
1924	648,527	4,346,478	5,504,300

* Hsieh, pp. 14–15, and V. K. Ting and W. H. Wong, *General Statement on the Mining Industry,* Special Report on the Geological Survey of China, No. 1 (June, 1921) (Peking, Commercial Press Works, 1921), p. 18.

There were two main shafts in Anyuan. The larger shaft was 3,000 meters long and 4.5 meters in diameter. The second was 170 meters in depth and 4 meters in diameter. The coal was hauled out of the mines by an electric train—the first used in China. There were in addition 2 coal-washing plants where the coal was sorted by size for cooking purposes. Three hundred Otte-Koepe type coke ovens lined the railroad.[29] The colliery also operated a large machine-and-bridge shop, an iron foundry, and repair shops. A 600-kilowatt generator supplied the power needs of the various operations.[30]

Because of the tremendous pressures on the tunnels, timbers and bricks were used to brace the walls and ceilings. The pressure was so great that the timber had to be constantly replaced. The policy of the company was to let the roofs fall in until they were so low that they interfered with the miners' work.[31] This problem is reflected in the two available expense ledgers of the company. According to the ledger for August, 1916, lumber was the second most expensive item.

[29] "The Pingsiang Colliery: A Story of Early Mining Difficulties in China," *The Far Eastern Review,* XII, No. 10 (March, 1916), 375–76.

[30] Hoyt, pp. 316–17.

[31] "The Pingsiang Colliery," *The Far Eastern Review,* XII, No. 10 (March, 1916), 375–76.

According to Hsieh, 1.754 taels equaled somewhat more than 2 silver yuan. This would indicate that the costs per ton were approximately the same in 1916 and in 1919. Unfortunately, the items in the two accounts are not consistent, and thus there are few additional conclusions one can draw from these accounts.

The labor policy of the Hanyehping Company was similar to that of most industrial firms in China. The company spent on its labor force the least the market would bear. The result was that its workers remained unskilled and unruly. "The local men were opium smokers and did not want to work regular hours. The men from Luyang were a disorderly, lawless lot, and those from Tayeh thought they could draw pay without working," grumbled Gustava Leinung, the first manager of the Pingsiang Colliery. The management explained to visiting foreign journalists that the Chinese must be driven "to doing right and habitually disobey orders unless constantly watched.' " [32]

Leinung started off without contractors, but the size of the operation soon demanded some sort of supervisory system. Thus Leinung, only six months after the operations began in 1898, picked out a number of miners whom he knew and offered to make them contractors. In less than a year, these men no longer worked themselves, but rather moved into the city and only appeared at the mines on the first and fifteenth of the month, when they rode in on sedan chairs dressed in silk finery. [33]

At one point, prior to 1906, Leinung tried to break the power of the contractors since their exploitation of the workers was leading to labor unrest, directed not only against the contractors but also against the company. Prior to this time both the workers' food and housing had been supplied by the contractors. Leinung thus built huge mining quarters with kitchens and stores. The contractors threatened to strike, but Leinung managed to isolate the individual contractors and succeeded in getting one to inform on the others. He then paid off the ringleader and forced him to leave. [34]

Leinung's general policy seemed to be to keep the work force as small as possible and the hours as long as possible in order to keep the wage bill down. During a six-month absence of Leinung in 1906, his subordinate had allowed more miners to be hired and for the work shifts to be shortened from twelve to eight hours. When Leinung returned, he reinstituted the twelve-hour shifts, "convinced

[32] *Ibid.*, p. 377.　　　[33] *Ibid.*, p. 378.　　　[34] *Ibid.*, p. 379.

Table 5. Pingsiang Colliery Expense Account for August, 1916 *

(Production for this month was 82,793 tons)

	Expenditure (*in taels*)	Expenditure per ton (*in taels*)
Chinese personnel salaries	7,389.223	0.088
Foreign personnel salaries	2,876.040	0.034
In and out of shaft rations	73,385.173	0.088 [*sic*]
Machinery parts	3,968.169	0.047
Lumber	26,298.530	0.317
Various materials used in shafts	1,481.201	0.017
Labor and materials for repairs and replacements	6,480.278	0.078
Electricity	3,444.420	0.041
Coking coal for boilers	2,438.893	0.029
Room and board for workers in native mines	3,323.333	0.040
General office expenses	11,691.827	0.141
Engineering office expenses	2,239.015	0.027
Miscellaneous expenses	317.223	0.003
Total	145,333.325	1.754

Expense Account for 1919 *

(Production for this year was about 750,000 tons)

	Expenditure per ton (*in silver yuan*)
Wages of miners engaged in ore extraction	0.360
Odd-job wages (In and out of shaft combined)	0.370
Lumber	0.350
Other materials	0.790
Electricity costs	0.091
Repairs	0.037
Expenses of opening up pits	0.033
Miscellaneous	0.160
Total	2.226 [*sic*]

* Hsieh, pp. 44–46.

that he would get much more work out of the men if he reverted to the twelve-hour shift and reduced the number of men." [35] This provoked a strike, but it was put down. Shortly afterward there was an uprising in the area, led by the Ke Lao Hui and the T'ung Meng

[35] *Ibid.*, p. 380.

Hui against the local governments.[36] The uprising started at Anyuan, where the Ke Lao Hui members had become contractors and thus gained a great influence among the workers.[37] The uprising, however, failed.

In 1915 the company again called in troops to put down another strike led by the Ke Lao Hui. This strike was directed at the German engineers who had given protection to contractors who were in the habit of beating the workers. Public indignation had been aroused and the workers went out on strike. One worker was killed by the troops.[38]

The Workers

The number of workers in Anyuan has been estimated at several different figures. P. S. Heintzleman, the American Consul General at Hankow, states that there were 393 men on the general staff and between 5,000 and 6,000 miners, in May, 1922.[39] Li Jui, the official biographer of Mao, estimated the number in 1922 at twice that amount—over 12,000 miners.[40] Ts'ai Shu-fan, who had been in charge of propaganda during the 1922 strike, told Helen Foster Snow that there were 13,000 miners.[41] One reason for the discrepancy is the contract labor system. It was common for companies not to know how many workers were being employed by the contractors. For this reason it is logical that the Communist estimates are nearer the truth since they were involved in organizing the workers and thus probably had a more accurate idea of how many there were.

In addition to the miners, there were, according to Li Jui, 4,500 railroad employees in Anyuan. A portion of the railroad employees

[36] The Ke Lao Hui was a widespread secret society. These societies were often anti-Manchu. The T'ung Meng Hui, a revolutionary organization dedicated to overthrowing the Manchu dynasty, worked with them. They succeeded in 1911.

[37] C. Miner Lewis, III, "The Opening of Hunan: Reform and Revolution in a Chinese Province, 1895–1907" (Ph.D. dissertation, the University of California at Berkeley, 1965), pp. 202–7.

[38] Teng Chung-hsia, *Chung-kuo chih-kung yün-tung chien-shih* (A Short History of the Chinese Workers Movement) (Peking, Liberation Publishing Co., 1949), p. 4.

[39] Heintzleman, *Trade Information Bulletin*, II–78, No. 26 (1922), 5.

[40] Li Jui, p. 180.

[41] Nym Wales [Helen Foster Snow], *Red Dust* (Stanford, Calif., Stanford University Press, 1952), p. 84.

and some of the Hanyehping employees were actually engaged in heavy manufacturing.[42] Since Pingsiang *hsien* was far from the source of machinery supplies, repair shops and machinery and appliance manufacturing had been developed on the spot. Steam engines, compressors, pumps, lathes, and almost everything in the heavy machinery line except electrical machinery were produced in the area. There was a foundry which could turn out castings weighing up to 3 tons.[43]

The railroad employees worked on the Chuchow-Pingsiang line, which is usually referred to as the Chu-Ping railroad. It was one of the earliest railroads in China, having been completed in 1906. The 56-mile-long railroad was built under the direction of Chang Chihtung and was financed by American capital.[44]

Wages were low and working conditions were poor all over China. Nevertheless, as in most countries, including the United States, the miners frequently worked under the worst conditions. Firstly, they had to contend with the contract labor system. While to the managers this was a method of supervision and a convenient way of dealing with workers, the workers saw it as most oppressive. The contractor was paid according to the quantity and quality of the work done, and he subsequently paid the wages to the workers.[45] Li Jui estimates that a contractor made about 150 yuan a month—100 yuan of which he paid to the overseers. The general overseer was collecting about 2,000 yuan a month.[46] In principle the contractors supervised 50 miners, but it was claimed that they in reality only hired 30 men to do the job of 50, and pocketed the wages of the 20 nonexisting workers.[47]

Workers were housed in small dormitories, with 50 to 60 men to a house. The beds were in triple tiers, and the eating facilities were most unpleasant places.[48]

[42] For descriptions of the industry in Anyuan, see "The Pingsiang Colliery," *The Far Eastern Review*, XII, No. 10 (1916), 375–77; see also Hoyt, pp. 315–17.

[43] *Ibid.*

[44] Chang Kai-ngau, *China's Struggle for Railroad Development* (New York, John Day Company, 1943), p. 35.

[45] "The Pingsiang Colliery," *The Far Eastern Review*, XII, No. 10 (1916), 377.

[46] Li Jui, p. 180.   [47] *Ibid.*

[48] See Li Jui, p. 181, and the account of Tang Shou-i as told to Anna Louise Strong, *China's Millions* (New York, Knight Publishing Co., 1935), p. 101.

Health and safety precautions were minimal. Workers worked twelve to fourteen or fifteen hours a day, lacked proper clothing, and according to a Rockefeller Institute report, were disease-ridden. Due to prolonged contact with infected earth, 81.6 percent of the surface miners and 90.2 percent of the pit workers suffered from intestinal worms (ankylostomosis).[49] There was a small hospital on the grounds, but it was the size of a small bungalow.[50] None of the workers' accounts mention it, and Li Jui states that there was no effort made to provide medical care for the workers.[51]

Cave-ins, floods, and fires were described as frequent.[52] The last major disaster at Anyuan which had come to the attention of the central government occurred on August 18, 1917, at 6:00 in the evening. One overseer, a man known as Wang Chün-ch'en, was killed, along with 26 miners. The cause of the fire was not determined, but it was thought to have been either a case of the miners' lamps igniting the gas in the mines or the self-ignition of sulphur.[53]

Detailed statistics for casualties at Anyuan are not available, but one can form a general impression from the reports of two other mining companies. At the mines of the Penchihu Coal and Iron Company, from 1912 to 1923, there were 13 fires and 3 flood disasters. During the same period 26,044 miners were injured and 853 killed. At the Fushun mines, between 1912 and 1923, there were 650 workers killed or injured.[54] There was a saying among the Anyuan miners that "A man goes into the mines at dawn, and he doesn't know if he will come out again at night." [55]

Most workers in China during this period were peasants who had recently migrated to the cities.[56] Others were recruited from areas which had been industrialized in an earlier period, and a few were from the handicraft sector of the economy.[57] The patterns of origin at Anyuan coincided with this national tendency. The workers came mainly from three sources—Hunan peasants, Tayeh miners (who were often first generation workers), and from Luyang.[58] Luyang

[49] This report was cited by Jean Chesneaux, in *The Chinese Labor Movement 1919–1927,* H. M. Wright, trans. (Stanford, Calif., Stanford University Press, 1968), p. 79.

[50] "The Pingsiang Colliery," *The Far Eastern Review,* XII, No. 10 (1916), 378.

[51] Li Jui, p. 181.   [52] *Ibid.,* p. 180.   [53] Hsieh, p. 69.

[54] *Ibid.,* pp. 71–72.   [55] Li Jui, p. 180.   [56] Chesneaux, pp. 47–52.

[57] *Ibid.,* pp. 42–43.

[58] "The Pingsiang Colliery," *The Far Eastern Review,* XII, No. 10 (1916), 377.

probably is a misspelling of Liuyang, a Hunan *hsien* to the northwest of Anyuan. The area around Hengshan, Hunan, is mentioned several times as the home of Anyuan workers.[59] Liu An-i, a peasant who lived in Hengshan, was said to have been politically influenced by Anyuan workers visiting their homes shortly after the strike. After 1923 he became a peasant organizer, and was said to have widely publicized the "help given poor people" by Liu Shao-ch'i and Li Li-san at Anyuan.[60] Another source stated that Pingsiang peasants participated in the Anyuan workers' movement at its inception, but that later they were alienated. The regional differences between the workers and the local peasants, complicated by a fear of landlord retaliation, undermined the early cooperation.[61]

There are available two rather detailed stories of Anyuan miners. Tang Shou-i was forty years old in 1927 when he was interviewed by Anna Louise Strong. He, an illiterate Hunanese peasant, was sent to work in the mines when he was seventeen because his family lacked enough land to support themselves. He explained that his room and board were provided by the contractors and that the company provided a bathhouse. He slept in an unheated shack with 40 other men, which in the summer was infested with insects and mosquitoes. The meals were rice, flavored with vegetables, which he claimed were bought wholesale and often rotted before they were used.[62]

Tang describes participating in a strike which he dated as "the end of the Kwanghsu reign," which is undoubtedly the 1906 strike which Leinung, the German engineer had provoked by increasing the work hours from eight to twelve hours a day.[63]

Tang gave a rather detailed account of his wages. It is useful to examine them since he had worked at the mines for more than twenty years, working his way up from an unskilled laborer to a skilled miner. Tang pointed out that the wages remained frozen after 1913 —the midpoint in the period of rapid price rise.

Perhaps Tang Shou-i, who was thirty-three in 1922, was atypical. Ts'ai Shu-fan, who was interviewed by Helen Snow at Yenan,

---

[59] Chung-kung Hunan-sheng wei-yuan i-ch'uan-pu, *Hunan ke-ming lieh-shi-chuan* (Revolutionary Martyrs of Hunan) (Changsha, 1952), pp. 113–14.

[60] *Ibid.*

[61] Mr. David Tseng has kindly supplied me with this information. Mr. Tseng, now a resident of Palo Alto, California, grew up in Anyuan, where his father was employed by the Chu-Ping railroad.

[62] Strong, p. 101.   [63] *Ibid.*

Table 6. Per Diem History of Tang Shou-i's Wages *

	Cash	Gold
Starting wage (1904)	120	2.5¢
Resumption of 12-hour day (1906)	160	3.5¢
Became a skilled miner	300	6¢
Later	360	7¢
Shortage of labor (1913?)	400	8¢
After the strike of 1922	750–1000	15–20¢

* These wages should be compared with the price of daily necessities shown in Table 2.

described the workers in 1922 as being quite young. The majority, he said, were between the ages of fourteen and twenty-three. Ts'ai perceived a generation gap among the miners, picturing the young ones as radicals and the older ones as conservatives.[64]

Ts'ai was a second generation worker; his father and uncle had been employed at the Tayeh mines before transferring to Anyuan. After going to school for two years, he entered the mines as an apprentice when he was fifteen. Helen Snow described Ts'ai as frank, outspoken, critical, and hot-tempered.[65] One might also add that he must not have listened to the older workers since he states that the 1922 strike was the first in the Anyuan mines, completely ignoring the strike led by the Ke Lao Hui in 1915, or the 1906 strike which Tang Shou-i described. Perhaps it is an indication that most of the workers were new to the mines in 1922, and probably Hunan peasant youths, since Ts'ai stated: "The workers had no idea of such a method before this time, and were surprised and happy to discover the use of the strike." [66]

Ts'ai picked out the German engineers as one source of the workers' discontent, not only because they beat the workers but also because of their large salaries. Ts'ai described his own salary as a manual laborer on the motors, pumps, and trams as $3 (yuan) a month, the average salary as $6 or $7 a month, and the salary of the German engineers as $1,000 to $2,000 a month.[67]

[64] Wales, *Red Dust*, p. 84.   [65] *Ibid.*, p. 83.   [66] *Ibid.*, p. 84.

[67] *Ibid.*, pp. 83, 85. Ts'ai may have had an exaggerated idea of the salary of the German engineers. As Table 5 shows, total payment in the month of August, 1916, for foreign personnel was 2,876.04 taels. While the exchange rate between taels and dollars (*yuan*) varied, at most this would have paid

There is, in addition, a short account of an Anyuan miner by the name of Hsieh Huai-teh. Hsieh, who was born in Hengshan *hsien,* Hunan, in 1887, was a part of the small sector of the working class which came from the traditional handicraft trades of China. He joined his father in the blacksmith trade when he was ten. When he was twenty-one, in 1908, he became a miner at Anyuan. Hsieh was later to be very active in organizing the workers' club, and in October, 1922, he was sent along with Chiang Hsien-yün to organize the lead mines at Shuikoushan.[68]

A very elusive subject, as mentioned earlier in relation to the 1906 uprising and the 1915 strike, is the Ke Lao Hui. In 1906 the Ke Lao Hui and the T'ung Meng Hui led a revolt in three adjoining provinces—Liling and Liuyang, Hunan, and Pingsiang, Kiangsi.[69] Two members of the Ke Lao Hui, Shao K'e-ch'ang and Li Chin-ch'i, became bosses and grew quite powerful among the workers. This would imply that they were in a position to exploit the workers. Similarly, Li Jui states that the heads of the local secret society, that is the Ke Lao Hui, and the contractors and overseers operated gambling houses, brothels, and opium dens to press the last drop of profits out of the workers.[70]

On the other hand, Teng Chung-hsia states that the Ke Lao Hui led the strike of 1915.[71] While it was not unknown for contractors to go on strike, and to take the workers out with them, Teng's very short description seems to indicate that this was a strike against the contractors for beating the workers and against the German engineers for allowing and thus encouraging it. The only consistent interpretation, assuming that the Ke Lao Hui was consistent, is that the assumption of the contractor positions by the Ke Lao Hui in 1906 was a limited phenomenon, only involving two members, or that the Ke Lao Hui lost its hold on the contractor positions.

In addition to the Ke Lao Hui, there was at least one other form of traditional labor organization at Anyuan—regional fraternities (*pang*) among the workers. Liu Shao-ch'i and Chu Shao-lien's short

---

for only 2 engineers if they received what Ts'ai said they did. Ts'ai himself stated that there were 6 or 7 at the mine in 1922. On the other hand, most of the Germans fled Anyuan in 1911–12 and may have returned only a few at a time, in which case, there may have been only 2 or 3 in Anyuan in 1916.

[68] *Hunan ke-ming lieh-shih chuan* (Revolutionary Martyrs of Hunan), p. 114.

[69] Lewis, pp. 198–99.   [70] Li Jui, p. 180.   [71] Teng, p. 4.

work on Anyuan discusses these fraternities,[72] and Li Jui mentions that the first office of the Anyuan Workers' Club was next door to the Hupeh fraternity.[73] Teng Chung-hsia describes these organizations in general. They were usually made up of small merchants, workers, and coolies from one area, and served as mutual aid societies and employment agencies. Teng describes these organizations as "tools of the gentry," [74] and asserts that a particular fraternity's influence depended upon the contractors and other more prominent members. This type of regional organization should be distinguished from the *hui-kuan,* the regional societies of more prominent merchants and gentry.

The Chinese Communist Party and the Organization of the Anyuan Workers

The Communist Party of China held its founding conference in July, 1921. *The First Decision as to the Object of the Communist Party of China, 1921* began: "To form industrial unions is the chief aim of our party." [75] In accordance with this aim the document called for an institution for studying labor organization having four departments: the "history of the labor movement, the method of organizing factory laborers, Karl Marx's economic theories, and the present aspects of the labor movement of various nations." [76] While this first congress is usually singled out as having a sectarian policy of forbidding its members to join or to have any relationship with other parties, it nevertheless instructed its members to join and to work with unions which did not agree with their programs and the existing guilds and technical unions.[77]

While the party organization was clandestine, an open organization was formed to fill the need for coordination and direction of the labor movement, namely, the Labor Organizations Secretariat.[78] Its main functions were labor agitation and union propaganda.[79] Its headquarters was first located at Shanghai, when Chang Kuo-t'ao directed it, but after the May, 1922, First All China Labor Congress, it was moved to Peking, and Teng Chung-hsia became the general-secretary.[80] There were five branches—in Shanghai, Wuhan, Kwang-

---

[72] Chesneaux, p. 123.   [73] Li Jui, p. 183.   [74] Teng, pp. 2–3.
[75] Ch'en Kung-po, *The Communist Movement in China,* with an introduction by C. Martin Wilbur (New York, Octagon Books, Inc., 1966), p. 103.
[76] *Ibid.,* p. 105.   [77] *Ibid.,* p. 103–4.   [78] Teng, p. 38.
[79] Chesneaux, p. 178.   [80] Teng, p. 38.

tung, Chinan, and Changsha—each with a branch secretary. The major aim at this point was the legal recognition of trade unions.

In 1921, Mao Tse-tung, who was almost twenty-eight-years old, was appointed Hunan party secretary and head of the Hunan branch of the Labor Secretariat. He had been working with labor for no more than six months at the time, although he had had experience in student organizing and agitating.[81] Mao, like other young Communists during this period, had a rather elementary grasp of Marxism. In a letter to a friend in Paris, he described the world as "made up of one-third 'capitalists' and two-thirds 'proletarians.' "[82]

Mao's ideological deficiencies, however, did not interfere with his work. Shortly after returning to Changsha, he and five other labor organizers, including the anarchists Huang Ai and Lung Jen-ch'üan, paid a short visit to Anyuan under the pretext of touring the mines.[83]

Mao and the others had an introduction to the Anyuan workers from the railway workers they knew in Changsha and Chuchow,[84] and thus they established their first contact with the Anyuan miners and railway workers in September, 1921. The painting current during the Cultural Revolution, in which Mao is depicted in a scholar's blue gown, carrying a broken umbrella, just as he reaches the summit of a hill, is a representation of this visit. The caption of the painting reads: "In the autumn of 1921 our great leader Chairman Mao went to Anyuan and personally lit the revolutionary fires of Anyuan."[85]

Mao and his group remained in Anyuan for one week—long enough to talk with the workers and survey the living and working conditions. Li Jui points out quite reasonably that Mao immediately recognized this large concentration of a modern industrial proletariat as virgin soil for the workers' movement and thus concentrated a great amount of his attention as head of the Hunan Labor Secretariat on Anyuan.[86]

The reaction of the workers, according to much later reminiscences, seems to be primarily amazement at the idea that students were interested in workers and that students desired to live at a level comparable to that of the workers. Their comments are filled with

[81] Stuart Schram, *Mao Tse-tung* (Middlesex, England, Penguin Books, Ltd., 1967), p. 64.

[82] *Ibid.*, p. 64.   [83] Li Jui, p. 179.   [84] *Ibid.*

[85] The artists who created this work were said to be Liu Ch'un-hua and others. It was distributed by *People's Daily, China Pictorial,* and *China Reconstructs.* For example, see *China Reconstructs,* XVIII, No. 2 (February, 1969), 17–19.

[86] Li Jui, p. 181.

incidents that demonstrate the students' unassuming manner and Spartan living standards, including the clothing worn, the food eaten, and the meager accommodations that the students insisted upon.[87] The main topic of conversation during this initial trip appears to have been the value of education and the idea of setting up a work-ers' school in Anyuan.[88]

In January of 1922, the first Communist cadre was sent to Anyuan to live. Li Li-san, who had been expelled from France three months previously for participating in a student demonstration which had seized a university building,[89] was a native of Liling. Liling was the Hunan *hsien* directly west of Pingsiang, through which the Chu-Ping railroad passed.

Li was the son of an impoverished school teacher. He had had seven years of schooling in Liling and Changsha before departing for France as a work-and-study student. He attended the College de Montargis and St. Charmond, where he was active in socialist study groups and other student activities. Li had worked in an iron factory and thus had some contact with European unions.[90]

Li is always described as an energetic person, with great forensic talent.[91] In spite of his later fall from grace, he is the Communist student most frequently mentioned in later accounts by Anyuan workers. Chang Kuo-t'ao describes him as too impulsive, requiring the steadying hand of more stolid personalities such as Liu Shao-ch'i.[92]

Very little has yet been uncovered about Li's intellectual develop-ment prior to 1922, except that he was deeply influenced by the

[87] "An-yüan-k'uang shih p'ien-tuan" (Fragments of History from the An-yuan Mines) *Hung-ch'i p'iao-p'iao,* XII (May, 1959) 147–70 *passim.*

[88] Li Jui, p. 179.

[89] Donald W. Klein and Anne B. Clark, *Biographic Dictionary of Chinese Communism* (Cambridge, Mass., Harvard University Press, forthcoming).

[90] The biographical information for Li Li-san was drawn from Klein and Clark; James Pinckney Harrison, Jr., "The Li Li-san Line and the Chinese Communist Party in 1930" (Master's essay; New York, Columbia Univer-sity, 1960) pp. 7–8; Howard L. Boorman, ed., *Biographical Dictionary of Republican China* (New York, Columbia University Press, 1968), II, 310–12; *Who's Who in Communist China* (Hongkong, Union Research Institute, 1966), pp. 350–53; Strong, pp. 90–91.

[91] Liu Shao-ch'i, *Collected Works of Liu Shao-ch'i, 1958–1967,* with an introduction by Chang Kuo-t'ao (Hongkong, Union Research Institute, 1968), p. iv.

[92] *Ibid.*

revolutionary activities of the T'ung Meng Hui in Hunan. An older schoolmate of his, and a member of the T'ung Meng Hui, Sun Hsiao-shun, introduced Li to the policies of the T'ung Meng Hui shortly before the revolution in 1911.[93] Li met Mao for the first time in 1917 when they were both students in Changsha,[94] but their friendship did not develop at that time.

Mao sent Li to Anyuan with the instruction to work for a legal workers' movement.[95] Li's cover was the mass-education movement launched in 1921 by leaders of the Chinese Young Men's Christian Association with American backing.[96] Mao instructed Li to make contacts with the local gentry so as to obtain legal status. Li proceeded straight to the district magistrate's office in Pingsiang to obtain permission to set up a school. The magistrate put out an official report approving of the mass-education program.[97]

The first school set up by Li was a day school for the workers' children. The workers themselves were rather dubious about a school for themselves, but they were willing to send their children. Through the children's classes Li was able to establish rapport with a few parents, and by March had founded a night school for workers.[98] When the night school opened it had only about 10 students, among whom was the worker Ts'ai Shu-fan. Ts'ai later became a prominent party member.[99] According to reminiscences, there were two major reasons for the miners' reluctance. First, the miners, already working at least twelve hours a day, considered reading and writing and arithmetic, the three subjects taught, to be of little use to manual laborers. However, one worker, and perhaps he was representative, feared the school and the teachers. Having had some experience with a village school teacher, he conceived of schooling as beatings and intimidation.[100] However, the cadres were reported to have expended great efforts in overcoming these fears. They greeted the students at the door, remembered their names after only one introduction, never scolded or ridiculed, and generally tried not to assume a superior attitude.[101]

The Hunan party secretariat paid Li 20 yuan a month, with which he paid his own expenses and those of the school.[102] In addition, the

---

[93] Klein and Clark.   [94] Schram, p. 37.   [95] Li Jui, p. 181.
[96] Schram, p. 68.   [97] Li Jui, p. 182.   [98] *Ibid.*
[99] Wales, *Red Dust*, pp. 83–84.
[100] *Hung-ch'i p'iao-p'iao,* XII (May, 1959), 157.   [101] *Ibid.,* pp. 157–58.
[102] Li Jui, p. 182.

workers themselves had to pay some of the expenses for pens, paper, and ink, if they could afford it. Classes were held both during the day and at night so that both workshifts could attend.[103] The materials used were not those prescribed by the Y.M.C.A., but rather special mimeographed materials.[104] The object was to teach the basic thousand-character vocabulary, but the content began with the labor theory of value and proceeded with explanations of class struggle, Communism, the Russian revolution, and the alliance of workers and peasants.[105] A worker, Yuan P'in Kao, described his first lesson in the labor theory of value, taught by Liu Shao-ch'i as follows.

LIU: You work at the foreign-style coking ovens—Who's your contractor there?

YUAN: Ch'uan T'ao-tsao.

LIU: Does he treat the workers well, or badly?

YUAN: All right, I guess.

LIU: What's good about him?

YUAN: When there's a fight he always wins.

LIU: (*Laughing*) He never loses?

YUAN: Never. He can always take up for us. When we fight with the other work sites, he helps.

LIU: What's this! Who do you fight with?

YUAN: The other workers at the foreign coking ovens, or the ones at the native coking ovens.

LIU: I see, and what other good points does he have? . . .

YUAN: When he gambles, he's very sharp—he uses a washbasin filled up with silver.

LIU: (*Laughing*) Well! I can see that you workers have many advantages.

YUAN: No! It's all true!

LIU: True! Old Yuan, think a minute—When he fights, who does he fight with? And when he gambles, where does all the money come from?

YUAN: (*After thinking a while*) Well, from the work of the coking ovens, cart by cart. He can't do so much by himself, so he hires other people to do it.

[103] Wuhan Unit of the Marxist-Leninist Night School, ed., *Chung-kuo Kung-ch'an-tang tsai chung-nan te ti-ch'ü ling-tao ke-ming tou-cheng te li-shih tzu-liao* (Materials on the History of Revolutionary Struggles in Central-South China Led by the Chinese Communist Party) (Hankow, Central-South People's Publishing Co., 1951) p. 57.

[104] Wales, *Red Dust,* p. 84.

[105] Since Ts'ai was discussing this matter in 1936 or 1937, it is possible that the worker-peasant alliance was an afterthought.

LIU: And why don't you get the money for it? Why is it that you don't even have anything to eat?

YUAN: We don't make much money.

LIU: Why haven't you thought of making more?

YUAN: I'm all alone. It's impossible. (*To himself:* It's just fate.)

LIU: It's not impossible. It's because you workers aren't united. . . .[106]

The lessons in Marxist economic theories were thus taught very concretely, and it would appear from this exchange that the personal relationship between the contractor and the workers was one obstacle the students had to overcome.

The school provided an excellent means of organizing. Whenever a new prospect showed up, the cadres would inquire about certain organizationally interesting data—where a man worked, what his wages were, how many were in his family, and basically how he was managing.[107] Whenever anyone appeared from a work location not yet contacted, they could make a special effort to enroll this person and, in this way, over a period of months, have contacts with most of the work sites.

On May 1, 1922, the same day that the First All China Labor Congress was opened in Canton, the Anyuan Mine and Railroad Workers' Club was officially founded. Li Li-san was elected chairman, and a worker, Chu Shao-lien, was elected vice-chairman.[108] With a membership of 300, a clubhouse was set up next door to the Hupeh fraternity.

As the number of students grew and the level of instruction advanced, Mao sent additional cadres to Anyuan. Chiang Hsien-yün arrived in May, 1922, after the official founding of the club. Chiang was born in Hengyang *hsien,* Hunan, where he attended the Third Normal School. Having been a prominent student leader during the May Fourth Movement, he was one of the first that Mao recruited into the party branch set up in Hengyang.[109] Later Chiang was sent to the lead mines at Shuikoushan, Hunan, to organize workers there. In 1923 he went to Kwangtung where, in 1924, he joined the first class and distinguished himself at the Whampoa Military Academy. During the Northern Expedition, Chiang was a regimental commander in the Fourth Army. What might have been a notable career ended abruptly when he was killed on the Honan front in 1927.[110]

[106] *Hung-ch'i p'iao p'iao,* XII (May, 1959), 158–59.

[107] *Ibid.,* pp. 158–59.　　[108] Li Jui, p. 183.　　[109] *Ibid.,* pp. 212–13.

[110] *Ibid.*

With the official founding of the club and the expansion of the school, the officials of the mining and railroad offices became alarmed and made an attempt to destroy the club. Statements began circulating labeling the club a seditious organization and ordering its immediate dissolution. There were demands that Chu Shao-lien be expelled from the area, and the officials tried to intimidate and then bribe Chiang Hsien-yün.[111] These efforts succeeded only in angering the workers. A meeting of workers' representatives was called, and they decided unanimously to resist.[112]

Tensions mounted over the summer, primarily because the company had not paid the workers' wages for several months.[113] In July, the Hanyang Ironworks, a part of the Hanyehping complex, went out on strike. After five days they succeeded in getting a wage increase and improvements in working and living conditions.[114] The news of this created a great deal of interested discussion at Anyuan.

At some point between May and September, 1922, Liu Shao-ch'i was sent by Mao to Anyuan. While there is still some doubt, the most probable date is September. Li Jui states that Liu was specially sent by Mao to lead the strike in September.[115] Boorman states that Liu returned to China from Russia in the spring of 1922 and that "several months later" he was sent to Anyuan.[116] Most significantly, Chang Kuo-t'ao, whom Liu was working with in Shanghai, and with whom he organized the First All China Labor Congress,[117] states that Liu went to Anyuan in September.[118]

In 1922, Liu Shao-ch'i, the son of a peasant landowner, was about twenty-four-years old. After receiving a classical education at home, he attended middle school in Changsha, just as Mao and Li had. In 1920, in Shanghai, he enrolled in a Russian language class and soon after that joined the Socialist Youth Corp.[119] Liu's own description of his intellectual development at the time is: "I only knew that socialism was good, [had] heard about Marx and Lenin, and the October Revolution, and the Bolshevik party, but I was not clear what socialism was and how it could be realized." [120] In 1921 Liu and 7 other students were sent to study at the Far Eastern University in

111 *Ibid.*, p. 183.   112 *Ibid.*

113 *Chung-nan li-shih tzu-liao*, p. 58.   114 Li Jui, p. 183.

115 *Ibid.*, p. 184.   116 Boorman, pp. 405–11.

117 Nym Wales [Helen Foster Snow] *The Chinese Labor Movement*, p. 29.

118 Liu Shao-ch'i, p. iii.   119 Boorman, pp. 405–11.

120 Klein and Clark.

Moscow. Liu described this trip in a rather dismal manner. Conditions in Russia had still not recovered from civil war, and Liu found himself chopping logs along the railroad across Siberia to provide fuel for the train. Liu's comment was: "Some of us wavered in [our] confidence in socialism on this account, but the confidence of the rest of us in socialism was further strengthened." [121] In 1922 he returned to Shanghai and worked with Chang Kuo-t'ao in the Shanghai branch of the Labor Secretariat. Chang described Liu as bookish, taciturn, thoughtful, and persevering. "Some people," Chang said, "found him a bit too glum and devoid of youthfulness." [122]

The Strike

By September the situation in Anyuan was growing tense. At this propitious moment, Mao returned to Anyuan to confer with the party cadres because he felt that the opportunity for a strike was fast approaching. The organization among the workers was expanded rapidly and preparations were made for the strike.[123] Mao evidently returned to Changsha before the strike was actually called, for Li Jui describes a letter received by the club from Mao on September 12. His instructions were only two: maintain an implacable struggle through agitation among the workers and obtain the widest possible public sympathy.[124]

The company and events elsewhere tripped the wire set up by the workers' club. The company decided to crack down and stated that they were going to call in troops to dissolve the union. The union replied with three conditions that the company had to meet to prevent them from striking: 1) The offices of the mines and railroad must petition the executive government offices to protect the club. 2) The company must provide the club with a 200-yuan-a-month subsidy. 3) The company must pay all the wages owed the workers within one week.[125] The company was intimidated by the intransigence of the workers and agreed to recognize the first two conditions, but

[121] *Ibid.*   [122] Liu Shao-ch'i, p. i.   [123] Li Jui, p. 183–84.
[124] *Ibid.*

[125] *Ibid.* Li Jui states that Liu Shao-ch'i and other cadres decided upon these three demands. However, according to the *Chung-nan li-shih tzu-liao* (p. 58), which was published eight years before Li Jui, in 1951, Li Li-san represented the workers when these three conditions were put forward.

claimed that due to financial difficulties they could not agree to the third.[126]

At almost the same time the news reached Anyuan of the strike at Wuchang of the Hankow-Canton railroad employees. There, on September 10, when a troop of soldiers found workers trying to obstruct work by lying on the rails, the soldiers opened fire, killing 10 workers and wounding 20. Many other workers drowned while trying to find safety in a nearby river.[127] The morale of the Anyuan workers was such that instead of discouraging them, the news only "added oil to the fire." [128]

At this point the club had succeeded in organizing almost all of the mines and railroad shops. On September 12, 1922, a meeting was called, during which Liu Shao-ch'i analyzed the situation. Liu had three major points.[129] The class consciousness of the workers was at a high level. The club enjoyed great prestige among the workers, and most of them were organized. Secondly, China was in the midst of a strike wave which added impetus.[130] The strike on the railroad was already affecting lumber supplies at the mine, weakening the company.[131] Thirdly, Liu calculated that the mining and railroad offices were unprepared and split over their tactics. The conclusion was to call a strike.

The strike order was given on September 13. The next day no one went to work at the mines or the railroad shops. Only those people considered necessary for the general safety of the area were allowed to work.[132] Ts'ai Shu-fan stated that pickets were put up to keep the "old workers" away, and propaganda teams went from dormitory to dormitory talking to the workers and persuading them to join. "Luckily," he said, "we persuaded the men in charge of pulling the

---

[126] Li Jui, p. 148.

[127] Chesneaux, p. 191. Li Jui (p. 184), states that 70 were wounded and 6 killed.

[128] *Ibid.*   [129] *Ibid.*

[130] This strike wave began in February, 1922, with the seamen's strike in Hongkong. The American consul in Tientsin gave a list of 88 strikes which occurred during 1922, the Anyuan strike being No. 48. See Records of the Department of State Relating to Internal Affairs of China, 1910–1929, 893,504–893.5045/83, "The Labor Situation in China," 893.504/15, a report prepared by Consul J. C. Huston. The wave ended in February, 1923, when the warlords Wu P'ei-fu, Ts'ao K'un, and Hsiao Yao-nan put down a railroad strike by military force. See Chesneaux, pp. 208–9.

[131] This was kindly pointed out to me by Mr. David Tseng.

[132] Li Jui, p. 185.

whistle to go on strike, and as no siren ordered the men to work, nobody went." [133]

Just to make sure, some workers cut the electricity wires, so that the electric carts could not run. After piling up the coal cars at the mouth of the pits, the workers agreed to let people out, but they would not permit anyone to enter. They implanted tricornered flags in the pile of carts. Written on the flags were the words: "Before we were beasts, but now we are men." [134]

The workers advanced 27 demands,[135] according to Liu Shao-ch'i and Chu Shao-lien, who took part in leading the strike. Li Jui states that there were 17 demands made, but that they were consolidated into 13 demands, all of which were granted.[136] The 13 consolidated demands were as follows.

1. The club shall be changed into a union; and the offices of the railroad and mines shall recognize the right of the union to represent the workers in negotiations with the two offices.
2. In the future, the two offices shall not fire any workers without the agreement of the union.
3. Beginning with this month, there shall be four statutory Sunday holidays every month.
4. The company shall provide leave for statutory holidays, illness, marriage, and funerals. During these leaves, the company shall continue to pay regular wages.
5. Every December the workers shall receive a bonus equal to one month's salary.
6. Those workers who are injured on the job must be supported by the company for the rest of their lives, according to the amount of their wages.
7. All back wages must be paid to the penny.
8. The workers shall receive their wages for the duration of the strike.
9. Starting with this month the offices shall pay a 200 yuan per month subsidy to the union for regular expenses.
10. The managerial personnel shall no longer be able to beat or abuse the workers.
11. The miners' wages shall be increased across the board at 50 percent.
12. The contractors will not be permitted to keep more than 5 percent of a worker's pay, and the overseers will not be allowed to keep

[133] Wales, *Red Dust*, p. 84.   [134] *Chung-nan li-shih tzu-liao*, p. 58.

[135] Chesneaux, p. 190, citing Liu Shao-ch'i and Chu Shao-lien, *An-yüan lu-k'uang kung-jen chü-lo-pu lüeh-shih* (A Short History of the Anyuan Miners' and Railwaymen's Club) (Anyuan, 1923).

[136] Li Jui, p. 186.

more than 15 percent. All "private labor" done for the foreman and contractors is abolished.

13. All wages below 8 fen per day must be increased to at least 1 chiao 8 fen per day.[137]

There exists another list of demands, but this one is not so clearly demarcated, and it lacks enumeration.[138] These demands are described as the 13 demands, but obviously include items which do not appear in the consolidated demands. It is conceivable that these demands were those left out in consolidation. The following are those that differ from the 13 demands already enumerated.

1. The workers shall have freedom of speech and assembly.
2. Disturbances among the workers shall be the responsibility of the workers' club to settle, and the mining and railroad offices shall not interfere or inquire about them.
3. The *hung-chang* (profit accounts) must be made public.
4. Work shifts shall be eight hours.
5. Electric lights shall be supplied.
6. Those who had to work during the strike for safety reasons will get double pay for the duration of the strike.
7. The families of workers killed on the job receive 72 yuan (including the coffin). This is to be increased to one-year's wages.
8. Those who are disabled on the job shall get a monthly wage of 7½ yuan. (Those who still can produce, still must produce according to their ability.)
9. If the parents or wife or children of a worker should die, the company must provide a casket.
10. A one-week leave for weddings and funerals.
11. Welfare, cooking coal, and electricity shall be provided free of charge.

Faced with these demands, Wang Hung-ch'ing, the head manager, called in Fang Pen-jen and his troops from the city of Pingsiang where they were garrisoned. The workers were undaunted and proceeded, under party urging, to propagandize the troops—with some results.[139] At one point, Wang had Fang station the troops right at the workers' club. Several thousand workers clashed with the soldiers and succeeded in pushing them away.[140]

[137] All demands except item twelve are a direct translation from Ch'en Ta's study, *Chung-kuo lao-kung wen-t'i* (Problems of Chinese Labor) (Peking, Commercial Press, 1927), p. 236. Item 12 is stated as explained by Chesneaux, p. 190.

[138] *Chung-nan li-shih tzu-liao*, p. 59.   [139] Li Jui, p. 186.

[140] *Chung-nan li-shih tzu-liao*, p. 58.

The company, already suffering from a lumber shortage due to the railroad strike, was faced with a threat from the workers: "If you don't [accept] our demands, we will strike for a long time and destroy the mine. You know that if the pumps are stopped for even one day, the mine will be flooded." [141] Since Fang's troops were not reliable, and the company feared the losses of a prolonged strike, on the third day they called in the local chamber of commerce to mediate.[142] The negotiations, which lasted two more days, were made up of three parties—the companies, the chamber of commerce, and the union, represented by Liu Shao-ch'i and Chiang Hsien-yün.

In line with Mao's instructions to gain the widest possible public support, the club sent letters to various newspapers of the area. The following appeared in the *Weekly Review of the Far East* on September 30, 1922.

"We get only 200 cash a day. If we buy rice, we can afford no clothing. We have to be content either with hunger or nakedness or exposure. We work ten hours a day in dark dungeons like animals, and are subject to flogging and scolding." These are the statements of some 20,000 workers of the Pinghsiang Colliery and the Chuchow-Pinghsiang Railway in Hunan in a strike declaration this week. Seventeen demands were presented to the mining and railway authorities through the Mining and Railway Workmen's Club, and after consideration and discussion, the demands were in the main agreed to, and the strike was called off. The demands include an increase in wages, superannuation arrangement, full pay when disabled and maintenance of the workmen's club.[143]

The consolidated 13 demands were all granted—with some revisions. The following changes were made.

3. Four paid Sunday holidays were changed to two Sundays per month.
5. The bonus was to be one-half of one month's salary, not the entire month's salary as demanded.
7. The miners would receive their back pay, completely, within five months, while the railroad workers would receive it immediately.
11. The wages would be increased separately, and would be paid in silver.[144]

While the union did not win all of its demands, the victory was unquestionable. Tang Shou-i's wages, for example, approximately

---

141 Wales, *Red Dust*, p. 84.   142 Li Jui, p. 186.

143 "News from Central China," *Weekly Review of the Far East*, XXII, No. 5 (September 30, 1922), 168.

144 Ch'en Ta, p. 237.

doubled overnight.[145] It was the first major victory for the Hunan Labor Secretariat.

The actual leadership of the strike, recently hotly contested in Peking, appears to have been neither that of Mao nor that of Liu Shao-ch'i. All the sources published or obviously collected before 1951 credit the "on the spot" leadership to Li Li-san. There is no question, however, that both Liu and Mao played important roles— Mao as an over-all director, instructor, recruiter, and coordinator; Liu, as leader of the union in 1923 and later. He did play a leadership role in the strike, but he did little of the organizing which made it possible. It is also fairly obvious that Mao picked the site and decided the strategy, and perhaps some of the tactics. But the long-term, personal organization at Anyuan before the strike in 1922 was mainly the work of Li Li-san.

After the strike, the club's victory was consolidated, and the structure of the club was reorganized. A 10-man-cell system was set up. Each cell had a representative-of-10, and each 10 cells had a representative-of-100. At every work site there was a general representative. These general representatives, each representing 1 work site, belonged to a General Congress of the Whole.[146]

The most complete list of officers available includes a general director, a director in charge of those who worked in the mines, a director in charge of those worked outside the mines, a director in charge of railroad employees, a secretary, and the heads of the education committee and the cooperative.[147] All sources agree that Li Li-san was elected general director, that Chu Chin-t'ang was director in charge of those who worked inside the mines, and that Chu Shao-lien was the director in charge of railroad workers. Li Jui states that Liu Shao-ch'i was elected special emissary,[148] but another source states that he was director in charge of those who worked inside mines.[149] Committee directors named were Chiang Hsien-jung (secretary),[150] Ts'ai Tseng-chun (education),[151] I Li-jen (cooperative

---

[145] See Table 6. [146] Li Jui, p. 186.

[147] *Chung-nan li-shih tzu-liao,* p. 59. [148] Li Jui, p. 186.

[149] *Chung-nan li-shih tzu-liao,* p. 59.

[150] This might be Chiang Hsien-yün. The *Chung-nan li-shih tzu-liao* (p. 59), from which the list was obtained, states that he was a commander in the Northern Expedition, but that he was killed at Wuhan. Li Jui (pp. 212–13), states that Chiang Hsien-yün was killed on the Honan front.

[151] Ts'ai Shu-fan told Helen Snow that the strike was led by Ts'ai Ch'en-

manager), and Mao Tse-min and T'ang Sheng-ch'ao (also cooperative managers).[152]

After its victory and reorganization the Anyuan Mine and Railroad
Workers' Club secured the first structure built for workers led by
the Communist party in all of China. Combining a portion of their
newly won wages, they financed the construction of a new two-story
club house, and set up a consumers' cooperative.[153]

Conclusion

There are at least three possible interpretations of the role the
students played at Anyuan. One, expressed by the American Consul
J. C. Huston, gives the primary responsibility to the Communist
students. With reference to the 1922 strikes, in general, he writes:

Unmistakeable evidences of Bolshevik handicraft are everywhere apparent, and instead of the workers themselves taking the lead, we find that
the various strikes have been engineered by young students having no
particular experience in the industry in which the strike is called.[154]

Helen Snow gives another interpretation. With reference to the
Communist students, she states:

They were only a spark set to tinder, and it was spontaneous combus-
tion. The Chinese are peculiarly capable of cohesive organization, and
the workers had been held back by sheer lack of information. Once the
ideas and methods were supplied by the Communists, they learned
quickly and were loyal to their cause, hence few splits occurred in their
ranks. . . . The students merely told the workers what unions and strikes
were and the workers acted. . . . The students supplied the ideas and
the over-all strategy, but the workers organized themselves. Their role
was important because most of the workers were illiterate.[155]

A third interpretation, offered by the American consul at Hankow,
puts the least emphasis on the role of the Communist students. His

---

chün and Li Li-san. It is possible that Ts'ai Ch'en-chün and Ts'ai Tseng-chun
are the same person. See Wales, *Red Dust,* p. 84.

[152] This list of officers comes from *Chung-nan li-shih tzu-liao,* p. 59. Mao
Tse-min was a brother of Mao Tse-tung.

[153] *Ibid.,* p. 160.

[154] United States Government, Records of the Department of State Relating
to Internal Affairs of China, 1910–1929, 893.504–893.5045/83. "Labor Situation in China," by American Consul J. C. Huston, 893.504/15, p. A.

[155] Wales [Snow], *The Chinese Labor Movement,* pp. 11–12.

explanation was that the low standard of living and a further deterioration had provoked the strike wave.[156]

In the case of Anyuan, it is possible to imagine a strike occurring again in 1922, over the nonpayment of wages and the beatings, even if there had been no student leaders. But it would probably have been like the earlier strikes—spontaneous, with very limited demands, and achieving, at the most, a partial victory. The sophisticated, class-delineated organization, designed in industrialized countries to deal with modern industry; the wider scope of the demands; and the revolutionary vision were all introduced by the leadership of the students. However, one should not put undue emphasis on the students, ignoring the past history of various sorts of strikes and the generally wretched condition of Chinese workers. If it were not for these conditions, the spark struck by the students would have ignited no prairie fire.

This, however, only explains in a general way this first strike wave. Most of the workers' movements in China were crushed in 1923. Only Anyuan stood out as a vigorous survivor of organized workers' power, with the exception of those unions in Canton where Sun Yat-sen returned and assumed some power in 1923.[157] Furthermore, the party organization in Anyuan, forced underground in 1928, continued to function, at least until 1930.[158]

The source of the later success of the Anyuan workers in withstanding the counterattack of the reaction lies in the organizing done during this period. The choice of the Pingsiang Colliery as an organizing site gave them three advantages from the beginning. Their target was a rather antiquated Chinese industry situated on a provincial border somewhat distant from provincial centers of power.[159] Nevertheless, this element can be overemphasized since, as the history of the mines indicates, troops were called in three times prior to 1923. In addition, there was no serious opposition or competition during this period from other modern forms of labor organizations. The dialect problem did not appear to have arisen among the workers, since most came from Hunan, as did the organizers. Li Li-san was essentially a native of the area.

---

[156] Records of the Department of State Relating to Internal Affairs of China, 1910–1929, 893.504–893.5045/83, "Labor Conditions in the Hankow Consular District," prepared by P. S. Heintzleman, 893.504/17.

[157] Chesneaux, pp. 213, 220–21.　　　[158] Li Jui, pp. 189–90.

[159] *Ibid.*, p. 196.

Most significantly, at Anyuan, the students avoided the two most common errors committed by the Labor Secretariat elsewhere—failing to extend the union organization down to the lowest levels and failing to recruit working class cadres into the party. The Communist students at Anyuan, through the intelligent use of the school and 10-person-cell type of organization thoroughly organized most of the workers. Anyuan was thus one of the few places in China where the rules promulgated by the Secretariat were actually carried out.[160]

Secondly, the students did an excellent job of recruiting talented workers into the party. By the end of 1923, according to the reminiscent statement of Ts'ai Shu-fan in 1937—which may not be accurate —400 young workers from sixteen to twenty-three years of age had been recruited into the Communist Youth Corps, and around 100 workers had been recruited into the party itself. By 1925, there were about 300 party members, and the Communist Youth Corps had about 500.[161] Several later became well known, like Ts'ai Shu-fan. Ts'ai became a general in the Red Army and was Commissioner of the Interior and Commissioner of Judicial Affairs for the liberated areas in Yenan. Anyuan, or "Little Moscow" as it was called throughout China,[162] grew in this way from the visionary project of one of the last viceroys of the Ch'ing dynasty into one of the major bases and command schools of the Communist revolution.

The collieries and the industrial complex which they served never fulfilled the dream of their original founders, Chang Chih-tung and Sheng Hsuan-huai. What steel was produced for Chinese use, before the complex was sold in financial bondage to the Japanese economic empire, did not serve as invincible armor for the old regime. The enlightened conservatives sought to change some things so that others could remain the same, but as history unfolded, a new group of leaders laid other seeds which together with unnumbered similar seeds, developed into an organization that helped to destroy the old utterly.

160 *Ibid.*, p. 196.   161 Wales, *Red Dust*, p. 85.
162 Chesneaux, p. 221.

Appendix

BIG OIL PAINTING "CHAIRMAN MAO GOES TO ANYUAN": A BRILLIANT FLOWER OF ART BURSTING IN CULTURAL REVOLUTION

An oil painting entitled *Chairman Mao Goes to Anyuan* was created amid the triumphant songs of wresting all-round victory for the great proletarian cultural revolution. This oil painting of large dimensions is another brilliant flower of art sparkling with Mao Tse-tung's thought. The broad worker, peasant and soldier masses highly appraised the painting when they saw it and described it as "another fruit of the unprecedented great proletarian cultural revolution, and a new victory for Chairman Mao's revolutionary line on literature and art."

The painting takes us back to the autumn of 1921. Our great leader Chairman Mao, fulfilling the tasks of the Chinese revolution and carrying with him the hopes of the Chinese nation, strides the hills of Anyuan with his head held high against the wind-driven clouds. The red sun lights up the vast earth of the motherland with its infinitely brilliant rays.

Over forty years ago, the Chinese people were weighed down by the three big mountains of imperialism, feudalism and bureaucrat-capitalism. The state was rotten to the core and society was in utter darkness. Like a clap of thunder, the Communist Party of China came into being in 1921. In the autumn of that year, Chairman Mao came to the Anyuan coal mines in Kiangsi Province where he initiated and led the general strike of 17,000 railway workers and coal miners, which ended in great victory for the workers. He planned the world-shaking Autumn Harvest Uprising and organized the Anyuan workers for this great armed struggle. Chairman Mao led the Anyuan workers from one victory to another on the road to the armed seizure of political power, the only correct revolutionary road. This painting genuinely mirrors the great historical event of Chairman Mao going to Anyuan and successfully portrays the all-illuminating image of our great leader Chairman Mao.

After the great leader Chairman Mao had opened up Anyuan as the cradle of the Chinese workers' revolutionary movement, China's Khrushchev, a speculator in revolution, wormed his way into the Anyuan mining area in September 1922. He did his utmost to oppose Chairman Mao's revolutionary line and committed many counterrevolutionary crimes. But for many years this arch renegade and scab leader tampered with the revolutionary history of Anyuan and shamelessly advertised himself as the "leader of the Anyuan workers' movement." He gathered together a gang of ghosts and monsters to glorify him in various literary and art forms in order to secure him a place in history.

In the great proletarian cultural revolution, millions upon millions of armymen and civilians throughout the country expressed their mortal hatred of China's Khrushchev for committing towering crimes, and voiced their great indignation at this arch renegade and scab leader for his shameless act of tampering with the revolutionary history of Anyuan. Inspired by the great revolutionary practice of Chairman Mao going to Anyuan, a group of Red Guards, young teachers and students of several Peking colleges collectively produced this oil painting. These young people, cherishing infinitely profound class feelings for the great leader Chairman Mao, created this invaluable work of proletarian art in a space of two months and more.

The Restructuring of State Education in Buganda before Colonial Overrule

JACOB VAN LUTSENBURG MAAS

Scanning the landscape of precolonial African societies, sociologists and historians today are intrigued by the immense variability in the rapidity with which these societies adopted, either partially or completely, Western-inspired innovations in such aspects of the social structure as education, religion, and administration. Recently this initial fascination has brought forth efforts to explain the variability. Frequently such explanations are sought primarily or even exclusively within the value systems attached to key roles in these societies. Thus, for example, Philip Foster in his *Education and Social Change in Ghana* attributes Ashanti's presumed "initially high resistance to innovative forces originating outside" of itself to the conservative "nature of its chiefly authority." This hypothesis he seeks to verify through a brief comparison with Buganda. There, following Apter and Fallers, he is able to find a strong "assimilative capacity" particularly in the king's despotic authority which presumably led to that society's immediate, eager acceptance of educational and other practices introduced by Western missionaries.[1]

Even if this writer could agree with the accuracy of the descriptions of these contrasting norms, he would have great difficulty in following the implicit, unidirectional, causal connections from *x*,

---

[1] P. Foster, *Education and Social Change in Ghana* (London, Routledge and Kegan Paul, 1965), pp. 25–27. See also Foster's references: L. A. Fallers, "Despotism, Status, Culture, and Social Mobility in an African Kingdom," *Comparative Studies in Society and History,* Vol. II, No. 1 (1959); and D. E. Apter, *The Political Kingdom in Uganda* (Princeton, Princeton University Press, 1961), pp. 84–107.

the static presence of a particular role set and value system to *y*, significant changes in major social institutions. Such explanations constitute unwarranted and unfruitful short cuts based on an over-simplified picturing of these precolonial societies as socially undiffer-entiated and held together by value consensus in a condition of more or less quiet equilibrium. Under such imputed stable conditions, social change results in the final analysis simply from the motivated acts of individuals or of the community as an entity, without need for reference as to how motives are shaped by changes in social conditions (whether internal or external) of the actors. Therefore, Buganda accepts Western innovations because of its assimilative capacity whereas Ashanti cannot because it is said to lack that capacity—a limp tautology instead of a tight argument. No such model can hope to cope adequately with on-going social change. But then, perhaps Foster's unconscious intention was to describe Ashanti—unjustifiably, I suspect—as near as possible to a convenient, historical *tabula rasa* from which it would be relatively easy to get on with *subsequent* change in the colonial period.

To avoid foreclosing the possibility of some continuous social change, that is, some continuity from before to after colonial over-rule, it is necessary to allow at least for the possibility of partial autonomy and conflicting interests between the various organized groupings of a precolonial social structure—and not to be misled by the official ideology of near totalitarian value consensus enforced from top down by absolute authority.

It is always an empirical question to establish which are the social forces causing the principal conflicts in each society. It is not, as we often all too simplistically imagine, merely a matter of the leaders having first the right instrumental values in order then for the society to will changes.

The approach to the study of social change suggested and adopted here is indirect, more arduous, and complex. Were the approach of looking immediately at roles and values for explanations equally powerful, sociology would never have arisen.

In this essay, I attempt such an institutional analysis in order to explain the rapidity of response in an African society to Western-inspired innovations, especially in education. I have chosen Buganda as my case study as it is the African society with which I am most familiar and the one which Foster and others have pointed to, with-out any dispute, as having accepted such change rapidly.

First, it is necessary to reformulate the problem somewhat before any explanation can be suggested and argued fruitfully. Foster's purpose is to explain what is called the "transfer of institutions" between two nations, particularly in a colonial relationship. However, as already mentioned, there is at least an implication in this term of a *tabula rasa* situation in the recipient society, which is graphically confirmed by the absence of any conscious effort to uncover in the recipient society the presence and degree of elaboration of the institution about to be transferred by the dominant power! Specifically, the implication is that in these societies not only was education in the family or clan insignificant to macro-level social change but also there existed no specialized, societal-level institutions to take educational functions out of the hands of the family and put them into those of the state. Such an assumption logically slants to the conclusions drawn from Foster's analysis of both Ashanti and Buganda as it is insensitive to the possibility of conditions and institutions in the precolonial situation dramatically affecting the course of subsequent attempts at innovation.

To obviate this theoretical bias it is necessary to pose the problem not in vague terms of *transfer* but in terms which allow the recipient a more active role, for example, the restructuring of educational arrangements which already could have existed (in the kin group or at a "higher" level), through the adoption of foreign-inspired techniques.

There is also in Foster's formulation a very questionable de-emphasis of the climate and structure of power relations between the potential donor and recipient nations as these would shape the ease or perhaps even possibility of close contact, much less *transfer*. This variable too must be scrutinized deliberately and entered into the explanatory framework.

For the sake of succinctness, I chose to present my argument or change-model, in the form of a proposition. But what follows is not to be construed as a testing of the proposition which would necessitate a proper sample of the universe of cases. I am tempted, instead, to consider the case of Buganda as a Weberian ideal-typical precolonial society ready and able to absorb change under favorable conditions. Due to space limitations, a careful explication of the major concepts is not possible. But it is hoped that the explicit character of the argument itself combined with the use of these concepts in the full context of the case study will suffice to clarify any terminological or conceptual questions.

THE ARGUMENT

A. The greater the structural differentiation or modernization

i.e.,

1. The greater the differentiation of status between the governing hierarchy and the subjects whom they govern
2. The greater the bureaucratization or rationalization of governing authority
3. The greater the development of specialized institutions, outside the primary group, e.g., in education
4. The greater the status group consciousness of students separate from other status groups

And

B. The more favorable the structure of international relations with potential sources of innovation

i.e.,

1. The more the pressure to seek outside technical support against threats to national security
2. The more readily available the sources of this aid
3. The less explicitly official and the more voluntary in character those bringing technical innovations

And

C. The more those who bring these innovations are allowed to enter, subvert, and gain control of existing institutions and processes of selection and training for the governing hierarchy, without first seizing over-all political control

And

D. The more coercive power is won by the group whose status interests are most enhanced by the imported techniques, that is, the students-become-administrators

Then

E. The more rapid and the more voluntary the adoption of foreign-inspired changes in educational (and other) institutions, resulting in a restructuring of the state system of education

For purposes of periodization the analysis covers two broad eras in Buganda's precolonial history which are worth demarcating in advance. Briefly these are:

1. The growth and expansion of the kingdom of Buganda until the mid-nineteenth century both in demography and territory,

and in the development of a state hierarchy to cope with the problems of reintegrating new social groups

2. The intensification in the last half of the nineteenth century of contacts with the world beyond the East African interior, with tremendous social repercussions from these contacts. The first of these contacts were with Arab and Swahili traders from the coast who principally sought ivory and slaves in exchange for cloth, beads, and guns. The second wave of alien visitors were Christian missionaries from Britain (Protestant) and France (Catholic).

Let us approach these periods rather schematically, abstracting general social trends from the complexity of events.

The Changing Social Structure before 1850

BUREAUCRATIZATION OF THE RULING ELITE

The over-all effect of the first four centuries of Buganda's history (commencing roughly in the fifteenth century A.D.) was to transform a loose confederation of several jealous primordial clan structures into a protonational society with a central kingdom administration, the state. This process of integration, barely keeping pace with a steady expansion of borders to incorporate more such autonomous clan units or even outlying sections of neighboring societies, was accomplished through a centralization of authority under a charismatic leader, the Kabaka. His precise origins remain clouded but, presumably, were akin to a *primus inter pares* among the several aboriginal clan heads.

By the middle of the nineteenth century, it seems fair to say that Buganda possessed at least an incipient bureaucracy, with which the state was able effectively to resist internal pressures towards disintegration or external threats of incorporation into other states. Not only had the kings asserted authority over the primordial clan heads through appointment of their own district chiefs, or *bakungu* but they had successfully taken steps to curb the tendency of these new chiefs to develop independent power bases. To begin with, they made sure to reserve for themselves the appointment of the immediately subordinate subdistrict chiefs, depriving the bakungu of powers of patronage.

Secondly, and more profoundly, with increasing frequency in the nineteenth century they instituted departmental chiefs, *batongole,* whose responsibilities, rather than diffuse and territorial, were functionally specific, for example, to head one of the following: the standing army, the canoe navy, the corps of palace pages, tax collectors, house builders, canoe makers, messengers, transporters, potters, and the like. The problem of allocating *ex officio* estates to provide basic support for these officials and their departments was handled in the Norman fashion of creating unconsolidated estates. But the special genius in this arrangement was twofold: a) to create these new dispersed estates out of land expropriated from the jurisdiction of the clans, thereby further weakening them and b) to provide that, in the case of military departments, the new batongole did not muster their men under the bakungu but brought them directly to the capital, thus effectively undercutting the latters' customary leadership of peasant militia.

Thirdly, the means with which to pay, at least partially, for the services of the bureaucratic chiefs were developed through various forms of national currency. For our purposes the exact form of this "money" means little so long as it is relatively unperishable and reusable, and so long as the ruler, and preferably *only* the ruler, can pay subordinate officials so that they need not and indeed cannot be self-sufficient and troublesome. Examples of such "money" were royal warrants to permit special goods-collecting tours for meritorious officials; collection of fines from law breakers (also a policing power); royally initiated predatory raids on neighboring peoples; and most important, monopoly on the importing of scarce and attractive items such as cloth goods and especially guns. Although each of these functional equivalents of a national currency was hardly completely immune from abuse by untrustworthy chiefs, skillful use of all four could provide the king with sufficient control over the flow of goods to permit him to develop his own "exchequer" with which to remunerate his own staff.

Having achieved these necessary preconditions for a fully bureaucratic administration before the arrival of alien influence, there remained but one more: writing or some other mnemonic device to accelerate the transmission of information over time and space. Meanwhile, Buganda possessed the most specialized bureaucratized administration imaginable for a preliterate national society. Thus, in retrospect, it is hardly surprising that when literacy and its accompanying institutions were introduced by the Arabs and Europeans, the Buganda should accept the same with such ease. It almost seems, as it were, that they had been waiting for them.

Two brief quotations from Max Weber succinctly summarize the dilemma faced by kabakas of the nineteenth century in particular: "It is the fate of charisma, whenever it comes into the permanent institutions of a community, to give way to powers of tradition or of rational socialization." With few exceptions the kings of Buganda saw greater advantage in consolidating their power through forming a rationalistic bureaucracy than in relying on traditional loyalties and constraints alone. No doubt their actions rather than deliberately planned were short-term, *ad hoc,* cumulative "solutions" to the problem of maintaining their own prerogatives and the integrity of the burgeoning kingdom, but the unintended and critically important effect was to create a new specifically *national* status group of universalistic bureaucrats. Identifying themselves naturally with the national unit as opposed to any region or clan, these new chiefs, the batongole, were thus in a position to undermine the king's last stronghold of power—his former monopoly of nationalist symbolism and legitimacy. It is this qualitatively different situation which makes the nineteenth-century power struggles in Buganda so complex and interesting. In fact, the kabaka had never been a true despot, frequent allusions notwithstanding, but he was to be even less of one now. "Of all those powers that lessen the importance of individual action, the most irresistible is rational discipline." [2]

STATUS DIFFERENTIATION AT MID-CENTURY

The obvious, basic social divisions had long since been among slaves; the mass of peasantry; and the small, governing hierarchy whose activity was to protect, integrate, and expand the state and manage the national economy more and more bureaucratically. However, it was in the subcleavages within the gradually enlarged ruling stratum that most of the forces for social change took shape in the late precolonial period. Consequently, these strains have been the principal focus of our concern and must continue to be.

On the eve of the arrival of the Arabs and Europeans, we find a situation where two status groups are struggling for greater freedom of action in governing the rest of the country: on the one hand,

[2] H. Gerth and C. W. Mills, *From Max Weber* (New York, Oxford University Press, 1958), p. 253.

bakungu and batongole in uneasy cooperation in their like status as chiefs and, on the other, the kabaka, still trying, as always, to create room in which to maneuver. The interests of the chiefs fell under one rather broad category: as in any bureaucracy, they sought occupational and personal security through a regularization of their terms of service to the state, and in the process of attaining that end they provided an inpediment to autocracy and charisma. The critical area of occupational security was the criterion for selection and dismissal. It seems that the only one ever to receive universal endorsement from those who seek office is that of meritocratic achievement as observed in performance, as opposed to selection on the basis of various ascriptive factors which are inherently and irrationally discriminatory against some contenders.

The interests of the kabaka, on the other hand, were in diametric opposition. He sought to avoid any recognition of occupational rights for his staff in regard to meritocratic selection which, in effect, would have guaranteed them status group privileges that Weber terms *prebends*.[3] As much as possible, he tried to impress on his subordinates a personal loyalty to him, in appreciation of his patronage, rather than to their impersonal functions. This tendency led the king to the brink of refeudalization or neotraditionalism, to stem the gravitational pull towards rationalization.

In apparent desperation, the last few independent kabakas attempted to maintain their prerogatives again and again by reshuffling and repersonalizing power through raising up new groups of officials in rapid succession, the last of which finally seized the initiative to overthrow Kabaka Mwanga in the so-called "Christian Revolution" of 1888–89. By then the chiefs, and particularly the student-pages in the palace in line for appointments, had become quite aware of their indispensability to the operation of the state bureaucracy. The cumulative shift over the last centuries had brought the kabaka to the point of no return. All that was necessary for the outward symbols of power to change hands, as in substance they already had, was for the chiefs or the students to appraise the new situation, affirm a monopoly over the newest techniques of administration (plus a distinctive ideology wedded to those techniques), and then boldly to "stand their ground"—and the acknowledgement of power would flow to them.

As we shall see, beginning in the late 1870s and especially by the

[3] *Ibid.*, pp. 203–4.

1880s the students were situated better than the chiefs to be united in their motivation to take such group action as a revolutionary "bund." Although the chiefs occasionally displayed enough status solidarity to stand up to the kabaka in council, they were basically too satisfied and accustomed to the *status quo* to risk the potential chaos that could and did erupt after a *coup d'état*—especially when coupled with the increasing presence of untrustworthy outsiders. Contrarily, the student-pages found it difficult to develop any such commitment to a situation which did not permit the fuller expression of their increased self-awareness as an identifiable group with priviliged access to scarce new skills and norms introduced by missionaries, both Arab and European.

FORMAL INSTITUTIONS OF EDUCATION

One of the great myths derived originally from early missionary accounts but still permeating anthropological discussions of precolonial African societies (and one to which Foster's general interpretation falls victim), is that "traditional education" was largely a matter of socialization into tribal behavioral norms, usually left in the trust of older family members and occasionally supplemented by initiation rites for whole age-cohorts marking their transition from puberty to adulthood. Roughly speaking, this type of education is essentially a matter of genetic inheritance within the individual with a minimum dosage of social learning provided adequately by the fairly narrow circle of kinsmen from the older generation. No doubt there were many smaller African societies where occupational and social differentiation between men was so negligible as to render unnecessary any specialized, extrafamilial educational arrangements. However, as should be apparent from this discussion thus far, Buganda was not that kind of society. Although the family, as anywhere else, inevitably did carry out a socializing function, in Buganda as in all other bureaucratically organized societies, many of the most important educational tasks tended to get "pulled" out of families and into increasingly specialized agencies, or "schools." In noncaste societies, such as Buganda, such institutions had also to perform the delicate and contentious operation of selecting those candidates from all social strata who best met whatever desiderata—meritocratic or otherwise—were requisite to the achievement and fulfillment of a higher status.

Semispecialized educational institutions recruiting from beyond the boundaries of kingship groups historically tend to develop as appendages to the centers of bureaucratic political and economic power. In medieval northwestern Europe and the Arab world the schools and universities grew out of the respective ecclesiastical institutions, cathedrals, monasteries, and mosques. In early Buganda (as in China and Japan) the schools originated in the bureaucratic establishments of kings or nobility.

The mandate given to the schools by the bureaucracy is to transmit specialized expertise and to inculcate the norms with which that expertise is to be applied. As Parsons points out, the content of particular subject matter committed to memory is of less significance than is the main outcome of education, which is learning how to interact with whom and under what conditions in one's future role and status as an adult. Where bureaucracy is the main mode of adult social organization—at least for the most powerful segment of the adult population as was increasingly the case in Buganda—education itself will tend to be organized along bureaucratic lines. In such schools the main criteria of evaluation will be impersonal and universalistic, as opposed to the particularistic evaluation of kinship groups.[4]

Coming from societies where the main body of specialized skills taught in the schools was derived from literacy (and written numeracy), late nineteenth-century Western observers in Buganda were unable, as well as ideologically unwilling, to see any "real" education going on in the palace-schools of a preliterate but proto-bureaucratic society. Had they thought more closely about the actual function of much of the great rush of activity they steadily observed in the palace, they would have noticed the teaching and learning of "useful arts" which, though not based on literacy, were of such skill that the average family elder could not transmit them to his son. Learning was focused essentially on three rather broad areas of the art of governance appropriate to the stage of economic and political development in which Buganda found itself.

First of all, as might be expected in an age of territorial expansion and in an economy based on a highly militarized mode of acquiring additional wealth, a prime value was placed on organizational leader-

---

[4] T. Parsons, "The School Class as a Social System: Some of Its Functions in American Society," *Harvard Educational Review*, XXIX (1959), 297–318; reprinted in A. H. Halsey, J. Floud, and C. A. Anderson, eds., *Education, Economy, and Society* (New York, The Free Press, 1961), pp. 434–55.

ship and coordination of large agglomerations of armed men, coolness under duress, and prowess as a warrior. Secondly, in a nonconstitutional monarchy where such a large residue of power still centered on a charismatic king, priority was given to such cultural skills of court life as flattery, obedience, political cunning, polished speech and etiquette, and, when asked for, sagacious advice. Finally, as civil rulers over men, recruits to chiefships would be required to prove their worthiness by mastery of (presumably) an evolving body of customary law and by ability to adjudicate disputes among their commoners with some degree of disinterested skill.

It was in these three areas of future responsibility that hundreds of adolescent or young adult student-pages, the *bagalagala,* would be expected to compete in displaying their achievements during their several years at court. Their examiner was the king or chief—or their special deputies—in whose palace the student was trying to prove himself. Their classroom was the highly politicized, competitive, and often dangerous real world of the palaces, the highways, the battlefields. Their "teachers" were primarily occupied as men of action—but with the beginnings of specialized student organizers and wardens. Their preliterate learning techniques were essentially those of apprentices: powers of observation and interpretation; efficient performance of required tasks; and an ability to profit from the criticisms of others' and one's own performance.

One further point concerning the institutional setting of education needs to be made. The various student-pages were never physically or psychologically together as a single group at any one time, but were divided both geographically and by a status hierarchy. To wit, every district chief would have student-pages at both his district headquarters and at the townhouse he was required to keep at the capital. Many palace establishments were situated in the immediate environs of the capital: in addition to the townhouses and the kabaka's palace there were those of the queen mother, the kabaka's sister, and the prime minister, or *katikiro.* As might be assumed there was a ranking in status between these palace establishments. And within the kabaka's palace, there was a status gradation between the hundred or more full student-pages who often but not always came from the more privileged families of various chiefs, and the thousand or so junior-pages, or *bassalosalo,* who were usually drafted from peasant homes and who performed the more menial tasks with less chance of promotion to an official adult position.

Such a situation of spatial and status separation naturally worked against the creation of a full, status-group consciousness and solidarity among all those who shared approximately the same relation and interests vis-à-vis the major authority figures.

The Impact of Alien Influence

MUSLIM TRADERS AND THE CHALLENGE TO AUTHORITY

The first noticeable result of more direct trade relations with the coast in the 1840s and 1850s was a nearly perfect monopoly by Kabaka Suna on the import and redistribution of scarce prestige items such as various cloths for new uniforms, beads, utensils, and, especially, guns and ammunition. The modern arms were used both to reward supporters and to obtain for export more slaves and ivory from weak neighbors.

During the subsequent reign of Kabaka Mutesa (1856–84), religious and other cultural influences such as literacy gradually came to be felt as Arab traders fulfilled their avocational role as missionaries and Mutesa found good cause to lend them a ready ear. Throughout the 1860s, the kabaka was able to watch from a safe distance while his northern neighbor, Bunyoro, fell victim to a steady assault on its own northern flank. Semilegal slave traders had begun to encroach on Bunyoro from the Sudan, leaving havoc in the wake of their uncontrolled use of superior firepower, while the Egyptian khedive was less than successful in hiding his intention of outright imperialist annexation of the whole Upper Nile Basin. By 1870 when the first probing party of Khartoum traders reached Buganda, the only power in the region to which Mutesa could turn with hope of help to offset this very real threat to Buganda's autonomy was Zanzibar, still far enough away not to be a threat itself.

It is difficult not to connect these political approaches to Mutesa's increasing willingness to heed the religious suasions of the Zanzibari visitors to his court. Having already begun to learn Arabic and Kiswahili along with officials at the court, in 1867, he adopted and decreed at least the outward forms of Islam, such as its calendar, appropriate greetings in Arabic, and the eating of properly slaughtered meat. Orders were also given out to construct mosques throughout the country, while several of the Swahili at court were appointed to chiefships, and the king was not perfunctory in enforcing his wishes on his people.

By 1875 the spread of at least the outward manifestations of Islamic religion had become great enough to cause the kabaka concern, particularly as the largest concentration of converts existed within the ranks of his own student-pages. Over the decade leading up to 1875, the rationale for a benign attitude towards Islam was eroded by changing circumstances. Although the Egyptians continued to loom beyond his northern horizon, Zanzibar proved uninterested in committing itself to firm diplomatic support for a trading partner which lay beyond its logistical reach, while in 1875 a new, more attractive possibility for an alliance appeared in the person of Henry M. Stanley.

Stanley's proved military skill in assisting Mutesa defeat a traditionally hostile group of offshore islanders and his enthusiastic presentations of the strengths and advantages of Western civilization and Christianity—especially when compared to Islam—made a marked impression on the kabaka. When he made the offer to call on his countrymen to come to Buganda to introduce their skills, skills which the kabaka not surprisingly saw as primarily mechanical and even military in nature, the kabaka could at last see nearing fruition his wish for an effective alliance with a strong but safely distant power. Zanzibar, the Arab and Swahili traders, and Islam, all paled noticeably by comparison.

However, it is hardly likely that the converts to "religion" in his court, especially the student-pages, would have shared this particular perspective on this new, alternative source of foreign innovation and influence. From accounts of Baganda Muslim martyrs, it seems highly plausible that these young men would have perceived Mutesa's slackened interest in their "religion" and his invitation of some unknown, but highly suspect, outsiders as a threat to their recently gained monopoly of foreign-inspired skills.[5] That eventually they would be able to tap this new source of further innovations as well is not likely to have occurred to them until time and exposure could transform their initial, uninformed reaction from one of mistrust to one of receptivity.

Late in 1875 or early the following year, a minor incident between the king and the young Muslim converts transformed that threat into a dramatic confrontation. In the ensuing circumstances, the converts gambled on the hope that through a show of unity they

[5] A. Katumba and F. B. Welbourn, "Muslim Martyrs of Buganda," *Uganda Journal*, XXVIII, No. 2 (1964), 153.

would persuade the kabaka to remember his previous espousal of the same body of skills and norms which they now sought to defend and thus continue to give them his support—still very much their principal guarantee of continued status advantage. However, they overestimated their powers of persuasion and mistook the kabaka's earlier religious pretensions, expressed at a time when circumstances required them, for a permanent commitment. Their gamble proved to be premature, as a comparison between the aftermath of this bloody episode and the one to come in ten years involving Kabaka Mwanga and the Christians clearly shows.

One valuable accomplishment, however, did come out of this first test of forces. For the first time significant numbers of student-pages had begun to overcome their spatial and status differences to join in a common group identity and effort, even though it was to be put down severely. This process of forging a group consciousness powerful enough to overcome previous atomization would continue at an even faster pace during the decade to come when "religion," in the form of Christianity, again presented itself in much greater force in terms of manpower, logistical support, new technical skills to offer, and quite amazing self-confidence in its charismatic sense of mission. By comparison, Islam and its part-time Arab and Swahili trader exponents would appear somewhat decidedly half-hearted and amateurish.

CHRISTIAN MISSIONARIES AND THE RESTRUCTURING OF POWER AND EDUCATION

Although Mutesa was eager to receive the missionaries for whatever practical help they might have to offer him and his administrative staff against Buganda's enemies, he soon sensed that he had to maintain a close, jealous watch over their potentially seditious teachings, no doubt in response to his recent experiences with the converts to Islam. A specific point of contention between himself and the missionaries was over what kind of pupils were appropriate for learning the new skills. When willing to countenance their teaching—which was not always—he and his chiefs made certain to confine the ranks of pupils to those relatively privileged young men already in court, whereas the missionaries had quite different expectations. One of them wrote:

It is . . . I believe, among these peasants that the efforts of the missionary will be most successful, and that here again, as in numberless other instances, history will repeat itself, and the earliest and sincerest converts will be drawn from among the poor of the country.[6]

But, whatever historical precedents the missionaries originally had in mind were not to be duplicated so easily here. If one took the *entire* social order into consideration, as they had here, it gradually became apparent that the spread of Western education, far from promoting a total, truly revolutionary status reversal between peasants and aristocrats, would actually serve to entrench the broad lines of status differentiation. But one could hardly expect the Buganda governing hierarchy to sit back and allow its status privileges to be eroded through offering scarce skills first to the sons of peasants. However, considering just the ruling stratum itself, a more moderate but still very significant status reversal along generational lines was to result from the missionary efforts.

After the first several years of the missionary presence, it was becoming increasingly obvious to most of the major chiefs that their worst fears were approaching reality. As increasing numbers of converts and catechists among the student-pages gathered round them, the missionaries came to be regarded as "chiefs" by friend and foe alike.

In effect, through encouraging the transfer of "client affiliations," the missionaries were striking very deeply into the heart of the regenerative mechanism of the national political structure. Once they could capture control over the processes of selection, recruitment, and training in the palace schools, a permanent place for Christianity in Buganda was virtually assured, with the young students as future chiefs in the vanguard. To guarantee the success of this effort they explicitly hoped from very early on to create "national schools" at the mission headquarters,[7] thereby drawing together into one or two central institutions those who had hitherto been somewhat scattered. As long as it was still politically necessary, they had to function under the king's official sponsorship. But, before long, they were operating subversive schools within the shadow of the palace, as original sponsorship inevitably changed to suspicion and intermittent opposition and they and their followers were forced to become increasingly secretive in meeting on their own at the missions.

[6] C. T. Wilson and R. W. Felkin, *Uganda and the Egyptian Soudan* (London, Sampson, Low, 1882), I, 193.

[7] A. M. Mackay, *Mackay of Uganda* (London, Armstrong, 1890), p. 106.

Little could the Buganda realize it during the 1880s, but, in retrospect, it is obvious that the missionaries were thinking and acting in a much larger frame of political reference than the still-untraveled Buganda could imagine in their wildest fantasies. While the kabaka and his people still held, though perhaps with decreasing conviction, to the sincere belief that Buganda was the center of their universe, the missionaries' very audacity expressed a sometimes foolhardy but always impressive confidence in the industrial and military might of Europe, which could increasingly be theirs to call on in some dire circumstance.

There is little reason to doubt that exposure to the missionaries helped the growing band of converts to enlarge their own frame of reference to daring proportions. The very literal depiction of the kingdom of God which the missionaries drew for them served gradually to undermine their simple faith in the omnipotence of their earthly king. The eye-opening example set by the missionaries that to young Buganda must have been seen as an openly defiant, disrespectful, and delegitimating posture towards men of authority apparently encouraged them into the unrealistic expectation that they too could behave similarly and with impunity. Even if they were to suffer the fate of previous martyrs for transgressing traditional decorum in the cause of the new religious-social-political order, they had a final refuge, the promised reward of everlasting life. The new "religion" offered a new, absolute, highly principled, rigid and eternal world view to a group whose life chances in the highly competitive conditions of court were until then sometimes promising but always insecure. It also accorded its members a distinctive, matching life style which set them apart from those who did not pursue it, with a new calendar, new ethical parameters, new architectural forms, a new language with a written literature, and new role models; in brief, the content and boundaries of a new moral community of men.

The process of building this community is worth tracing through various shifts in the mode of interaction among student-pages who became its members. Before the period of Arab influence their behavior was dominated by role-striving with the intention of acceding to the rather few positions left behind by their retiring elders. As demand far outstripped supply, peer interaction naturally was characterized by rigorous competition and divisiveness. The gradual discrediting of these traditional role-models, upon the arrival of a small group of highly unconventional and yet influential aliens, effectively displaced the adult generation of leaders from their normal central position in the student-pages' interaction network. But just as the youth were about to be cut loose into an anomic drift, this rather outlandish group of role-figures were available to fill the vacuum. However, the set of relationships they established with the missionaries, and between themselves under their guidance, were necessarily of a somewhat if not totally different kind from the previous atomized, status-striving pattern of interaction. Although this process of transfer of reference and allegiance tended to be quite brief in the life of the average individual student, its effect on the consciousness of the status group as a whole was both profound and enduring.

To wit for the first time a tightly woven network of relations was established among all status members as equals. Since the missionaries held no life-and-death powers for punishment and reward, as the king had, and since they could not stimulate a frenzied competition by holding out limited achievement opportunities (such as chiefships), there was no built-in tendency toward a re-atomization of peer relations. Instead every young man who came to the missionaries could acquire the skills and life style of "religion" with a modicum of study and exemplary behavior without automatically depriving others of the chance to attain them. In fact, the "supply" of achievement, amazingly, was very "elastic." Quite unlike the monolithic reward structure in the king's bureaucracy, now there were three possible sources of achievement: the Catholic and Protestant mission as well as the Muslim trader "community," competing with each other to *offer* their rewards to all sincere comers.

Had Kabaka Mwanga, who succeeded his father in 1884, been as secure as his father in his monopoly over the distribution of rewards and power, it is quite possible that the Christian persecutions of 1885–86 would never have occurred. After some of his most trusted and beloved pages were hastily accused and summarily executed for spying in court for the missionaries, Mwanga rather belatedly realized that momentary suspicions, largely inspired by his own enemies in the court, were serving to undermine his much needed support among the younger generation. For, as patently compromised as the student-pages were in their loyalties, Mwanga's own unstable power position would not permit him to kill off the flower of Buganda youth; he still depended on them to withstand the pressures from potentially seditious older chiefs who sought to turn history back on itself by liquidating the lot—the missionaries, their converts, *and* the king who weakly tolerated them both.

The Christian converts among the student-pages found themselves in a position strikingly similar to their fellow "religionists" of ten years before. Like the Muslims, they had entered into their new status as students of religion with the evident encouragement of Mutesa, who wished for increased technical sophistication of his national cadres. Equally, it was predictable that they would view Mwanga's sudden withdrawal of support as a threat to all that they felt they had won. But, by 1886 conditions had come around to supporting the feasibility of the strategy of united resistance which had been catastrophic for the Muslims. This time a new king, very unsure of himself, was only barely holding his power. Ten years of the shifting of institutional affiliations of young people away from the various palaces and towards the missions had caused a steady, unmistakable erosion of support for the major chiefs. These full-time missionaries were more committed than the Arabs were to a permanent foreign presence in Buganda. They were willing to make very real short-term sacrifices, believing that over the long term they could, if necessary, draw on almost unlimited resources at home with which to become firmly established against almost any local opposition. Finally, the process of regrouping and institutional reorganization by the student-pages outside the walls of the palaces which formerly divided them had had sufficient time in which to generate a stronger status-group self-awareness to the point where they could become a tight-knit conspiratorial "bund" woven around their own charismatic leaders in the persons of the missionaries and a few of the older more devout converts.

When in 1886 some of the Christian students accused of subversion were subjected to the usual sanction of torture and execution, the remainder—the vast majority—came away finding that both their numbers and their obvious indispensibility to the king were as great as ever. Almost immediately after the executions the wavering kabaka reversed his policy drastically by creating and equipping three new unprecedented regiments for the youths of the three religions. Each regiment was placed under the leadership of former student-pages, some of whose wounds from the recent tortures literally were just healing. They were provided with estates appropriated from the *ex officio* holdings of chiefs in the immediate environs of the capital and then allowed to pillage the land of other chiefs with impunity. In the process, the kabaka had sacrificed his monopoly over the flow of a key commodity—firearms—in order to secure needed support.

But in 1888 Mwanga's old suspicions of the students were aroused once more, and he clumsily tried to conspire against them. By now it was apparent to the rapidly increasing number of all three types of religionists that they could never again rely on the support of Mwanga. Their only course was to unite to drive from the throne their last obstacle to the attainment of power and then install a puppet prince of their own choosing. In this they succeeded almost effortlessly.

However, for the next several years the three religious factions jockeyed among themselves to win control over the majority of political positions in the country, each hoping for the support of a foreign patron-power. The Muslims having alienated popular support by religious fanaticism and lacking logistical support were in the weakest position and the first to be eliminated. This left a struggle between the Catholic and Protestant factions which was decided only shortly before the inception of colonial rule in 1894 by predictable British intervention on the side of the Protestants. The Catholics' cause was undermined when their foreign patrons, French and German, were outmaneuvered in the international diplomatic and military arenas.

Conclusion

Some historians have referred to the events beginning in 1888 as the "Christian revolution." In view of the immediate effect of the coup, which was simply to bring to power rather early a group of men who were already in line to assume power under the kabaka. This usage of the term *revolution* appears too free and misleading in what the term should imply for status reversal on a total societal scale.[8] Nevertheless, there is no question that within the ruling hierarchy there were some very profound changes resulting from the struggle. Through their successful gamble the new generation of chiefs were paid off handsomely with the opportunity to set their own more regularized and bureaucratic terms of service. Government activities were to be organized along even more rational, functional lines in

---

[8] C. C. Wrigley, "The Christian Revolution in Buganda," *Comparative Studies in Society and History,* II (1959), 1.

keeping with the long historical trend traced earlier from charismatic to bureaucratic modes of authority.

Secondly, through a new generation of the elite coming to power earlier than the normal pace of promotions would have allowed, Buganda, alone among all East African societies on the eve of colonialism, was in a position to benefit from leadership by a corps of "modernists" who looked upon the prospect of collaboration with alien overrule with unusual confidence. Whereas in many other areas the missions arrived on the scene jointly or even well after the colonial administrators and soldiers, in Buganda the effect of the prior arrival of the missionaries (and to an extent the Arabs) was to bring together and to help prepare a cadre of leaders who would be able to absorb the shocks of imposed colonial rule, thereby preserving intact their country's sense of national integrity and self-confident ability to cope with rapid change. Had the colonial administrators arrived in Buganda well before the missionaries, it is at least doubtful that the Buganda leadership—and Buganda as a whole—would have fared quite so well under colonial overrule as is generally agreed to be the case.

The contrast with the contemporaneous experience of the neighboring kingdom of Bunyoro is highly instructive. There, before the appearance of missionaries, diplomatic hostilities with British envoys of the Egyptian khedive prejudiced the chances of developing trustful relations with subsequent unofficial visitors. Thus early missionaries following on the heel of heavy-handed official visitors did not tarry long at the Omukama's capital: they had neither an invitation to come nor the confidence to try to stay. In fact the first missionaries to carry out work in the kingdom arrived only after the British conquest, in effect, as part of the total regimen of military occupation.

But it is certainly not intended to ascribe sufficient causation for Buganda's ability to accept change readily merely to the missionaries' active influence, for one must then ask why the missionaries chose to come to Buganda in particular as the place to begin their efforts in the East African interior. The answer to that question must lie in the extent and depth of differentiation and specialization in the social structure even before 1875. The several dimensions of this modernization process were listed in our introduction and were surveyed in the second section. It is plain from all accounts that the missionaries sought to reach Buganda because it was at that precise moment the most powerful and structurally differentiated society in the interior. Should it be converted to Christianity hopefully it could serve as a model for surrounding, weaker societies. Obviously, as the most developed society it would have other things being equal, the greatest "assimilative capacity". The apparent but superficial obviousness of this relationship can make attempts at its fuller explanation seem pointless. But are they? A main point of this essay is that subsequent historical developments, especially international, had to be favorable as well for successful assimilation to take place.

With such a highly elaborated administrative apparatus already in existence the missionaries could achieve success not by any crude conquest but by selecting (unconsciously, perhaps), entering, subverting, and finally controlling and eventually restructuring the very regenerative mechanism of the society—the main educational institution of the state at the capital. Here was a social organization which could absorb and channel rather than succumb to the impact of sudden change—change which would tremendously accelerate social processes and structural shifts *already* in existence. The weight of this impact then provided the extra push with which to alter the internal balance of power (through the 1888 coup) in a direction favorable to even further absorption, adaptation, and change under the impact of colonial administrators and commercial interests, who were far more dynamic in the long run, and less accommodating to local sensibilities than the early missionaries. From such a perspective the greatest change of all resulting from the missionary impact was in the accelerated *rate* of change of the structural features under our scrutiny.

Thus we arrive at the conclusion that the independent variables sketched in the introduction were indeed at work in promoting the rapid and partly voluntary adoption of Western inspired innovations especially in education. In the first place, the degree of modernization in terms of status differentiation, bureaucratization, institutional specialization, and status group consciousness was promotive of such innovation. But on top of this, the structure of Buganda's relationship with potential sources of innovation in modern literacy-based techniques was relatively favorable: a delicate combination of pressure to seek outside technical aid which was readily available, and the lack of political military intimidation from an overbearing official presence by the aid-donors, at least in the early stages. These bearers of technical innovation were able to subvert and gain control of the existing institutions and processes of selection and training for "high level manpower," without first taking over-all control of the state. Finally, the most direct recipient and beneficiary of this technical advice, the status group of "students soon to be administrators," was able to seize political and military power from conservative forces, thereafter to collaborate with the foreign tutors in ushering in a new social order with a renovated system of education, increasingly differentiated from political institutions.

An investigation of the source material on Ashanti employed by Foster has shown that a re-analysis along the lines of this study leads to quite different conclusions from those which he arrived at. Along the dimensions of the first independent variable, Ashanti reveals virtually no significant difference from Buganda. However, there is tremendous difference between the experiences of the two countries along the second independent variable which by itself appears to explain satisfactorily their startling variance in the acceptance of innovations. Ashanti's first contact with the outside world was aborted by a prolonged and insurmountable impasse in relations between itself and the key foreign power in the area, Britain, because of Britain's pre-existent alliance with Ashanti's traditional enemies, the coastal Fanti peoples. When Buganda had had difficulties with Egypt she was able to call for help from Zanzibar and European missionaries, but no such option existed for Ashanti. Instead, missionaries who probed Ashanti were turned back for their suspicious and undeniable connections with the British. The diplomatic hostility was resolved by a long series of military confrontations culminating in defeat and colonial subjugation by the British. It is hardly surprising, therefore, that Ashanti like Bunyoro was not in a position to accept innovations in foreign-inspired technical skills on its own terms and initiative, even though it may have been prepared in terms of degree of internal development.[9]

[9] Forthcoming: "Educational Reorganization in Precolonial African Societies: A Recomparison of Buganda and Ashanti," *Comparative Education Review* (June, 1970).

Political Participation in Soviet Local Government

THEODORE H. FRIEDGUT

The Concept of Political Participation

Since the earliest days of political theory the number of persons
participating in the ruling of a state has been a key to the definition
of that state's political system. Aristotle's threefold classification
served for centuries as a quantitative basis for political taxonomies.
More sophisticated examination of political participation relates also
to the point at which citizen participation impinges on the political
process. In differentiating between a citizen culture and a subject
culture, Almond and Verba define the politically competent citizen as
one who has a role in the formation of general policy, while the
subject has no role in rule-making and exerts no policy-making influence but is called into action only when policies are being applied.
The differentiation between these stages is both legitimate and significant in determining the quality of citizen participation in any system;
yet we must bear in mind that participation in policy implementation
may in turn generate strong pressures for influence on policy determination. It is a stated tenet of Soviet government theory that ultimate responsibility for policy determination and implementation must
be lodged with the same body, and this is the rationale behind the
recent tendency to broaden the competence of various public bodies
connected with the soviets to include some policy-discussing and
legislative functions. In practice, however, this principle applies more
to formal structures than to functional arrangements and is intended
to unite the legislative and executive powers in the executive committees of the soviets. The legislative power of the local soviets is
exercised under strict hierarchical surveillance; a local soviet has,
for instance, neither independent sources of revenue nor autonomy
of resource allocation. Similarly, the electoral process though in-

volving extensive mass activity, affords a minimum of individual influence in the normal course of events.

Thus citizen involvement in policy implementation in what Soviet writers call "control and inspection" functions leads to creation of institutions which in the course of their development broaden their scope and become involved in various areas of legislative and low-level policy-forming activities. These are as yet minor functions of the various auxiliary organs of the local soviets and have no established stability or legitimacy as public representative organs. Nevertheless, the extent of their activity and the direction of their development are of great interest as an instance of development of potential centers of political activity within what was once regarded as a monolithic totality ruled exclusively by a small central elite.

Even more important for an analysis of the nature of citizen participation in Soviet politics is the tension created within the political system by the regime's attempt to keep politics and government strictly separate, involving the citizen in policy application while excluding him from policy determination.

Avoidance of the tyranny of a single central power, whether ruled by one or by many, has been the central theme of American governmental evolution since the days of the Federalist Papers. Much of both ancient and modern democratic political theory has been constructed in a similar vein, positing a plural, counterbalanced state structure with numerous sources of information and political leverage and a multiplicity of nonstate interests and associations. William Kornhauser, for example, describes what he calls the mass society in which the lack of autonomous structures bring every aspect of society under control of the central state organs, thus preventing the development of those bodies which might serve to nourish critical values or independent thought. Thus, if we discern the urge for broader autonomy in social and political groupings at the level of local government in the USSR, we may have a valuable focus for evaluating the potential for adaptability of the Soviet political system to new challenges and of the possible consequences of growing or repressed openness in Soviet public life in coming years.

Lenin's concept of government and administration, much of which is still prominent in Soviet theory and practice, was built on the expectation of mass citizen participation in administration combined with party control and "democratic centralism" in policy-making. Drawing chiefly on Marx's critique of the Paris Commune, Lenin hastily completed work on his *State and Revolution,* setting out the organization principles of the Communist state in anticipation of the coming revolution. Its focus was strongly antibureaucratic and almost anarchistic. It proposed the abolition of ranks, the institution of workmen's pay for civil servants, and the subjecting of all officials to citizen recall; it suggested frequent rotation of office to encourage mobilization of all available citizens into the ranks of public administrators. The slogan "Every cook a Commissar" was not taken lightly during the early phase of the revolution, when the term of election to local soviets was only three months.

Even today the objective of simplifying local administration down to processes of "control and accounting" practicable for any reasonably enlightened citizen is held as an ideal, though there is still much controversy as to how this is to be accomplished. In addition, an examination suggests that the participation of the Soviet citizen in electoral activities, as well as his relation to governmental institutions during his public service, in its function within the political system differs greatly from similar activities in America for all that many of the forms followed may be similar.

This essay focuses on Soviet elections as embodying the principal characteristics of the political system. They involve virtually all adult citizens in some phase of the electoral process without significant relaxation of the control which is the foundation of the system. The elections draw upon the most active Soviet citizens to serve in the representative councils—the soviets which have given the country its name. These are the bodies which carry the local administration to the citizens and bring their needs to the regime. Their selection and acceptability to the citizen body is one of the bases of the functioning of the Soviet system.

The Soviet Citizen and His Electoral System

The hierarchy of soviets, from the bicameral Supreme Soviet of the USSR to the most remote village council, encompasses some 50,000 elected bodies with over 2,000,000 members. Elections to the Supreme Soviet and the Republic Supreme Soviets are held every four years and never fall in the same year as elections to lower soviets. All other soviets are elected for two-year terms.

Despite the fact that this requires elections to be held three years out of four, the Soviet Union's political life is not election-oriented, as is that of the United States. Though the election campaigns elicit great attention and activity while they are in progress, they provide not a turning point or "moment of truth" for Soviet political leaders but rather an opportunity for the reaffirmation of loyalty, a demonstration of unity, and an emphasis on continuity. Election issues are almost never mentioned as such before the official opening of the campaign, and they fade quickly from sight as soon as the campaign is ended.

Nevertheless, the elections have a definite function in Soviet politics. They involve large numbers of people in activity supportive of the regime. They bring the policies of the government into direct and live contact with the citizenry through the system of election meetings and home canvassing. They serve to test the ability of the regime to mobilize the population into demonstrations of support and, in the final analysis, provide the disgruntled citizen with a legitimate, if generally symbolic, form of protest. This last feature is made possible by the rule that any candidate must secure an absolute majority of the votes cast before being certified as elected. Thus, by having a majority of voters strike out the candidate's name, the electorate may defeat him.

The rate of rejection of candidates in Soviet elections is minimal —something under 1 in 10,000—and such failure of any prominent candidate is almost inconceivable. Yet the rejection of a candidate remains the prerogative of the electorate and, particularly on the village level, may serve as the ultimate popular sanction against incompetence or corruption. In this discussion of the actual election procedures I shall pursue this manifestation of the voter's sovereignty further.

PREPARATIONS OF THE ELECTION APPARATUS

The Soviet election campaign is typically brief—approximately two months. In 1963, for instance, the Supreme Soviet of the RSFSR announced on January 6 that elections would be held on March 3; and this has been the approximate span of time allotted to organizing and campaigning in subsequent elections as well.* Formally, this is about the same length of time as the contest between the two major

* The suggestion has been made in the Soviet press that since campaign techniques have been practiced and mastered in recent years, the campaigning period could be further shortened—a somewhat bewildering application of "plan fulfillment" criteria to political life.

Presidential candidates in the U.S. Actually, the period of the American primaries and of preconvention politicking is an integral part of the American election campaign. American politics, however, may be divided into two separate streams: the campaign vis-à-vis one's rival candidates, on the one hand, and his campaign vis-à-vis his constituents, on the other. There is not even the vaguest parallel to the first in the Soviet system, though many of the customs and institutions of the second are not unfamiliar to the Soviet voter.

The first step in the election procedure is the establishment of the election commission at each level from the Republic down to the village. The commissioners are generally prominent citizens, and at the Republic level the commission is typically headed by a person such as the chairman of the Republic's trade union organization or the rector of a university.

The formal functions of these committees are much the same as in any other electoral system. They oversee observance of election regulations, correct nomination procedures, the delineation of election districts, and preparation of the voters' lists. Ultimately the election committee in each voting precinct must supervise balloting procedures and scrutinize the ballot count.

This chain of electoral commissions involves large numbers of citizens in what is basically nonpartisan civic activity. They are acting as protagonists of the system rather than of any candidate, good citizens fulfilling a duty to the state. Soviet sources indicate that 2,155,207 commissions were active in 1969, involving 8,698,765 persons out of a total electorate of 149,775,884.

In a multiparty electoral system, the scrutineers at the polls are partisans, overseeing fair play on behalf of their respective parties as part of the entire system of competition. In the Soviet Union, where the concept of factional competition of views has been rejected, the elections become an affirmation of the identity of the regime and the public's best interest. The role of the election commissions in all their tasks reflect this public and nonpartisan character.

In their work, the electoral commissions must supervise the executive committees of the local soviets in adjusting the boundaries of election districts in keeping with population shifts and in updating the electoral rolls on the basis of local housing office registers. The Soviet press gives publicity to their work, chronicling the formation of commissions at various levels and their success in detecting and correcting such errors as the formation of electoral districts on the basis of number of voters rather than over-all population. The importance of such points goes beyond the technical, however, for if one of the functions of the election campaign is to demonstrate the regime's ability to mobilize the population in style and to deliver a 99 percent vote as proof of unity, then the electoral rolls and voting districts are of basic importance and the work of the electoral commissions becomes a serious trust. The Soviet government sets great store by the use of symbols, and the arrangement of impeccably correct conditions for the holding of the elections is a symbol of some importance in the demonstration of Soviet democracy to its own citizens and to observers from abroad.

THE ELECTION CAMPAIGN

The nearly 9 million election commissioners are only one branch of the election apparatus. In addition, there are "agitators' collectives" in each election district, groups of propagandists whose job is to bring the "issues" of the campaign to the people. Such collectives consist of a nucleus of 3 or 4 people directing the election campaign propaganda through the so-called "red corners" found in factories, schools, and public institutions; through voters' clubs; and ideally every Soviet home. These are open and active supporters of the list of candidates named by the "bloc of Communists and non-Party people," and the fact that the candidates are unopposed detracts not at all from the presentation of the national and local achievements and goals on which the campaign centers. We have here, then, another 8 to 10 million persons engaged in active election work. The work of the agitators' collective is concentrated on the *agitpunkt* (political indoctrination center) where tasks are assigned, literature is made available, and the various phases of electioneering are specified and checked. Agitpunkty are everywhere. The rural county (*raion*) of Bezhetsk, for instance, has a population of 25,200 and includes 1 town soviet and 22 village soviets. In the 1967 elections it had 55 agitpunkty, 15 of them in the town and 40 in the farms of the surrounding county. This means that the collective of each agitpunkt was responsible for slightly fewer than 500 people, of whom, if the nationwide ratio of eligible voters to total population holds good, only about two thirds were of voting age. While it is difficult to determine whether there is any fixed ratio of agitators to population, the above ratio does not seem unusual in that Ulyanovsk, a city of 265,000, divided into 3 urban wards, had 660 agitators and propagandists from the Ulyanov auto factory alone. At a ratio of 3 or 4 agitators to 500 population this would be enough to cover a good portion of the city. The network of agitpunkty not only covers the USSR but reaches out to ships at sea as well. Each Soviet merchantman and warship has its electoral commission and its agitpunkt, headed by senior officers. In this way each and every Soviet citizen is brought into the election campaign and participates in some fashion, however attenuated, in the politics of the country.

The organization of election propaganda is, however, more than a matter of setting forth governmental policies, and the job of the agitator is—at least formally—both to explain and to listen. Thus, *Izvestia* carried the following description of the agitator's function: "The people must understand the Party's work and line, and the Party must know the people's needs." The most intensive implementation of this work comes in the final ten days of the campaign when house-to-house visits are carried out by the agitators. Each agitator may be responsible for visiting 10 to 30 families, depending on the nature of the election district in which he works. In urban areas this may not be very difficult, as 2 or 3 families may share a single apartment, and these may be covered in a single visit. The elicitation of citizens' criticisms of administrative shortcomings and the pinpointing of urgent needs and demands during the local election campaigns are the final links in the long chain of discussing government plans and their implementation, which in Soviet elections takes the place of any discussion of policy choices. Deputies "report" to their electors, executive committees of soviets call plenary sessions to evaluate their work and to sum up their localities' performance in fulfilling national and local plans, and so on up to the pinnacle of the Soviet hierarchy. In this context newspapers often criticize local soviet executives who "have not used the election campaign to the full extent to eliminate serious shortcomings in the activities of cultural institutions and daily services, communal economy, transport, trade and public catering enterprises." Along with this criticism from above, citizens' groups are encouraged to formulate requests for action to be presented to the candidates which the candidates are obliged to accept as mandates from the electorate. In fact, action on many of these citizens' demands must be deferred or abandoned for lack of funds or materials in the framework of the local plan of development and supply. Nevertheless, these requests of the citizenry, dealing mainly with personal and immediate communal needs, become part of the formal record of election meetings, and the percentage of these requests met by the deputy is one of the quantitative measures of his effectiveness. This system is often pointed out as an indication of the Soviet government's solicitude for and responsiveness to its citizens. Such requests are usually made publicly at the election meetings in the presence of the candidates, and it is another of the agitator's tasks to see that these meetings are well-attended, that requests be presented in the proper positive spirit, and that as many citizens as possible hear the candidate at a meeting and meet him and other leading citizens at the voters' club.

The specific content and extent of popular participation in election meetings varies understandably with the individual candidate and the level of soviet for which he is running, but attention to needs on the local level is an ever-present theme in official election presentations. Thus, even when Nikita Khrushchev made a nationally broadcast speech during his 1963 campaign for election to the RSFSR Supreme Soviet from Moscow's Kalinin District, he began by reviewing progress in overcoming the district's housing shortage and speaking of the production accomplishments of the district's industrial enterprises before turning to national and international problems.

Meetings with candidates of national stature are, as they tend to be in any political system, largely formal, but meetings with candidates for local soviets appear to be marked by free exchanges between the audience and the rostrum. This is the result of the deputy's representing a relatively small and homogeneous district, thus engendering a sense of familiarity. It is also a result of the attempt to select local candidates from among the most active and publicly known personalities of the district. This is a fundamental part of the campaign to revitalize Soviet local government which began in 1957 and appears to be continuing to this day. Reapportionment of the electoral districts has resulted in a steady rise in the number of elected deputies from 1,550,000 in the 1957 elections to the recent number of about 2,071,000.* There is, however, a drawback in this constant proliferation of deputies, for it has never been easy to find men of good caliber to fill local deputies' posts, and the difficulty

---

* This number, derived from Moscow *Izvestia*, March 22, 1969, is made up as follows: 2,070,539 deputies elected, 145 deputies rejected, 5 candidates withdrew before election day, 6 elections disqualified for irregularities, elections in 15 Uzbekistani soviets (2 county, 1 city, 12 village, and 1 settlement soviets) postponed because of bad weather.

mounts with the increasing number of jobs and the demands made on the incumbents. A visiting Soviet professor noted recently that the fact that a person has a good name and a reputation as a conscientious citizen does not necessarily mean that he is endowed with the ability to handle the administrative and organizational duties of municipal management. Given the scope of government activity in the Soviet Union, where almost every aspect of everyday commerce and service is dominated or monopolized by the state, the quality of the deputies on the local level and their success in anticipating and answering the needs of the citizenry must play a large part in developing the internal strength of the Soviet political system. Additionally, the elected deputies are the heart of some 20 million citizens who are mobilized to carry on the "voluntary" mass public activity initiated and directed by the local soviets, relieving some of the strain on the paid bureaucracy. In view of the effort made to select prominent candidates and bring them into contact with the public, the finding that less than 10 percent of the citizens of Irkutsk knew their local ward deputies by name seems surprising. It indicates the gap between the theory and successful practice which plagues the effectiveness of local government.

THE NOMINATION PROCESS

Nomination is, in effect, the decisive phase of elections in the Soviet Union, much as it used to be in certain elections in what was once "the Solid South" in the U.S. Only one candidate is nominated in each election district, and nomination may be considered very nearly tantamount to election. The question of participation in the nominating process takes on some importance in the light of this situation, as does the need for understanding what political significance remains in the act of balloting if the election is in effect decided at nomination time.

The role of the Communist party in determining nominations is of some interest here. Regarding national figures who are nominated in more than one district—though by law they may stand as a candidate in only one district—a formal announcement may appear in one of the central newspapers stating that these figures will accept assignment by the party Central Committee to a particular district, declining gratefully the honor of the other nominations. This would seem to be the pattern on the lower levels as well, where it appears that although the Communist party as a body does not place the names of candidates in nomination, it exercises a veto right over any proposed candidacies, and its representatives supervise the preliminary private discussions which lead to the public nomination meeting. The visiting Soviet professor ascribed this reluctance to accept open responsibility for nominations as a precautionary measure intended to protect the prestige of the party should a particular candidate prove to be a failure. Additionally, though he noted that the recall was less frequently used today than in the Twenties, when "many" deputies were recalled, a *Pravda* article (April 14, 1967) notes that during the precedng two years more than 800 local deputies were in fact recalled, and an *Izvestia* article (September 15, 1968) states that 498 were recalled in 1966 alone. The exercise of the right of recall with regard to a deputy is probably facilitated when it cannot be said to be in conflict with a decision initiated publicly by a specific party group or official. Lastly, the party makes nomination an affair of general public responsibility to bolster the image of the candidate as representing the "bloc of Communists and non-Party people" rather than a straight party nominee. Neither are the candidates all Communists. In the 1969 local elections 55 percent of the deputies elected were not party people.

Just as the entire election process is conceived as an affirmation of unity and continuity in Soviet society (expressed, for instance, in the statement, "We believe that once again the elections will show our strength, our unity, our stability under the banner of the Leninist Party"), so is the selection of each deputy viewed as a focus of the unity of the people and the regime. Moreover, an attempt is made to involve as broad a cross section of the population as possible in this process without endangering the prearranged results. Party control is an essential part of the nomination process, but party direction without parallel activization of individuals and groups in the community, organized at every point of social contact—and first and foremost at places of work—would miss one of the prime objects of the election process.

Although formal nomination meetings are held in factories or in mass public rallies, the choice of candidate is made some time in advance, after a series of discussions typically involving the trade-union membership, the leaders of the local soviet, and the local party leaders. At the village level these discussions are relatively simple and appear to center chiefly on the problem of finding sufficient qualified candidates who are not already intensely involved in public service. One problem facing local government in the USSR is that its leading figures are busy men. A recent survey revealed that some 40 percent of local deputies have two or more public assignments in addition to their duties in the local soviet.

At the city or provincial level, the selection of a candidate may involve coordination among several groups at different work places in search of a single candidate to be presented at all the local meetings. The choice of the appropriate candidate is a weighty matter, for though he will not be a significant policy-maker—nor will he in most cases have a great deal of legislating to do—the deputy in a local soviet has a representative and organizing function which requires considerable tact, persistence, even ingenuity, for he is the man who must note and eliminate any friction between the regime and the citizen. In addition, rejection of the candidate at the polls or his recall subsequent to election can only reflect to the detriment of those who proposed him as a candidate, damaging the whole image of enthusiastic unity around which the election revolves.

Thus the pre-election period is marked by calls for intensive discussion in small groups, in shops and kolkhoz brigades "to confer and arrive at a common opinion about the comrades and only then to nominate the one candidate at a meeting of the collective." This point recurs with each new election; it was emphasized once again in the 1967 elections when the chairman of the Central Election Commission of the RSFSR called the nomination process "the most responsible phase of the election campaign.

The nomination brought before a mass public meeting is therefore assumed to have been decided well in advance, and there is generally little surprise or competition even when an additional "honorific" nomination of a national leader is made. The result is that if all goes smoothly the election campaign is given a festive beginning, demonstrative of all the alleged virtues of Soviet government and citizenship. The candidate is generally not present during the nomination but is represented at the meeting by an official supporter who places his name in nomination on behalf of the collective and recites his virtues to the audience with supporting speeches from local dignitaries such as the chairman of the soviet, the factory manager, or a local party dignitary.

There have, however, been exceptions to this supposedly standard form of nomination, and we learn from one Soviet source that the acclaim with which the prearranged nominee is usually greeted may be replaced by a rank-and-file uprising resulting in the rejection of of the proffered candidate. Although no specific details of the subsequent procedure are given, the article implies that a substitute was put forward and nominated at the same meeting. Another case of interest mentioned in the same source concerns two factory assemblies which disagreed regarding the nomination of a candidate— the incumbent chairman of a district executive committee. Having voted, one to accept him and the other to reject him, the two collectives conferred, finally deciding to reject the incumbent and nominate a new candidate for the coming elections.

What are we to make of these phenomena within the framework of the Soviet political system as it is generally understood? Were they to occur in the context of New York City politics, we would look for the emergence of a reform bloc against the ruling machine. Is this to be totally ruled out even at the lowest levels of Soviet politics? The above examples, exceptional as they evidently are, would indicate that there may on occasion be a higher level of political excitement in Soviet elections than has generally been granted by outside observers. Certainly they give us cause to re-examine the nomination process more closely to determine whether these cases were a phenomenon of a particular period (both were mentioned in connection with the 1957 elections) or represent an integral part of Soviet local politics. The existence of all the institutions of representative politics and the mobilization of the population in the election campaign could sometimes result in genuinely or studiedly naïve citizens taking the slogans of democracy seriously and ignoring the rituals imposed from above.

An additional phenomenon in Soviet elections which is generally unexplained in the literature is the dismissal of candidates after their nomination but before election. A discussion of such cases claims that these candidates were dismissed and replaced by others "at the demand of the voters," and that this was due to insufficient all-round discussion of the candidates' qualifications before nomination. This source records 297 such cases in the 1955 elections to the various soviets of the RSFSR and notes that there have been such occurrences even with nomination for Republic Supreme Soviets and for the Supreme Soviet of the USSR. There is no indication as to whether this is a case of the citizens rebelling against arbitrary nominations by local leaders or whether it is a belated veto by higher authority; nor any indication as to how pressure was applied for this switching

of candidates—whether by petition to higher party levels, intraparty
mechanisms of control, or some other method. There is indication,
however, that this is a recurrent problem, for the hortatory editorials
appearing before each election day lay great emphasis on a full
discussion of each candidate's community and production activities
and an attentive hearing of the voters' criticisms of his background.
The editorials take pains to note that this should be done before his
registration as a candidate with the election commission. While
such indications of respect for public opinion are too slender to
support ponderous conclusions—300 cases in a total of some 2
million deputies is as yet a negligible proportion—we once again
have some indication of a hitherto unexpected type of political activity in the Soviet system.

It is worth noting that comparatively few people—and these are
all officials of party or state organizations—play an active role in
choosing the candidates to be presented in nomination. The participation of the ordinary citizen is limited to approval (except for the
occasional instance of dissent) in the public nomination meeting.
Unlike the balloting, the nomination is completely open and the
expression of dissent must be a public rather than private act. One
might expect that the exclusion of the citizen from any participation
in the choice of the person to be nominated would necessarily follow
from the closely controlled nature of the political system; yet the
practice in China, where the electoral system appears to have drawn
many of its features from Soviet practice, shows that this is not
necessarily so. J. R. Townsend notes the Chinese emphasis on direct
contact between the leadership and the masses in the elicitation of
popular participation. With this principle in mind, nominations are
called for and discussed at all levels of the population down to small
groups organized by residence. A multitude of possible nominees are
discussed until the party-desired result of a single approved candidate
for each set is obtained. Though the ultimate result is the same as
that in the Soviet Union, the method followed in winnowing out the
candidates is one of personal discussion with the citizenry by political
activists, rather than deals in a "smoke-filled room" as in the Soviet
case.

One may argue that the nominating system in a party caucus
in a British constituency or in American political conventions is no
more broadly participatory in any effective sense; yet the difference
in the function of the nominations and their place in the environment

of a multiparty system gives an entirely different perspective to the matter. The virtual exclusion of the citizen from that portion of the electoral process which is termed critical by protagonists of the system is strong evidence of the predominance of control as a characteristic of the entire political system.

From the candidate's point of view, his nomination is most definitely a public honor. For the greater part, nomination as a deputy in a local soviet case of "the office seeking the man" rather than vice versa. Deputies serve without remuneration except for travel and lodging expenses incurred when attending sessions of the soviet —a minimal amount in the case of local government. The deputy continues with his regular work, whether in factory, farm, or office, except for daytime sessions of the soviet or work connected with soviet business. Thus, the bulk of the deputies' activities represents an encroachment on leisure time, accepted by the incumbent as a step in a public career, as an earnest of public commitment, as a party assignment, or as public honor and recognition. The ultimate stated aim of Soviet government is to have every citizen participate actively in governing himself, and there are areas in which up to 25 percent of the adult population have been active in some phase of local government. This creates an atmosphere in which acceptance of the burdens of public service becomes a normal part of life, with the perquisites of honor, attention, and "being in" serving as an attraction to offset the burdens.

It is with reference to this element of honor and public trust that Soviet sources often address themselves to the question of the single-candidate system. A Soviet professor remarked that a direct confrontation of two candidates in each constituency would result in an alienation of the 2 million losing candidates in every election. In his view, the losers would be insulted by the implication that they were less trustworthy or less capable than the winners, since there would be no policy differences for the voters to judge. Upon further discussion, however, he noted that the possibility of multi-seat constituencies with perhaps 7 candidates vying for 5 seats, had been considered. The adoption of such a suggestion would, of course, involve a change in many basic aspects of Soviet elections and the quality of citizen participation. The emphasis on complete unity; the idea of a single correct state policy; the nomination process as the locus of decision in the elections; the role of the public as a purely supportive and demonstrative force with no real power to indicate policy preference:

all these would be basically altered by abandoning the single-candidate system. In short, the single-candidate system is an integral part of the culture of Soviet elections, and any change in this could only be part of a much deeper change in the political values prevailing in the USSR.

The involvement of the public in the election campaign is extensive and serves for both the individual citizen's edification and that of the candidates. As mentioned above, teams of agitators reach into literally every home, and the "red corners" and wall newspapers of the factories and public institutions are easily harnessed to the election campaign. More personal contact is provided by what appears to be a relatively new institution, the voters' club. The club is the site of informal meetings with the candidates or other leading officials at which the citizens are encouraged to raise questions or bring requests regarding local or national issues. These evenings are rounded out by the serving of light refreshments and entertainment to help draw a crowd, much in the manner of the open-house evenings held by American candidates. This type of attempt to bring the candidate into direct contact with the public was further "Americanized" in the 1967 elections when a television agitpunkt was opened with direct lines available from the viewers to the candidates in the television studio. The establishment of such points of citizen-candidate communication is, however, not spontaneous, nor is it left to the candidate's initiative. The agitators and propagandists who run these and other campaign activities are drawn from the active core of various permanent bodies. They may be deputies themselves, Communist party officials, workers in the local soviet, or members of the "Society for the Dissemination of Political and Scientific Knowledge."

While some few individuals or small groups may conceivably escape participation in electoral meetings and campaign-related discussions, every effort is made to get a full turnout for the vote itself. As Derek Scott points out, the onus of registration is not on the citizen, but on the local soviet. This is an indication of the state's interest in individual participation.

The act of balloting is the citizen's individual affirmation of his interest in the regime, and not appearing is construed as either apathy or opposition, the one as impermissible as the other. As the individual voting precincts are small, sometimes covering no more than 70 or 80 voters, it is not difficult to maintain control of the population and assure a full turnout. An illustrative anecdote deals with the residents of a house who proclaimed a boycott of the elections in protest against bureaucratic procrastination regarding a hole in their roof. Negotiations and promises failed to soften their stand and only late on election day when tension had mounted considerably did the group appear at the polls remarking diffidently as they balloted that so small a matter as a leaky roof should not lead one to turn against the Soviet regime. To heighten the symbolic importance of balloting and the image of full unity, portable ballot boxes are taken to critically ill voters, and helicopters have been used to ensure isolated herdsmen their right to cast a vote. Those who expect to be absent from home on election day may vote in advance, not an uncommon practice in many countries, but those who must travel unexpectedly may obtain a certificate of their right to vote and cast their ballot in whatever district they find themselves on election day.

The balloting process itself has been likened to a religious ritual. The voter approaches the ballot box, which is generally set on a low dais, flanked by vases of flowers and watched over by a portrait of Lenin. The act of depositing the ballot slip becomes almost an obeisance. Should he wish to be demonstrative of his support of the candidates, the voter may take his ballot directly to the ballot box without availing himself of the polling booth provided so that he may consider the printed instruction on the ballot to "strike out the names of those candidates for whom he does not wish to vote, leaving only one name." Despite the fact that there is only one candidate for each seat, this instruction normally appears on the ballot, though at one time it had been dropped. In the late Thirties, voters were specifically instructed to enter the polling booth as part of the election procedure, but this instruction has been dropped. The proportion of voters using the booth is evidently small, varying among different groups in the population. Max Mote sets the proportion of booth users observed by him in Leningrad as 1 in 10, while Peter Juviler, writing on the basis of earlier observation, notes a range varying from 2 percent to 5 percent in an "ordinary" urban precinct, up to 24 percent in a precinct populated by Moscow University students. Even this seemingly low percentage of booth users far exceeds the percentage of negative votes cast. We may ask why a Soviet citizen should make use of the voter's booth if he has no intention of striking out the candidate's name. Many possible reasons could be offered, but none substantiated. It does, however, seem reasonable to believe that, whatever the most frequent motive or motives may be, they involve some degree of feeling that the voter ought to have the independence to exercise his choice if he so desires. Table 1 indicates the extent of dissent as registered in the 1969 elections in the RSFSR.

We have now seen that the Soviet citizen has little if any influence over the outcome of his elections. Although large numbers of citizens are activated in the organization of elections, and almost all citizens are touched by some phase of campaigning, the citizen as such has

Table 1. Dissenting Votes in 1969 Elections to Local Soviets

Type of soviet	Votes against nominee	Percentage voting against nominee	Spoiled ballots *	Rejections
Territory (Krai)	30,472	0.31	70	0
Province (Oblast')	305,733	0.30	521	0
Autonomous Province (Avtonomnaya Oblast')	3,366	0.31	6	0
National Region (Natsionalnyi Okrug)	3,783	0.65	—	0
County (Raion)	198,345	0.26	149	3
City (Gorod)	326,957	0.40	642	3
Urban Ward (Gorodskoi Raion)	165,834	0.42	231	0
Village (Selo)	182,634	0.30	217	135
Settlement (Poselok)	61,433	0.47	109	4

Source: *Izvestia,* March 22, 1969.

* A spoiled ballot must be considered as the result of opposition to the candidate—for no action is required of the voter to affirm the choice of the nominee.

at most a very marginal voice in the nomination and only the option of rejecting the one candidate running when he votes. Only in pre-election meetings with the candidates can he give some voice to his particular requests, and this, in the circumstances of Soviet politics, severely restricts the range of issues open for discussion. Nevertheless, criticism and dissent are allowed and even approved within the framework of possibilities described here. The elections thus are neither a point of change nor of choice. They are a demonstration of unity, a rallying point at which continuity is pledged, and a testing of the apparatus by which Communist rule is maintained and administered.

Conclusions

The political life of the USSR is marked by the separation of policy-making from policy-implementation. The former is reserved to the upper echelons of the CPSU, while an attempt is made to mobilize as large a portion of the citizenry as possible into playing active roles in the latter. Election campaigns are intended as symbols of unity and continuity, and no effort is spared to rally the citizenry into support of these goals. The Communist party and the soviets are tested as to their mobilizing abilities in this rallying of the citizens.

The elections, though not significantly an instrument of choice, provide legitimation for the representatives of the population, who must transmit the regime's demands to the citizens and attempt to articulate their needs to the regime and, on a simpler level, tend to the many needs which they have, a large part of which are a result of the totally administered nature of Soviet society. This has brought new importance to the role of the deputy and increases the need for finding and training suitable candidates to fill the growing numbers of deputies' positions.

Within the basic parallel framework of soviet and party organs, there have been many attempts to realize Lenin's prescription of involving the mass of citizens in the administration of Soviet society. While the emphasis today has shifted from replacement of a paid professional bureaucracy to supplemental volunteer groups organized under the supervision of deputies of the soviets, the elements of broad mobilization and central control have remained constant. These are the essence of participation by Soviet citizens in their governmental processes.

It should be recognized, however, that this control-based system of mass mobilization carries within it destabilizing elements of its own. As the educational and cultural level of the country rises, the mobilization of the public and the regime's demands for active participation may provide a locus for coalescence of demands upon the regime. Increasing sophistication of the citizenry will almost inevitably result in a consciousness of a lack of autonomy and substantive choice in determination of local affairs. The theme of trust in administrators, trust in the peasants, trust in youth has already been raised in the Soviet press. The common claim of these different groups is that they have reached a level of social and political maturity at which they are capable of self-sustaining activity without strict central control. Yet this demand for broader limits of discretion, which we may designate as an intrasystemic demand for citizen competence, although most important for the future development of citizen participation in the Soviet political system, is only the most constructive of several possible forms of social reaction to the problems engendered by the imperfect performance of a manipulative and control-oriented system.

Soviet materials offer us endless examples of purely *pro forma* activity which can only widen the gap between appearance and reality in the operation of the Soviet system. The repression of citizen competence at the same time that citizen participation is unremittingly urged upon an increasingly sophisticated population which lives in an increasingly diverse and diverting environment, must militate towards the increase in what we may call the "cop-out" tendency. This lowering of the saliency of politics in the citizen's consciousness creates further tensions, for it stands in opposition to a principal regime value.

The third type of reaction is perhaps more complex than the other two. It involves both rejection of the realities of control and manipulation and rejection of the premise of nonconflict of interests within Soviet society, while demanding literal realization of ideal-type values now only nominally espoused by the regime as expressed in the patristic writings of Marxism and the Constitution of the USSR. Such demands—which might eventually range from a multiplicity of candidates to open nominations or multiple parties—if entrenched within the citizen organizations of local government, would offer a basic challenge to the system and, as such, are likely to be met with the strictest possible repression. They are, however, of importance both to decision-makers within the system and to students of it as signals of the extremities of political sentiment to be found among Soviet citizens. In the determination of forms of citizen participation in government, these demands serve to strengthen the credibility and attractiveness of those advocating broader intrasystemic competence as a reform capable of improving the performance of control, penetration and support without dismantling the institutions or values regarded as essential by the regime. An analogous process has been the adoption in economics of the diluted "Libermanist" reforms, which retain many of the basic economic forms existing in the USSR, rather than the more extreme versions of market socialism advocated by other prominent economists.

One of the conscious goals of the Soviet regime has been the diminution of differentiations of interest and outlook among various sectors of Soviet society by postulating an overriding common interest of Soviet citizenship. This is indeed the picture of the mass society suggested by William Kornhauser, in which elites have no autonomy and non-elites no independent group life. Yet this attempt to create a monolithic social unity breaks down on all sides upon contact with the many-sided nature of human activity as well as the necessities of stimulating and directing the cumbersome and complicated machinery of administration which directs and serves this mass society. Stalin maintained the functioning of this system at a much simpler stage of its development through application of unlimited exhortation and unbridled police terror. Current efforts to build a basis of citizen criticism and correction of the administration lead to the growing recognition of competing special interests rather than their diminution, and as various segments of Soviet society are officially encouraged to focus their expertise on the inadequacies of the administration's performance, the value of this expertise rises in the social scale, providing prestige and protection for the social group possessing it. This prestige and protection, providing a measure of limited freedom from control, is a prerequisite for the fostering of independent critical values and group autonomy. We thus return to the conflict between unity and pluralism, between citizen participation and subject participation.

We are led to believe that the present state of Soviet society is unstable and that the tension in it militates in the long run for important changes in the direction of pluralism of social values and forces. However, this tendency has yet to find substantial legitimation within the controlling sector of the society and runs counter to pressures created by international forces as well as by continuing domestic shortcomings in the economic sphere. Control will therefore continue to be the dominant regime consideration in the development of citizen activity in Soviet government.

It should be noted, however, that the social framework erected by the regime to foster its values and policies, serves to encourage the coalescence of independent opinions. The "transmission belts" of

Soviet society may sometimes be thrown into reverse, bringing popular demands to the regime, rather than regime demands to the people. While citizen participation in the elections is centered on support and affirmation rather than policy choices, we note pressures for the broadening of the citizen's scope and for both added competence in the fields granted him and broadened limits of participation.

The United States and the Yemen Crisis in 1962

JOSEPH A. STORK

The Middle East had been relatively quiet since 1958. That year, with the landing of United States troops in Lebanon, seemed to be a watershed for the American policies of the 1950s, characterized by the Baghdad Pact and the Eisenhower Doctrine. A return to normal diplomatic relations with the United Arab Republic took place in the last moments of the Eisenhower Administration. The outline of a policy of cooperation with and neutrality among the Arab states formed a legacy for the Kennedy Administration. The first serious challenge to this approach came in September, 1962, in Yemen.

On the night of September 26, Colonel 'Abdallah al-Salal led a revolt of the Yemeni army against the Imam Mohammed al-Badr and proclaimed Yemen a Republic. The incident precipitated a crisis which involved the diplomacy of the United States for the first time in the Arab world since the Lebanese-Iraqi crisis in the summer of 1958. What ensued was the most serious diplomatic encounter of the Kennedy Administration in the Middle East.

The upheaval in Yemen was a challenge to American economic and strategic interests in the Arabian peninsula and, as such, engaged the attention of the crisis managers in Washington. The dispute, as it quickly evolved, appeared to range the military—mostly arms clients of the Soviet Union—against the traditional, pro-Western monarchies. In addition to the threat of conflict and instability in the area, such polarization seemed to assist an increased Soviet role and presence in the Arab world. The immediate question facing the United States was whether to grant recognition to the Salal regime. This dilemma brought into sharp relief the priorities of American policy in the Arab world. An analysis of the decision to recognize the new Republic provides the means for understanding and evaluating these competing priorities as they reveal themselves in conflict.

The question of recognition was not easily or quickly answered, despite later charges that it was granted precipitously.[1] Before the question was finally resolved three months after the coup (December 19, 1962), the conflict ignited by the coup had developed into a debilitating civil war and had gone beyond the borders of one small country to involve in varying degrees, the United Arab Republic, Saudi Arabia, Jordan, and Great Britain. Yemen had become, in effect, a microcosm of the difficulties and contradictions of United States policy in the Arab world.[2] Recognition had become of correspondingly greater significance both as an instrument and as an expression of United States policy.

Traditionally, diplomatic recognition is regarded as a legal act based upon the fulfillment of objective criteria such as control of the machinery of state and national territory, stability as indicated by the lack of substantial resistance, and the ability and disposition of the new government to fulfill the international obligations of the state.[3] The *Digest of International Law,* prepared for the State Department, tells us:

> The usual and normal practice is that the government of the state from which recognition is sought awaits the receipt of a formal communication from the new government confirming the establishment of the new state or government and requesting recognition.[4]

On October 7, 1962, it was reported that the revolutionary government had complied with this procedure, stating its intention to comply with previous international obligations.[5] The new regime sought American recognition as a legal acknowledgment of its status.

Recognition is also an act of policy whose dynamic aspects are sometimes obscured by static legal concepts. As expressed in the British comments on the International Law Commission in 1949: "There is bound to be considerable scope for political judgement in deciding whether an entity fulfills the conditions for recognition as a

[1] Particularly by syndicated columnists like Joseph Alsop, pro-Israel Senators like Jacob Javits, Thomas Dodd, and Kenneth Keating, and Arab monarchs, Saud and Husein.

[2] John S. Badeau, *The American Approach to the Arab World* (New York, Harper, 1968) p. 123.

[3] Margaret Whitman, *Digest of International Law* (Washington, D.C., 1963) p. 69, and Ti-chiang Chen, *The International Law of Recognition* (London, Stevens, 1951) p. 124.

[4] Whitman, p. 48.   [5] New York *Times,* October 7, 1962.

state." [6] The same point was made by the Inter-American Council of Jurists. "The question as to whether and when a new government that comes into existence is to be recognized is a matter entirely within the discretion of the recognizing government." [7] For the newly arrived incumbents, diplomatic recognition contributes to their prestige and stabilization, is a guarantee against hostile intervention, and increases the chances for economic and political credit. In this instance, all of the interested parties—Yemen, Saudi Arabia, the United Arab Republic, Jordan, Great Britain—were aware of the possible consequences of recognition. There was international political pressure for and against such a decision on the part of Washington. The controversy that later developed around the recognition of the al-Salal government has been compared to the one that surrounded the support of Egypt in 1956.[8] It is testimony to the high political content of the decision. An explication of that policy involves a discussion and evaluation of all the various interests and pressures that had to be dealt with.

Yemen emerged as a sovereign state in the disintegration of the Ottoman Empire after World War I. American recognition, however, did not come until 1946, and a resident legation was not established until 1959, as a countermeasure to economic, military, and technical cooperation initiatives by the Soviet Union and the Chinese People's Republic. In 1959, and in 1962, the mere fact of competition elsewhere granted an importance to Yemen that its size, location, and resources did not warrant. In the years when any coup or struggle, no matter how remote, had to be recorded as a national asset or liability, Yemen could not be ignored. When the revolution came to Yemen, the concern and interest of the United States could be predicted, even if its decisions could not.

The delay and the timing of recognition were parts of United States policy. The republicans actively sought recognition from the beginning in order to bolster their internal and international stature. There appeared to be no reason for supporting the forces of the imam, and there were ten in the diplomatic circle who grieved his passing. The limited American presence in Yemen up to this time had been motivated chiefly by the desire to counter Soviet and Chinese influence and to encourage modernization, in that order.

[6] Whitman. [7] *Ibid*, p. 5.
[8] Dana Adams Schmidt, *Yemen, The Unknown War* (London, Bodley Head, 1968), p. 188.

Both designs, it would seem, would be facilitated by an unambiguous diplomatic presence. The first reports of the United States chargé d'affaires, Robert Stookey, after the coup, indicated that most of the country was in republican control.[9] The accounts of the first journalists to enter the country disclosed no signs or patterns of resistance, and the new government had specifically noted its adherence to its international obligations.[10] The delay was not chiefly a question of formal criteria. The answer must follow from a consideration of the forces for and against recognition.

One United States official, then serving in Saudi Arabia, suggested[11] that although there was little regard or concern for the disappearance of the ancien régime, the political murders of members of the royal family and some of the ministers of government added no stature to the insurgents. But this was no more sanguinary that the standard operating procedure of the imam, and the proponents of progress might note, along with Abdallah al-Salal, that the condemned were no longer beheaded, but shot. It was also observed that the alleged requests for recognition were made in the form of demands and that Mr. Stookey had refused even to transmit them until they were put in a more acceptable form. Also at issue was the alleged noncooperative and harassing behavior of the new officials toward the United States representative. There is no corroboration for these explanations, however, including the accounts of James Cortada, who succeeded Stookey as chargé in February, 1963, or of Dana Adams Schmidt, no friend of the republicans.[12]

A significant element in the arguments against recognition soon became the fact that there was indeed some Yemeni opposition to the new government, and this factor was strengthened by the subsequent re-emergence of Iman Mohammed al-Badr, who was thought to have been killed the night of the coup. As previous attempts at revolt in 1948 and 1955 indicate, there was good reason for trying to eliminate the imam and thereby remove a likely catalyst for reaction. There is no guarantee, however, that even if the republicans had succeeded in eliminating al-Badr, they would have spared traditional tribal opposition to that regime. Deputy Prime Minister Abdal-

[9] New York *Times,* October 7, 1962.
[10] *The Times* (London), October 9, 1962.
[11] In a private conversation.
[12] James Cortada, *The Yemen Crisis* (Los Angeles, 1964), pp. 6–9; and Schmidt.

Rahman al-Baydani, in addition to claiming general support, noted on October 9 that this included the largest tribal confederations, the Hashid and the Baqil, a statement which is notable, if not for its accuracy, at least for the awareness of the problem.[13] Sayf al-Islam al-Hasan, uncle of al-Badr and erstwhile rival to his throne, had immediately left his post at the United Nations to return to Yemen "to restore order." [14]

Republican claims of tribal support were not entirely spurious, particularly in the initial months following the coup. The recently deceased Imam Ahmad had done much to alienate some tribes; they hardly expected more than vacillation from al-Badr. Their support, however, was not the result of any ideological ardor or political commitment. In addition to their innate opposition to any significant societal transformation, the Zaydis could be expected to rely on their warlike attributes to oppose the development of a system which would favor the better educated, more adaptable Shafi'is.[15] In other instances, tribal support was based even less firmly in the traditional feuds which had nothing to do with the imam or the imamate. If one's traditional enemy joined the royalists, that was reason enough to join the republicans. Even more tenuous was the cooperation elicited through cash subsidies, a method of support as traditional as it is flimsy.[16] One does not have to go outside Yemen to explain the coup, and there is no evidence for the assertion that it was conceived and directed from Cairo with the objective of establishing an Egyptian base on the peninsula. There is nothing sinister about the alliance which was quickly formed between Salal and Egypt. Prerevolutionary ties, both official and clandestine, between the two countries were considerable; Yemen was considered to be in the Egyptian camp, as expressed in the voting patterns of the League of Arab States and the United Nations.[17] The existence of a sizable

[13] See the Chronology in *The Middle East Journal* (Spring, 1963), pp. 141–42.

[14] New York *Times,* October 9, 1962.

[15] William R. Brown, "The Yemeni Dilemma," *The Middle East Journal* (Autumn, 1963), p. 365.

[16] Kathryn D. Boals, "Yemen: Modernization and Intervention," a paper presented to the Middle East Studies Association in Austin, Texas, November, 1968 (mimeo). Also see Peter Somerville-Large, *Tribes and Tribulations* (London, 1968), pp. 136–55 *passim.*

[17] Robert MacDonald, *The League of Arab States* (Princeton, Princeton University Press, 1965), p. 79.

Free Yemeni movement in Cairo made it natural for the new leaders to look to President Nasser for diplomatic support and material sustenance.[18] They were able to cite the Jiddah Pact of 1956 to justify the military assistance asked for, although the Saudis used this same pact to justify their own support for the other side.[19]

The chief link between the two countries after the coup was the intense revolutionary character of the political, economic, and social objectives they shared. Diplomatic recognition came on September 29, and the decision to offer more concrete support was made at about this same time.[20] Reports of Egyptian arms and advisers in or on the way to Yemen were frequent in the first days of October. In conjunction with this material support, there was considerable talk in the first few weeks of some of union or federation with the U.A.R., but Cairo soon indicated that it was not ready for such a move.[21] Coming just a year after the split with Syria, the decision to intervene in Yemen was probably influenced by that event in curious ways. On the one hand, it created the need for President Nasser to reassert his prestigious role in the Arab world. At the same time, it had the effect of confirming the concept of union as something which can take place only after there has been a revolutionary transformation of the political and economic structure of a country. This view, that union must reflect rather than create the transformation, was soon to be articulated in the unity talks with Iraq and Syria in the spring of 1963.

The reluctance to forge a formal union did not prevent the Egyptians from attempting to contribute substantially to the transformation of Yemen. The lack of a coherent ideology, the shortage of trained men, the absence of modern institutions—all these were areas in which the Egyptians felt they could provide assistance. Indeed, the civil war and Egyptian military involvement have all but obscured the nonmilitary dimensions of the U.A.R. relationship with Yemen. In education, public administration, fiscal reform, and other areas, Egypt made considerable contributions towards the development of a more modern society. The enormity of the task has dwarfed their significance.

Once the Egyptians decided to lend support to the new govern-

[18] Badeau, pp. 126–28.

[19] Manfred Wenner, *Modern Yemen: 1918–1966* (Baltimore, Johns Hopkins University Press, 1967), p. 187.

[20] Badeau, p. 127.   [21] New York *Times,* October 7 and 16, 1962.

ment, they saw that the most pressing and immediately threatening problem facing the modernizers was the developing disaffection and growing armed resistance among tribes to the north and east. The fears and antagonisms of the Zaydis towards the Shafi'is were exploited by the Sayyid ruling class in general and the royal family in particular.[22] If they were not to suffer the fate of earlier coups, the republicans needed help. The standing army was relatively small, and its reliability unknown. To avoid being overthrown before they could even begin to come to grips with the problems, it was natural for them to turn to the United Arab Republic, and, given its avowed position of progressive leadership in the Arab world, it was natural for the U.A.R. to respond. As a result, there was some concern in Washington over the role of the U.A.R. and at least part of the debate over recognition focused on whether al-Salal was his own man and the coup was a genuinely Yemeni attempt to create a new political order.[23]

The considerable role which the Egyptians played in the months following the coup can account in some part for the delay in American recognition, but by itself did not warrant the extensive diplomatic involvement which did occur. This was the result of the hostility of Saudi Arabia to the new and radical political entity on its borders, as expressed in the arms and money sent to sustain the royalist faction. The Egyptian presence in Yemen might by itself account for the Saudi involvement, but hostility towards the new regime was a fact from the first days of the revolution. King Saud was sensitive to the implications of an antimonarchical revolt on the peninsula. Although there was no organized resistance to Saudi rule within the kingdom, there was considerable disaffection with the rule of Saud himself. The history of the internal affairs of Saudi Arabia during the preceding years was essentially the history of a struggle for power within the royal family. There was no violence, and its outward manifestations were few beyond some changes in office, diplomatic assignments, and a growing controversy over the issue of constitutional reform.

After the death of King Abd al-'Aziz in 1953 there was competition between Saud, who had succeeded to the throne, and Emir Feisal, who was his junior but much more capable. Having been invested as crown prince, Feisal took over much of the executive power

[22] Boals, "Yemen."   [23] New York *Times,* October 7, 1962.

in 1958 after Saud had been exposed in financing a plot to assassinate
President Nasser. Feisal's fiscal policy of retrenchment later alienated
powerful interests within the royal household as well as certain
tribes. This aided Saud in staging a comeback. The third faction
within the royal family was that small group of emirs led by Talal,
who advocated some measure of constitutional reform while retain-
ing the monarchy. This group had the support of the still small but
growing intelligentsia and the commercial and professional middle
class in Hijaz. Feisal did not favor this approach, and, in fact, much
of his support came from traditional and conservative religious leaders opposed to the incompetence and profligacy of Saud and his
sons. The king was shrewd enough to campaign for the support of
those favoring constitutional reform, but, after he had maneuvered
Feisal's resignation as prime minister in December, 1960, nothing
more came of this professed support.

Emir Talal and his opposition to Saud's regime became public in
the weeks just before the Yemen coup. While traveling outside the
country, he telegraphed congratulations to Nasser on the occasion
of the successful firing of some Egyptian-made rockets. Saud reacted
by confiscating Talal's property. At a Beirut press conference, Talal
ascribed this breach of the Islamic code to his constant advocacy of
constitutional reform while serving as finance minister. Saud's response was to take Talal's passport away, who thereupon went to
Cairo to organize the opposition of other expatriates.[24]

King Saud's reaction to the coup in Yemen was instinctive and
immediate. Some United States officials maintain that this hostility
would have remained dormant had it not been for the Egyptian
intervention. Yet, as early as October 2, *The Times* (London) noted
that "speculation continues about the strong tribes in the northern
Yemeni highlands and Saudi Arabian attempts to get them to rise
up against the new republican government." In a few days it was no
longer a matter for speculation. On October 3, the republicans issued
a warning to the Saudis against supporting or sheltering the imam
and the royal family. If the imam had not survived, King Saud probably would have backed another member of the royal family, like
Sayf al-Islam al-Hasan, who was already in Jidda claiming enough
tribal support to oust the "treacherous clique" in San'a. On the
same day, the first of several Saudi pilots defected to Aswan with a

[24] New York *Times,* August 16, 1962; *The Economist* (London), August
25, 1962.

planeload of American arms allegedly destined for the royalists.[25] Once Hasan and the imam had taken refuge with the kingdom, for Saud it became a question of *sharaf*—one does not turn away one who comes seeking help.

In trying to assess the question of who provoked whom, of whether the Egyptians had poured in troops, calling for a Saudi response, or whether it was the considerable support and assistance provided by Saud, along with the troops he had massed along the border, which prompted President Nasser to send his expeditionary forces, the answers would probably remain ambiguous even if one had access to all the facts. Each side used these alliances to castigate the other as puppets and extol themselves as the representatives of the Yemeni people. It can hardly be doubted, moreover, that this syndrome involved more than political chicanery: the republicans were convinced that the real motivation behind the tribal opposition lay in the arms and money of the Saudis and the British. On the other side, the rapid and extensive support of President Nasser persuaded the Saudis and the imam that the revolution was, *au fond,* part of the Egyptian imperial design for the Arabian Peninsula. King Saud suspected that the threat to his royal integrity was based on his huge oil reserves and the relative poverty of his revolutionary brethren. What is clear is that in the first days after the coup the sides were taken and each move by the other was interpreted as requiring and justifying an escalated response.

The opposition of King Husein of Jordan to the Yemen revolution can be ascribed to many of the factors cited in the discussion of Saudi Arabia, although oil and a proximity to Yemen were not among them. Husein, like Saud, feared the ideological motives of his republican opponents in fostering the concept of Arab unity and promoting regicide and revolution as a means to that noble end. Within the only surviving Hashemite Kingdom, political opposition was much more substantial than it was in Saudi Arabia. The majority of the population consisted of Palestinians who were particularly receptive to Cairo propaganda. On many occasions in the past, only the personal resourcefulness of King Husein preserved his position, and he was wary lest the forces of republicanism might move against him once more. The revolution in Yemen was seen in this light, and, if only because of "the enemy of my enemy is my friend" attitude, the king was disposed to help the deposed.

[25] *The Middle East Journal* (Spring, 1963), pp. 141–42.

In addition, relations with the United Arab Republic had not been good prior to the crisis over Yemen. A truce in the propaganda war which had been in effect after August, 1959, broke down the following winter. Jordan's quick recognition of Syria in 1961 did nothing to improve things. A rapprochement with Iraq began to take the shape of an informal coalition against the U.A.R. Several times in the summer of 1962, Jordanian Prime Minister Wasfi al-Tall charged that the Jordanians had uncovered Egyptian-inspired plots to assassinate Husein.[26] Just prior to the Yemen revolution, the meeting of the Arab League in Shtura, Lebanon, in August, revealed and contributed to the deep fissures of inter-Arab politics. The meeting had been called to hear Syrian charges of Egyptian interference in Damascus politics, but the U.A.R. took the initiative in demanding apologies from Syria and, getting none, walked out.[27] Amid rumors and threats that the U.A.R. might quit the league altogether, the Syrians and Jordanians accused President Nasser of slackening his opposition to Israel as the price of continued United States support and aid, and they interpreted his walkout as playing into the hands of the Zionists and imperialists by weakening the common Arab cause. These events point up the fact that there was considerable opposition to the United Arab Republic, that this was being articulated well before the Yemen crisis, and that the beleaguered U.A.R. could be expected to seize the chance for a committed ally such as was presented by the coup. They might also explain why the league was never utilized in the first years of the dispute, despite Syria's proposal to do so in early November.[28]

The Jordanian alliance with Saudi Arabia preceded the threat from the south, even though Saudi Arabia had not taken the initiatives against Nasser in the dispute within the league. The shared bitterness of the two kings towards the Egyptian president was articulated in a communiqué of August 29, 1962, announcing a military and economic merger of the two countries.[29] To all appearances, Jordanian support of the royalists in Yemen was limited to the diplomatic and propaganda spheres, although several Jordanian pilots, including the chief of the air force, defected to the U.A.R.[30] On several occasions the Jordanians threatened to intervene actively

---

[26] *The Times* (London), August 9 and 19, 1962.
[27] New York *Times*, August 24, 1962; *The Economist*, September 1, 1962.
[28] *The Times* (London), November 7, 1962.
[29] New York *Times*, August 30, 1962.   [30] *Ibid.*, November 14, 1962.

and gave unqualified diplomatic support and encouragement to Saud, al-Badr, and al-Hasan.[31] The royalist embassy in 'Amman became the chief outlet for news of royalist offensives, victories, and assorted propaganda. The defection of the pilots and the earlier resignation of the vice-president of the Development Board, Kamal al-Sheir, indicates that support was also financial and military. At the time of his resignation, al-Sheir gave his government's Yemen policy as the reason.[32] Two days later, he became more explicit and countered official denials by maintaining that there were several hundred Jordanian officers in Yemen or in Saudi Arabia in direct connection with the conflict. Moreover, this support had resulted in a supplementary military budget of $3 million.[33]

The other Arab states remained out of the conflict. Aside from the kings—Saud, Husein, and Hasan of Morocco—they quickly granted recognition, but engaged in no other forms of support. There remained one other very interested party, however. Related to the confrontation of the U.A.R. and Saudi Arabia was the position of the British at the southern end of the peninsula. The traditional instability of the Yemeni-Protectorate border would now be compounded by the anti-imperialist propaganda that could be expected to come from Cairo and be echoed in San'a, amplified by the traditional irredentism of the Yemenis. In the beginning, al-Salal made some attempts to encourage or at least not discourage British recognition by muting calls for union with the protectorate after an initial flush of enthusiasm in that direction.[34] He was conscious of the need to avoid any provocation that might bring about British intervention, and he saw the need of eliminating them as a source of funds and arms to the dissidents.[35]

Such intervention was forthcoming. Dana Adams Schmidt wrote from Jidda in the middle of November about the growing momentum of the royalists, noting that along with arms, equipment, and money from Saudi Arabia and Jordan, they also had "British equipment that has been slipped across the border from the South Arabian Federation at Beihan." [36] Several weeks later, he interviewed al-Hasan, now the royalist premier, in a cave in Beihan.[37] David Ver-

---

[31] *Ibid.,* October 17 and 22, 1962; *The Times* (London) November 5, 1962.
[32] New York *Times,* October 18, 1962.   [33] *Ibid.,* October 21, 1962.
[34] *The Economist,* October 20, 1962; *The Times* (London), October 9, 1962.
[35] *Ibid.,* October 16, 1962.   [36] New York *Times,* November 13, 1962.
[37] *Ibid.,* December 2, 1962.

rier, a British journalist from the area, told me that British assistance was in fact much more substantial than that of Saudi Arabia. Ambassador Hart agreed that British support was considerable, although he doubted it exceeded that of Saudi Arabia, given the volume of the latter. All this prompted the republicans to bomb supply and staging areas in Beihan in late October.[38]

The British denied charges of interference and protested the attacks on protectorate territory, but the arms and funds were getting across. On one occasion, when Deputy Prime Minister al-Baydani charged that British arms were still entering from Beihan, the British government announced the delivery of £1.5 million sterling worth of military supplies to the federation army.[39] The revolution, after all, had come just at the time of the merger of Aden with the western protectorate to form the South Arabian Federation. The internal opposition to this plan, consisting mainly of Yemeni trade unionists, had been vocal and violent. With the end of the anachronistic oppression to the north, the imamic obstacle to a movement for unity on the part of Adeni radicals no longer existed.

The federation scheme had been seen as an answer to the territorial claims of Yemen.[40] The British proposal was approved by the legislative council of Aden on the eve of the revolution.[41] Almost immediately a delegation of anxious sheikhs from the federation flew to London to confer with Colonial Secretary Duncan Sandys.[42] With them was the agent for the western protectorate and one of the architects of the federation plan, Kennedy Trevaskis. They asked for, and apparently got, more British troops for their borders, British officers for their own troops, so as to eliminate the danger of homegrown coups, and more funds.[43] Officials who were familiar with the problems surrounding British policy on the peninsula felt that British recognition of the republicans would focus attention on some sort of Greater South Arabia, and this would probably mean the end of the base at Aden. All the British political and diplomatic stratagems in South Arabia both before and after the coup were designed to accommodate the lingering presence of the "Gibraltar of

---

[38] *Ibid.,* October 23, 1962; *The Times* (London), October 23, 1962.
[39] *The Economist,* December 8, 1962.
[40] Kennedy Trevaskis, *Shades of Amber* (London, Hutchinson 1968), p. 43.
[41] *The Middle East Journal* (Spring, 1963), p. 105.
[42] *The Times* (London), October 5, 1962.
[43] *Ibid.,* October 11, 1962.

the East," [44] the largest bunkering port in the world and one of the largest R.A.F. stations as well.[45] This called for a friendly, stable Yemeni government, and the British were confident that the United States shared this concern.[46]

Official British policy [47] emphasized the need for a British military presence in Aden to safeguard oil interests in the Gulf, and in this the Labour opposition concurred.[48] The underlying assumption of this policy is that the United Kingdom has a special responsibility for the defense of Western interests and the maintenance of peace in the Indian Ocean and the Persian Gulf, including East Africa.[49] Another significant part of the British rationale is the necessity of honoring treaty obligations towards the sheikhs of the protectorates. The Colonial Office, from all accounts, was opposed to the recognition of the new regime at all costs. They left no doubt that they would regard such a move as a betrayal of their allies in the federation.[50]

After the revolution this policy came under increasing criticism from the press and presumably underwent the further scrutiny of the Foreign Office, where it seemed that the debate in the State Department was being repeated with a British accent. Great Britain had already retreated from base to base, from Suez, and from Kenya, each one once regarded as essential to the British global position. Having devised the South Arabian Federation as an answer to demands for decolonialization, the British were not about to take further steps to come to terms with what they saw as "the mordant spirit of revolution . . . on the prowl, threatening the established foundation of our Middle East power." [51]

In sum, the interests of allies and other friendly countries in the area were not all congruent with those of the United States. The dilemma was dramatically encapsulated by a paragraph in *the New York Times,* on October 7, noting that the armies of Saudi Arabia, Jordan, and Great Britain stood poised on the borders, ready to intervene. That dispatch may have been overly dramatic, in that the several countries were not about to rush into Yemen in full battle

---

[44] Trevaskis, p. xv.   [45] *Spectator,* July 26, 1963.

[46] Charles Johnston, *The View from Steamer Point* (London, 1968), p. 161.

[47] As stated in the Defense White Papers of 1960 and 1962.

[48] New York *Times,* May 13, 1964.

[49] Gillian King, *Imperial Outpost: Aden* (London, 1967), pp. 5–10.

[50] Johnston, pp. 105, 124.   [51] Trevaskis, p. 36.

regalia. A more accurate description suggests a more subtle but equally explosive configuration. Troops did not go into Yemen, by all accounts, except those of the United Arab Republic, but by October 7 the battle had been effectively joined.

The Middle-East policy of the Kennedy Administration was already evoking criticism and comment well before the Yemen crisis, especially with regard to the U.A.R. United States assistance, mostly agricultural products under PL 480, were blamed by some for providing the wherewithal for the purchase of Soviet MIG aircraft.[52] Israeli concern over the detrimental effects of any *modus vivendi* between the United States and the U.A.R. had prompted a visit to Tel Aviv by one of the President's special assistants, Myer Feldman, in late August.[53]

The rise in hostility towards President Nasser within and among the other Arab states was significant chiefly because it seemed to assume the United States as placing its hopes in and money on the Egyptian leader.[54] In the context of the line-up for and against the new regime in Yemen, it was clear that a decision by the United States to recognize al-Salal could be construed as a move supporting Nasser. This became increasingly so as the republicans became more completely identified with the Egyptians. While the United States might have its own reasons for recognizing al-Salal, the vindication it would represent for Nasser was not an insignificant factor.

By the same token, any decision could not ignore the American interest in maintaining a working relationship with the U.A.R. The influence of a country like the United States in the Arab world is a crucial but nebulous thing. In many instances, mutuality of interests is obvious enough. In other cases it is less well-defined. For the United States, a polarization of the powers behind opposing countries or alliances would not serve the purposes of clients or mentors, particularly in a crisis of this sort. The Kennedy Administration shared the opinion that movements for political, social, and economic change could not be ignored except at the peril of those who value stability most.[55] Kennedy had been seeking a more progressive American image in the area. Recognition of the Yemen Arab Republic could help augment some needed diplomatic mobility in the Arab world.

[52] *Congressional Record* (June 29, 1962), Vol. 108, Pt. 9, pp. 12237–38.

[53] New York *Times,* August 22 and 24, 1962. The visit was billed as private, not official.

[54] *Ibid.,* September 23, 1962.   [55] Badeau, p. 19.

Mobility and influence are only important if we ask: For what? They are not ends in themselves, and in this case they were seen as means for dealing with some very specific interests. The primary interest and concern which the United States perceived as threatened by the crisis was the stability and general well-being of the Saudi Arabian government. For if the U.S. had no economic interests in Yemen *per se,* the operations of American oil companies in Saudi Arabia provided sufficient impetus for the United States to involve its prestige and diplomatic efforts in maintaining stability and a modicum of tranquillity on the rest of the peninsula.

The accessibility of oil was an indirect but not inconsiderable factor in responding to the crisis. Oil imports to this country from the Middle East were minimal, but the NATO countries and U.S. bases and fleets were highly dependent on Middle Eastern oil. The U.S. could not be disinterested in the effects of any impairment of the military and industrial capabilities of its allies. The instability of Saudi rule and the lack of an alternative to the royal family made the fragmentation of the kingdom a potential danger. In addition, United States companies controlled 60 percent of the proved resources in the Middle East and had full control of Aramco in Saudi Arabia. The disintegration would inevitably effect the small oil-rich states and protectorates along the Gulf littoral of the peninsula as well.

In 1963, petroleum accounted for 32 percent of all United States direct investment abroad, but produced 55 percent of the income from this total direct investment. Petroleum investments in Asia and Africa, which means the Middle East and North Africa, were only 10 percent of the total direct investment abroad, but accounted for 35 percent of the same total income.[56] In 1966, trade and investment in the Middle East and North Africa produced a net inflow of $1.66 billion into the United States,[57] a sum lent added importance by the general balance of payments problem. *The Wall Street Journal* has offered the observation that Aramco's crude oil reserves are "more than twice as large as those contained in the entire United States" and that public scrutiny of their closely guarded books "would probably show that it has the highest profit margin of any billion-dollar plus corporation in the world." [58] A report by the Arthur D.

[56] *Survey of Current Business* (September, 1967), p. 45, Table 6.
[57] George Lenczowski, *United States Interests in the Middle East* (Washington, D. C., 1968), p. 39.
[58] March 14, 1966.

Little firm for OPEC disclosed that between 1956 and 1960, the average yearly net profits on the investments of Aramco was 61 percent, based on net earnings, minus taxes, in relation to investment.[59]

Any developments that put the continued existence and stability of the present regime in doubt called for United States involvement to counter the threat.[60] Emir Feisal was in Washington at the time of the coup and had lunch with President Kennedy the first week in October, where it can be presumed that he made a strong case against recognition.[61] As the Egyptian presence grew more pronounced and when Feisal later assumed responsibility as premier and after Egyptian bombs had fallen on Saudi villages near the border in November, this opposition grew more firm. On November 6, Saudi Arabia broke off relations with the United Arab Republic, thus making the issue more clearly an Egyptian-Saudi confrontation.[62]

Some U.S. officials believe that the Egyptians came into Yemen with every intention of bringing down the Saudi Arab regime. They feel that the Egyptians were probably misled by reports of discontent within the kingdom to suppose that their presence, along with some forays and bombings and some inaccurate arms drops would be enough to catalyze a popular movement that would overthrow the monarchy and replace it with a republican government with a penchant for economic and political reform. This view maintains that Egyptian bombings across the border were neither retaliatory nor accidental in nature, but rather calculated probings.

President Nasser did not seem reluctant to use the events in Yemen to embarrass the Saudis by helping to establish a radical alternative next door. It is also possible that he was unduly optimistic with regard to a possible revolution in Saudi Arabia, as the drop of arms in Saudi territory seems to indicate. This hope was the fear of Saudis and Americans, that the days of the House of Saud were numbered. But the burden of proof remains with those who maintain that Nasser seriously entertained an Egyptian expedition into Saudi Arabia. The geography of the peninsula would be quite enough to stop any army the Egyptians could field, even if the Yemeni royalists were less successful.

The State Department appeared to consider that the chief threat

[59] Published in *Il Punto*. See *The Middle East Journal* (Spring, 1963), p. 105.
[60] Badeau, p. 25.   [61] New York *Times*, October 7, 1962.
[62] MEJ, p. 133. *The Middle East Journal* (Spring, 1963), p. 133.

to the Saudis stemmed from their commitment to the royalists rather than directly from the Egyptians. The subdued but persistent conflict between Saud and Feisal, with the public prodding of Talal as a backdrop, testified to the strains of dissatisfaction with Saud's handling of policy both domestic and foreign. The post-haste involvement with the insurgent royalists created new strains on the fabric of governmental stability. The loyalties of various groups and factions to the House of Saud had deteriorated to the point where they were no longer a sufficient bulwark against any indigenous or foreign revolutionary effort.

Opposition to Saudi policy in Yemen came from those members of the Cabinet who were not members of the royal family. Some argued for recognition of the republican regime; all opposed support for the imam and his retinue. Much of the armed forces in the middle levels of command also opposed the king, though not openly. They did not think it would be in Saudi Arabia's interest to identify itself so clearly with reaction. At the same time, they feared the effects of such a drain on the economy which was already in serious trouble as a result of Saud's mismanagement. This concern was shared by more conservative factions as well. They also worried about the outcome of any military confrontation with the relatively modern and well-equipped army of the U.A.R. Political instability would follow defeat. In this connection, the defections of three Saudi planes and their crews in the first week of October was viewed as ominous.[63]

In the middle of October, Saud, probably under duress, recalled Feisal to form a new Cabinet and serve as premier. This was viewed as a favorable development in Washington, where Feisal was regarded as a shrewd and capable leader. This did not immediately change the course of Saudi policy, though, and the pressures of the crisis were not alleviated. Feisal, like Saud, saw a real threat in the Egyptian presence to the south. In the beginning of November, he dismissed the six commoners who had been in the Cabinet. This indicated that the Saudi commitment to the royalist cause would be strengthened, and with Feisal's backing, if not his sponsorship.

The crux for the United States thus appeared to be one of satisfying both the Saudi and Egyptian positions and thereby maintaining an uneasy peace outside the borders of Yemen. The question of recognition came to be perceived as a means to that end. Specifically, it might stabilize the republican regime, allowing it to dispense with

[63] *Ibid.,* p. 132.

Joseph A. Stork

extensive Egyptian military assistance. Egyptian disengagement might convince the Saudis to end their support of the royalists. Without Saudi support, the opposition would be incidental and not serious. Just as the confrontation had grown by mutually reinforcing steps, so too would it hopefully diminish.

With regard to the interests of Jordan and Great Britain, the former was not central to the debate over recognition. Washington had the same fears for Jordan as for Saudi Arabia. Stability had never been more than a relative condition in the volatile politics of Jordan. Moreover, in the event of any insurrection, the involvement of Israel and a great power confrontation became a danger. However, this was obvious and it was not as difficult to convince King Husein that his best interests lay in disengagement as it was to convince the Saudis. Use of the substantial U.S. aid fund as a means of overcoming any reluctance in this regard was also a possibility not at hand with Saudi Arabia.[64]

The question of recognition was more relevant in dealing with Great Britain. From the start a deference to the wishes of that ally was used to explain the American delay.[65] Officially Great Britain continued to maintain that recognition was contingent upon the full control of the republican government. British policy in this period has been described as "searching for reasons to do nothing." [66] When, towards the end of November, there had been a noticeable pause in claims by al-Salal to protectorate territory, the British seemed to require a categorical disavowal of such ambitions. In a sense, the revolution had touched the core of the problem of British policy in the middle East: should Britain accommodate itself to radical Arab nationalism or should its policy be based on the defense of existing interests and the fulfillment of existing commitments.[67]

British policy-making is hardly a monolithic enterprise, but in this instance there was a solid, influential body of opinion logically based in the past that demanded nonrecognition, and got it. Thus Tom Little describes Colonial Secretary Sandys as "ready to fight the Foreign Office or any members of the Cabinet guilty of what he considered wooly thinking in regard to a deal with left-wing Arab nationalism." In his policy, if not in his attitude, Sandys was backed by the authorities in Aden and the federal rulers, who perceived the

[64] New York *Times*, October 8, 1963.   [65] *Ibid.*, October 7, 1962.
[66] Trevaskis, p. 182.
[67] Tom Little, *South Arabia* (London, Pall Mall, 1968) p. 94.

threat to their designs.[68] With this in mind, the question of republican control and British clandestine intervention becomes inseparable. Little's account, sympathetic to the Colonial officials, describes their plight and implies their solution:

The situation was at its worst in early October because there was no evidence of any royalist resistance to the republic, and therefore it seemed inevitable that the republic would be recognized by Britain. . . . In Aden the populace was solidly on the side of the republic. . . . Even in the tribal areas the message was having its effect. . . .

When it became known that there was royalist resistance and that Imam Muhammad al-Badr was alive and speaking, the situation somewhat improved, at least as far as the British government was concerned, for it was now much easier to argue against recognition.[69]

On several occasions, U.S. recognition appeared to be forthcoming, only to be postponed for one reason or another, such as deference to an ally [70] or some bellicose statement by al-Salal.[71] If United States recognition was to work, however, in being the first step down the rungs of escalation, there had to be some assurance that the other parties would descend accordingly. The daily in recognition, therefore, seems to have been the result of the U.S. trying to get the parties concerned, the U.A.R., Saudi Arabia, and Britain, to agree to a schedule of moves that would end outside intervention and bring an end to the pressures on the Saudis and the potential of a larger war.

One of the first public moves in this direction came near the end of November when President Kennedy sent letters to al-Salal, Nasser, and Feisal with suggestions for ending the conflict on the basis of self-determination.[72] President al-Salal welcomed Kennedy's offer of mediation, while al-Badr protested that he had not been consulted.[73] Emir Feisal rejected the U.S. proposals, specifically an appeal to end assistance to the royalists. In his reply to Kennedy, Feisal noted that Saudi Arabia still regarded the imam as the legal ruler and his government as the one supported by the Yemeni people. Moreover, he was confident of a royalist victory.[74]

President Nasser, in his reply, denied any intention of occupying Yemen. The Egyptian leader went further and tried to define for

[68] *Ibid.,* pp. 95–96.   [69] *Ibid.,* pp. 96–97.
[70] New York *Times,* October 7, 1962.   [71] *Ibid.,* November 17, 1962.
[72] *Ibid.,* November 22, 1962; *The Middle East Journal* (Spring, 1963), p. 104.
[73] *Ibid.,* p. 143.   [74] New York *Times,* November 30, 1962.

himself the consequences of United States recognition, which was part of the offer to mediate. As Nasser saw it, such a move would be evidence of American good faith and nonintervention and in addition it would be an important lever in getting Saudi Arabia and Britain to cease their aid.[75] Cairo Radio's protests to the contrary notwithstanding, the U.A.R. was very much interested in obtaining American recognition for their Yemeni allies, although they may have exaggerated the effect of such a move on their Saudi and British opponents.

By the middle of December, it was becoming increasingly difficult for the United States and its aid programs to remain in Yemen without granting recognition, and it was probably this pressure that finally brought it to pass on December 19. On several occasions al-Salal had threatened to turn to the Soviets for aid [76] and had broadly hinted that the AID mission might be terminated. Russian arms shipments and other forms of assistance had been stepped up after the coup, and in a sense the Soviet presence and its possible expansion was the underlying motive for American involvement. The United States felt that it had to stay in Yemen both to forestall further Soviet influence and to negotiate some sort of truce with the contending area powers.

When recognition finally came, it was not a negotiated solution, but only set the scene for further diplomatic efforts. In the first place, the Saudi Arab Government still declined to agree to any timetable for terminating its aid, insisting that the removal of all Egyptian forces was a precondition. Great Britain, in some ways the chief cause for the delay, indicated that there was no early prospect for their recognition. By December, a decision could no longer wait. The precise timing of the decision was left to be worked out between the United States, the Yemen Arab Republic and the United Arab Republic. On December 18, the Y.A.R. issued a statement which included a reaffirmation of its international obligations and its intent to live in peace and harmony with its neighbors. Later the same day, the U.A.R. supported that with its own statement and "signified its willingness to undertake a reciprocal expeditious disengagement and phased removal of its troops" contingent upon the termination of Saudi and Jordanian support for the royalists. United States recognition came the next day, in a statement that took full note of the Yemeni declaration and welcomed the U.A.R. statement as well,

[75] *Ibid.*, December 2, 1962.   [76] *Ibid.*, October 12, 1962.

seeing them both as "a basis for terminating the conflict over Yemen." [77] The United States took particular note of the Treaty of San'a with Britain in 1934, apparently still hopeful that the British would climb aboard.

United States recognition was technically based on republican control of most of the country and adherence to international obligations. Its motives were to provide the basis for a continued American presence in the country and influence with all the parties. A careful reading of the statements and a consideration of the negotiations that produced them make clear that recognition was not based on any reciprocal moves by other governments. Specifically, Egyptian withdrawal would have to be negotiated on the basis of Saudi and British disengagement. The minimal objective of United States recognition was to maintain influence and provide the widest possible setting for further diplomatic initiatives.

The broader objectives of United States presence in Yemen were to preserve and protect the stability of the Saudi Arab government, to enhance rather than to disturb the close working relationship with the United Arab Republic that had been built up over the previous four years, and to prevent the increase of Soviet or Chinese influence in the area. The essential concern of the United States was, in the words of Assistant Secretary of State Phillips Talbot, to keep "the Yemen conflict and its repercussions from spreading"; [78] to contain the revolution and the civil war.[79] This was designed to meet all the policy objectives in some measure. It was especially relevant to the first: Saudi stability and the maintenance of its vast oil reserves for United States use. Oil interests did not determine the specifics of the policy in the Yemen crisis, but they did force the development of a policy that would avert a confrontation whereby the United States would have to choose Saudi Arabia and Britain over the U.A.R., with only military options for dealing with the threat. Recognition was the first of several concrete moves to dampen the war, maintain Saudi rule, and eliminate threats to U.S. economic and strategic interests and those of its allies.

[77] *The Middle East Journal* (Spring, 1963), p. 151.
[78] In a letter to Senator Hickenlooper. *Congressional Record,* July 30, 1963, Vol. 109, Pt. 10, pp. 13668–69.
[79] Badeau, p. 120.

Humphrey Marshall in China, 1853: The Failure of an Independent American Policy

DALE K. ANDERSON

The 1850s were an important decade in China's foreign relations. By 1860 a new treaty settlement and the second Anglo-Chinese War had given Western nations the right to residence in Peking, greatly increased the number of treaty ports, and opened China's interior to foreign penetration. Widespread internal discontent produced numerous local uprisings throughout China, one of which developed into the Taiping Rebellion, probably the greatest civil war in world history, which devastated vast areas of China's heartland and took perhaps 20 million lives. Before it was suppressed in 1864, a rival dynasty reigned for eleven years at Nanking, threatening Manchu rule. The turmoil in the Yangtze valley disrupted foreign trade at Shanghai, which was rapidly replacing Canton as China's most important commercial entrepôt. In addition, disturbed conditions within China seemed to present the Western nations with an opportunity to obtain, either from the hard-pressed Manchu government or from the new regime at Nanking, further commercial concessions and an improved diplomatic and legal status for their nationals.

Great Britain, with the largest commercial stake in China, was the nation most willing and able to take decisive action to obtain the commercial advantages it regarded as necessary and to protect its citizens and their commerce against threats of rebellion and the disruption of trade. In this endeavor the British government, simultaneously faced with a growing crisis in the Crimea, sought the cooperation of the other treaty powers. Particularly on the issue of protecting foreign interests in China, British views on the exigencies of the situation began, during 1853, to diverge from those of Humphrey Marshall, the American commissioner to China, who attempted to formulate an independent American policy. Such a policy, however, could not succeed. Isolated as the foreigners were in the treaty ports, any hope that they could overcome the intransigence of officials practiced in the art of "using barbarians to control barbarians" and improve conditions for trade depended upon cooperation among all the treaty powers, and especially with Great Britain. The American commissioner also found himself with little direction, encouragement, or support from Washington, with a small, poorly staffed and financed, and disorganized consular establishment, and thus in a weak position to act independently. The fact that Marshall's policy may have been formulated in part because of an anti-British bias further weakened its effectiveness and contributed to its failure.[1]

When Marshall arrived in China in February, 1854, he was the third choice of what was by then a lame-duck administration and could expect to be replaced any time after the new administration came into office in March.[2] Secretary of State Marcy and the State

---

[1] Marshall's hostility to both Britain and France is indicated in the heading he added to the draft of a joint proclamation in April, 1853, soon after his arrival at Shanghai. It read: "The citizens of the United States of America and the subjects of Great Britain and France." John King Fairbank, *Trade and Diplomacy on the China Coast: The Opening of the Treaty Ports, 1842–1854* (Cambridge, Mass., Harvard University Press, 1953), I, 416.

[2] This is not to say that Marshall was not a well-known figure in American politics. Supposedly, he had an appointment to the Supreme Court and had turned down an appointment as minister to Central America before accepting the post in China. Humphrey Marshall (1812–72) was born into a less illustrious branch of the well-known Kentucky Marshalls, his grandfather being a cousin of Chief Justice John Marshall. Marshall was commissioned a lieutenant mounted ranger following his graduation from West Point in 1832, but a year later he resigned his commission to study and practice law, first in Frankfort, his birthplace, and after 1835 in Louisville, where he was elected to the city council in 1836. He maintained his interest in military matters, however, being active in the state militia, rising to the rank of lieutenant colonel, and in 1836 organized a Kentucky company to fight in Texas, but the victory at San Jacinto was won before it left the state and it was disbanded. During the Mexican War Marshall organized and served as colonel of the First Kentucky Cavalry.

Marshall's career in national politics began with his election to Congress in 1849, where he became prominent as a Whig spokesman. After his return from China, he was reelected to Congress as a Know-Nothing. In 1859 he declined to run again, but opened a law practice in Washington until the Civil War, in which he served as a brigadier general in the Confederate Army and was elected to the second Confederate Congress. See entry in Dumas Malone, ed.,

Department seem to have paid little attention to developments in China and therefore gave the commissioner to China wide latitude in decision-making but little assurance of support.[3] Marshall's tasks were made even more difficult by the handicaps under which he operated. Yeh Ming-ch'en, the governor-general of Kwangtung and Peking's commissioner for foreign affairs, had for several years followed a policy of noncooperation and marked antiforeignism, and Marshall, like the other foreign representatives in China, found his attempts to obtain an interview effectively blocked. Unlike the French and British ministers, he could not call on naval vessels to transport him between the five treaty ports or even to protect American interests in China against the dangers posed by insurgents, and Washington was of little help in mediating the resulting disputes with the commander of the Far Eastern fleet. In a time of turmoil and rebellion, Marshall found himself with few resources to deal with the problems he faced and the questions that arose.

Upon his arrival in Hong Kong, Marshall requisitioned a naval vessel to take him to Canton to present his credentials to Governor-General Yeh. Yeh pleaded that he was in Hupeh leading an army against the Taiping rebels, but promised to "select a felicitous day" for "a pleasant interview" as soon as he had some leisure.[4] Noting that the French minister had been waiting fifteen months for such a "felicitous day" to arrive and that his own predecessors and the British representative had suffered similar treatment, Marshall decided to go to Nanking and demand to present his credentials to the governor-general of Liang-Kiang, as provided in the Treaty of Wanghia. "The indifference, if not contempt, with which the Chinese officials treat the functionaries of foreign powers, can scarcely be known to the central authority," he exclaimed. "If so, the permitted repetition of such bearing must operate to produce a conviction on the Chinese mind that injury and insult may be multiplied with impunity." [5] His plan, however, had to be postponed when the *Saratoga* was suddenly withdrawn by Commodore Aulick, who refused to

---

Dictionary of American Biography (New York, Charles Scribner's Sons, 1933), XII 310–11.

[3] On January 9, 1854, Marshall wrote that he had received no reply to any of his dispatches since April 1, 1853! *House Executive Document* No. 123, 33d Congress, First Session (hereafter *HED 123*), Marshall to Marcy, January 9, 1854, p. 336. See also *ibid.,* Marshall to March, January 25, 1854, p. 368.

[4] *Ibid.,* the Chinese Commissioners to Marshall, February 3, 1853, p. 14.

[5] *Ibid.,* Marshall to Secretary of State, February 7, 1853, p. 10.

release another vessel to take Marshall to Shanghai.[6] Charging that he had been "exceedingly embarrassed" by the commodore's peremptory action, which had rendered him virtually helpless to fulfill his duties as commissioner, Marshall began an acrimonious exchange with Aulick. The latter, while expressing his willingness to cooperate with Marshall "in all matters of public interest," asserted his responsibility to judge how far such cooperation accorded with his instructions from the Navy Department and declared that the "opinion of the Commissioner alone" could not justify his detaching any portion of his squadron for other service.[7] Apparently unwilling to use one of the British steamers plying between Canton and Shanghai, Marshall appealed his case to the State Department and retired to Macao to await orders from Washington or Aulick's departure from China.

In the meantime, he set about regularizing the functions of the American legation in China.[8] Preparatory to setting up a system of quarterly reports from each of the five consulates, Marshall called for information on annual American trade since 1844 at each of the treaty ports, on the judicial proceedings of the consuls and any receipts or expenditures related to them, and on Chinese emigration from the ports or their vicinity. It is not surprising that Marshall, a slaveowning Southern planter, was concerned about the effects on Southern agriculture and industry of the importation of large numbers of Chinese coolies to fill the growing demand for cheap labor in the West Indies and Cuba, as well as in Australia, California, and various parts of South America, following the abolition of the slave trade. Stressing that the Chinese were hard-working and frugal, accustomed to a tropical climate, skilled at raising sugar, cotton, and rice, and able to live at wages far less than the cost of purchasing and maintaining slaves, Marshall feared that their immigration to the West

[6] Aulick was away from the squadron when Marshall arrived and the *Saratoga* was placed at Marshall's service by Commander Walker. Aulick may well have been angered by the imperative tone of Marshall's request, which was addressed only to "the Commanding Officer of the United States Squadron in the East India station" and demanded that he "furnish me, at Macao, immediately, a suitable vessel-of-war from the naval force under your command on this station, to convey me to such point as it may be necessary for me to visit, in order to enter upon my official intercourse with the court of China." *Ibid.*, January 17, 1853, p. 18.

[7] *Ibid.*, Aulick to Marshall, February 5, 1853, p. 20.

[8] See especially *ibid.*, Marshall to Secretary of State, March 8, 1853, pp. 78–82.

Indies would "create a competition against which it must be difficult to struggle" and "must depress the entire planting interest of the United States." Since it was against the laws of China for its citizens to emigrate, he suggested that "to manifest the disinclination of the United States to the progress of this emigration," the American consuls be ordered to refuse clearance to American ships carrying Chinese emigrants.[9] Marshall did not seem to realize that such a step would probably have served only to drive the legal trade to other flags and, as in the opium trade, to lead to increased smuggling of coolies outside the treaty ports. Furthermore, his hope that Great Britain would thereby be induced "to halt in this scheme so at war with an established principle of American policy" was clearly a vain one, since Britain's chief concern was to eliminate the abuses and corruption involved in the coolie trade, which provided the West Indies with a constant supply of the cheap labor they so vitally required.[10]

Marshall also took up several matters which had concerned his predecessors in China and which would remain to plague his successors. One of these was the inability of missionaries in Fuchow to take possession of a leasehold for which they had paid in advance. The Treaty of Wanghia (1844) stipulated that all such transactions be made with "due regard to the feelings of the people in the location thereof," and the Chinese authorities argued that a single objection constituted grounds for withholding title. Marshall recommended that this be made a test case to enforce compliance with a broader interpretation of the treaty article providing for the right to lease and purchase property, which would otherwise be rendered meaningless.[11] No response from Washington was ever received, and his protests to Governor-General Yeh met only with the bland response

9 *Ibid.*, p. 80.

10 The British government had been growing increasingly disturbed over the adoption, with the connivance of Chinese authorities, of fraudulent means to obtain emigrants and over the shocking conditions and extremely high mortality rates which prevailed on the coolie ships. While desirous of regulating the trade to prevent smuggling and improve conditions on the ships, it was fearful that restrictions on British shipping would simply drive the trade to the ships of other countries. In addition, "their beneficent activities were to an extent paralysed by the difficulty of co-operation with Chinese authorities." On the British coolie trade, see W. C. Costin, *Great Britain and China, 1833–1860* (Oxford, At the Clarendon Press, 1937), pp. 168–76.

11 *HED 123*, Marshall to Secretary of State, March 8, 1853, p. 78.

that the appropriate authorities in Fukien had been ordered to investigate thoroughly, but since rebels there were "creating disturbances," a reply could not be expected immediately.[12]

A second problem was the repeated refusal of the Chinese authorities at Canton to enforce payment of the balance of an award made by a joint claims commission for the destruction by a mob in 1845 of property belonging to the Reverend I. J. Roberts.[13] Declaring that the issue had been settled in 1848 by Commissioner Davis and Hsü Kuang-chin, then imperial commissioner, Yeh was adamant that "there is no occasion at this time to resume the discussion of it." [14] Unless the claim were enforced, Marshall felt, the United States "may as well tear up the treaty," and he recommended the adoption of any means short of war to enforce payment. The establishment of the provisional system for customs administration at Shanghai in September [15] provided Marshall with an opportunity to secure the claim "without necessarily disturbing commercial operations in any degree, and yet having all the effect of a resort to reprisals," and he ordered the consul to withhold the necessary amount from the duties he received from American shippers.[16] Apparently this was not done, however, and when similar threats were made by the consuls at Amoy and Shanghai in 1856, Washington ordered that such highhanded tactics cease.[17] The issue remained unsettled until Reed's negotiations for treaty revision in 1858.

Another matter of concern was the need for "greater facilities and power for maintaining peace and order among American seamen" at Shanghai, where the presence of footloose sailors and deserters was fast turning the port into a brawling, dangerous city. Aware that Chinese jails were not strong enough to confine them, American seamen defied all law. In addition, many deserters joined the Taiping

[12] *Ibid.*, Yeh to Marshall, September 16, 1853, pp. 283–84.

[13] For the background of this case, see Te-kong Tong, *United States Diplomacy in China, 1844–60* (Seattle, University of Washington Press, 1964), pp. 91–92 and 99–103.

[14] *HED 123*, Yeh to Marshall, September 16, 1853, p. 283. In reality, the question had merely been posponed while it was referred to Washington. See *ibid.*, Marshall to March, October 10, 1853, pp. 277–78.

[15] On the provisional system, see below, pp. 293 ff.

[16] *HED 123*, p. 283.

[17] Tyler Dennett, *Americans in Eastern Asia: A Critical Study of United States' Policy in the Far East in the Nineteenth Century* (New York, Barnes & Noble, Inc., 1963), p. 328.

forces or fought with the insurgents who captured Shanghai in September, 1853, but in the absence of adequate jails, there were no means to restrain them. Marshall repeatedly urged the appropriation of funds to lease or purchase land and erect jails at Shanghai and Canton and to build a permanent consulate at each of the five ports.[18] A year later his successor, Robert McLane, again protested the lack of consular jails, which had forced him to confine American criminals in a cell at the British consulate.[19]

Marshall was embittered by the contrast between the British and American consular establishments in China. The latter made no provisions for permanent offices or residences for either the minister or the consuls, whose salaries were entirely inadequate to cover such expenses. When in the south, the commissioner customarily resided at the Portuguese colony of Macao, while the consulate at Shanghai was in the offices of Russell and Company, the leading American firm (and the largest American shipper of opium) [20] in China, whose head customarily served as the American consul. William Cunningham, vice-consul during Marshall's term, was a partner in this firm. The first full-time consul, Robert Murphy, was not appointed until 1854, and during most of Marshall's year in China, three of the consulates (Canton, Shanghai, and Amoy) were staffed by vice-consuls who had been deputed to serve in the absence of their business partners, the regularly appointed merchant-consuls. Missionaries served as unsalaried consular deputies at Ningpo and Fuchow. In July the consulate at Amoy was closed when Consul Charles Bradley, who had returned to his home in Connecticut the previous year, withdrew the vice-consular authority from his son; just before leaving China, Marshall appointed Charles Bradley, Jr. acting consul, but the latter apparently declined the post.[21] Letters arrived from the Department of State addressed to a "Dwight Webb, esq.,

[18] See *HED 123*, Marshall to Marcy, July 30, 1853, pp. 224–25; December 8, 1853, p. 326. Apparently Consul Griswold had also written to the State Department on this subject. See *ibid.*, Cunningham to Marshall, July 23, 1853, p. 229.

[19] Senate Executive Document No. 22, 35th Congress, Second Session (hereafter *SED 22*), McLane to Marcy, August 20, 1854, p. 168.

[20] Unable to obtain an American naval vessel, Marshall refused several times to travel to Shanghai in a British opium steamer and repeatedly denounced the British for trading in opium.

[21] *HED 123*, Marshall to Charles W. Bradley, Jr., December 29, 1853, p. 327.

United States consul at Fuhchowfoo," who had never been heard of in China let alone served as consul at Fuchow. Finally, Dr. Peter Parker, the secretary of legation, insisted upon his right to receive sealed, official communications from the State Department, touching off an angry exchange with Marshall.[22] All in all, it was haphazard establishment.

Marshall expressed particular anxiety over the lack of adequate provision for Chinese interpreters and writers at the American consulates, declaring that British foresight in supplying and training competent interpreters gave them an advantage in "the means of acquiring information and in communicating it to the Chinese in the language of the latter" that would, "by degrees, enable the officers of that power to exercise a controlling influence over the determination of questions which your corps of consuls will not understand." [23] Although Marshall's implied suspicions were totally unjustified, American representatives were plainly handicapped in trying to deal with and understand the Chinese. Whereas the British Superintendancy of Trade at Hong Kong and its consulates at the treaty ports employed 7 Englishmen as Chinese secretaries and assistant secretaries and 14 Chinese writers, he was provided with only the services of a single secretary-interpreter, Dr. Parker. Parker pleaded ill health and returned to a lucrative medical practice in Canton two months after accompanying Marshall to Shanghai, thereafter agreeing to hold his appointment only so long as his duties could be fulfilled in Canton. The Reverend M. C. Culbertson, who replaced him, was too busy to serve as secretary and his meager knowledge of Mandarin, the dialect spoken at Shanghai, made his limitations as an interpreter "painfully manifest" whenever Marshall had to deal with Chinese officials.[24] For a time he hired a young Cantonese as a Chinese writer and, although the boy could not write the formal style required for official correspondence, was very pleased with his services as translator and interpreter.[25] Marshall urged that such individuals be attached permanently to the legation and encouraged by promise of promotion to further their training and ability; but Marcy's order that no foreigners be employed in American legations required Marshall to

---

[22] *HED 123*, especially pp. 232–39, 245–48.
[23] *Ibid.*, Marshall to Secretary of State, March 8, 1853, p. 82.
[24] *Ibid.*, Marshall to Parker, August 2, 1853, p. 238.
[25] *Ibid.*, Marshall to Secretary of State, May 26, 1853, p. 141.

discharge his new assistant.[26] His suggestion that the position of secretary-interpreter be split between two individuals and the salary raised to attract qualified and capable persons to the posts [27] was also ignored.

One issue which was settled amicably, despite Marshall's hostility to the British authorities, was the knotty problem of the administration of the foreign settlement in Shanghai. This had plagued Anglo-American relations ever since the first American consul attempted in 1845 to raise the American flag within an area in which Great Britain claimed it had been given exclusive jurisdiction. The United States had protested that to grant such a right to any single government abridged the right, guaranteed to American citizens under the treaty, to rent or purchase land freely. In 1853 the British government accepted the American contention and agreed to the adoption of a set of land regulations which placed the foreign settlement under the joint jurisdiction of the foreign consuls and the Shanghai taotai,[28] thus reaffirming Chinese sovereignty over the settlement, with an elected municipal council to determine questions of taxation, wharfs, roads, and the like. Marshall amended the British draft to limit somewhat the role of the consuls, expand the authority of the municipal council, remove prohibitions against Chinese residence in the settlement, and protect Chinese rights in selling or leasing property. His

[26] *Ibid.,* Marshall to Marcy, September 15, 1853, p. 257.

[27] Marshall pointed out: "Dr. Parker could not live on his salary from the government and could not afford to hold the place he occupies, were his services entirely to be yielded to the business of the legation. Many book-keepers in the heavy mercantile houses receive $4,000 to $6,000 per year; an ordinary clerk receives $2,500 to $3,000; a tea-taster, whose only genius is his palate, obtains a higher salary by far than is paid by the United States to the secretary and interpreter of this legation." *Ibid.,* Marshall to Secretary of State, May 26, 1853, pp. 139–40.

On the capable group of British interpreters, many of whom later served as ministers and consuls in China, see Fairbank, p. 166. McLane also complained of the inadequacy of the American consular establishment. See *SED 22,* McLane to Marcy, August 20, 1854, pp. 165–68.

[28] The taotai, or provincial intendant of circuit, had jurisdiction over two or more subprovincial divisions and held a rank of 4a in the 9 ranks (each of which had two levels) of the imperial bureaucracy. The taotai whose jurisdiction included a treaty port was also superintendent of customs for that port. Since Shanghai was not a provincial capital, the taotai was the highest resident official at the port. See Earl Swisher, *China's Management of the American Barbarians: A Study of Sino-American Relations, 1841–1861, with Documents* (New Haven, Far Eastern Publications, 1953), pp. 2–3.

amendments clearly benefited both the Chinese and the nationals of various nations in the foreign settlement and were accepted almost in their entirety by London. The code was promulgated by the three treaty powers in 1854.[29]

Commodore Aulick's departure provided Marshall with the opportunity to sail for Shanghai in the *Susquehanna*. It was clearly his intention to depart at once for Nanking, either to present his credentials to the governor-general there or, if, as expected, the city had fallen to the Taiping rebels, to inform himself as to their "character, purposes, and prospects." [30] After capturing Wuchang, the capital of Hupeh province, in January, the Taiping forces moved rapidly down the Yangtze, occupying the major cities, including Anking, the capital of Anhwei province, and enlisting or impressing at least half a million of the impoverished and discontented population along their 400-mile route through the Yangtze valley.[31] By early March, they were on the outskirts of Nanking, the ancient capital of China, although word of its fall on March 19 was not received in Shanghai until after Marshall's arrival on March 27. To most foreigners and many Chinese its capture seemed to herald the imminent collapse of the Manchu dynasty.

Whether Marshall actually attempted to sail to Nanking is a matter of controversy among historians. No report of his activities during April exists, for the only copy of his dispatch No. 12, written sometime between March 28 and April 28, was lost in a shipwreck on May 2; he professed to be unable to remember its contents "with sufficient exactness to repeat them," although he claimed they were of little importance.[32] In view of his earlier altercation with Aulick, Marshall may well have decided to carry out his plans at once, lest the *Susquehanna* be taken for the Japan expedition upon Perry's arrival in China.[33] Such an attempt at that particular moment, how-

[29] For the background of this issue and the draft code, see *HED 123*, Marshall to Marcy, July 26, 1853, pp. 210–23. The code as finally adopted is in *SED 22*, July 8, 1954, pp. 158–65. The settlement has been fully discussed by Dennett (The Settlement of the Shanghai Land Question," pp. 194–205) and will not be further discussed here.

[30] *HED 123*, Marshall to Secretary of State, March 19, 1853, p. 87.

[31] See Franz Michael, *The Taiping Rebellion: History and Documents, Volume I: History* (Seattle and London, University of Washington Press, 1966), pp. 69–70, and Appendix I, Map 5.

[32] *HED 123*, Marshall to Marcy, May 30, 1853, pp. 163–64.

[33] This is precisely what happened. When Perry arrived in Hong Kong, he was incensed by the absence of the *Susquehanna*, which he intended to use as

ever, would have seriously compromised American neutrality vis-à-vis the Taiping and imperialist forces.[34] Just before the fall of Nanking, the governor of Kiangsu province, through the Shanghai taotai Wu Chien-chang, asked the British, French, and American consuls for warships to aid in preventing the capture of Nanking, and, despite their refusal, Wu continued his efforts to obtain Western gunboats.[35] He did succeed in chartering at least 1 armed opium receiving ship from Russell and Company, arousing the ire of Sir George Bonham, the British minister, who wrote to the Foreign Office:

In my opinion it is much to be regretted that such a step should have been taken, as it can only complicate matters; it being highly probable that other foreign vessels will follow in the same path. Moreover, it must not be forgotten that neither the insurgents nor the inhabitants in the vicinity of Nanking know anything about the ships and flags of Western Powers, and to them it will of course appear that the vessel in question is one out of many obtained by the Taoutae from foreign Powers. . . . I cannot allow this opportunity to escape, without once more recording my sentiments as to the bad policy, in every respect, of allowing merchants to hold Consular appointments, and in the case now reported we have, I think, a strong and apposite illustration of the inconveniences likely to arise from the practice being allowed to continue in full force.[36]

his flagship. He immediately set sail for Shanghai to reclaim the vessel and thereafter adamantly refused to place any American naval vessel at Marshall's disposal. Soon after the expedition sailed for Japan, the last vessel was withdrawn from Shanghai, despite the fact that the disturbed conditions posed a constant threat to Americans and their property. The continuing conflict with Aulick and Perry that marked Marshall's entire tenure in China are examined in a very sympathetic article (not discussed in detail in this essay) by Chester A. Bain, "Commodore Matthew Perry, Humphrey Marshall, and the Taiping Rebellion," *Far Eastern Quarterly*, X, No. 3 (May, 1951), 258–70.

[34] Bain has theorized that Marshall realized this and therefore preferred not to report the attempt to the State Department. *Ibid.*, pp. 261–62.

[35] A second request about March 21 urged the consuls to consult with each other about dispatching "the vessels of war which may have already arrived at Shanghae, together with that stationed there, to Nanking, that they may . . . make a combined attack, solemnly binding themselves to extirpate the rebels, in order to gratify the public mind and open the paths of commerce, . . . to sweep away every remnant of rebellion and give tranquility to the country, to the great happiness of myself, the Chinese officials and people." House of Commons, *Accounts and Papers, 1852–1853:* Vol. 13, LXIX, "China" (hereafter cited as House of Commons), the Shanghai Taotai to Consul Alcock, pp. 3–4.

[36] *Ibid.*, Bonham to Russell, March 28, 1853, pp. 650–51.

Bonham clearly regarded Marshall's alleged attempt to go to Nanking in the same light, fearing that it would "induce a belief in the rebel mind that foreigners intend to side with the Imperialists," [37] as a memorial to the emperor of May 28 indicates was indeed the case.[38] It may be that a decision to go to Nanking was influenced by Bonham's opposition to the plan and his somewhat sympathetic attitude toward the Taipings.

Other contemporary sources provide further evidence that the attempt was made. Bain quotes two British accounts to the effect that the *Susquehanna* ran aground near Chinkiang, about 100 miles up-river.[39] Some credence is given to these reports by Marshall's dispatch to the State Department reporting Bonham's departure for Nanking and commenting that he had "heard of the vessel between Chinkiang-foo and Nankin, so that his excellency has accomplished what I essayed in vain to perform in the steamer Susquehanna," [40] though this may refer merely to his desire to make the trip. Another version is given by Bonham, who reported to the Foreign Office that the *Susquehanna* had left for Nanking and returned to Shanghai three days later, after being aground for twenty-four hours 10 miles from Wusung.[41] The best evidence, however, is an account written for the *North China Herald* by Lewis Carr, a member of the legation staff, which Commissioner Robert McLane enclosed in his report on his

---

[37] Bonham to Hammond, April 13, 1853, quoted in Costin, p. 181. A month later, when the British expedition sailed for Nanking, it was clear that no official aid would be given to either side, and Bonham took pains to stress this to the rebels as well. Bonham's account of his voyage is in House of Commons, pp. 21–44.

[38] Reporting on the possibility of hiring foreign warships to aid against the Taipings, General Hsiang Jung, one of the most important imperialist generals at that time, stated that in an interview with Wu Chien-chang, Marshall had said "the warships from his country which had come to take part in the war had gone to the mouth of the river, struck shallows and returned. Now they had gone to fight in Japan and could not be hired to fight rebels." Swisher, p. 191. Fairbank also cites several memorials indicating that Wu had boasted that he had persuaded the Americans to provide the support of the *Susquehanna*. See Fairbank, II, 40 *n* 34.

[39] Bain, pp. 261–62.

[40] *HED 123*, Marshall to Secretary of State, April 28, 1853, p. 98.

[41] Costin, p. 181. Wusung was about 15 miles from Shanghai, at the point where the Whangpu River, on which Shanghai is located, flows into the Yangtze. It served as the receiving station for opium ships trading at Shanghai. See Hosea Ballou Morse, *The International Relations of the Chinese Empire, Vol. II: The Period of Submission* (London, 1918), map facing p. 80.

voyage to Nanking in the *Susquehanna* the following year. Carr states:

> It may be remembered, that in the spring of last year, the *"Susque-hanna,"* with Colonel Marshall on board, started on a similar expedition, and although Captain Buchanan was told by all who professed to know anything of the navigation of the river, that it would be futile to attempt it in so large a vessel, he was still willing to make the effort; more particularly as at that time very great interest was felt touching the remarkable events in the interior.
>
> The ship grounded on the Blonde shoal soon after getting into the river; the disappointment was naturally very great to all on board, and especially to Captain Buchanan, who would, at that time, have persevered and gone on had not the services of the *"Susquehanna"* been needed in the Japan Expedition. He returned therefore, with reluctance, intending to embrace the first opportunity to attempt it anew.

Carr goes on to say that when McLane decided to go to Nanking in the *Susquehanna,* which Perry had placed at his disposal, Buchanan was "only too glad to have another opportunity." [42] It is highly unlikely that Carr had not discussed the earlier attempt with Captain Buchanan before making such a statement. Marshall's better judgment would seem to have been outweighed by his eagerness to carry out his plan before Perry might thwart it,[43] and perhaps by his hostility to the British and Sir George Bonham.

Marshall continued to try to reach Nanking, but Perry stubbornly refused to provide a ship for his use. Eventually Marshall's position was sustained by the State Department, although not until after he had left China. A reprimand of October, 1853, from the Secretary of the Navy ordered Perry to place a war steamer under McLane's control, and the following month he was again ordered to cooperate with McLane "in the execution of his mission to China." [44] Unlike

---

[42] *SED 22,* p. 64. This account is usually identified as a clipping from the *North China Herald* rather than a report prepared for submission to the newspaper by a member of the expedition, as McLane and Carr clearly indicate.

[43] On the other hand, it might be argued that Perry would hardly have missed the opportunity to create an issue over the grounding of his flagship, had such an event occurred.

[44] Bain, p. 269. Marcy's instructions to McLane read: "Should you deem the presence of any considerable part or the whole of the naval force under [Perry's] command on the coast of China necessary to enable you to carry into effect the objects of your mission, you will communicate your views thereon to the commanding officer thereof. He will receive instructions in regard to rendering to you such assistance as the exigencies of the public interest may

Marshall, McLane was thus able to sail to Nanking. Even though such a trip would not have changed Marshall's conclusion—that the Nanking regime's attitude toward foreign intercourse was not likely to differ from that of Peking and that ultimately America's interests lay in supporting the Manchu government, the same conclusion McLane reached a year later—Marshall was right to insist that American policy must be formulated on the basis of his own observations and could not be based solely on British or French reports. Granted that his insistence was in part based on unfounded suspicions of British policies and goals, and chagrin that he had failed where Bonham had succeeded, it was not to be expected that the representative of the second most important nation trading in China would have taken any other position.

Unable to obtain firsthand information, however, Marshall was forced to rely on the reports of Bonham and others who successfully visited areas held by the Taipings and of the refugees streaming into Shanghai and Canton. In addition, many reports and translations of Taiping literature were printed in the weekly *North China Herald* published at Shanghai, or in the Hong Kong *China Mail,* some of which Marshall enclosed in his dispatches to Washington. Some copies of the *Peking Gazette* (*Ching Pao*), which contained memorials, imperial edicts, and news of the movements of the Taiping and imperialist armies,[45] were received in Shanghai. Despite his confinement to Shanghai and the secondhand nature of his information, Marshall's dispatches relating to the Taiping Rebellion show him to have been a keen observer of events in China.[46]

---

require, if it can be done without abandoning the principal end of his expedition or seriously hazarding its success. The President does not propose to subject him to your control, but he expects that you and he will coöperate together whenever, in the judgments of both, the interests of the United States indicate the necessity or the advantage of such cooperation." *Senate Executive Document No. 39*, 36th Congress, First Session, Marcy to McLane, November 9, 1853, p. 3.

[45] Such reports were very slanted, since they were made by the commanders of the imperial armies whose lives and careers might be forfeit if defeats were reported. (See, for example, *HED 123*, Marshall to Marcy, December 8, 1853, p. 327.) Nevertheless, it was impossible to cover up the sorry performance and repeated defeats of the imperialist forces. A colonel in the First Kentucky Cavalry who had fought with distinction in the Mexican War, Marshall followed the military movements of the rebel armies with interest.

[46] Even Rutherford Alcock, the British consul toward whom Marshall, as we shall see, was particularly antagonistic, praised the quality of Marshall's

Little was known of the Taipings until late in 1852, and no firm policies toward them were formulated by the American or other foreign governments or their representatives until after the fall of Nanking. Although attitudes toward the rebels varied widely, the frustrations felt by most foreigners as they attempted to deal with Chinese officials within the confines of the treaty ports gave rise to great hopes that the establishment of a new dynasty might bring about a change in their situation in China. These hopes were fed by reports that the rebels had embraced Christianity. Daniel Spooner, the American consul at Canton, was probably speaking for most foreigners when he wrote Marshall on March 13: "I hope Teen-Tih [47] will be successful, and upset the present dynasty. We cannot be worse off; and he is said to be a liberal man." [48] Marshall's first dispatch from China reported that the insurgent leader was expected to capture Nanking and "assume the diadem of empire," [49] and subsequent dispatches throughout his residence in China reflect his pessimism concerning the prospects for the survival of the regime in Peking. On May 26, he advised Washington that "the rebellion must thus far be regarded as a successful effort against the existing government" and reported rumors of new revolts in Kwangsi and Fukien.[50] His last

---

dispatches: "for his sound judgment and statesmanlike views, with a clear insight into what was passing around him in China (always excepting a certain monomania he brought with him from Kentucky about the British and their aims and plottings) . , . he is deserving of very high praise. We doubt whether the whole body of [British] interpreters—educated men, familiar with the people and the language—have ever produced anything to be compared with [Marshall's] dispatches." Unsigned article by Alcock reviewing Marshall's published correspondence in *Bombay Quarterly Review* (October, 1855), quoted in Fairbank, p. 416.

[47] Early foreign accounts often refer to the Taiping leader as *T'ien-te-wang* (King of Heavenly Virtue). Whether a leader with this title ever actually existed is argued by historians. Some claim that there were originally two Taiping chiefs, the founder Hung Hsiu-ch'üan, who bore the title *T'ien-wang* (Heavenly King), and the *T'ien-te-wang*, Hung Ta-ch'üan (no relation to Hung Hsiuch'üan), a man who was captured and executed in April, 1852, by the imperialists, who published his confession. See Ssu-yü Teng, *New Light on the History of the Taiping Rebellion* (New York, Russell & Russell, 1966), pp. 20–28; and William James Hail, *Tseng Kuo-fan and the Taiping Rebellion* (New York, Paragon Book Reprint Corp., 1964), pp. 50–74 (Chapter 3, "The Suppressed Leader").

[48] *HED 123,* Spooner to Marshall, March 13, 1853, p. 96.

[49] *Ibid.,* Marshall to Secretary of State, February 7, 1853, p. 12.

[50] *Ibid.,* Marshall to Secretary of State, May 26, 1853, pp. 142–43.

report, on January 9, 1854, again states the possibility that the government at Peking would be overthrown and the Manchus forced to flee.[51]

At the same time, his attitude toward the rebels at Nanking became more and more cynical. Unlike certain missionaries and merchants who enthusiastically viewed the Christianity professed by the Taipings [52] as "persuasive evidence that the moral bread which was cast upon these waters in bygone time is now returning after many days" and as heralding the rise of "a more enlightened civilization in China," Marshall regarded their pseudo-Christianity as a combination of absurd beliefs and the designs of "a cold and crafty agitator" who had revamped the religion taught by the missionaries to attract the impoverished and discontented to his standard of revolt.[53] While expecting no change for the better to emanate from Nanking, Marshall thereafter regarded the rebellion as "but the *initiative* of a revolution which, after successive efforts, will effect a great change in the condition of China, and will sweep away the ridiculous forms as well as the hoary vices of the despotism which for centuries has weighed China below her proper level in the family of nations." [54]

Writing in the same vein on June 21, he stated his conviction that while "there never has been, in the history of mankind, a worse government than that which for some years past has afflicted China," its opponents promised little improvement. Nevertheless, he recommended that the Western powers "unite . . . in a timely interfer-

[51] *Ibid.*, Marshall to Marcy, January 9, 1854, p. 337.

[52] For a survey of missionary attitudes toward the Taipings, see John B. Littell, "Missionaries and Politics in China—The Taiping Rebellion," *Political Science Quarterly,* XLIII, No. 4 (December, 1928), 566–99. Littell shows that missionaries were far from unanimous in supporting the Taipings. On the Christian sources and content of Taiping ideology, see Eugene Powers Boardman, *Christian Influence Upon the Ideology of the Taiping Rebellion, 1851– 1864* (Madison, University of Wisconsin Press, 1952).

[53] This is strikingly similar to the thesis advanced by Hail and some other recent Taiping historians that Hung Ta-ch'üan (see fn. 47 above) was a secret society leader named Chu Chiu-t'ao who, realizing the revolutionary potential of Hung Hsiu-ch'üan's teachings, joined the Society of God Worshippers (the religious organization out of which the Taiping army developed) with large numbers of his followers, becoming cosovereign as the *T'ien-te-wang,* and attempted to utilize the organization for his own antidynastic aims. Not long after Hung Ta-ch'üan's capture in April, 1852, all secret society members who refused to adhere to Hung Hsiu-ch'üan's doctrines were expelled from the Taiping forces. See Hail, pp. 50–74.

[54] *HED 123,* Marshall to Secretary of State, May 26, 1853, pp. 141–42.

ence" to end the civil war and restore trade by "sending their diplomatists to Pekin *or to Nankin.*" [55] Marshall did not indicate whether the "diplomatists" were to be accompanied by a military force, but he clearly was advocating that the United States recognize and attempt to negotiate with a *de facto* government in Nanking should Peking, despite the internal threat to its control, continue its policy of stubborn resistance to intercourse with foreign nations.

Following the capture of Amoy, in Fukien province, by a band of Small Sword Society members [56] on May 19, Marshall asked Washington what policy he should follow. Even if he were to recognize a new *de facto* government at Amoy, should customs duties, collected according to a treaty signed with the Peking government, be paid to the rebels? What position should he take if such "free cities" were established at various places in China? [57] He also noted the likelihood that the Taipings, in return for recognition by the Western powers, might agree to sign treaties of amity and commerce, permit foreign ministers to reside at Nanking, establish religious toleration and individual freedom, and open the Yangtze to foreign commerce.[58] What should his response be?

But there was a deeper reason for his concern than merely to be prepared with an American policy in such a contingency, for he feared that Great Britain might assume a protectorate over the new

[55] *Ibid.,* Marshall to Marcy, June 21, 1853, pp. 183–84.

[56] Secret societies have been important at various times in Chinese history, becoming particularly strong during periods of internal weakness and dynastic decline. During the nineteenth century many anti-Manchu secret societies, founded after the overthrow of the Ming dynasty in the seventeenth century and aiming at its restoration, sprang to new life. One of the largest of these was the Triads (*San-ho-hui*). This brotherhood is often difficult to identify, since it had many semiautonomous branches scattered throughout China, often with different names and each having its own secret organization, ritual, signs, and language—according to Fairbank, not unlike the Masonic order. The Small Sword Society (sometimes translated as the Small Knife/Dagger, the Short Knife or Short Sword Society) had been particularly active among Cantonese and Fukienese sailors and boatmen who had migrated to Shanghai, and had been causing trouble for the local authorities for several years before capturing the city in 1853. See Fairbank, pp. 406–7.

[57] *HED 123,* Marshall to Marcy, May 30, 1853, pp. 167–68. These were questions which were to arise again when Shanghai was captured in September and to which, in the absence of guidelines from Washington and of control over naval vessels, Marshall was forced to find answers as best he could.

[58] Marshall later listed these as the conditions under which he would recommend intervention on behalf of Peking. See below, p. 285.

government in Nanking and thereby be able to obtain rights to navigation on the Yangtze and commerce at an inland port. "I do not doubt," he added, "that with that view her war with Burmah has been waged and her Indian empire extended. The portage from the Ihrawaddy to the Yangtze Kiang is very short." [59] American policy, he felt, must be ready to forestall such an eventuality. He soon found his fears confirmed. On June 8, in a "confidential" N.B. to Marcy, Marshall wrote that Bonham, on his visit to Nanking, had received from "the high ministers" of the Taiping emperor "an imperial letter, which treated of the navigation of the Yangtsze, expressed great good will towards western nations, and alluded to the willingness of the taipingwan to establish liberal commercial intercourse. Sir George Bonham," he added darkly, "never dropped even a hint to me of any such transaction, and doubtless has communicated it only to her Majesty's government." That this did not take place and that Bonham had no such designs in mind is clear from his report to the Foreign Office on his trip to Nanking,[60] but henceforth Marshall's policy was to be guided by his convictions concerning British intentions.[61]

[59] Costin has somewhat unfairly attributed this statement to the suspicion and jealousy of a backwoodsman, declaring that "there is no trace of such a suggestion in the records of the Foreign Office, nor was it likely that a trade route comparable in value to the Pacific could be dreamt of between Burmah and the Yangtse." (Costin, p. 182.) T. K. Tong, however, found in the National Archives a report from Commissioner Everett that Sir John F. Davis, then British minister plenipotentiary, had in 1847 asked Ch'i-ying, the Chinese imperial commissioner, for the opening of a direct route to Burma. Tong points out that it was not until 1861 that an expedition up the Yangtze discovered that the distance from the Yangtze to the Irrawaddy was more than just a short portage. See Tong, p. 128.

In June, 1854, the Reverend E. C. Bridgman, who accompanied McLane to Nanking, prepared a report on the Yangtze, based on Chinese sources on the geographical and statistical surveys made by the Jesuits in the seventeenth century. Bridgman states that "it is well-known" that the sources of the Yangtze, the Irrawaddy, and the Bramaputra were "in one and the same region, and that, too, one of no very wide extent," *SED 22*, p. 93. At the turn of the century Great Britain pressed for the right to build railroads from Burma into Yunnan and Szechwan in order to tap the Yangtze valley trade from the west. See Morse, *Vol. III: The Period of Subjection, 1894–1911* (London, 1918), pp. 98–99.

[60] *HED 123*, Marshall to Marcy, June 8, 1853, p. 177.

[61] Marshall's fears were in part due to the favorable attitude of Thomas Taylor Meadows, the British interpreter at Shanghai, who had made three trips to areas occupied by the Taipings and whose articles in the *North China*

In a second "confidential" dispatch on July 10, Marshall lay down what Dennett has lauded as the "second plank" in American policy towards China—that "the highest interests of the United States are involved in sustaining China." [62] In addition to his fear of British penetration, he now saw in the rumors of Russian offers to aid Peking against the rebels evidence that Russia too aimed to establish a protectorate over China. The United States, he believed, should make

almost any sacrifice . . . to keep Russia from spreading her Pacific boundary, and to avoid her coming directly to an interference in Chinese domestic affairs; for China is like a lamb before the shearers, as easy a conquest as were the provinces of India. Whenever the avarice or the ambition of Russia or Great Britain shall tempt them to make the prizes, the fate of Asia will be sealed, and the future Chinese relations of the United States of America may be considered as closed for ages, unless *now* the United States shall foil the untoward result by adopting a sound policy. It is my opinion that the highest interests of the United States are involved in sustaining China—maintaining order here, and gradually engrafting on this worn-out stock the healthy principles which give life and health to governments, rather than to see China become the theatre of a widespread anarchy, and ultimately the prey of European ambition.[63]

Such an intervention, which aimed, by opposing British and Russian ambitions, only "to preserve the nationality of China; to revivify her, [and] to elevate her people," he regarded as "a mission of humanity and charity"—but one, it should be noted, accompanied by great

---

Herald were then quite favorable to the rebels. In line with his earlier recommendations that qualified interpreters be attached to the American consulates in China, Marshall wrote that Meadows's fluency in the language would enable Great Britain to mold Nanking's "first steps to suit the policy" of the British government (*HED 123,* Marshall to Marcy, May 30, 1853, p. 168). Meadows and the *North China Herald* did not change their attitude until mid-1854, long after Marshall had expressed the opinion that the West had nothing to gain from supporting the insurgents. See Michael, pp. 105–6.

[62] Dennett, p. 207.

[63] *HED 123,* Marshall to Marcy, July 10, 1853, p. 204. That Marshall's fears of Russian ambitions, although apparently based on a false rumor, were not unjustified can be seen from Russia's constant encroachment on Chinese territory in Ili and along the Amur River, and its claims to territorial compensation for its ambassadors' mediation on China's behalf with Great Britain and France in 1858 and 1860. See Morse, *Vol. I: The Period of Conflict* (Shanghai, 1910), pp. 472–78, 525–26, 613–14.

benefits for the United States. While the U.S. would impart to China its knowledge of naval architecture and help to apply in China its own experience in steam navigation on inland waterways, Americans would lead the way in the commercial development of the interior of China. The United States stood to gain the most from the resulting efflorescence of commerce at Shanghai, for its transcontinental railway would end just across the Pacific from that port. The knowledge it shared with China would enable the latter to develop a navy to enforce its revenue laws and put an end to the illegal traffic in opium —and thus to the basis of British predominance in the commerce of the Far East.[64]

It was a rosy picture. But apart from the fact that it would have reversed America's traditional policy of neutrality and nonintervention, particularly in events outside the Western hemisphere, Marshall attached such preconditions as to make any interference totally out of the question:

When the Emperor of China shall proclaim an amnesty for past political offences to all the rebels who shall at once return to their homes and avocations; freedom of religious opinion, and religious worship throughout the realm; freedom to citizens of nations having treaties of amity and commerce with China to pass and repass through his dominions at will, without distinction of place; when the Emperor shall install a department of foreign affairs, which can meet the ambassadors of foreign countries; when, in fine, the Emperor shall open the Yangtsze and its affluents to steam navigation, and shall devise some just mode of regulating the same by registry or license; and, finally, when *he shall become a subscriber to the laws of nations*—then, and not till then, would I suggest any interference whatever.[65]

Given China's attitude toward foreign nations, it obviously was not likely to acquiesce in these demands. On the contrary, intervention would have been, and ultimately was, a necessary precondition to attaining them. Neither Washington nor Marshall would have been willing to recommend such a step.

Marshall's view of events in China having been thus formulated, it is not surprising that when he received instructions from Marcy in September urging "cordial relations and free conference" with the

[64] It is perhaps noteworthy that immediately after this dispatch was written, the Shanghai land question was amicably solved, with Great Britain renouncing any claims to sovereignty or jurisdiction there.

[65] *HED 123*, Marshall to Marcy, July 10, 1853, p. 205.

British,[66] his reaction was pessimistic. *"China gives to England no privilege that is not extorted by fear,"* he charged.

This prejudice has been confessed to me by Chinese officials; and the reluctance to allow a privilege to England has been assigned, privately, more than once, as a reason for refusing to concede more to the United States. . . . Great Britain has exhibited in her eastern conquests neither fear of Heaven nor love of justice among men.[67]

Marshall's suspicions clearly made him easy prey for the Chinese technique of manipulating the barbarians.

Apart from this Anglophobia, however, Marshall's observations on the rebellion were remarkably penetrating. While a few other foreigners also noted the pretensions of the new dynasty at Nanking and its implications for the commercial hopes of the West, few so early saw one of the reasons for the ultimate defeat of the Taiping

---

[66] Bonham had recommended to London a policy of neutrality, in order to avoid prolonging the struggle, which he expected to result in a Taiping victory. He also hoped to gain more liberal commercial benefits from Nanking. (Costin, pp. 160–61.) Marshall, on the other hand, advocated neutrality in the hope of gaining trade concessions from Peking, writing: "The Emperor will receive *from events* a stronger impression than could be made upon his mind by a timely and facile release of his southern capital from danger." (*HED 123,* Marshall to Secretary of State, March 28, 1853, p. 98.) Both sides, of course, would want to keep their options open so long as the outcome of the struggle was uncertain.

With war clouds gathering in the Crimea, the British government decided to pursue a policy of strict neutrality and cooperation with the other treaty powers in China. Before replying to Bonham's inquiry, Clarendon invited the cooperation of the French, American, and Russian governments with a view to using the opportunity offered by the upheaval in China to obtain benefits for their commerce. The French minister in China had from the beginning adopted a neutral posture, though his sympathies were with the imperialists, in part perhaps because of the Protestant doctrines espoused by the rebels. In addition, Anglo-French cooperation in the Crimea provided a policy that might easily be extended to China. France therefore agreed readily. Russia was unenthusiastic, but promised to instruct its minister to cooperate. Lacking knowledge of conditions in China, Marcy was agreeable but cautious; he instructed Marshall as follows: "Without knowing what course the British authorities may deem it expedient to take in furtherance of the object in view, the President does not enjoin upon you co-operation but only cordial relations and free conference with them." (See Fairbank, pp. 413–14; also Dennett, 213–14.) Shanghai had fallen two weeks before this instruction was received, and Marshall's anger and apprehension had been further aroused by British actions during the resulting crisis.

[67] *HED 123,* Marshall to Marcy, September 21, 1853, p. 269.

rebels—their failure to attract the allegiance of China's educated elite, the scholar-gentry. Aware of China's strong Confucian heritage, Marshall saw that the gentry would not rally to a cause that rejected the beliefs and customs of that tradition and that any attempt on the part of the Taiping emperor to assert his control and to reform the existing institutions of government and society would constitute a threat to "the substantial men of China," who would oppose him not to support the dynasty but to protect their ancient institutions and privileges. In anticipating the ultimate overthrow of the Manchu dynasty, he could not have foreseen the rise, after 1856, of the remarkable group of statesmen, such as Tseng Kuo-fan, Tso Tsung-t'ang, and Li Hung-chang, who preserved the dynasty for another fifty years and postponed the long period of revolution and chaos that Marshall predicted. His stand against the Taipings set Marshall against the many foreigners who vainly believed that current events would soon result in more enlightened intercourse between China and the world.[68]

To obtain concessions from Peking, Marshall believed it was first necessary to gain access to the imperial ear (which he was convinced he did not have through the officials in Shanghai and Canton) by sailing to Tientsin and demanding that an imperial commissioner be appointed there to discuss American grievances with him. Although Marshall was not proposing a cooperative venture, this was the same strategy pursued by McLane and Bowring the following year and in the four-power expedition of 1858. The plan was blocked by Perry's withdrawal of the entire fleet for the expedition to Japan and subsequently by his adamant refusal to place a naval vessel at Marshall's disposal for this purpose. There is some justice in Marshall's complaints that, had the emperor invited him to Tientsin or Peking, he would not have had the means to go—obviously a most embarrassing

---

[68] *Ibid.*, pp. 265–68. One of these was Commodore Perry. In December, 1853, after again refusing Marshall's request for a ship to take him to Nanking, he added: "I must be the judge of the necessity of using the force at my disposal in intermeddling in a civil war between a despotic government, struggling for its very existence, and without the power of enforcing its own laws, or of sustaining its treaty engagements, and an organized revolutionary army gallantly fighting for a more liberal and enlightened religious and political position; and hence my undeviating policy, whatever have been my sympathies for the revolutionists, of practising myself, and enjoining upon all under my command, a studied regard to neutrality and non-interference." *Ibid.*, Perry to Marshall, December 29, 1853, p. 352.

position! But the chances of such an invitation were virtually non-existent, and Marshall certainly knew it. Even if he had proceeded on his own to the Peiho, hindsight indicates that, like McLane the following year, he was unlikely to have gained any concessions from the Chinese, who had proved themselves masters of the tactics of delay, obstruction, and vague but meaningless promises. Soon after his arrival in China, Marshall himself had written that "the Chinese government *acts upon the principle of assuming so long as assumption will be tolerated, and concedes justice only in the presence of a force able and willing to extort it.*[69] The lesson he had learned at Canton could only have been reinforced by any attempt to deal directly with the central government in the north.

Marshall's repeated threats to go to Tientsin, just as the Taiping armies were launching a drive northward on Peking, did produce compliance with his demands for an interview with I-liang, the governor-general of Liang-Kiang (Kiangsu, Chekiang, and Anhwei, 3 provinces of east-central China). This is apparent from I'liang's memorial to the emperor forwarding Marshall's credentials, in which he justified his reception of Marshall by his fear that "in the face of the violence of the rebels and the stringent measures of the various provinces, if the said barbarians were allowed to go to Tientsin it would inevitably arouse the suspicions of the people living along the coast." [70] The interview took place on July 4, 1853, but aside from gaining, after more than six months, the Chinese government's acknowledgement of his right to present his credentials to the Liang-Kiang governor-general, little was accomplished.[71] An edict of July

[69] *Ibid.*, Marshall to Secretary of State, February 7, 1853, p. 11.

[70] Memorial received June 16, 1853, in Swisher, p. 193.

[71] Since I-liang's capital, Nanking, was in rebel hands, the interview was held at K'un-shan, a district city in Kiangsu about 40 miles west of Shanghai. It is doubtful, however, that I-liang would have set the dangerous precedent of meeting Marshall at Nanking, had he been able to do so, but would rather have held the interview at some location nearer the coast.

Marshall's record of the visit is a fascinating account and well worth reading for his observations on the Chinese people, on I-liang (who was one of the great statesmen of mid-nineteenth-century China), and on the countryside through which he traveled to K'un-shan, and its products. His comments on the prospects for trade at Shanghai were American commerce to be allowed into the interior of "eight of the richest provinces of the empire, in which are abundantly produced cotton, hemp, teenching, rice, all the cereals, tobacco, flax, teas, lead, coal, mica, and several varieties of marble," must have stimulated dreams in Washington of vast, untapped markets, immeasurable resources, and limitless profits across the Pacific. See *HED 123*, Marshall to Marcy, July 6, 1853, pp. 189–98.

20 ordered I-liang to refer all future requests to Governor-General Yeh in Canton, and the *status quo* was resumed.

Marshall's policy towards Peking was based on two wrong assumptions. The first was that the Hsien-feng emperor was kept in seclusion as a result of the "artful management" of the mandarins.[72] It is true that, in contrast to Western nations, full details of his ministers' dealings with the foreigners were not related to the emperor, and he was therefore unaware of many important issues involved. Nevertheless, he agreed fully with their policy of nonintercourse and noncooperation.[73] Second, Marshall did not realize that the Manchu government was more afraid of the barbarians on the coast than of the rebels in Nanking. As an alien dynasty whose power was based on conquest and whose Confucian heritage placed no value on the commerce prized by the West, it had no reason to believe that foreign aims in China were any different from those which had led to the founding of the Ch'ing dynasty itself, or that they were not part of the cycle in which barbarians periodically conquered and ruled China. Peking had no intention of voluntarily altering the regulations which had thus far proved so effective in confining the barbarians to the treaty ports, far away from the heartland of China and its capital.[74]

One problem that the ministers to China from every country faced was that of forcing their citizens to remain neutral. We have already noted Marshall's disagreement with those who expected the dawn of a new day in China. His particular *bête-noir* was the missionary who wanted to take to the Taipings those Christian doctrines which Hung Hsiu-ch'üan had overlooked.[75] Although an 1848 American law made aiding an insurrection against the Chinese government a capital offense, three missionaires attempted to visit Taiping territory. The first was Charles Taylor, who in June, 1853, took Chris-

[72] *Ibid.*, Marshall to Secretary of State, March 19, 1853, p. 88.

[73] There is abundant evidence of this in the documents on this period in Swisher, pp. 191 ff. See, for example, the edict of September 1, 1853, ordering Yeh to handle Marshall at Canton and immediately to devise "means of blocking and controlling him as circumstances allow. If there are further demands, hold rigidly to the treaty as before and stop his wanton ideas. It is important not to allow the development of further complications." Swisher, p. 199.

[74] On China's attitude towards these barbarians from the sea, see Fairbank Chapter 1, "The Problem of China's Response to the West," pp. 3–22.

[75] On this aspect of Taiping Christianity, see "The Christian Component: What the Taipings Took" and "What the Taipings Failed to Take," in Boardman, pp. 52–115.

tian books and pamphlets to Chinkiang. When an imperialist attack on the city was launched while he was there, he returned to his boat for medicines and surgical instruments to allay Taiping suspicions that he was an imperialist spy. Marshall condemned as "acts of the most reprehensible character" Taylor's presenting one of the Taiping leaders with a pistol and a spy glass and leaving a musket behind. Believing Taylor ignorant of the 1848 law, however, he took no measures other than to order him not to publish an account of his adventures in the *North China Herald.*

A similar attempt by W. A. P. Martin failed when he was captured by imperialist forces. That he was taken for one of their foreign officers is indicative of the widespread violation of neutrality by foreigners. Marshall did little to combat such activities, except to order Vice-Consul Cunningham to issue a notification to American citizens enjoining them against infractions of the treaties and American law, in response to a request from the Shanghai taotai that foreigners be prevented from providing arms to the Nanking rebels.[76]

His most famous exchange was with the Reverend I. J. Roberts. Hung Hsiu-ch'üan had studied at Roberts's mission in Canton for two months in 1847, but left without being baptized.[77] In 1853, he invited Roberts to come to Nanking. Roberts asked Marshall whether he would violate any American or international law by going "in the capacity of a minister of the Gospel, merely to preach to him and his followers the unsearchable riches of Christ?" In an eloquent reply, Marshall asserted that such a mission could only impart new zeal to the rebels and declared: "the camp of the insurgents, and the moment when the sceptre of empire trembles in the balance, are neither fit place nor time for you or others—the citizens of a friendly power—to seize upon to display to the followers of Tienteh 'the unsearchable riches of Christ.'" Were Roberts to violate the treaty under which he was permitted to reside in China, he would be worse than a heathen. As a Christian missionary, Marshall pointed out,

. . . Yours is a life dedicated to a labor of love, which justly attracts the benevolent sympathies of all christendom; but, my dear sir, that life would lose "its lustre and perfume" whenever you blend with the surplice of the priest the robes of the political reformer, and seek a proper theatre for your ministrations of the Gospel amidst the flaunting banners and glistening spears of men whose energies are centred upon the task of overthrowing the dynasty which rules their country.

[76] *HED 123,* Notification of June 20, 1853, p. 189.   [77] Boardman, p. 14.

. . . The intemperate zeal, or the improper interference with politics of Christian missionaries, in past centuries, closed the eastern empires of China and Japan against intercourse with western nations. Just emerging from their protracted seclusion, it would be most unfortunate for themselves and the world that the first display before the eyes of China and Japan should be the torch of civil war, lighted upon the altars of their country by Christian teachers of religion! [78]

Marshall's exhortations failed to convince Roberts, who was resolved to go to Nanking, and Marshall was powerless to stop him. [79]

A more serious problem was posed by the fall of the walled city of Shanghai in September. As imperialist forces besieged the city, arms were freely supplied to both sides by foreigners in the foreign settlement just outside the north wall, and many foreigners actively obstructed imperialist attempts to recapture the city. Alcock later wrote that "open sympathy, counsel, food, guns, and ammunition, passed daily from a foreign settlement, held sacred from the intrusion of imperial troops on the ground of absolute neutrality, into a blockaded city, with the professed object of prolonging the defense against the Emperor's forces!" [80] Marshall seems to have been more concerned about British attempts to neutralize the foreign settlement and did little more than urge American citizens to remain neutral. [81] The truth is that there was probably little else he could have done. Even Alcock, whose police powers were much greater, came close to admitting the helplessness of all the foreign consuls when he stated that only public opinion could prevent the traffic in arms. [82]

The walled city of Shanghai fell to a Small Sword Society band on September 7, 1853. That evening the Chinese customs house, located in the foreign settlement, was looted. [83] A British marine

[78] Roberts's inquiry and Marshall's reply are found in *HED 123*, pp. 184–88.

[79] Roberts's attempt to reach Nanking in 1853 failed, and he did not arrive until 1860. The episode is described in Littell, pp. 581–88.

[80] Fairbank, p. 432; see also, p. 430; and *HED 123*, Marshall to Secretary of State, October 30, 1853, p. 292.

[81] This is discussed below. See also Fairbank's (pp. 431–32) discussion of Wu taotai's later impeachment on charges of having conspired with the rebels and the barbarians and his connections with Russell and Company, the firm in which Consul Griswold and Vice-Consul Cunningham were partners. I find his evidence much more persuasive than T. K. Tong apparently does (p. 140).

[82] Fairbank, p. 430.

[83] Marshall stated that he was present on the morning of the seventh when the customs house was first broken into, by a British merchant seeking to

guard was placed on the gutted customs house the next day, and Consul Alcock declared the foreign settlement closed to both the imperialist and insurgent forces. In deploying British troops, Alcock apparently made no effort to consult the Americans. Marshall was angered by what he considered the British consul's highhanded action in posting British troops at all entrances to the foreign settlement and charged that his suggestion that a common defense plan be adopted was ignored.[84] It is unlikely that any joint defense could have been worked out between Marshall and the British, given their opposing views of the situation. The British, arguing that nature's law of self-preservation was higher than any treaty, insisted that troops had to be used to maintain the neutrality of the foreign settlement in order to prevent loss of foreign lives and property.[85] Marshall re-

recover some merchandise seized for a violation of the Chinese revenue laws; thereafter several other British merchants took away cannon and gun carriages stored at the customs house as security against debts they claimed were owed them by the inspector of customs. Only then did the Chinese rabble start to loot. T. K. Tong's statement that the British had purposely put the customs house out of operation, however, can hardly be deduced from Marshall's account. See Tong, p. 136.

[84] *HED 123*, Marshall to Marcy, October 30, 1853, p. 288. A basis for such cooperation did exist. After the fall of Nanking, separate British and American volunteer corps had been organized to aid the naval forces in protecting the foreign community at Shanghai, and particularly to guard merchandise worth some £2 million which had been accumulating in warehouses in the foreign settlement as a result of the disruption of trade in the Yangtze valley. These corps were soon combined into a joint militia and a permanent three-man defense committee was set up, Cunningham serving as one of its members. A meeting of all the foreign residents had voted to adopt various defense measures under the leadership of the committee, including the digging of a ditch (later known as Defense Creek) along the western side of the settlement, thereby enclosing it completely. See Morse, *Conflict*, pp. 458–59; House of Commons, pp. 657–63.

After September 7, this Committee of Cooperation assumed political administration of the foreign settlement under the protection of British troops (Tong, p. 155). The fact that Alcock, as chairman of the committee, became virtual dictator over the foreign community could not but have heightened Marshall's opposition to such an exercise of political administration on Chinese territory. The committee is never mentioned by Marshall, who concentrated his attacks on Alcock.

[85] See *SED 22*, "Minutes of a public meeting of foreign renters of land . . . on the 11th day of July, 1854," pp. 128–31. These minutes, which give the British view of the crisis in September, 1853, were written by Alcock and contain a memorandum from Sir James Stirling, the British naval commander-in-chief.

torted that foreigners in Shanghai had remained unmolested during the uprising, he himself had walked through the city unharmed on the day it was captured, and one of the rebel leaders had assured him that the foreign settlement would not be attacked; the use of foreign troops was therefore an unnecessary violation of China's sovereignty. Calling for firm adherence to treaty rights and obligations, he urged Americans to remain neutral, stay out of the line of fire, and trust their government to obtain indemnity for any losses they might incur.[86] In view of the futility of past endeavors to collect such indemnities from the Chinese government, the British position was certainly more realistic, if less honorable and legally justifiable. Marshall's stand is somewhat puzzling in view of his earlier statement that China would yield nothing except under duress. Unlike the French, whose troops relieved British forces guarding one entrance into the foreign settlement, Marshall refused to ask the naval guard from the *Saratoga* to come ashore after September 10, when he considered the immediate danger over. Given the presence of British and French troops and Alcock's determination to protect British citizens and property by such methods as he felt were necessary, Marshall had little choice but to acquiesce in the situation, although he continued to protest bitterly and offer whatever resistance he could to British policies.

Marshall did cooperate with Alcock in reaching a preliminary agreement on the payment of customs duties in the absence of the imperial authorities.[87] At the time of the capture of Amoy, Marshall raised the question with the State Department but never received a response. On September 9, Marshall and Alcock agreed that the treaties were still in force and that for the present British and American ships would be cleared after promissory notes for the full amount of customs duties owed had been collected by the British and American consuls respectively. Similar regulations were to be posted by Alcock and Cunningham, but, as finally issued, they contained one important difference: the British rules contained a stipulation that the promissory notes would be payable "provided the sanction of H.B.M.'s Government to that effect be received," thus leaving up to the Foreign Office in London the final decision as to whether pay-

[86] *HED 123*, Marshall to Secretary of State, October 30, 1853, p. 289.

[87] Marshall later claimed that he first suggested the deposit of promissory notes to Alcock and Cunningham. Even if this were true, it was certainly in line with the thinking of Alcock, who had attempted to institute such a system earlier that year. See below, p. 294.

ment could be required. It has been charged that Marshall's desire to support the imperial government led him to omit a similar proviso; but British officials customarily referred such questions to London, while the latitude the State Department normally gave its representatives in China justified Marshall's making such a decision on his own. Alcock later said the clause was added to the British announcement upon the insistence of the British merchants while he was "prostrate with sickness" and presumably in no condition to resist.[88]

The fact that British shippers might never have to repay the promissory notes, as was generally predicted, whereas Marshall clearly intended to require Americans to fulfill their obligations under the treaty was a distinct disadvantage to the American merchants. The disruption of the domestic market following the Taiping advance into the Yangtze valley in the spring produced a drastic drop in imports, while exports increased rapidly. The result was a trade imbalance which required increasing imports of treasure. The Spanish Carolus dollar of the reign of Charles IV was the only silver Chinese merchants would accept, and its disappearance in Europe and hoarding in China resulted in silver becoming virtually unobtainable. Even the opium trade had been reduced to a barter basis.[89] In March of that year Alcock had attempted to institute a provisional system, clearing British ships upon deposit of some form of security against part or all of export duties owed. This was a clear violation of the treaties, no other foreign consul followed his lead, and the experiment was dropped a month later.[90] The merchants in Shanghai viewed the capture of the city as an opportunity to obtain relief from the increasing difficulties of the currency situation by declaring Shanghai an open port. Bonham would have preferred to follow the precedent set at Amoy, where no customs duties were collected until the customs house was reestablished in December, 1853, a month after the imperialists regained control of the city. There was very little trade at Amoy, however, and customs revenues were not as important there as at Shanghai; therefore, he chose to refer the question to London rather than to assume responsibility for reversing Alcock's decision. By the time the Foreign Office's reply—that duties should be paid, by all nations trading in China, to whatever Chinese government had established itself in Shanghai or be returned to the merchants—was

[88] Fairbank, pp. 418–19.
[89] For details, see Morse, *Conflict*, pp. 466–68.   [90] Fairbank, p. 404.

received in mid-January, many events had intervened to change the provisional system.[91]

The difficulties that this provisional system would face became clear even before it went into effect. On September 8, the British merchant serving as Prussian consul cleared a Prussian vessel on receipt of a written promise that he would not be held liable for any demands for payment of duties that might be made by the Chinese authorities.[92] It was obvious that while British and American shippers would be required to pay duties under the provisional system, the ships of other countries would be able to depart freely without payment of duties or deposit of promissory notes. On September 12, four of the largest American firms trading at Shanghai protested the new trade regulations, arguing that since the imperial government no longer provided the protection guaranteed under the treaty, Shanghai should be declared a free port. They also objected strenuously to the requirement that duties be paid to a rival merchant in his capacity as vice-consul and that he should be able to requisition their business records to ensure compliance with the system.

"The treaty is not dead," Marshall declared; "for, if it were, I should have no business here, your country no privileges, you no safety for your persons or property. The obligations of both parties to the contract survive the invasion of Shanghai by the horde which now holds it in possession." The treaty could not be abrogated in Shanghai and enforced in Canton, nor could the merchants expect in the future to demand indemnity for any losses unless they had fulfilled their own obligations under the treaty. Thus far, he reminded them, he had not heard that they had suffered any losses, therefore they could not charge the government with failing to fulfill its obligations. Furthermore, in the absence of evidence to the contrary, a consul appointed by the president was presumed to fulfill his duties conscientiously and honestly, and Marshall saw no cause to change any of the regulations.[93]

On September 20, Marshall wrote to Governor-General I-liang to inform him of the measures that had been adopted to clear ships from the port of Shanghai, explaining that his aim had been to prevent losses which might lead to claims against the emperor while at the same time "preserving the duties due, under the treaty, for your

[91] *Ibid.*, pp. 416–20.　　　　　　[92] *Ibid.*, p. 419.

[93] *HED 123*, American merchants to Marshall (September 12, 1853) and Marshall's reply (September 14, 1853), pp. 257–63.

Emperor, when his officers are not able to collect or ascertain them." [94] On October 8, I-liang replied that Wu had been instructed to return to Shanghai and resume his duties as collector of customs in conformity with the treaty regulations,[95] and a few days later Wu himself reappeared and notified the British and American consuls that from the ninth of October "the custom-house business is now carried on as usual, according to the regulations," but with a borrowed seal, his own having been lost to the insurgents and therefore "discontinued." Should he be recognized? Cunningham asked Marshall.[96]

To Marshall the answer was simple: Official notification had been received that an official appointed by the Chinese government, with which the United States had signed a treaty, had returned to Shanghai and was ready to resume his functions. Marshall saw no reason to question his authority, and "exact fidelity" to America's treaty engagements demanded that Wu be allowed once again to administer the customs. Alcock, however, disagreed. On the grounds that Wu's presence in the foreign settlement would constitute a violation of neutrality, Alcock refused to allow him to return to the customs house and informed him that the question of duties would be discussed only after the imperial administration had been reinstated in the walled city. When Wu threatened to collect the duties owed by levying internal duties on Chinese merchants, Alcock responded that such action would lead to "acts of reprisal" disastrous to China's interests.[97] The argument was then dropped, but Marshall

[94] *Ibid.*, Marshall to I-liang, pp. 273–74. In pointing out American good will towards China, Marshall also stressed the fact that, immediately after the capture of Shanghai, he had given protection to Wu taotai at the American consulate (i.e., Russell & Co.) as an *"office of humanity,"* rather than as an attempt to interfere on behalf of one of the belligerents. See also *ibid.*, Marshall to Marcy, September 15, 1853, pp. 255–56.

[95] *Ibid.*, I-liang to Marshall, October 8, 1853, pp. 297–98.

[96] *Ibid.*, pp. 299–300.

[97] *Ibid.*, Marshall to Secretary of State, October 30, 1853, p. 286. See also Fairbank, pp. 423–25. The British argument was that to recognize Wu's authority and permit him to enter the foreign settlement might provoke a rebel attack upon the settlement, requiring foreign resistance and endangering the property the community had adopted self-defense measures to protect. To allow him the protection of either foreign troops or his own guards would be violations of neutrality. The British probably feared that Wu would resume his attempts to enlist foreign aid against the rebels. They also pointed out that Wu's function as inspector of customs could not be separated from his duties

was incensed and determined to force recognition of the taotai's authority. Marshall's decision was probably prompted equally by his growing suspicion of British intentions in China, which had been fueled by the posting of British guards and Alcock's attitude towards the taotai, by British refusal to permit armed guards, "a mere escort, usual to his rank and station," to accompany either the rebel or the imperialist commanders on official visits to the foreign settlement or to allow imperial ships to anchor in front of the customs house,[98] and by what he viewed as lax treatment of a British subject who had been seized en route to Nanking.[99] Neutrality may be the avowed policy of the British government, he wrote to Washington, but the actions of its representatives in China can only lead "to the conclusion that there is another policy in view." Only the threat of resistance by the United States, he believed, deterred Great Britain from seizing Shanghai and gaining control of trade in the entire Yangtze valley. "Practice in British India, at the Cape, in the Caribbean, in Burmah, has familiarized this power with the best methods, through the instrumentality of a protectorate, to acquire substantial dominion over weak and unwarlike peoples." It was his duty to forestall such an eventuality, while maintaining his neutrality in the present struggle, and in so doing "to impress the authorities and people of China with a conviction that the love of justice, the cultivation of friendly relations with other nations, and unswerving fidelity to the sacred obligations of treaties, were and are prominent characteristics of the foreign policy of the United States." [100]

Marshall therefore ordered Cunningham to notify Wu and the American merchants of Shanghai that as of October 28 the American consul would cease to collect promissory notes. Unable to take

as taotai, which he was no longer in a position to fulfill, hence the requirement, which so incensed Marshall, that Wu recover his regular seal before he resume collecting the customs duties. This was hardly their fundamental argument, however.

[98] Since the customs house was in the foreign settlement and the foreign anchorages had been neutralized as well, the British argued that imperialist ships could not be allowed into the anchorage. Furthermore, foreign shipping would be endangered if the imperial fleet were fired upon or attacked by the insurgents.

[99] *HED 123*, Marshall to Secretary of State, October 30, 1853, p. 289. Marshall really had no right to censure the British in this regard for, as we have seen, he had imposed no penalties on Americans who went to Nanking.

[100] *Ibid.*, pp. 290–91.

possession of the customs house, Wu told Cunningham that one or two boats would be moored in the Whangpu River to serve as a customs house and requested that he continue to clear American ships under the provisional arrangements until the boats could be procured. Cunningham was adamant, pointing out that he could not withdraw his notification to the American merchants, and demanded to know the arrangements under which ships were to be cleared. When October 28 dawned, Wu had not replied, and Cunningham turned to Marshall for further instructions. Marshall replied that those ships which were already loaded might be cleared under the provisional rules. For those who wanted to pay in sycee, Cunningham was to take a declaration indicating the duties owed and officially demand that the inspector of customs accept the duties and give the ship port clearance; should he refuse to do so, Cunningham was to protest as a violation of the treaty such an embargo upon American shipping and permit the ship to depart, unless the inspector indicated a willingness to pay a fair demurrage for delaying the vessel's departure.[101] Several ships were thereafter cleared under the provisional rules.[102]

Whether the floating customs house ever functioned is uncertain. Marshall complained to the State Department that the boats were "twice driven from their anchorage . . . by a British man-of-war." [103] On several occasions boats moored at locations suitable for intercepting ships into and out of the harbor were driven off for fear that they would be attacked by the rebels. It is clear that any attempt on the taotai's part to assert his authority was hindered by foreign desires to protect their shipping and maintain their neutrality. As Cunningham describes the problem:

Can it be expected that where the collector has no oversight of the great bulk of the merchantmen visiting the port, no notice of their arrivals or departures, interdicted even from sending boats to make inquiries,—for the boats must be armed for their own protection and all armed boats have been turned from the foreign anchorage by the British force,—he will be able to perform his functions with regularity? It is tying a man's hands and feet in the water and upon the result denying that he can swim.[104]

[101] For this correspondence, see *ibid.*, pp. 299–305.
[102] *SED 22*, Cunningham to McLane, May 4, 1854, p. 361.
[103] *HED 123*, Marshall to Secretary of State, October 30, 1853, p. 291.
[104] Cunningham to Alcock, January 30, 1854, quoted in Fairbank, p. 426.

It was not long before the floating customs house disappeared. On October 29, the Austrian vessel *Robert* left Shanghai, where there was no Austrian consul, without paying duties or posting bond. Having just been ordered to resume payment in specie, American merchants were alarmed at the advantage given to shipping under other flags. The same group of American firms thereupon addressed a letter to the consuls of Great Britain, France, Portugal, Holland, Prussia, and Hamburg inquiring whether they recognized the authority of a customs house in Shanghai and where it was situated. Receiving a unanimously negative reply,[105] they protested Cunningham's recognition of the customs house and appealed to Marshall to permit their vessels to be cleared on the same basis as those of other nations. Declaring that the American consul had been officially informed of the reestablishment of the customs house whereas the other consuls had not (on this occasion Marshall chose to overlook the fact that this was certainly not true of Great Britain), Marshall was adamant that American merchants would be required to pay duties to the inspector of customs as provided under the treaties.[106] At that point, however, Marshall decided to return to Canton,[107] and Cunningham apparently returned to the system of collecting promissory notes. Desiring clearance for its barque *Jennet,* Smith, King & Co. wrote to Cunningham stating it was their understanding that "it will be sufficient for shippers to give promissory notes for the amounts due by them, and that, as consignees of the ship, it will be our business to place these in possession of the Chinese collector." Wu formally acquiesced in Cunningham's demand that American shippers be granted clearance upon deposit of promissory notes, as British shippers were permitted to do,[108] with the proviso "payable

---

[105] The farcical nature of this inquiry is not revealed in Marshall's correspondence. T. C. Beale, a British merchant, served as both the Portuguese and Dutch consuls; the Hamburg consul was William Hogg, another British merchant; the Prussian consul was D. O. King, a partner in one of the firms signing the letter. Fairbank, p. 425.

[106] For this inquiry, dated October 31, 1853, and Marshall's reply of November 1, see *HED 123*, pp. 312–14.

[107] He stated that he desired to seek an interview with Yeh to discuss their conflicting interpretations of the treaty and questions arising from "the strange course of the British consul at Shanghai," to confer with Bonham at Hong Kong in the light of Marcy's recent instructions, and to await the arrival of his successor at Hong Kong. *Ibid.,* Marshall to Marcy, November 21, 1853, p. 311.

[108] See correspondence, *ibid.,* pp. 330–31.

if the sanction of the United States government is obtained." [109] Cunningham later said that as a result of a misunderstanding on the part of the shippers and the consular clerk, the notes were deposited with the consulate rather than the inspector of customs. The vice-consul thus returned to Alcock's provisional system,[110] and Marshall's attempt to defeat the British consul and restore the authority of the inspector of customs failed.

In the final chapter of Marshall's battle over the customs dues Shanghai was declared a free port. Apparently disregarding the fact that Cunningham had returned to the provisional system, Marshall wrote Governor-General Yeh pointing out that the United States alone had been willing to resume payment of duties as usual. He declared that so long as ships of other nations were allowed to depart without paying duties [111] and British ships were allowed to clear on the deposit of promissory notes of dubious value, it was his duty under the most-favored-nation clause of the treaty to permit American ships to depart without clearance or payment of duties.[112]

[109] *Ibid.,* Cunningham to Marshall, December 24, 1853, p. 364.

[110] *SED 22,* Cunningham to McLane, May 4, 1854, p. 362. It is unlikely that the system was ever really abandoned in practice. The earlier joint protests asked for the *right* to be cleared on the same basis as ships of other countries; this was the first time that actual clearance was demanded. See *ibid.,* pp. 360–63. Also Wetmore & Co. to McLane, July 15, 1854: "It thus appears that the floating custom-house *was not a bona fide establishment;* all vessels which had commenced loading prior to the 28th of October cleared under the provisional regulations; those which *subsequently* arrived *did the same,* the vice consul raising no objection and tacitly admitting the failure of measures which he was instrumental in originating. Henceforth no notice whatever was taken of the *floating custom-house;* the boats remained but a day or two near the spot designated, engaged with the rest in several desperate attacks upon the suburbs, and, if not destroyed, were subsequently lost to view." *Ibid.,* p. 373.

[111] Obviously because France was a treaty power, Marshall particularly stressed that French ships were allowed to depart without payment of duties. The reply of the French consul to the query of the American firms, stating that he did not recognize the existence of a Chinese customs house and considered himself "fully at liberty to allow the entry and despatch of the ships of my nation free of all duties," was published in the *North China Herald* (Morse, *Submission,* p. 14). Marshall's argument was somewhat specious, however, since there was no French shipping at Shanghai during the period of the provisional system (Fairbank, p. 436), although the *Robert* and several other vessels sailing under the flags of nontreaty nations had departed without paying duties or depositing promissory notes.

[112] See correspondence between Marshall and Yeh, *HED 123,* pp. 340–47.

One wonders why Marshall suddenly decided to bring an end to the provisional system by in effect declaring Shanghai a free port. Why did he shift to an emphasis on the advantages which would accrue to American commerce once Shanghai became a free port, so in contrast to his earlier expression of a desire to ensure the customs revenues for China and to provide, in the fulfillment of America's treaty obligations, an example of friendship and adherence to the law of nations? One reason may have been a fear for the effect of his requirements on American trade, although American merchants were operating on virtually the same basis as the British. Since British and American ships carried more than 85 percent of the trade at Shanghai,[113] American shipping had not been placed in a particularly unfavorable position, and it was hardly likely that the American government would require payment of American promissory notes if the British notes were disallowed by the Foreign Office. A stronger reason perhaps is indicated in his comment that if Shanghai were made a free port, "retributive justice will overtake Great Britain," for the resulting shift of trade from Canton must decrease the value of Hong Kong. Even if Britain were to respond by making Canton a free port, American shipping would profit equally.[114] However honorable his intentions towards China might otherwise have been, it would seem that, in his attempts to abolish the provisional system, whether by recognizing the authority of the Chinese customs or abolishing the customs altogether, Marshall was also motivated by his hostility towards Great Britain, which he had labeled many months before as America's "chief rival" for the commerce of the Far East.[115]

Marshall's hope that Britain and France would "continue to hold their present counsels" and refuse to pay duties to the Chinese inspector of customs was not in vain. On January 4, in the absence of any indication from Governor-General Yeh that the *Robert's* duties would be collected or Britain made to cease clearing British ships under a system other than payment in silver as required by its treaty with China, Marshall ordered Cunningham to declare Shanghai a free port. In the long run, his resistance to British customs policy, by first supporting the Chinese customs and then abolishing it, served

[113] Fairbank, pp. 427 and 436.
[114] *HED 123*, Marshall to Marcy, January 9, 1854, pp. 334–35.
[115] *Ibid.*, Marshall to Secretary of State, April 28, 1853, p. 102.

only to weaken the taotai's position.[116] In January, the Foreign Office ruling was received stating that British promissory notes were payable if the shipping of other nations had been subject to the same regulations. Thus Alcock's position, already weakened when the ships of nontreaty nations departed freely, was made untenable by Marshall's action.

Marshall's mission ended as it had begun, in a vain attempt to obtain an interview with Governor-General Yeh at Canton and in controversy with the commander of the Far Eastern fleet over his right to requisition a naval vessel to transport him to Shanghai and Nanking. Learning first through a Washington newspaper that his successor had been appointed, Marshall left China on January 27, 1854. Most of the problems which he had faced were left to his successor, who would also be forced to operate under most of the same handicaps.

Marshall's policy of using this period of turmoil to obtain advantages for American commerce while preserving China's rights and sovereignty against foreign encroachment was a failure. In part this was due to his lack of support from Washington and the inadequacy of the American consular establishment in China. A more important reason, however, was the fact that any hope of obtaining concessions from China depended upon cooperation with Great Britain, and such cooperation was made extremely difficult, if not impossible, by his undisguised hostility to Britain. The benefits of such cooperation were shown in the drafting of the Shanghai municipal code. His suspicion of British aims in China was also an important factor in undercutting Alcock's regulation of the customs system and, ultimately, in weakening China's claims to the customs revenues. Furthermore, despite his genuine concern to preserve China's sovereignty, his policy of demanding strict fulfillment of the treaties by China as well as the United States was unrealistic, in view of China's attitude towards the treaties in the past.

On the other hand, despite his limited knowledge of China, Marshall showed a keener awareness of the nature and significance of China's rebellion than did most Westerners at the time. He soon

[116] *Ibid.*, Marshall to Cunningham, January 4, 1854, pp. 365–67. The British, of course, did the same. By then the tea and silk season was over and a change in the customs system could be made. In February, a new Chinese customs house was established and recognized by the consuls in Shanghai. See Fairbank, pp. 434–36.

realized what came to be the basis of American policy towards China, that the preservation of a unified China against domestic and foreign threats was important to the United States. The preconditions he attached to his recommendation of intervention to further such a policy made it, as was so often true of America's China policy in subsequent years, more a statement of intent than a program of action.

Soviet Foreign Trade: Law, Practice and Financing

CHARLES J. MOXLEY, JR.

The Soviet Union's foreign trade turnover in 1966 was $16,754 million, including $7,913 million of export and $8,841 million of import. In 1966 the Soviet Union ranked sixth among the world's trading nations in amount of trade. Nonetheless, Soviet trade makes up less than 4 percent of total world trade.[1] Soviet foreign trade has been a smaller percentage of its Gross National Product (GNP) than that of any other nation in the world with the possible exception of Red China.[2] Soviet trade in 1966 represented less than one third of that of the United States for the same year.[3] Moreover, in 1966 about 70 percent of Soviet trade was conducted within the Communist world, and approximately 55 percent of this was carried on with COMECON countries. This is not at all exceptional, but is rather a typical percentage of Soviet trade to be carried on with the Communist bloc.[4] Of the remaining 30 percent of Soviet trade in 1966, a little more than three fifths was with the industrial West and the remainder with the developing nations.[5]

Thus, Soviet economic policy is one in which trade does play a great role. The Soviets have espoused the economic policy of autarky, which entails the drive for economic self-sufficiency, and, to a great

[1] United Nations, *1967 Statistical Yearbook* (New York, 1968), pp. 384–87.

[2] See, F. Holzman, ed., *Readings on the Soviet Economy* (Chicago, Rand McNally, 1962), p. 707. This autarkic trade policy is typical not just of the Soviet Union but of the Communist nations generally. F. Pryor, *The Communist Foreign Trade System* (Cambridge, Mass., M.I.T. Press, 1963), p. 25; Stolte, "The USSR and the World Trade Conference," *Bulletin of the Institute for the Study of the USSR,* XI, No. 10 (October, 1964), 18.

[3] See, United Nations, *1967 Statistical Yearbook,* pp. 384–87.

[4] *Vneshnaya Torgovla SSSR, 1918–66* (Moscow, 1967), pp. 70–71.

[5] *Ibid.,* pp. 62–63, 70–71.

extent, only the import of those goods which it is necessary to import and the export of goods in order only to import.[6]

The Law of Soviet Foreign Trade

STRUCTURE OF SOVIET FOREIGN TRADE

The Soviet Union conducts its foreign trade through a state monopoly.[7] The Council of Ministers has the ultimate responsibility in the field of foreign trade and has exclusive jurisdiction over the creation of foreign-trade organizations and the determination of their responsibilities. The Council of Ministers has delegated the direct responsibility for the supervision, regulation, and control of foreign trade to the Ministry of Foreign Trade.[8]

The Ministry of Foreign Trade. The Ministry is part of the government of the Soviet Union and as such is not a juridical person,[9] but enjoys sovereign immunity.[10] It is part of the Council of Ministers of the Soviet Union, which is the highest executive and administrative organ of state authority.[11] The Minister of Foreign Trade is a member of the Central Committee of the Communist Party of the Soviet

[6] For an historical review of the basic trends of Soviet foreign-trade policy, structure, and partners during the several distinctive periods of development thereof, see, R. L. Allen, *Soviet Economic Warfare* (Washington, D.C., Public Affairs Press, 1960); A. Baykov, *Soviet Foreign Trade* (Princeton, Princeton University Press, 1946); Z. Brzezinski, *The Soviet Bloc* (New York, Praeger, 1965); A. Bergson and S. Kuznets, eds., *Economic Trends in the Soviet Union* (Cambridge, Mass., Harvard University Press, 1963); M. Florinsky, ed., *Encyclopedia of Russia and the Soviet Union* (New York, McGraw-Hill, 1961); *The Gallatin Annual of International Business* (New York, American Heritage, 1965); V. Katkoff, *Soviet Economy 1940–65* (Baltimore, Dangary, 1961); M. Kaser, COMECON (New York, Oxford University Press, 1967); P. Lydolph, *Geography of the U.S.S.R.* (New York, Wiley, 1964); *Narodnoe Khozyzystvo v 1960 Gody* (Moscow, 1961), p. 744; Olsiekiewicz, "Trade and Liberalization," *Bulletin of the Institute for the Soviet Union* (June, 1964), p. 6; A. Nove, *The Soviet Economy* (New York, Praeger, 1965); and Pryor, *The Communist Foreign Trade System* (Chicago, Rand McNally).

[7] *U.S.S.R. Const.,* arts. 11, 14; K. Grzybowski, *Soviet Private International Law 72* (Leyden, A. W. Sijthoff, 1965); H. Berman, "The Legal Framework of Trade Between Planned and Market Economies: The Soviet-American Example," *Law and Contemporary Problems,* XXIV (1959), 482, 484.

[8] Grzybowski, p. 72.   [9] Berman, p. 486.

[10] B. Fensterwald, "Sovereign Immunity and Soviet State Trading," *Harvard Law Review,* LXIII (1950), 614, 634–39.

[11] *U.S.S.R. Const.,* art. 64; Berman, p. 486.

Union.[12] The actions of the Ministry of Foreign Trade are thus subordinate to the Council of Ministers, the Party Presidium, and other higher organs of the Communist party.

The ministry exercises broad direct responsibility.[13] Working within the limits of the over-all national plan, national policy, and existing commitments, it has responsibility for the over-all planning of Soviet foreign trade.[14] Through its planning department, it participates in the preparation of the draft plan for submission to the Council of Ministers.[15] In preparing this draft plan, the Ministry of Foreign Trade must coordinate all the lower-level plans of the importing and exporting corporations, which draft their plans based on those of the producing organizations and the selling and purchasing departments.[16]

The Ministry of Foreign Trade has the responsibility of drafting and participating in the negotiation of foreign trade agreements.[17] It makes and administers the national tariff policies and issues licenses for the export and import of goods.[18] It controls the trade delegations (*torgpred'stva*) which act in a sovereign capacity as a part of the Soviet government.

The ministry creates and controls the foreign trade associations or combines and determines the scope of their statutory activities, issues their charter, and generally supervises and controls them.[19]

[12] Pisar, *A New Look at Trade Policy Toward the Communist Bloc* (Washington, D.C., U.S. Government, 1961), p. 19.

[13] H. Schwartz, *Russia's Soviet Economy* (Englewood Cliffs, N.J., Prentice-Hall, 1958), p. 579.

[14] Spubler, "The Soviet Bloc Foreign Trade System," *Law and Contemporary Problems,* XXIV (1959), 420.

[15] Schwartz, p. 579; Baykov, p. 24.

[16] Spulber, p. 421; Baykov, p. 24; R. Allen, pp. 282–84; Berman, pp. 497–99; C. Schmitthoff, "Commercial Treaties and International Trade Transactions in East-West Trade," *Vanderbilt Law Review,* XX (1967), 355, 359; "New Civil Code of the RSFSR—A Soviet View; A Western View," *International and Comparative Law Quarterly,* XV (1966), 1090.

[17] Spulber, p. 420; Berman, p. 486; Grzybowski, p. 72; Schwartz, p. 579.

[18] Berman, p. 486.

[19] *Ibid.;* Grzybowski, p. 73; See A. M. Smirnov and N. N. Liubimov, eds., *Vneshviaia Torgovlia SSSR* (Foreign Trade of the U.S.S.R.) (Moscow, 1954), p. 77, where a general list of the powers and functions of the Ministry of Foreign Trade is given. The Ministry in fact even has the power to modify or cancel terms of contracts made by the combines; Genkin, "Pravovoe polozhenie sovetskikh eksportnykh i importnykh ob' 'edinenii za granitsei," *Problemy Mezhdunarodnogo Chastnogo Prava* (1960), pp. 7–8.

The presidents and vice-presidents of the combines are appointed by the Minister of Foreign Trade and are subject to his authority on a continuing basis.

Before 1935, the Ministry of Foreign Trade carried on most of the trade of the Soviet Union through the trade delegations. Under the old system, the delegations acted abroad, negotiating and concluding contracts, and generally promoting the development of Soviet foreign economic relations. Their areas of competence are not restricted to specific commodities.

However, in 1935 the technique and organization of Soviet foreign trade was significantly changed as follows:

Trade delegations were assigned controlling and supervisory functions, given administrative responsibility for issuing import and export licenses, and were relieved of conducting foreign trade operations. This task was assigned to the foreign trade associations with a seat in Moscow. Unless contracts and agreements between parties provided otherwise, Soviet arbitration organizations became the forum, and Soviet private international law the proper law for Soviet foreign trade transactions.[20]

Thus, after 1935 the combines became the main contract-making agencies, although the trade delegations remained the "formal commercial policy executors and controllers of Soviet foreign trade activity".[21]

Foreign Trade Corporations (Combines or Associations)

Thus, since 1935 the actual operation of the Soviet foreign-trade monopoly has been carried on in most countries through the combines. This has been the case in the United States where the foreign-trade organizations have worked either directly, through commercial representatives, or indirectly, through Amtorg Trading Corporation, a New York corporation, the shares of which are held in escrow by the Bank of Foreign Trade in Moscow.[22] Most of the trade transac-

[20] Grzybowski, p. 39; see *Sobranie Zakonov i Rasporiazhenii Raboche-Krest'ianskogo Pravitel'stva SSSR, 1924–38* (1935), art. 367.

[21] J. Triska and R. Slusser, *The Theory, Law, and Policy of Soviet Treaties* (Stanford, Calif., Stanford University Press, 1962), p. 332; Pryor, p. 53; R. Mikesell and J. Behrman, *Financing Free World Trade with the Sino-Soviet Bloc* (Princeton, Princeton University Press, 1958), p. 63.

[22] When it recognized the Soviet Union in 1933, the United States refused to accept the assignment of trade commissioners with diplomatic status to the

tions carried on through Amtorg are characteristically implemented through contracts made directly with the foreign-trade corporations.[23]

Besides concluding contracts with foreign commercial interests, the combines are responsible for promoting and implementing Soviet foreign trade. These combines act within the over-all plan of the Soviet economy, serving as intermediaries between Soviet domestic producers, consumer and distributional enterprises, on the one hand, and the foreign buyers and sellers on the other.[24] They assure the delivery by national domestic suppliers of goods for export, and the receipt and acceptance by domestic customers of the imported merchandise. This trade function of the combine is obviously a most important one since no ordinary Soviet enterprise may legally import or export.

The relationship of the combines to the Soviet domestic enterprises is one of customer and supplier and the role is formalized through

---

United States, *Foreign Relations of the United States, The Soviet Union 1933–39* (Washington, D. C., U.S. Department of State, 1952), p. 51; J. Stevenson, "The Legal Position of Soviet Foreign Trade Organizations in the United States," in *The Law of The U.S.—U.S.S.R. Trade* (Washington, D.C., Association of American Law Schools, 1965), pp. 52–53, the major reason for this U.S. position was the desire to prevent the Soviet claim of sovereign immunity in trade transactions; Berman, p. 518; Stevenson, p. 51. However, there seem to be no state or federal laws which significantly limit the business activities of the Soviet foreign trade combine or its affiliated corporations in the U.S.; *Ibid.*, p. 56, the foreign trade corporations are subject to the jurisdiction of our courts and may not invoke sovereign immunity; *Ibid.*, p. 57; there are, in addition, other Soviet enterprises which in limited circumstances are empowered to enter into foreign-trade operations. Examples are *Sovexportfilm, film,* which is subordinate to the Ministry of Culture of the USSR, or *Skotoimport,* which is subordinate to the Ministry of Food Industry; Knapp, "The Function, Organization and Activities of Foreign Trade Corporations in the European Socialist Countries," in C. Schmitthoff, ed., *The Sources of the Law of International Trade* (London, Stevens and Sons, 1964), p. 59; see Berman, p. 489; see P. Cherviakov, *Organizatsiia i Technika Vneshnei Torgovli SSSR* (Organization and Technique of Foreign Trade of the U.S.S.R.) (Moscow, Foreign Trade Publications, 1958), pp. 41–43. (This book is translated and condensed by Scott in *10 Soviet Legal Studies* [1959], pp. 393, 394–96.)

[23] Apparently only the new and inexperienced U.S. trader will demand that the contract be signed directly with the Amtorg Trading Corp. Interview with Mr. Tom Hoya, Columbia University School of Law, New York, N.Y.

[24] Nove, p. 43; Mikesell & Behrman, p. 63.

the conclusion of special contracts between the combines and the domestic enterprises.[25]

The 31 combines are organized according to the group of commodities in which they specialize.[26] Each has a monopoly in a particular area of the export-import economy, and no other state enterprise will have competence in this field.[27] For instance, *Raznoimport* imports and exports products such as light metals, rolled light metals, rubber, and synthetic rubber products. *Promsyr'aimport* imports and exports ferrous metals and alloys, railroad material, steels, pipes, and hardware.[28]

An important instrument of the Soviet monopoly of foreign trade from which the combines are largely exempted is the licensing system. The combines are generally given basic or general permits for exporting and importing the goods within their charter jurisdiction, or general permits for up to a certain amount of the total export or import turnover.[29]

LEGAL STATUS OF THE COMBINE

As indicated, the Council of Ministers has exclusive jurisdiction in the creation of foreign-trade organizations and in the determination of their responsibilities. The direct responsibility for the supervision, regulation, and control of foreign trade lies in the Ministry of Foreign Trade. The ministry creates combines upon the instructions of the Council of Ministers.[30]

Thus, the combines are in effect extensions of the Soviet government. However, under Soviet law they are juridical persons,[31] which consequently can sue and be sued, can own property in their own names, and can make contracts enforceable against themselves.[32]

---

[25] Spulber, p. 442.

[26] H. Berman, "A Reappraisal of U.S.–U.S.S.R. Trade Policy," *Harvard Business Review*, XLII (July-August, 1964), 139; Nove, p. 53.

[27] Knapp, p. 62. [28] Cherviakov, pp. 41–42. [29] Knapp, p. 58.

[30] Grzybowski, pp. 72–73.

[31] "Fundamentals of Civil Legislation of the USSR and Union Republics" (hereinafter cited as "Fundamentals"), in *Law in Eastern Europe*, VII (Leyden, A. W. Sythoff, 1963), p. 265, art. 11; see D. Ramzaitsev, "The Law of International Trade in the New Soviet Legislation," *Journal of Business*, L (1963), 229, for a consideration of the sections of the "Fundamentals" relevant to Soviet foreign trade; see *Sovetskii Yezhegodnik Mezhdunarodnogo Prava* (1963), p. 417; Knapp, pp. 62, 63, 66.

[32] "Fundamentals," art. 13; Berman, p. 483; Knapp, p. 64.

However, the combine does not enjoy the "general capacity of having rights and performing duties in law" as a natural person would have. Rather, it has a special capacity, exclusive in its limited area of monopoly control as defined by its charter.[33] Fundamentals' article 12 provides that a juridical person has legal capacity as determined by "the purposes laid down for its activity." Article 11 provides that "a juridical person operates on the basis of a charter (by-law)." Thus the legal capacity of Soviet juridical persons is of a special nature, such that it may be exercised solely within the limits laid down by its charter. However, Ramzaitsev, a leading Soviet writer in the foreign-trade field, asserts that this limited capacity of the Soviet foreign-trade corporation presents no obstacle to foreign trade with the Soviet Union since, he says, there has not been a single instance of a Soviet foreign-trade corporation exceeding its legal capacity.[34]

The question presents itself, however, of the extraterritorial effect of the Soviet definition of the limited capacity of the foreign-trade combine. Does it have absolute extraterritorial effect, such that it cannot be defeated in a common-law court by the doctrine of apparent or ostensible authority? Grzybowski asserts that "there seems to be no doubt that the provisions of the charter of a foreign trade enterprise, and the foreign-trade regulations which determine the mode of the conclusion of contracts and the legal capacity of Soviet foreign-trade associations, will have effect also vis-à-vis their partners abroad".[35] Ramzaitsev indicates that the general provisions of private international law provide that the legal status of a juridical person is determined by the law of the country to which the juridical person belongs and that consequently the Soviet rules concerning the capacity of Soviet legal persons and the responsibility for their commitments must be applied, irrespective of the place where the combine performed any legal act.[36]

---

[33] *Ibid.*, pp. 62–63.   [34] *Soveteskii Yezhegodnik*, p. 417.

[35] Grzybowski, p. 77.

[36] Ramzaitsev, p. 230; *Sovetskii Yezhegodnik*, p. 417; see also Grzybowski, p. 80; L. Lunts, *Nekotorye Voprosy Mezhdunarodnogo Chastnogo Prava* (Some Problems of Private International Law) (Moscow, Uchenye Zapiski, 1955), VIIuN, No. 3. However, I must note the potential tension between this Soviet rule of the extraterritoriality of the status of the Soviet combines, on the one hand, and the common-law rule of apparent authority, on the other. See Knapp, p. 64; See. Mentschikoff, "Principles of Law Bearing upon Contracts Between Soviet Trading Organizations and American Business Enterprises," in

Section 13 of the Fundamentals covers the extent of the liability of the juridical person on its obligations. It provides that the state is not liable on the obligations of juridical persons, nor are the juridical persons liable on the obligations of the state.[37] It provides further that

A juridical person is liable on its obligations to the extent of its property (or, if a State body with legal personality, to the extent of the property allotted to it) so far as such property may be taken in execution of judgment under the legislation of the USSR and the Union Republics.[38]

Thus, the Fundamentals, sections 11–13, define juridical persons and indicate that the combine is a juridical person with all the concomitant implications of this. However, the charter of the combine will characteristically provide that the combine is liable to compulsory execution according to the general legislation of the USSR.[39] In fact, the area of assets that are *extra commercium* and cannot be taken in execution of judgment under the legislation of the USSR is great, extending to fixed assets, real estate, and capital equipment. However, the combines are established with a capital of a set amount, which capital is subject to execution.[40]

Although the property of the combine is under section 21 of the

---

The Law of U.S. Trade (Washington, D.C., Association of American Law Schools, 1965), XVIII, 20–21. Tuttle suggests as a solution to these difficulties that the United States conclude with the Soviet Union a treaty pursuant to article 129 of the Fundamentals, which treaty would supersede the other terms of the Fundamentals and, in particular, would neutralize the provisions of article 128: "A foreign law shall not apply where application contradicts the fundamental principles of the Soviet system." W. Tuttle, "Soviet-American Trade: Some Problems of Socialist Law Requiring Treaty Clarification," *Santa Clara Lawyer,* VII, 188; "Fundamentals," art. 129, provides as follows: "Rules laid down in any international treaty or agreement to which the USSR is a party are to be applied in preference to different rules otherwise applicable under Soviet civil legislation." In this essay, however, I am not concerned with the conflicts rules of law *per se,* but rather with the question of the nature and power of the combine within the Soviet legal system.

[37] Knapp, p. 56.

[38] Ramsaitsev, p. 231.

[39] Genkin, "Pravovoe Polozhenie Vsesoiuznykh Vneshne Torgovykh Ob' 'edinenii," (The Legal Status of All-Union Foreign-Trade Combines), in Genkin, ed., *Pravovye Voprosy Vneshnei Torgovli SSSR S Evropeiskimi Stranami Narodnoi Demokratski* (Legal Questions of Foreign Trade of the USSR With European Countries of People's Democracy) (Moscow, 1955), pp. 53, 71.

[40] K. M. Genkin, ed., *Pravovoe Regulirovanie Vneshnei Torgovli* (Moscow, 1961), p. 47; Grzybowski, p. 75.

Fundamentals state property of the USSR, the combines "have the operational management of the State property alloted to them, and exercise the rights of possession, use and disposition of such property within the limits laid down by law in accordance with the objectives of their operations, their planned tasks and the purpose of the property." [41] These rights of possession, use, and disposition of property given the state organization are the same as those given an owner of property by section 19.[42] Article 21 is the legal authority of the combine to sell property of the state under its management.

Thus, the legal nature of the combine is defined by the preceding chapters of the Fundamentals. However, this is only a small part of the answer to the question as to what regime of law the combines are subjected. This question is a perplexing one which does not seem to be adequately answered in the literature.

The Soviet constitution by its terms purports to be the highest legislation in the country. However, the Soviets have not regarded their constitution as a fundamental statement and guarantee of basic governmental structure and of established rights. To the contrary, they have regarded the constitution as a policy statement of the goals of the government and of the party for the future. The fact that the Soviet constitution does not serve as a basic document of established rights and governmental structure is evidenced by the absence of provisions for judicial review of legislative enactments.[43] This is also indicated by the frequency and type of amendments of the constitution and by the forms and procedures for amendment. Theoretically, the highest ranking legislation in the Soviet Union is the "law" (zakon). This is enacted by the legislature of the Soviet Union, the Supreme Soviet, consisting of the two houses, the Council of Nationalities, and the Council of the Union. However, during the months each year when the legislature is not in session,

[41] Ramsaitsev, pp. 231–32.

[42] *Ibid.; Sovetskii Yezhegodnik,* pp. 417–18.

[43] Although the Soviet constitution of 1923 gave the authority to the Supreme Court of the USSR to render an opinion, pursuant to the prior request of the legislature, as to the conformity with the constitution of legislation of the constituent republics, this limited form of judicial review was removed from the 1936 constitution. J. Hazard and I. Shapiro, eds., *The Soviet Legal System* (Dobbs Ferry, N.Y., Oceana Publications, Inc., 1962), Part I, p. 27; P. Romashkin, "A New Stage in the Development of the Soviet State," *Sovetskoe Gosudarstvo i Pravo,* No. 10 (1960), p. 31, in Hazard and Shapiro, eds., pp. 33–35.

the Presidium of the Supreme Soviet may make "provisional measures" through "decree" action. Although the decrees of the Presidium of the Supreme Soviet do not acquire the status of law until they are ratified by the Supreme Soviet, this distinction seems to have become virtually meaningless since the decrees are given the same effect as law and are apparently never denied ratification when ratification is sought.

In addition, the Council of Ministers of the U.S.S.R. and of the union and autonomous republics issue "orders" and "directives" on the basis of and in execution of existing laws.[44] Also, the ministers of the USSR issue "orders" and "instructions." The local soviets of toilers' deputies and of their executive committees also issue "decisions" and "orders." Occasionally, the Council of Ministers of the USSR and the Central Committee of the Communist party of the Soviet Union issue "joint orders," designed to mobilize broad popular support. These different acts of Soviet state organs are issued on the basis of and in execution of existing laws and in conformity with them and are subordinate to the "laws." [45]

The Soviet legal system seems to attribute rather little significance to custom as a source of law. Likewise, the Soviet Union follows the traditional approach of the Romanist system of Continental Europe, as opposed to the common-law system, and rejects the idea of the binding effect of court decisions.

The determination of the role of the Communist party as a source of law in the Soviet Union is, of course, a difficult and perhaps impossible one to answer. However, it is clear that the organizational structure of the government renders rather simple the effectuation of influence, since the party members predominate at the higher levels of government. In addition, the Soviet goal is the expansion of the role of the party and retraction of the governmental role.[46]

In considering the over-all structure of Soviet law, it is, of course, necessary to take cognizance of the federal nature of the Soviet governmental organization.[47] The federal government has jurisdiction to determine the fundamental principles of criminal and civil legis-

[44] Hazard and Shapiro, eds., p. 28, citing J. Hazard, "Constitutional Problems in the USSR," in J. K. Pollock, ed., *Change and Crisis in European Government* (New York, 1947).

[45] A. S. Fedoseev, *Osnovy Sovetskogo Gosudarstva i Prava* (The Basis of the Soviet State and Law) (Moscow, 1958), pp. 37–41.

[46] Romashkin, in Hazard and Shapiro, eds., p. 34.   [47] *Ibid.*, p. 32.

lation. Federal law takes precedence over the law of the Union Republics, pursuant to article 20 of the constitution, which provides as follows: "In the event of divergence between a law of a Union Republic and a law of the Union, the Union law prevails."

From all this, it seems the major sources of relevant law that in different ways and areas govern the combines are:

1. The constitution and legal action taken in implementation thereof establishing the foreign trade monopoly

2. The general civil law as reflected in the Fundamentals and in the Republic laws

3. Special foreign trade legislation (civil law provisions)

4. General administrative law, that is, the hierarchical system wherein the combines are subject to the authority of the Ministry of Foreign Trade and the Ministry of Foreign Trade in turn to the Council of Ministers

5. The administrative law of the plan, which is in effect law under the Soviet system.[48] The plan defines the position of the combine in the national economy.

6. International treaties

A clear definition of the respective areas of application of these six different sources of Soviet foreign-trade law is far from being readily determinable, from the literature available at the time.

However, it seems reasonably clear that there is presently no definitive answer to the role of the general civil law in Soviet foreign-trade law. The Soviet civil law does not provide a uniform set of rules applicable generally in standard legal relations. In a sense foreign trade is outside the civil-law system in the Soviet Union. Grzybowski points out:

The characteristic feature of Soviet civil law is that it is constructed along lines dividing various categories of persons according to the classes of goods and economic assets which may be the objects of their legal transactions. This division is indeed the core of the public order in the Soviet Union, and the foundation of its social and economic regime. However, foreign trade transactions are conducted in total disregard of those basic principles of Soviet civil law, as they involve various classes of persons and the passage among them of goods and commodities in a manner impossible in internal commerce.

He goes on to point out that Soviet foreign-trade combines deal in goods that are *extra commercium* as far as the rest of the Soviet

[48] See fn. 59 below and accompanying text.

economy is concerned. For instance, they can deal in capital goods, buying and selling them abroad, and can make contracts concerning the construction of factories and power stations with private organizations and firms abroad. By the same token, the foreign corporation or legal personality can acquire interests in property which are *extra commercium* for Soviets in the same situation.[49]

There are Soviet publicists, however, who advocate that the provisions of the Soviet civil code be applied strictly to foreign-trade transactions. Pereterskii and Krylov, for instance, both writers of considerable authority, take the position that contracts concluded abroad, but to be performed in the Soviet Union, must conform with not only the foreign law but also the Soviet civil codes. They state:

For instance, if the contract provided for the transfer on the territory of the Soviet Union of things which are excluded from legal commerce, it cannot be considered valid in the eyes of Soviet law, even if the contract is legal under the law of the place where it was concluded.[50]

Grzybowski, however, points out that in actual practice the Soviet civil codes have not been regarded as so applicable. In an attempt to reconcile the codes with actual practice, he argues that

the concept of the unity of civil law in the Soviet Union appears to be totally artificial, unless the general statement contained in Article 3 of the Principles of Civil Legislation of 1961 is seriously considered as a device which incorporated foreign trade regulations into the general body of Soviet civil legislation.[51]

Article 3 of the Fundamentals provides: "Foreign-trade relations are governed by special foreign-trade legislation of the USSR and by the general civil legislation of the USSR and the Union Republics."

However, this theory of the integration of foreign-trade regulations into Soviet general civil law seems contrived. It seems clear that the general civil law only governs Soviet foreign trade in a most general way.

There are, however, several other articles of the Fundamentals that do deal with the foreign-trade combines, although in a general manner. Article 28 deals with the protection of property rights and article 30 with the question of the time at which the right to property passes from seller to buyer. Article 124 concerns itself with foreign organizations in the field of foreign trade. This section makes it clear

[49] Grzybowski, p. 83.

[50] *Ibid.;* I. Pereterskii and S. Krylov, *Mezhdunarodnoe Chastnoe Pravo* (Private International Law) (Moscow, 1959), p. 125*n*1.

[51] Grzybowski, p. 84.

that a foreign enterprise needs no special permission to carry on foreign-trade transactions and the attendant insurance and accounting operations in the Soviet Union. This is a correlative to the USSR government decree of March 11, 1931, article 12, entitled: "On the Procedure for Permitting Foreign Firms to Carry on Trade Operations on USSR Territory," which required special permission from Soviet authorities for a foreign enterprise to carry on actual operations in the USSR, as opposed to isolated commercial transactions.[52] Article 122 guarantees aliens the "national regime" with the exception of particular exemptions to be made by Statute of the USSR. Article 125 provides that the form of foreign-trade transactions made by the combines and the method for their signature are established by the legislation of the USSR "irrespective of the place of the transaction." Article 14 provides correlatively that the failure to abide by the forms established and the order of signature required for foreign trade transactions makes the transaction involved void.[53] Article 126 concerns itself with the law applicable to obligations under foreign-trade transactions. Article 128 concerns restrictions on the application of foreign law and article 129 with international treaties and agreements.

Thus, Soviet civil law is of limited application to the Soviet foreign-trade apparatus. In considering the scope of the Soviet civil law, notably the Fundamentals of Civil Law of the USSR and of the Union Republics, it is useful to look at some of the discussion that accompanied the enactment of the code. Many influential professors and administrators reasserted the position, which had been rejected by Stalin,[54] that the law should distinguish between "economic law" and "civil law." Economic law was regarded to be that law having to do with relations between public corporations; whereas, civil law was to extend only to relations between private individuals. However, the legislative drafting committee of the Council of Ministers decided against separating the rules relating to public corporations from the civil code, and the Fundamentals as enacted cover these economic relations. With stated exceptions the Fundamentals purport to include everything relating to property relations and those non-property relations linked with them. The purported rationale behind

[52] Ramzaitsev, p. 233.

[53] See *ibid.*, p. 234, for a brief statement of the current Soviet legislation establishing the required forms and order of signature.

[54] Hazard and Shapiro, eds., *The Soviet Legal System*, Part II, p. 99.

this adamant refusal to distinguish between economic and civil law is that all property relationships have one basis and are closely bound to each other and that consequently civil law must embrace within one unified complex all property relationships.[55] The position is further taken that to the extent to which the civil law as enacted does not specifically deal with relevant factors, these can be covered through the enactment of supplementary laws. This would seem to be the current law.[56]

However, the criticism of the failure to enact a separate body of economic law has continued, and it is significant in arriving at an understanding of the current structure of Soviet foreign-trade law to consider the criticisms that are made of the present scope of the Fundamentals. The position is taken by some that the Fundamentals fail to cover the matter of relations between public corporations in a satisfactory manner. In many cases even the most significant of relations between public corporations are treated only in the most general way or are left to prospective special legislation.

Thus, clearly we must look beyond the general principles of the civil law to understand the legal regime under which the combines function.

Laws governing the combines in a more specific way are the foreign-trade regulations. Grzybowski calls these "civil law provisions, a term which includes separate systems of rules concerned with relations between various classes of persons.[57] These regulations apply specifically to foreign trade and have a minimum connection with the general body of civil law unless they are regarded, as suggested above,[58] as incorporated into the Soviet general civil law by way of article 3 of the Fundamentals.

A further and major type of law to which the combines are subject is administrative law. The combines are in direct administrative subordination to the Ministry of Foreign Trade, which, as indicated above, issues their charters, determines the scope of their activity, and generally supervises and controls them, and has appointive and disciplinary power over their major officers. The ministry regularly

[55] V. Paniugin, "Comments on the Draft Fundamental Principles of Civil Law of the U.S.S.R. and of the Union Republics," *Sotsialisticheskaia Zakonnost,* pp. 13, 15 (No. 9, 1960), in Hazard and Shapiro, eds., Part II, pp. 111–12.

[56] *USSR Constitution,* art. 3.   [57] Grzybowski, p. 84.

[58] See fn. 51 above and accompanying text.

issues regulations to the combines concerning their activities. Moreover, the charter issued a combine by the ministry is a major governing force over the combine because it determines the scope of its activity.

Another major area of law over the combine is the economic plan. After the New Economic Policy (NEP) period of relaxation of the original Soviet policy and practice of maximum direction of industry from above, the Soviet Union in 1927 established the principle that the plan has the force of law and is obligatory on the combine.[59] The State Planning Commission arrives at the plan and sends the relevant parts of it to the relevant ministries, whereupon the ministries issue appropriate directives to the public corporation under them in pursuance of their parts of the plan.

The last major source of foreign-trade law is the treaty. This source is of importance because of article 129 of the Fundamentals which provides: "Rules laid down in any international treaty or agreement to which the USSR is a party are to be applied in preference to different rules otherwise applicable under Soviet civil legislation." [60]

IMPLEMENTATION OF SOVIET FOREIGN TRADE

In the actual implementation of its foreign-trade policies, the Soviet Union operates on several levels. In trade between socialist countries there are three levels of agreement. The states conclude long-term commercial treaties, which are implemented by annual agreements which guarantee in more particularity the rights and obligations of the states parties and sometimes even the amounts of goods to be traded. On the third level, the agreements are ultimately particularized and implemented through individual commercial contracts between the state trading corporations. In these contracts all the specifics of the exchange are determined.[61]

In Soviet trade with a state with a free-market economy, on the other hand, the international trade treaties do not establish an obligation to buy or sell any products at all. Rather they only constitute

[59] Hazard & Shapiro, eds., Part II, p. 97.

[60] See fn. 36 above, for Tuttle's suggestion that the United States should make more extensive use of this provision in its trade with the Soviet Union.

[61] C. Schmitthoff, pp. 355–60; Cohen, "Some Problems of Doing Business with State Trading Agencies," *University of Illinois Law Review* (1965), 520–23.

agreements to maintain the frameworks in which private companies can trade as they choose.[62] The respective states parties guarantee nothing in terms of actual trade, but only that they will issue any necessary export licenses in accordance with the treaty and will accord imports "most favored nations" treatment and will issue payment and foreign exchange permits for payment due as a result of individual trade operations.[63] The respective state trading organizations and private companies must locate their own trading parties and conclude any contracts they can negotiate.[64]

Trade agreements between countries with free-market economies and countries with state-planned economies have characteristically resembled formally contracts between state-planned economies, having such characteristics as year-by-year evaluation and reconsideration of the long-term agreement, so as to fit the terms into the annual plans of the respective states. However, by the same token, these trade agreements have resembled trade agreements between countries with free economic systems in that the states parties do not guarantee performance of any of the states parties.[65]

The fact that this type of agreement has developed seems to show that trade between free-market economies and planned economies is feasible. Many of the Western European countries have learned this lesson, although the United States has not.[66] It is time

[62] Schmitthoff, p. 355.

[63] *Ibid.* For a consideration of the typical provisions of a U.S. trade treaty, see H. Walker, "The Effects of Existing or Proposed International Trade Treaties and Agreements Upon Foreign Trade Between the USSR and the USA," *The Law of U.S.–U.S.S.R. Trade* (Washington, D.C., Association of American Law Schools, 1965), LXXIX, 79.

[64] Knapp, pp. 67–68; Cohen, p. 520.

[65] Cohen, p. 523; Schmitthoff, p. 355. "Most favored nation" agreements are meaningless in trade between a free-market economy and a state-trading economy because such agreements guarantee only the noninterference by the respective states of trade agreements arrived at by their respective enterprises. This type of agreement is obviously meaningless against a state trader, because it is the state in effect which is making the initial agreement. The United States has specifically abandoned "both the principle and policy of free trade with Communist countries." Berman, p. 527. See Gatt, *Basic Instruments and Selected Documents* (1952), p. 36, for the dissolution of the GATT committment between the U.S. and Czechslovakia.

[66] For a sharp contrast of the U.S. policy vis-à-vis foreign trade with the Communist bloc with that of our major Western European allies, see L. Herman, "The Economic Content of Soviet Trade with the West," in Baade, ed.,

that the United States came to look upon trade with the Soviet Union and the other Communist countries as an economic and not a political venture.[67] Also, in point of fact, the substantive external trade law of the Soviet Union does not differ fundamentally from the same law of the United States and other major trading countries of the world. Despite the differences of its internal legal structure, the Soviet Union follows internationally the commonly established and accepted international commercial laws and usages.[68]

There are, of course, many substantial impediments to increased trade between the United States and the Soviet Union.[69] However, it would seem that an increased understanding of the similarity of international commercial practice of the two states and of the struc-

The Soviet Impact on International Law (Dobbs Ferry, N.Y., Oceana Publications, Inc., 1965), pp. 127, 128–31; see, generally, Mikesell and Behrman, pp. 1–17.

[67] The proposed East-West Trade Relations Act, which would empower the President to make commercial agreements with Communist countries extending "most favored nation" clauses when in the national interest, stands virtually no chance of passage in the Congress as long as the Viet Nam war continues. See H. Berman and J. Garson, "Possible Effects of the Proposed East-West Trade Relations Act Upon U.S. Import, Export, and Credit Controls," *Vanderbilt Law Review,* XX (1967), 279; see "Report of the Special Committee on U.S. Trade with Eastern European Countries and the U.S.S.R," *Department of State Bulletin,* LIV (1966), 845; "Private Boycotts V. The National Interest," *Department of State Bulletin,* LV (1967), 446.

[68] C. Schmitthoff, "The Law of International Trade, Its Growth, Formulation and Operation," in C. Schmitthoff, ed., *The Sources of the Law of International Trade* (London, Stevens & Sons, 1964), I, 42; Schmitthoff, *Commerical Treaties,* p. 368.

[69] A list of the difficulties facing trade between the U.S. and the Soviet Union would include the following: 1) sovereign immunity; 2) choice of law; 3) arbitration provisions; 4) prosecution of international claims; 5) political factors; 6) protection of industrial rights; 7) arrangement for the establishment or expansion of U.S. trade and tourist facilities in the Soviet Union; 8) settlement of financial and property claims and improvement of consular relations; 9) assurance of market access and fair treatment; 10) agreement in areas of conflict of laws, e.g., on the questions of apparent or ostensible authority, and on the doctrine of impossibility of performance; 11) prevention of "prototype" purchases; 12) antidumping agreements; 13) diversification in terms of consumer goods and industrial goods of Soviet imports from the U.S. and exports to the U.S.; 14) assurance that any trade be carried on to the mutual advantage of the U.S. and the Soviet Union; 15) overcoming the problem that the Soviets do not really know what they have that is readily exportable to the U.S.; 16) currency and financing problems; and 17) restrictive U.S. export-import laws.

ture of the Soviet foreign-trade apparatus would somewhat enhance the prospects for the development of further trade relations between the states, especially in terms of influencing the United States people and more particularly the legislators to lessen the substantial restraints placed by this country on trade with the Soviet Union.[70]

Financing of Soviet Foreign Trade

An interesting aspect of Soviet foreign trade is the wide range of financing alternatives that have developed. Although data are rather scarce and detailed analysis has not been frequently attempted, the following main types of financing can be pointed to: [71]

1. payment in transferable currencies, such as the dollar or sterling
2. financing without a foreign exchange transaction by means of barter or private compensation
3. payment by debiting or crediting a bilateral clearing account
4. financing by means of a credit or gift

The first two types of financing, unlike the second two, do not generally require any special agreement between the countries as to means of financing.

A considerable portion of the agreement trade and some of the nonagreement trade between the West and the Soviet Union is carried on without any foreign exchange transactions at all, but rather through barter.[72] The barter is a relatively simple concept and, as the name implies, means generally contracts calling for the exchange of a specific quantity of one good for a specific quantity of another good. However, the concept in practice is not quite so simple, since

[70] See Berman and Garson, p. 279; see Metzger, "United States Governmental Regulation of Trade with the Soviet Union and Certain Other Countries," in *The Law of U.S.-U.S.S.R. Trade*, p. 33; also in Baade, ed., *The Soviet Impact on International Law*, p. 156.

[71] R. Mikesell and J. Behrman, *Financing Free World Trade in the Sino-Soviet Bloc* (Princeton, N.J., Princeton University Press, 1958), p. 30 passim; see also M. Trued and R. Mikesell, *Postwar Bilateral Payment Agreements* (Princeton, N.J., Princeton University Press, 1955), pp. 6–10; R. Mikesell, *Foreign Exchange in the Postwar World* (New York, Twentieth Century Fund, 1954), pp. 85–86; Comment, "Soviet Bilateral Development Assistance: The Legal Form and Structure," *Columbia Journal of Transnational Law*, VII (1968), 48.

[72] Mikesell and Behrman, p. 43.

the determination of value has to take into consideration the value not only of the goods transferred but also of such incidentals as freight and insurance. Moreover, since a perfect balance may not reasonably be anticipated, provisions must be made for accounts to serve to record the extent of agreement fulfillment at any given time, and especially at the termination of the agreement. In addition, of course, provision must be made for the eventuality of an imbalance after the contract has been otherwise fully performed.

The private exchange transaction is a transaction whereby compensation is arranged through the private importer in one country paying his own currency to the private exporter in the same country. Balance is provided when the adjustment is made in the other country between exporter and importer.[73] A private "global" compensation agreement is one by the terms of which a number of different commodities may be traded. Such agreement may provide that it is not necessary to balance individual transactions and may also establish a clearing account with a swing credit.[74]

The clearing-account type of financing involves the setting up of special accounts in the central bank of one or both partner countries, designed for the financing of certain trade transactions, as generally specified in the agreement. Although in the prewar period exporters had to wait to get payment until there were sufficient funds in the clearing account, derived from corresponding imports, the current practice is to provide for general credits or debits at any given time as the trade transactions occur, regardless of the actual trade balance at that time. The credits in clearing accounts are not generally held by commercial banks or firms and are not ordinarily transferable to third countries except by specific agreement by both countries.[75]

The unit of account used in the clearing account may be that of either of the parties or may well be that of a third country, often the dollar or sterling. Because of their limited transferability and uncertain value relative to cost, Soviet and other bloc currencies are seldom used in clearing accounts in East-West trade. Where the currency of one of the parties is used, the agreement sometimes provides for a revaluation guarantee in terms of gold or dollars.[76]

Generally, credit agreements will indicate the kinds of transac-

[73] *Ibid.*, p. 43n8.   [74] See *ibid.*, p. 47.
[75] See generally, Trued and Mikesell, *Postwar Bilateral Payments Agreements.*
[76] See Comment, p. 57.

tions which may be financed through the accounts. Moreover, credit provisions will be provided for, generally with specific provisions for a swing credit. The latter credits are often free of interest.[77] Obviously, in addition, there must be provisions for maintaining the balance and for settlements. There is a wide range of possible settlement provisions. Generally, the agreement will provide for either bilateral or triangular settlement. Thus, under a bilateral settlement agreement, there may be provisions for automatic liquidation in gold or transferable currencies of any excess balances when the swing credit is exceeded or for a regaining of balance through the use of trade controls.[78] As indicated above,[79] there are periodic reexaminations of trade agreements and payment provisions thereof. At trade negotiations, consideration is naturally given to the current status of the clearing balance. In addition, some clearing-house provisions' agreements provide for transfer, either by consent or automatically, of bilateral balances to third countries. Apparently, however, this type of multilateralism does not seem to have become common.[80]

The Soviet Union extends significant amounts of aid to the developing countries in the form of credits and occasionally gifts, such that now foreign economic aid constitutes a regular component of the Soviet national economy.[81] By the end of 1966, worldwide Soviet aid commitments in 68 agreements with 28 countries aggregated $4.82 billion, of which $4.6 billion was in loans in the form of medium- and long-term credits and $169 million in the form of grants.[82] Only approximately 6 percent of total Sino-Soviet bloc aid has been in the form of grants or gifts.[83]

It is instructive to look at the commercial and banking practices

[77] Mikesell and Behrman, pp. 36–37.   [78] *Ibid.*, p. 38.

[79] See fn. 65 above and accompanying text.

[80] Mikesell and Behrman, pp. 40–41.

[81] K. Müller, *The Foreign Aid Program of the Soviet Bloc and Communist China: An Analysis* (1967), p. 219.

[82] Comment, p. 48. See M. Goldman, *Soviet Foreign Aid* (New York, Praeger, 1967), p. 206; Muller, p. 215; C. Prochorov, *The Two World System and the Liberated Countries* (1965), p. 110; *Report on the Dimensions of Soviet Economic Power*, Study Proposed for the Joint Economic Committee, 87th Cong. 2d Sess. (Comm. Print 1962), p. 461.

[83] *Organization for Economic Cooperation and Development, Flow of Financial Resources to Less Developed Countries 1956–63* (1965), p. 5; see J. Berliner, *Soviet Economic Aid* (New York, Praeger, 1958); for general background on credit financing, see Trued and Mikesell, pp. 35 ff.

typical in East-West trade. As indicated above,[84] the actual substantive rules of Soviet foreign-trade law are remarkably similar to those of Western nations. So also the credit instruments and procedures used in financing transactions in East-West trade are similar to standard Western practices. Such standard procedures as use of the letter of credit, cash on presentation of documents, cash on delivery, time drafts on the importer, partial payment or full prepayment with orders, and open accounts are all used.[85]

The role of gold and free currencies is an important one in Soviet trade. The USSR's production and sale of gold are substantial, though the exact amounts are not known. The Soviet Union is in fact the only Soviet bloc country that has a major gold reserve. This gold reserve is regarded to constitute the ultimate financial bulwark of the Soviet Bloc, since the bloc countries generally have only very minimal foreign exchange reserves and the reliable credit facilities available are likewise exceedingly limited. Short of relying on the Soviet gold reserves, the bloc countries can make limited use of the loan facilities of the Soviet controlled banks in London (Moscow-Narodny) and Paris (Banque Commerciale Pour l'Europe du Nord) and the normal commercial facilities available up to six months from Western banks. Recently, the Soviet Union, in order to increase imports, has drawn on its gold reserves and has also relied on extended medium—term credit offered by the West. The United States, of course, has prevented any significant extensions of credit to the Soviet Union.[86]

As indicated, the United States now has no trade agreements with the Soviet Union, and all trade that is carried on is conducted by contracts between the United States contracting party and the Soviet foreign-trade corporation. If there were, in fact, a trade agreement between the United States and the Soviet Union, that agreement might well provide for specific modes of financing, probably involving a combination of the four alternative ways suggested above. In the absence of a trade agreement or of a specific payments agreement between the two countries, most trade between them is financed through the use of transferable currencies.[87]

---

[84] See fn. 69 above and accompanying text.

[85] Mikesell and Behrman, p. 45.

[86] Committee on Foreign Relations, U.S. Senate, *A Background Study of East-West Trade* (1965), p. 60.

[87] Mikesell and Behrman, p. 30.

Biographical Sketches

DALE K. ANDERSON received her B.A. degree from Vassar College in 1963, with a major in History. She was Secretary to the Director of the East Asian Institute until September 1968, when she resigned to work toward an M.A. in modern Chinese history. As a graduate research assistant of the East Asian Institute, she served as rapporteur for the Conference on Japanese-American Relations, 1931, held in Japan in July 1969 under the sponsorship of the East Asian Institute and the International House of Japan.

EDMUND BEARD received a B.A. with High Distinction and High Honors in American History from the University of Michigan. As an undergraduate, he was a member of Phi Beta Kappa, received a Jules Avery Hopwood Prize in Creative Writing, and assisted in geologic research in Southern Colorado under a National Science Foundation grant. He is presently a graduate student in Political Science at Columbia University where he has received an M.I.A. and where he holds a Herbert Lehman Fellowship. He has served as a State Department Overseas Intern in Tripoli, Libya, and was recently a member of the academic staff of the Institute of World Affairs Summer Seminar in Salisbury, Connecticut.

ALAN D. BERLIND was born in Brooklyn in 1934 and spent his early years in Woodmere, New York, where he attended Woodmere Academy. Graduated from Princeton University in 1956 with a B.A. in Sociology, he entered the U.S. Army and served for the better part of three years in Frankfurt, West Germany. A recuperative year on the Spanish isle of Ibiza preceded a year of courses in government at Georgetown University. In 1961, Mr. Berlind joined the Foreign Service. He has served in the American Embassy in Athens, on the Congo (Kinshasa) desk in Washington, and, most recently, in the American Embassy in Accra. His studies at Columbia's School of International Affairs and European Institute, sponsored by the Department of State, were designed to prepare him for a career specialization in Western European and Atlantic community affairs. Mr. Berlind is currently back in Washington with his wife, a native of Greece and a psychiatric social worker.

ROBERTA MARX DELSON developed her interest in Latin America while an undergraduate at Syracuse University. Her studies at the Maxwell

School of Citizenship and Public Affairs led to a graduation magna cum laude in 1966, and election to Phi Beta Kappa. Since entering Columbia that summer, she has held NDFL fellowships in either Spanish or Portuguese. During the summer of 1967, Mrs. Delson spent two months in Porto Alegre, Brazil, under the Metropolitan Summer Field Training Program. Her study of the city's Jewish community was accepted as a master's essay in the Department of Anthropology in 1968, when she also received the certificate of the Institute of Latin American Studies. Mrs. Delson is currently an advanced-certification level candidate for the Ph.D. in the Department of History and plans to conduct her thesis research on the modernization process in Curitiba, Brazil. Her career plans include college teaching and research on Latin America. Mr. Delson is a doctoral candidate in Vertebrate Paleontology in the Columbia department of Geology.

THEODORE H. FRIEDGUT received both his B.A. and M.A. in Political Science from the Hebrew University of Jerusalem. In September of 1967 he enrolled as a candidate for the Ph.D degree in the Russian Institute of Columbia University. From September of 1969 to February of 1970 he was an exchange student at Moscow University on the University of Toronto exchange program. During the 1970–71 academic year he will be lecturing in Political Science in the School of General Studies of Columbia University.

TREVOR J. HOPE, British born, completed his undergraduate education at the University of St. Andrews, Scotland, in Modern European History and Political Science, graduating in 1967 with an M.A. degree. Active in British politics, he was the political organizer for the Labour Party in the Rutland and Stamford constituency in the 1964 General Election. Mr. Hope was a member of the Student's Representative Council at St. Andrews University, 1963–64, and was selected to pay a visit to the Soviet Union in 1966 with a group from the Scottish Union of Students. Through Anglo-French and Anglo-Romanian cultural exchange programs he studied in France in summer 1965 and in Romania in summer 1967. In the fall of 1967 Mr. Hope came to Columbia University through the sponsorship of the English-Speaking Union. He was enrolled in the History Department and the Institute on East-Central Europe, where he worked as research assistant in the spring term, 1968. Mr. Hope taught two Modern European History courses in the Summer Session at Columbia in 1968 and a course in Modern British History along with a course in Modern European History in summer, 1969. He expects to teach Modern European History upon completion of his Ph.D.

KAREL F. KOECHER is a graduate of Charles University in Prague, Czechoslovakia, from which he obtained an advanced degree in Physics in 1958.

While still in Czechoslovakia, Mr. Koecher lectured in Mathematics at Czech Technical University in Prague; wrote for Czechoslovak television and several newspapers, and later worked as Contributing Editor in Prague Radio. In 1966, he was awarded an Indiana University Fellowship for graduate studies in Philosophy of Science. In 1967, he entered Columbia where he is a Ph.D. candidate in the Department of Philosophy and has earned a Certificate of the Russian Institute. In the United States, Mr. Koecher also worked as Special Consultant for Radio Free Europe and is now teaching at Wagner College in Staten Island. Mr. Koecher has translated into English, "The Dialectics of the Concrete," by Karel Kosík for the Reidel Publishing Company.

JACOB VAN LUTSENBURG MAAS is presently a doctoral candidate in Comparative Sociology of Education at Columbia University Teachers College. He received his B.A. degree from Washington University (St. Louis) in 1961 and an M.A. in Teaching from Oberlin College the following year. After teaching briefly in American high schools, he taught in a teacher-training college in Uganda from 1964 to 1967. Since then he has resumed graduate study at Columbia. In 1969–70 he will be carrying out his dissertation research in Uganda under a Fullbright-Hayes Fellowship on the growth of a modern educational structure in relation to the development of modern occupations in the colonial period.

CHARLES J. MOXLEY, JR., is a member of the bar of the State of New York. He received his J.D. from Columbia University School of Law and his M.A. in Russian Area Studies and B.A. in Political Science from Fordham University.

HARRIET Z. PASS is a native of Canada's capital. In 1964, standing first in the City of Ottawa at Senior Matriculation, she entered the University of Toronto as a student of modern languages: French, German, and Russian. The summer of 1965 she spent studying in Germany on a German government scholarship. After being an exchange student at Smith College during her third year, Miss Pass graduated from the University of Toronto with an Honor B.A. in Slavic Studies in the spring of 1968. She was awarded a Woodrow Wilson Honorable Mention and is a Faculty Fellow of the Department of History and an Honors Fellow of the Institute on East Central Europe at Columbia University. Her future plans include teaching in both her major field, Eastern European history, and her minor field, Jewish history. Combining her interest in these two areas, Miss Pass also hopes to do further research on problems in the history of the Jews in Eastern Europe. She has done extensive work on the Jews of Austria and Yugoslavia. For summer of 1969, she received a grant from the American Council of Learned Societies for language study and research in Yugoslavia.

JOSEPH A. STORK graduated from St. Vincent College in 1964. Between 1964 and 1966 he worked in Turkey as a Peace Corps Volunteer. He attended the School of International Affairs from 1967 to 1969. He received his M.I.A. degree in June 1969 and the certificate of the Middle East Institute the following October.

WILLIAM MILLS TODD was graduated in 1966 from Dartmouth College, where he received Summa Cum Laude honors and a Senior Fellowship in Russian literature. He studied at University College, Oxford, under a Reynolds Scholarship from Dartmouth and was awarded a B.A. with First Class Honours in modern languages. He has visited the Soviet Union in 1965 and 1967 and is presently a Faculty Fellow in the Department of Slavic Languages at Columbia University. Mr. Todd plans to teach at the university level when he has completed his doctorate in Russian literature with a minor field of comparative literature.

V. ANNA WILLMAN received a B.A. degree from Wellesley College in 1964 and an M.I.S from Claremont Graduate School in 1966. After two years as a research assistant in the Strategic Studies Center at Stanford Research Institute, she taught in the Social Sciences Department at Saint Paul's College in Lawrenceville, Virginia. She is currently studying for a Ph.D. in comparative politics at Columbia University. She plans to do research for her dissertation in Yugoslavia. Miss Willman will then teach and continue research.

LYNDA SHAFFER WOMACK, a member of the Junior Fellows (1964–66) and Phi Beta Kappa (1966) at the University of Texas, received her B.A. with Special Honors in Plan II in 1966. In August of that year she was an intern at the United Nations. Since arriving at Columbia, Mrs. Womack has been a Woodrow Wilson Fellow (1966–67); a Fellow of the School of International Affairs, from which she received the M.I.A. in 1969; and a Fellow of the East Asian Institute, from which she received the Certificate in 1970. She won the Julian Oberman Prize for Excellence in Chinese in 1967. She is currently a member of the Committee of Concerned Asian Scholars at Columbia University, and is working toward a Ph.D. from the Department of History in modern Chinese and Japanese history.